Praise for
Puzzling 2020
CONNECTING THE PIECES

"An interesting book describing personal reflections and Biblical truth about the Holy Spirit's work in our lives. These reflections are relevant and so needed in our present religious culture."

—Charles Simpson

"In my opinion, the author's third book is his best because it is aimed at every Christian's greatest problem... How to listen clearly to the Holy Spirit about the target of positive existence. He rebukes us all about our laziness, even craziness, about the ultimate targets of our life. A former USAF fighter pilot and an airline captain... 20,000 hours throughout the world... He uses flying coupled with scripture to encourage the puzzle of our flight through our creation. Every life and every flight is a journey to see if we know and arrive at our God-given destination. I've been there, and so has our author."

—Dr. H.D. McCarty, Brigadier General, USAF (Retired)

Puzzling 2020

CONNECTING THE PIECES

B. DWAYNE BELL

Copyright © 2022 B. Dwayne Bell

All rights reserved. No part of this book may be used or reproduced by any means, graphic, electronic, or mechanical, including photocopying, recording, taping or by and information storage retrieval system without the written permission of the publisher or the author except in the case of brief quotations embodied in critical articles and reviews.

Unless otherwise noted, all Scripture taken from the NEW AMERICAN STANDARD BIBLE®, copyright© 1960, 1962, 1963, 1968, 1971, 1972, 1973, 1975, 1977, 1995 by The Lockman Foundation. Used by permission.

Scriptures marked AMP are taken from the AMPLIFIED® BIBLE, Copyright © 1954, 1958, 1962, 1964, 1965, 1987 by the Lockman Foundation Used by Permission. (www.Lockman.org)

Scriptures marked NLT are taken from the HOLY BIBLE, NEW LIVING TRANSLATION, Copyright© 1996, 2004, 2007 by Tyndale House Foundation. Used by permission of Tyndale House Publishers, Inc., Carol Stream, Illinois 60188. All rights reserved. Used by permission.

Scriptures marked NIV are taken from the NEW INTERNATIONAL VERSION®. Copyright© 1973, 1978, 1984, 2011 by Biblica, Inc.TM. Used by permission of Zondervan.

Scriptures marked ESV are taken from the HOLY BIBLE, ENGLISH STANDARD VERSION® Copyright© 2001 by Crossway, a publishing ministry of Good News Publishers. Used by permission.

Scriptures marked KJV are taken from the KING JAMES VERSION, public domain.

Scriptures marked NCV are taken from the NEW CENTURY VERSION®. Copyright© 2005 by Thomas Nelson, Inc. Used by permission. All rights reserved.

Scriptures marked ISV are taken from the INTERNATIONAL STANDARD VERSION, copyright© 1996-2008 by the ISV Foundation. All rights reserved internationally.

Scripture quotations marked (CEV) are from the Contemporary English Version Copyright © 1991, 1992, 1995 by American Bible Society. Used by Permission.

Scriptures marked NKJV taken from the New King James Version®. Copyright © 1982 by Thomas Nelson. Used by permission. All rights reserved.

ISBN: 979-8-9875826-1-9 (Paperback)
       979-8-9875826-0-2 (Hardcover)
       979-8-9875826-2-6 (eBook)

Published in the United States of America.

Acknowledgment and Dedication

THANK YOU, JOE CARRUTH, FOR encouraging me to write and for the many thoughtful hours devoted to editing this book. Not only editing but many more coffee-shop hours and hours over lunch, you devoted sacrificially and unselfishly to help me focus while the vision for this book unfolded. Your countless hours serving me are only surpassed in value and appreciation by your well-founded and well-rounded worldview formed by a keen intellect, excellent education, your grasp of the Bible, and being the most well-read person I know. Above that, you touch me by the humble, gentle, sacrificial way you bring all that to bear on my life as your friend and support me in this effort to encourage people in their faith and kingdom living — seeking to give honor to the King. May He bless and keep you and yours forever.

I'm forever grateful for our friendship and the fantastic travel and kingdom experiences we've enjoyed, from our mission to Burkina Faso twenty years ago to a son's wedding in South Korea and a tremendous discovery and friendship tour of Israel three short years ago. You inspire me with your discipline, dedication, kingdom focus, and sacrifices demonstrating your love of people and life.

Photo Credits

Cover ~ Design by S.M. Savoy
Cover ~ Author photo by Dwayne Bell, Iceland 2018
Chapters ~ Puzzles worked by Elizabeth Bell and friends
Photos by Dwayne Bell, Spring Mountain, AR 2020-2022

Puzzling 2020
Connecting the Pieces

Puzzling — An Introduction xi
Puzzling Chapter 1   Getting Started 1
Puzzling Chapter 2   9/11 Twenty Years Later. 7
Puzzling Chapter 3   The Jewish New Year. 11
Puzzling Chapter 4   The Spirit and the Bride 13
Puzzling Chapter 5   The Holy Spirit In The Church. 17
Puzzling Chapter 6   BLM is a Crock. 25
Puzzling Chapter 7   The Lord Loves Justice. 29
Puzzling Chapter 8   Fault Lines of Social Justice 33
Puzzling Chapter 9   Epiphany 2021 35
Puzzling Chapter 10   A Word for a Wilderness 39
Puzzling Chapter 11   Race. 43
Puzzling Chapter 12   Grace to See. 49
Puzzling Chapter 13   A Gentle Breeze 59
Puzzling Chapter 14   The Spirit Without Measure 65
Puzzling Chapter 15   Christmas Puzzle 73
Puzzling Chapter 16   Epiphany 2022 77
Puzzling Chapter 17   Trust Is The Key 79
Puzzling Chapter 18   Two Witnesses 89
Puzzling Chapter 19   What We Carry. 99

Puzzling Chapter 20	Sex and Marriage	103
Puzzling Chapter 21	Marriage Failure	107
Puzzling Chapter 22	Divorce and Remarriage	123
Puzzling Chapter 23	Hell and Mr. Fudge	135
Puzzling Chapter 24	Sex In Perspective	143
Puzzling Chapter 25	Holy Spirit Perspective	163
Puzzling Chapter 26	Signs Before Jesus Comes	169
Puzzling Chapter 27	With Eyes Wide Open	177
Puzzling Chapter 28	Did God Say?	185
Puzzling Chapter 29	Hearing God	195
Puzzling Chapter 30	An Ass	205
Puzzling Chapter 31	An Apology	217
Puzzling Chapter 32	Pause for Revelation	227
Puzzling Chapter 33	Atheism Postmortem	239
Puzzling Chapter 34	Easter in Emmaus	251
Puzzling Chapter 35	Fault Lines and Deception	261
Puzzling Chapter 36	Spiritual Vision & Deception	267
Puzzling Chapter 37	Hopenots and the Song of the King	279
Puzzling Chapter 38	The Man of God	285
Puzzling Chapter 39	The Church	295
Puzzling Chapter 40	Living Stones	311
Puzzling Chapter 41	Martyrs	327
Puzzling Chapter 42	Slavery	333
Puzzling Chapter 43	Delusion from the Lord	343
Puzzling Chapter 44	Peter and Faith	355
Puzzling Chapter 45	The Fool	361
Puzzling Chapter 46	Stay in Your Lane - Men	373
Puzzling Chapter 47	Stay in Your Lane - Women	391
Puzzling Chapter 48	Prayer Privilege	405
Puzzling Chapter 49	Prayer Helps	417
Puzzling Chapter 50	The Threshing Floor	427
Puzzling Chapter 51	Wonder or Wander	433

PUZZLING CHAPTER 52	Prayer at Shiloh	441
PUZZLING CHAPTER 53	Disciple Prayer	451
PUZZLING CHAPTER 54	God's Prayer	463
PUZZLING CHAPTER 55	Passionate Prayer and Grace	469
PUZZLING CHAPTER 56	Cell Phones	477
PUZZLING CHAPTER 57	Church and Religion	487
PUZZLING CHAPTER 58	The Holy Bible	495
PUZZLING CHAPTER 59	Predestined	503
PUZZLING CHAPTER 60	Coffee Shop Problem Solving	511
PUZZLING CHAPTER 61	Value Life	519
PUZZLING CHAPTER 62	Your Fast	527
PUZZLING CHAPTER 63	Strange New World	535
PUZZLING CHAPTER 64	Israel ישראל	547
PUZZLING CHAPTER 65	See God and Live	561
PUZZLING CHAPTER 66	Blessings at Gerizim	569
PUZZLING CHAPTER 67	Twenty Years	585
PUZZLING CHAPTER 68	Quips and Quotes	601
PUZZLING CHAPTER 69	Summary	611
PUZZLING CHAPTER 70	Afterword	621
APPENDIX: Simple Time Line for Reference		627

Puzzling — An Introduction

2020 AD WAS A VERY PUZZLING year, with a puzzling pandemic, and other puzzling events that continued to mystify thinking people as they muddled through 2021 toward the end of 2022.

I didn't make the image of this puzzle! God did.

But then I suppose you could say the same thing of all puzzles and images. He made everything, and sustains everything by His power.

I'm just making a small puzzle, a painting from God's word the Bible, and history, and current events. And then I'm going to cut it into pieces, like a puzzle, so you can put it back together and see the image more clearly, because you've had opportunity to examine each piece in the process, to see how and if it fits. And see if the image of the puzzle when complete is true to the real thing — reality?

My intention is not to make a complex or 2000 piece puzzle, but a simple puzzle for children or beginning puzzlers, maybe 70 pieces, or 70 short chapters.

We'll see as we progress. But I want it to be simple not daunting. I want it to be doable, interesting, and fun. A bit mysterious? Yes! That's what puzzles are. How can all these pieces, different shapes and colors, fit together into an image — the image on the box? And how close will the image be to what is on the box?

Many times while working a puzzle, the puzzler will ask themselves, "How can this piece possibly be a part of this image?" Or they will think to themselves, "This certainly isn't going to look like the image on the box."

But it usually does! It surprises us. Not only that, but by spending time to notice the colors, details, and shapes of individual pieces or groups of pieces, we see more detail in the whole image than ever before. We see the image more clearly than before, with detail, color, and clarity that we miss if we blink or glance at the image and move on. Puzzles cause us to slow to the speed of life, and living, and being.

The Mysterious

It's mysterious how all of this happens. There is something in humans that love mystery. We are drawn to it. We are challenged by it, and we want to understand.

It makes us a bit childlike again, "Let's do it, Mom!" "Can we, Dad?" "Would you do it with me?" "Let's do it together!" Puzzles can be solitary or relational. They are a journey into seeing.

Not only do children love puzzles and are excited at their worth, I think God loves puzzles.

There is so much clarity in the Bible. It's the best selling book of all time for a reason. It's God's message to us for healthy, happy living. Also, it's a primer for knowing each other, knowing ourselves, and knowing God.

It's clearly inspired, from another realm, but intended for this realm — our realm, our lives, our day. And this is true no matter which day of our six-thousand-year human history you may have lived.

Truth of this kind is genius, concrete, time tested, forever settled in heaven, and is not dependent on what people think or do.

Yet some things in the Bible seem purposely obscured, not perfectly clear, and a bit fuzzy. They are like pieces to a puzzle that don't seem to fit. I used to rail at these things, thinking I had to solve those mysteries or come up with a solution of what God meant to say or really thinks about these matters.

As I've grown in years, and hopefully wisdom, I've come to see the folly and the hubris in my thinking.

It's a humanistic kind of thinking that was handed down to me from the church of previous decades and my recent spiritual fathers. But it's also a tendency in every human to want to help God out or to be like God themselves. So I must accept the responsibility for my own spiritual blindness in this area.

We do not need to help God! A better posture would be to sit in silence before Him.

The God who created 150 billion galaxies with 150 billion stars each including our star called the sun and the planet revolving around it we call the earth and home, probably doesn't need our help with anything.

The same Bible tells us He made it all, and He owns it all. It tells us He knows and sees at every moment every little detail about it. He is all knowing. He knows the number of hairs on your head, the exact number and condition of each of the estimated fifty billion birds on our planet, and the molecular structure of the blades of grass and the leaves turning red outside my window as I write.

Indeed, the Bible informs us that He sustains it all by the power of His word. That is, He continually tweaks it or breathes or speaks life and order into it or it would dissolve and decay, according to the second law of thermodynamics, a law He created to govern the part of His realm we call "the natural."

So, how is it that I've been duped into thinking that God needs my help? Couldn't a being so great, powerful, and majestic make all things about truth, love, and living absolutely clear if He intended to do so?

Of course He could, is the obvious answer. Then why the mystery about some things? Why leave some questions unanswered? Or at least fuzzy, so that the exact answer is not easily recognizable or may not be fully known?

Well in part, because He clearly loves mystery. And He knows we do. We're created in His image. Jesus taught in parables, stories made up with real life and spiritual applications telling us about living, motives, His plan, Himself, and His kingdom which is both now and forever. These are among the most beautiful stories ever told, and the most important mystery makers and mystery breakers.

Why He chooses to use mystery, and to be somewhat a mystery, is a mystery? But He does speak to that in His word, and I'll revisit it later as an important piece of the puzzle.

I intend to speak to some of the fuzzy things later, not necessarily to be any kind of final word on them, because how could I, if God Himself made them fuzzy? There will be puzzle pieces on marriage and divorce, heaven and hell, and election and free will. There will be purpose in the discussion and perhaps some insight and revelation. There could be revelation from God to you! That's my prayer. And in the end, this whole earth life is between God and you, isn't it? That's what it boils down to. As the Lord said to Job after a painful, puzzling saga in his life, "Will you really annul My judgment? Will you condemn Me that you may be justified?" (Job 40:8).

Deception and Delusion

I have not mentioned it yet, but deception and delusion will be a thread woven into many pieces of the puzzle. It's a big part of the reality and image of our day and lives. God said deception and delusion would be prevalent in the last days. He may have sent it? Be open to seeing and hearing this, if it's true. Be alert. Be watching, and engaged. It does add to the mystery, doesn't it?

A. W. Tozer discusses Isaiah 6, and points out Isaiah was told to speak to the people, but they wouldn't be able to hear. Tozer says of God's way for man: "It's a secret, but it's an open secret."

That's how I feel about everything in this book. It's all right there in your Bible. Why haven't you seen it? I don't know.

I'm writing this book to Christians primarily, who should be knowledgeable of the Bible, and be knowing God better each year, by reading it every day. But this book is also for truth seekers everywhere. Truth is truth, wherever you find it. It is through His word that we come to discern truth from lies and truth from error—indeed to "know the truth that sets us free" (John 8:32).

Jesus said, "I am the way, and the truth, and the life; no one comes to the Father but through me" (John 14:6). We have a spiritual enemy called Satan, "the father of lies," who came "to kill, steal, and destroy." Thankfully in the same passage, Jesus said: "...but I have come that you may have life, and have it more abundantly" (John 10:10). That's beautiful.

The early church testified to this truth and spread it throughout the Roman empire. It then spread from Europe to the rest of world. Christ's followers for the ensuing two thousand years have enjoyed this truth, prospered because of it, and held it dear.

That's what I'm writing about, or at least a taste of it. After all, it is a puzzle, and you must work it to see the image appear, hopefully with an accompanying degree of satisfaction, clarity, and vision.

Why am I writing? Why am I providing this simple puzzle for you to assemble and piece together for yourself?

It's partly out of personal heartbreak and hope for better days. I'll explain this in a moment.

It's partly out of a desire to help people live whole and free. From my sixty-nine years on the planet, and as things grow gloriously dark, I have found the best path in the good news of Jesus Christ. "In Christ Alone," as the early Irish Christians sang, and Paul wrote in

Colossians 1:27, "Christ in you, the hope of glory [goodness, eternal fulfillment]."

Another reason for writing and puzzling with you, is out of gratitude for God's goodness in my life and his incredible grace and faithfulness. I want to tell of God's goodness and faithfulness to the next generation, so they will put their trust in God.

Finally, I'm writing this as a matter of obedience. I feel the Spirit has impressed me to do so, with the promise of His help and illumination.

Joy In The Journey

I would also say that philosophy, theology, truth — the knowledge of the Holy — is the most enjoyable, satisfying, and invigorating part of my life. I enjoy solitude, silence, journaling, reading, meditating, and fellowshipping with other believers like never before. I get the most life out of this communion and community. It's the ancient path rediscovered, and I wish it for everyone. Seek Him "in spirit and in truth" and He will lead you into these joyful relationships.

The Heartbreak and the Power

The genesis of this book began seven years ago, or maybe earlier, as I pondered and journaled about the divide in our nation, our churches, and our families. How could people once so united be so divided, so loudly, and so quickly? Mysterious? Puzzling! It is also telling. Perhaps a clue to what's happening?

Examples abound in your realm and life, I'm sure! So I'll mention only two major examples for simplicity and brevity.

First, note the last election and the political scene in the USA today. I'll probably develop this as a piece of the puzzle and won't elaborate here. I don't put much stock in the political system or politics. I vote, and encourage my friends to vote. I support the candidate in each case who I feel, by their actions, has the better character and the better platform. And I pray. But that the church in the USA in this past election could be so divided, when reading the same Bible, is very mysterious, and telling. Allow me please to leave that for now and speak to it as a puzzle piece later. Suffice to say, churches, if they even addressed it, were very divided by the choices, as were friends, and even families on a widespread scale. I am aware that while politics isn't my hope for life or peace, it does touch our lives. Eventually, it can do so deeply. It now comes to mind that as my wife and I were eating breakfast at a Waffle House with our niece and nephew last Sunday, a big guy walked by brandishing in large letters on the back of his T-shirt, "Only You Can Stop Socialism." It seemed unusual and out of place, but in retrospect, it shows where we are as a nation.

Secondly, on a more personal and family level, I hear over and over, from parents and personal friends, "How can our children who were raised in church, and who we tried to send to the best schools, and for whom we modeled the Christian life as best we could, not be walking with the Lord? They're not going to church, and they have come to espouse the ungodly memes of the culture in our day." "Where did we go wrong?" "Why is this happening?" "How could this happen!?"

Why has this happened? That is a big question and the answer might not be simple. It could spring from many elements? But as I asked the Lord, and watched and prayed about this all-too-common occurrence, I feel He's given me some insight. And that would be the biggest motivation for writing about this puzzling development. And it would be my biggest hope, that the Spirit of God might use some, or all these puzzle pieces, to bring clarity, truth, and sharpness to the image of our present state, and restore hope and vision for the future, and real life in the authentic Christ.

I know of a recent conversation some parents had with their two adult children. This family has been very close, and by appearances, still is. But as the conversation about what the Bible says and what the culture says grew heated, then abated, it became clear the two lovely and lovable children, now young adults, successful in the world, espoused the morals and ethics of the culture and made their decisions based on these, not the Bible or what God says. They would, however, contend that their views and actions and beliefs lined up with the Bible, and how God sees things. After a long discussion, with everyone participating, the dad said to his son, "I think you'd have to say one of us is deluded or deceived, wouldn't you?" The son looked at his father, nodded and said, "Yes, I think you would."

They hugged and they affirmed they still loved each other. And they agreed to disagree until the Lord shined more light on the matter or helped all to see.

In one way, this is about as good of an outcome as one could hope for, but in another vein both parents and children knew that sharing life closely together, as a family, like they always had, was interrupted. And it was in danger of being lost. All the love, all the beautiful memories and experiences together, all the battles fought for each other and with each other, would likely be suspended if not lost, as now there were differences so great they weren't even sure who the real enemy was. And knowing how time slips away, like a turtle and also like a jet fighter, the loss of sharing love, intimacy, experiences, and dreams was felt by all. That is true loss.

That's heartbreak! That's something that strikes deep into the heart of the family, families in our churches, and families in our culture.

"Now abide faith, hope, and love, these three, but the greatest of these is love." This is true, of course. That's what the Word of God says in I Corinthians 13. I'm glad it also says "hope." Hope springs eternal. This is especially so when one knows God.

I'm glad in the same Bible we find the story of the lost coin, the lost sheep, and the lost son. The last story is commonly called the story of the prodigal son. Someone has said it could more accurately be called, the story of the incredible father. It gives me hope, for all the fathers and mothers out there, and maybe a good model? And it gives me hope for the prodigals.

For the same Bible teaches us that where sin abounds, grace abounds more.

Grace will be a common thread too, and as important a piece of this puzzle as deception. Let's begin to examine the pieces on the table, turn them over, group them, look for the ones with straight edges to assemble the border; whatever you normally do to start a puzzle? There is no certain order or strategy. Just find similar pieces and fit them into adjacent pieces where they belong. Repeat, look, sort, inspect, try one here or there. If you have patience and desire to see the image as it is, using your own powers of observation, you'll be richly rewarded. Enjoy!

PUZZLING CHAPTER 1

Getting Started

LET'S GET STARTED BY LOOKING at the image on the box. That helps as you try to come up with a strategy to put a puzzle together. Some people like to arrange the pieces into groups of like colors, shapes, or pieces that obviously go in a certain scene.

So let's do that, or at least let me give you a glimpse of the image so that you can decide where you want to start, while keeping in mind the scenes with the larger numbers of pieces.

There are three major areas. You can imagine them like the sea with its shades of greens and blues. There is also the sky with its shades of different blues, but also the oranges and reds of a sunset, with some clouds. Lastly in the big groupings there is the forest with shades of greens, different plants and trees, and a few animals. There are clearings in the forest, areas of people doing activities. There may also be a few colorful birds, some flags, and a handful of extra items, that fit into the puzzle, but are not easily recognizable as part of the major themes. They might not even look like they would fit. But all the pieces do fit.

They fit with the Bible narrative. They fit with a true historical narrative. They fit with what is going on in our day. I think you'll see it as it comes together. You may be challenged to look anew, at the Bible and the world around you with different eyes.

Here's a hint from the image on the box. The overall image I've entitled *Puzzling 2020, Connecting the Pieces*. This describes what the image is about. The three major groupings of pieces to the puzzle, like the sea, the sky, and the forest, are these: (1) **Where are we as a church and culture?** (2) **How did we get here?** and (3) **Where do we go from here, or how do we live in these puzzling times?** How do we live meaningful, enjoyable lives in the puzzling chaos of today and the uncertain future it portends?

Of course, I've included a table of contents, but it's fairly meaningless. It names some pieces of the puzzle and gives hints to their groupings, but they are not listed in any certain order or even by group. It's a puzzle! The joy is in the journey. The method is in the madness. I believe you'll see the image more clearly this way than any other way. And you'll be glad you worked this puzzle.

If I'm successful, the puzzle will be helpful to the kindergarten Christian, the elementary Christian, the high school Christian, the college Christian, the PhD Christian, the seminary-trained Christian, and the pagan on the street.

I know that's a pretty lofty goal. I can say it, because it doesn't depend on me. There are two major elements at play here: the word of God, or the Bible, and the Spirit of God, the Holy Spirit.

The Word and The Spirit

Ian Thomas, a British army major in World War II, later turned theologian said, "The Bible is the only book you can't understand unless you know the Author." There's a good bit of truth in that, but the mystery is how the Holy Spirit draws and illuminates a person as they read the Bible or are drawn to investigate its truths. While that part is not visible to us, it's not beyond us to experience His presence and truth. It's His job! He is able to separate the wheat from the chaff, the sheep from the goats, the silver from the dross, and cheap grace from costly grace, as Bonhoeffer teaches us and describes for us.

The Spirit is able and willing to do his part, and He's on the job 24/7. The better question is, "Do you want to know the truth? Do we want to know the God of Creation and His Son Jesus Christ, if it is all true?" If so, I believe He will lead you into truth. He says He will, in His word.

So this puzzle will rely heavily on the Bible and the Spirit. I felt the Spirit impress me in a thought that wasn't my thought, "Don't try to convince with long chapters or many words. Just say what I impress you to say, or you feel led to share. The readers will either believe it or they won't." I also heard this morning, probably because writing like this is a daunting task for me, "Have fun with it!"

So, I'm trusting the Holy Spirit to drive home to you, the reader, whatever truth or revelation He wishes. My only task is to listen to the Spirit, and be as true to the Bible as I can be. This I promise to do, with no bias or ulterior motive or compulsion other than what I have stated — to be helpful, and be true to the Bible. One of my favorite verses since I was a boy in Sunday school is: "Study to show yourself approved unto God, a workman that need not be ashamed, rightly dividing the word of truth" (2 Timothy 2:15).

Text Without Context Is Pretext

How do you interpret the Bible? It's not as hard as you think! Ask these three questions as you read, and read often! Expect the Holy Spirit to do the heavy lifting in the area of revelation and helping you understand. It does not depend on you perhaps as much as you think. You must only care enough to read, search, and ask questions, like a child.

One of the best educated Bible teachers I ever sat under told us to ask three questions when you read the Bible: (1) What did it mean then? (2) What does it mean now? and (3) What does it mean to me?

You'll be shocked at the wisdom, insight, and truth you will glean just from doing that. Then follow your heart and mind, and other teachers who have been studying for a long time.

I will give this one caution, mainly because of what I've already said about deception, and because God left some things fuzzy, probably for a reason. He probably did this so we would seek Him, the Giver of Truth, for the answers? He knew the dead ends in our search with pure motives would lead us back to Him.

This caution is really common sense. And it's already accomplished if you ask the three questions above. But it merits saying and keeping in mind for all your Bible study, all of your days. "A text without a context is a pretext." This is an axiom in the world of Bible study and interpretation, as it should be, and really must be! It will guard you from error and being carried away by your own logic, not fully informed, or from teachers of the word who quote things out of context for their own purposes, intentionally or unknowingly, because that's what they have been taught.

Paul an apostle of Jesus Christ, a Jewish lawyer very familiar with the word of God, learned by revelation that he didn't have as clear an understanding of the Scriptures as he thought. That came when he met the living Word of God, Jesus Christ, traveling from Jerusalem to Damascus. Paul praised one of the early churches (Berea) because: "they studied the Scriptures daily to see if what Paul was telling them was true" (Acts 17:11).

What do we mean by context? What audience is the speaker or writer addressing? What is the period in history? What are the circumstances or reasons for the writing or speaking? What is the outcome? Questions like these will answer the question, **"What did it mean then?"** Then meditate or think about the second question, **"What does**

it mean now?" See what comes to your mind as a meaning or application in our day? Ask the Spirit for any revelation He might have for you. Do that for the last question as well, ***"What does it mean to me?"***

If you're not familiar with the word "pretext," I suggest you look it up. I did and found I didn't know what it meant. The first definition I found was, "a reason given in justification of a course of action that is not the real reason." Hmm? That implies someone is trying to lead someone astray for some reason! Dictionary.com has as the first definition, "something that is put forward to conceal a true purpose or object; and ostensible reason; excuse." Do you see the deception connection? Don't let this happen to you. Guard against deception.

<u>Look at every Scripture you're going to take to heart in the context it's given. Then also make sure what you get out of it is consistent with the rest of God's word, the Bible.</u> You won't go wrong! And you'll have the Spirit to shine His light on it if you want to know the truth. He wants you to know. That's why He gave it. He will help you. But beware, He looks at your heart (I Samuel 16:7b). You should make it your highest goal to know His heart. It will be your highest good. Don't read your Bible to prove things, but with the hope, and for the purpose of knowing God.

One of my favorite passages is Proverbs 30. How could you not love a passage that starts out with these names, and ends with such a profound prayer?

"The words of Agur the son of Jakeh, the oracle.
The man declares to Ithiel, to Ithiel and Ucal:
Surely I am more stupid than any man,
And I do not have the understanding of a man.
Neither have I learned wisdom,
Nor do I have the knowledge of the Holy One.
Who has ascended into heaven and descended?
Who has gathered the wind in His fists?

Who has wrapped the waters in His garment?
Who has established all the ends of the earth?
What is His name or His Son's name?
Surely you know!
Every word of God is tested;
He is a shield to those who take refuge in Him.
Do not add to His words
Or He will reprove you, and you will be proved a liar.
Two things I asked of You,
Do not refuse me before I die:
Keep deception and lies far from me,…"

(Proverbs 30:1-8a).

Happy puzzling!

PUZZLING CHAPTER 2

9/11 Twenty Years Later

IN MY JOURNAL, I NOTED the following: I was up this morning at 6:00 A.M. with coffee pondering the fact that it's been twenty years since the fateful events of 9/11/2001 impacted New York City and shocked the world. I rode our four-wheeler to a high bluff on the end of the mountain to see the sunrise and meditate.

Does it seem twenty years later, there are more questions than answers? There are plenty of explanations for those who can see, whose eyes are open, spiritually open, to the puzzle before us and around us. "Unless the LORD builds the house, they labor in vain who build it; unless the LORD guards the city, the watchman keeps awake in vain" (Psalm 127:1). This verse certainly seems to apply to the post 9/11 United States of America. What do you think, if you've lived long enough to notice the difference?

A prayer just came to my mind, and I jotted it down in my journal. "Help us, Jesus, to see and deliver us from evil. Rescue us, and have mercy on us. Amen." "Rescue" was the central theme of the theatrical production, *Jesus*, that we saw in Branson with my sister and her husband Thursday afternoon. We need His rescue like never before in my lifetime. And we need His power for living in this day and hour.

"The walls are broken down, the gates are burned with fire, and the people are in great distress." Nehemiah, cupbearer to the king of Persia, recorded those words after he inquired of his brother, who had just arrived from Jerusalem, about the status of his home city. Twenty years after 9/11/2001, this seems like an accurate description of the church in America and America herself.

But to those who fear His name, these are only harbingers and signs that the Holy, the Almighty, is on the move. These are signs that His grace abounds more, and we can expect it because sin is abounding more. These are calls to paths of power, calls to light and living, calls to rebuild while facing spiritual enemies all around, and very near.

Do you see it? Do you hear it? I hope you do and that you will act in obedience to whatever the Spirit tells you to do. Godspeed! And enjoy the adventure of the times He has given you to live.

"They said to me, 'Those who survived the exile and are back in the province are in great trouble and disgrace. The wall of Jerusalem is broken down, and its gates have been burned with fire'"

(Nehemiah 1:3 NIV).

"God's law was given so that all people could see how sinful they were. But as people sinned more and more, God's wonderful grace became more abundant"

(Romans 5:20 NLT).

"But you will receive power when the Holy Spirit comes on you; and you will be my witnesses in Jerusalem, and in all Judea and Samaria, and to the ends of the earth"

(Acts 1:8 NIV).

"From one man he made all the nations, that they should inhabit the whole earth; and he marked out their appointed times in history and the boundaries of their lands"

(Acts 17:26).

PUZZLING CHAPTER 3

The Jewish New Year

IN MY JOURNAL SEPTEMBER 6, 2021, I noted: Sundown this evening begins Rosh Hashanah 2021 or 5782 on the Hebrew calendar, the new year. It also begins the Feast of Trumpets, ten days called "The Days of Awe," "Days of Repentance," the days of restoring relationships.

According to Wikipedia, traditionally, Rosh Hashanah is the "anniversary of the creation of Adam and Eve, the first man and woman according to the Hebrew Bible, and the inauguration of humanity's role in God's world."

There is only one commandment regarding Rosh Hashanah, "Blow the shofar." The sound of the trumpet lets us know something is happening — something wonderful. It is an invitation to once again give our attention to the Lord and usher in His presence.

Also, the year 5782 is right on the threshold of the 6000-year mark the ancient Jewish sages, and early church fathers thought would end man's rule in the earth and usher in the 1000 year reign of the Messiah, King of the Jews. Lactantius wrote: "As there have been 2000 years from Adam to Abraham, and 2000 years from Abraham to Christ, so there will be 2000 years for the Christian Era and then would come the Millennium (the remaining 1000 year reign of Christ on earth)."

Suppose the date of Jesus' crucifixion was April 3, 33 AD, as I've come to believe after researching the matter. If you add from that date 2000 years, you get 2033 as a possible starting time frame for the Millennium, probably in the fall, if the Feasts of Israel are God's prophetic timeline, as many suppose, around the Feast of Trumpets. If you subtract seven years for the seventieth week of Daniel or the great tribulation, you get 2026. According to many prophecy and eschatology scholars of the Bible, the church's rapture could come before or during these years. At any rate, 2000 years since Christ's appearing is coming quickly!

If you think that could be true, take up your trumpet! Speak out this message of truth. If you hear the trumpet, react, awaken, repent, draw near, and welcome your King! He is coming. He is near.

"Seventy weeks are determined upon thy people and upon thy holy city, to finish the transgression, and to make an end of sins, and to make reconciliation for iniquity, and to bring in everlasting righteousness, and to seal up the vision and prophecy, and to anoint the most Holy"

(Daniel 9:24).

"Now to the King eternal, immortal, invisible, the only God, be honor and glory forever and ever. Amen"

(I Tim 1:17 NIV).

"The kingdom of the world has become the kingdom of our Lord and of his Christ, and he shall reign forever and ever"

(Revelation 11:15).

PUZZLING CHAPTER 4

The Spirit and the Bride

A PIECE OF THE PUZZLE and phrase that's been coming to my mind lately is, "The Spirit and the bride say, 'Come.'" It's from the very last chapter of the Apocalypse (Revelation 22:17). It's such a beautiful phrase — peaceful, inviting, gracious.

The Bride is Christ's church. And when flowing in, or filled with His Spirit, she is most beautiful indeed.

Thoughts rush in here! The cousins' weekend comes quickly to mind. Two weeks ago, my girl cousins came to our cabin for a weekend getaway. These girls are beautiful, inside and out, and a joy to be with and behold.

At the risk of being too personal, a few other beautiful women come to mind. Miriam, Sophia, and a young woman from Hungary I sat beside on an American Airlines flight are examples of dozens of other chance encounters. I've had the joy of beholding and knowing such beautiful ones. They are mysterious, probably even to themselves. Even casually knowing and encountering such beauty is a treasured part of one's journey. Divina, Laura, and their mother from Honduras now come to mind, along with others. Beauty and mystery!

It's also a bit of a mystery that these beautiful ones long to be revealed and even to give themselves away to someone worthy, faithful, true, loving, gentle, strong, and kind. They look for a chance, a dance, a meeting of hearts, romance, an opportunity for such a relationship, as part of their destiny and fulfillment.

Once a bride has given herself to a worthy one, she is constantly in the process of being his. She is loving, serving, enjoying her position and the opportunity to reveal her inner and outer beauty to her man, lover, friend, protector, defender, and provider.

She also gives of herself and serves her children, other children, and friends. She helps the downcast and the poor who benefit much from her touch, smile, service, hospitality, care, kindness, and love.

Mystery! But experiential, something we can know, touch, experience over time in an earth-life, during our journey on the planet. It's undoubtedly a dance, imperfect but joyful, and the best part of our sojourn. Experienced rightly, or with the help of the Spirit, it's an immense joy for a husband and wife.

They are a gift from God, to each other, then to their families and friends. They are a gift even to strangers who catch a glimpse of their beauty and marvel, maybe not even realizing why they are smiling inside, at the sight of a happy couple holding hands or gazing into each other's eyes over coffee.

Well, I've wandered far from where I started, and maybe not continually in the right direction. But there is something special about a bride! The beauty, the charm, the glory that both men and women, husbands and wives, understand, admire, and hold as a paragon of value. They do so, even from vastly different perspectives.

At the end of the Apocalypse, doesn't it seem that it should read, "The king says come"? It is, after all, the Revelation of Jesus, the King, but in the last chapter of the Holy Bible, we find, "The Spirit and the bride say, 'Come.'" The Bride who knows the King of all power, wealth, glory, and honor intimately and is honored because of her favored position, and a beauty of her own enhanced by His Spirit, extends the invitation — Come.

I opened my Bible to look at that verse and its context. In the process, my eyes fell on the verse of the day: "Surely goodness and loving kindness will follow me, and I will dwell in the house of the Lord forever" (Psalm 23:6). This verse from the most famous chapter in the Bible seems to fit with this invitation.

My mind quickens, and my heart enlarges as I think about Ruth, Esther, Sarah, Naomi, Abigail, Mary, Mary Magdalene, Mary and Martha. Ponder with me the beauty of creation, the beauty of a woman, the beauty of the Lord, the beauty of love and grace — incredible and unique.

The last chapter of the Apocalypse is rich! So much joy and peace flood my soul while reading it, along with insights, like the rush you get when you put the last few pieces of a puzzle together after the long puzzling journey. The end is near. The mystery is almost complete.

"The now" and the "not yet" are in place at the same time. The King is in the process of making Himself and his kingdom clearly known and His dominance shown. But He is not threatening to His bride or sons and daughters, and His friends — all the ones He knows, His sheep.

Come, eat from the tree of life by the streams of living water. We begin Genesis with the tree of life in the garden and end with the tree of life in Revelation. What's in between is a journey, six days or 6000 years of human experience — humans interacting with their Creator King and His constant invitation to relationship, to be a part of His bride.

There are many 60, 70, 80-year journeys — microcosms, intimate, personal, miniatures of humanity's overall and overarching story on the planet. In our way, each of us relates in our day to our Creator as Solomon so clearly describes in Ecclesiastes chapter three.

Isn't it interesting that Solomon, the wisest man who ever lived after asking God for that grace, also wrote "The Song"? You could describe "The Song of Solomon" as an intimate look at the King and his lover, his Bride, and their journey. This Bride comprises those the King knows and keeps in relationship. This Bride is His church — most valuable to Him and beautiful.

A faithful bride, enjoying His graces and her position, flowing and growing in His Spirit, is the most beautiful and desirable being on earth. She knows her King intimately and has experienced his touch, kindness, riches, power, grace, and love.

This Bride, who knows the King best, gives her warm, genuine, loving, hospitable, generous invitation — "Come." She knows her King has set an unimaginable table for all! Gracious and loving is He. You are invited.

PUZZLING CHAPTER 5

The Holy Spirit In The Church

A PIECE OF THE PUZZLE is "The Holy Spirit in the Church."

In a men's group recently, the discussion about the Holy Spirit was excellent! Most of the guys were open to new truth and revelation as long as it was in the Bible, but having a Baptist background like me, I wondered how it would go? The same could apply to many denominations, as you will note.

"Why," it was asked, "does the church in the west, or we have trouble with the Holy Spirit?"

Honest answers proffered and discussed included:

1. Our educational system is Greek modeled, materialistic, and further influenced by the French Enlightenment, stressing the intellect and neglecting or rejecting the Spirit.
2. Our churches are affected and infected and have not understood nor taught what the Bible says about the Holy Spirit.
3. The Spirit is mystical and mysterious, so He's not easy to know if you have the mindset mentioned in 1 and 2 above.

4. Because of excesses seen or reported, we've been skeptical of those sects or denominations who claim to have experienced the Holy Spirit. Some have acted like they have some corner on Him, or have Him in their box, so we've rejected them and their teaching, likely throwing out the baby with the bathwater.

Why are our eyes and minds closed? We love the truth. Are we that afraid of error? Why wouldn't we trust God our Father to lead us into all truth? One of the most important truths is that we can and should have a relationship with the Holy Spirit.

Spiritual blindness is more rampant, embedded, and systemic in our lives and churches than we have thought! This omitted teaching and missing experiential relationship with the Holy Spirit is one area that demonstrates that fact. One member of our group just finished reading *The Heavenly Man*. It's about Brother Yun, a leader of the underground church in China, who was constantly led by the Spirit. My friend brings it up often, and I can tell the book has changed his thinking about the place of the Holy Spirit in the church and his personal life.

In Isaiah chapter six, we find another clue why we in the community of believers haven't known the truth about the Holy Spirit and are consequently spiritually dull. The Lord is understated and doesn't appear to those disinterested, but to those who are humble or desperate and hungry to know Him. Grace is free, but it is not cheap. Grace is costly, as Dietrich Bonhoeffer told the modern church in *The Cost of Discipleship*. He found the German church in his day asleep and deceived, like the Jewish nation of Isaiah's day. The Lord told Isaiah to speak to the people whatever he heard from the Lord, but also told him the people would not hear, by and large. They had grown dull of hearing because of idolatry and the lack of intimacy.

Jesus on The Holy Spirit

What did Jesus have to say about the Holy Spirit? "Much!" is the answer. I'll point out a few things for brevity. Let it serve as a springboard to do your own research and study. It's easy to see that the Holy Spirit was a significant focus for Jesus and an essential part of his plan for us.

"Nevertheless, I tell you the truth: it is to your advantage that I go away, for if I do not go away, the Helper will not come to you. But if I go, I will send him to you" (John 16:7 ESV).

"But the Helper, the Holy Spirit, whom the Father will send in my name, he will teach you all things and bring to your remembrance all that I have said to you" (John 14:26 ESV).

Paul on the Holy Spirit

The Apostle Paul had much to say and demonstrate about the Holy Spirit. In Acts 19, Paul on his way to Ephesus met a group of believers outside of town and asked them a meaningful, telling question: "Did you receive the Holy Spirit when you believed?" They replied, "No, we have not even heard that there is a Holy Spirit" (Acts 19:2 ESV). Doesn't that describe or define the church in the West? In America? In our city? We have not even heard whether there is a Holy Spirit, it seems.

At least we act like it. While we do experience the Holy Spirit from time to time, it seems we do so without being aware. It appears we are wired by God for 220 volts and are living on AA batteries.

There isn't awareness. There isn't the practice. There isn't the experience. There isn't the hunger. Biblical teaching on the Holy Spirit as an abiding part of our lives doesn't exist in many churches. The Bible teaches that God sent the Holy Spirit in Christ's name to dwell with us and in us, to be our Helper. Is He a part of your reality?

The Acts 19 account goes on to say there were about twelve men involved. That's not a significant number. God is not into big numbers, apparently. I wonder what kind of wonders these twelve accomplished after that experience and for the rest of their lives? Later in the same chapter, we read, "God was performing extraordinary miracles by the hand of Paul" (Acts 19:9 ESV). Paul continually said it was the Holy Spirit working through him.

We Should Know the Spirit

Back to our reality, the Holy Spirit goes about his work of refining us, convicting us of sin, righteousness, and judgment. He is molding us into the image of Christ, to be His friends and His bride, the church, the "ecclesia," the called-out ones. But it seems there is so much more available from Him for us and through us if we understand the working of the Spirit.

John chapter 3 is significant and instructive about the role of the Holy Spirit. Jesus speaks to Nicodemus, "The Teacher of Israel," a man schooled and skilled in the Bible, and tells Nicodemus there is more. Someone has said, "God not only left us a map; He left us a guide." The map is the Bible, and the guide is the Holy Spirit. Scripture completely supports this convergence. "That which is born of the flesh is flesh, and that which is born of the Spirit is spirit" (John 3:6 ESV). "The wind blows where it wishes, and you hear its sound, but you do not know where it comes from or where it goes. So it is with everyone who is born of the Spirit" (John 3:8 ESV).

How to Know the Spirit

Don't be overly amazed about this. Just experience it. Be willingly led by the Spirit wind as you come to apprehend or hear His leading and come to see what He is doing. Jesus told Nicodemus that he could.

And he's telling you that you can.

It's not hard! You don't have to understand it completely. In fact, you won't! John 3:8 and Proverbs 3:5-6 tell us not to lean on our understanding, rather expect to be moved by the wind of the Spirit. You have to sense it and follow those leadings and impressions. By training your senses through obedience to what you hear, you will improve. It's a sixth sense, one the world does not experience, but one the believer uses to see into the spiritual realm and bring heaven's goodness to bear on earth.

You will learn to recognize synchronicities. You will know to pay attention to some dreams and reject others. You will expect visions. You'll not be surprised when awakened at 3:33 AM anymore. You will get up and journal or meditate in silence and listen to what thoughts come to you. You will listen for what the Spirit might say. Through practice, you can learn to distinguish between your ideas and His thoughts. Through familiarity, you will learn to discern His voice from others, like you recognize the voice of a family member or close friend.

Hindrances to Knowing the Spirit

Does this spiritual exchange of information ever become foolproof? I'd say no, it does not. The Scripture would indicate that dark spirits can operate on these same frequencies or spiritual impressions. The Scriptures record that even "Satan can appear as an angel of light." So that scares many away from desiring honest dialogue with the Holy Spirit. But it shouldn't. Trust God, He's more powerful, and He is good. We know this spiritual communication is a fact of life, whether we want to bury our heads in the sand and ignore it or not. You have undoubtedly had bad dreams that disturbed sleep, for no rhyme or reason, and that scared you. They seemed disjointed with no discernible message. Do you think those came from God? Yet, we know that dreams can be valid from Scripture and shared human experience. They may warn us about something or someone. They may give us a glimpse into our destiny or what God intends for our future. We may need the help of interpretation or more dreams, but they don't scare us, and we don't forget them when we sense their validity.

Another thing that drives many with a western mindset away from this spiritual communication is the fear of making mistakes. What if I hear incorrectly? What if I hear from a dark spirit or my imagination? Fear of failure and fear of making a mistake robs us of life that might be ours. Trust God. Get to know Him through His record of interacting with people in the Bible. Then you will know if what you hear sounds like something He would say. But don't wait until you are a Bible scholar. Remember He also sent a guide, the Holy Spirit. He will help you. He will train you. He will show you the way you are to go. Sometimes it will involve courage. Obedience to what you hear will always require faith and trust. Each obedient action leads to better hearing, more confidence, more trust, more spiritual insight. Initially, the Spirit probably won't speak to you the same way He spoke to Moses, Elijah, the prophets, the apostles, or Jesus Himself. But He desires to speak and commune with you. It's both a gift and a learned skill to hear. It's to your great advantage to listen, obey, and enjoy that relationship of intimacy, seeing, and adventure — Godspeed on your journey.

The Joy of Knowing the Spirit

You will come to hear of someone having a word of knowledge and see it for what it is. You won't be surprised, seeing it as the Holy Spirit wanting to illuminate something or help someone. I know of many examples personally, but not as many as I would like to see and experience.

It only stands to reason that if you know it happens and that it's a valid expression or communication of the Holy Spirit, you're going to participate in it by faith. All of the gifts work by faith and leading, by leading and faith, by hearing and obeying. Afterward, the spiritual power flows, and you see it, sense it, and are in awe of it.

There are times you are not aware of it. Only the person receiving your word of encouragement, word of knowledge, or prayer, is affected deeply by it. They may not even show you this outwardly. But inwardly, between them and the Lord, they know and are moved or stunned by what is said, prayed, or laid bare. It will affect their life, if not immediately, in the days to come, as they surrender or come to know the Spirit themselves. God is very understated like that. Expect it often to work this way. Have faith that you delivered the message and trust God with the results. When people sense a message is supernatural or from God, they're seldom inclined to shoot the messenger. Relax, be humble, be caring, be loving, be gracious, be courageous. "… wisdom is proved right by her deeds" (Matthew 11:19b).

Again, it stands to reason that if you don't understand how the Holy Spirit works, even a little bit, or haven't seen Him in action, you're going to stand by and gawk. You'll be more in shock and doubt than a willing participant in God's grace as it's pouring out.

I have eight examples listed in the journal I'm referencing right now. And I'd love to share them as demonstrations of what I'm talking about because they're convincing and fun to recount. But I feel the Spirit impressing me not to do so, instead to let my words be few and leave the convincing between Him and you, the reader. He's reminding me of the Scripture, "Your ears will hear a word behind you saying, 'This is the way, walk in it'" (Isaiah 30:21a).

PUZZLING CHAPTER 6

BLM is a Crock

THIS LINE CAME TO ME in the early morning as I was lying in bed and contemplating all that I had been reading in Voddie Baucham Jr.'s *Fault Lines*. But it sounded sort of harsh and judgmental, so I didn't want to use it until I looked up the meaning of the word "crock."

> crock NOUN
> 1. an earthenware pot or jar, a broken piece of earthenware
> 2. (informal) something considered to be complete nonsense.
> VERB cause an injury to (a person or part of the body)

It fits what I thought when I first heard the phrase Black Lives Matter in light of Scripture and a world view informed by Scripture. It's nonsense and nothing that should be attractive to a Christian with a Biblical worldview. So it's shocking to me that many well-meaning Christians have fallen for the deception, including a few well-known Christian leaders. It's another gospel, such as Paul warned the early church against, and a very inferior one.

I'm not going to convince anyone who believes the Black Lives Matter deception with a few paragraphs, nor do I wish to try. I've done you the biggest favor I can by recommending possibly the best book written on the subject. The author treats the matter with excellent research and clarity, and with honor, respect, and kindness. The search for truth is up to you. You've probably heard the proverb: "The first to speak in court sounds right—until the cross-examination begins" (Proverbs 18:17 NLT).

I'll leave you with two thoughts from Voddie Baucham and his book. "So when Zambians began to ask me questions about the murderous and corrupt American police hunting down black men, I could not remain silent. I began to tell the stories and raise the issues that I will share with you…." He goes on to say that the United States is the least racially prejudiced country he's ever known or visited. After a twenty-five-year career as an airline pilot, and the last fifteen of it flying internationally, I wholeheartedly agree. So who came up with this narrative (lies unfounded in fact or by evidence)? Who? What? When? Where? Why? And what are the facts?

It would be best if you asked these questions and then decided what you believe. It's vital for you, for your church, for your culture, and for your country. Ask God in prayer to show you the facts and the truth of this matter.

Oh, one last thing! Be kind and loving when you discuss this matter. You usually don't fight fire with fire, but with water. You fight lies with truth, simple truth, spoken in love. And you trust God to do the heavy lifting. He's the only One Who can fix this deception. Pray that He will be willing and do so.

Continue to enjoy your life of adventure and love with Him and in Him. The world changer, Paul the Apostle, said of his mission: "For I determined to know nothing among you except Jesus Christ, and Him crucified" (1 Corinthians 2:2). He said his passion was this: "That I may know Him and the power of His resurrection and the fellowship of His sufferings…"(Philippians 3:10). It would seem profitable and wise to do the same.

Get to know Voddie Baucham
[https://youtu.be/hxnFE6DWbxo]

Hear a black theologian speak about this subject
[https://youtu.be/i60eQZPG5XM]

Hear a white theologian talk about this subject
[https://youtu.be/3MMU7f0Bdw4]

"But though we, or an angel from heaven, preach any other gospel unto you than that which we have preached unto you, let him be accursed" (Galatians 1:8).

"The first one to plead his cause seems right until his neighbor comes and examines him" (Proverbs 18:17).

PUZZLING CHAPTER 7

The Lord Loves Justice

SOME DEAR YOUNG FRIENDS OF ours recently had a new baby boy and named him Justice Malachi. On an Instagram post, his mom quoted Psalm 37:28:

"The LORD loves Justice...."

Lovely, and true!

It's a strong name, isn't it? Malachi is the last book in the Old Testament. You might say he is the last prophet beginning 400 years of silence before the first advent of the King, the Messiah, Jesus of Nazareth, King of the Jews. Then comes Jesus' forerunner prophet, John the Baptist, and the New Testament of the Bible. Malachi in Hebrew means "Messenger" or "Messenger of Yahweh."

The name "Justice" is powerful and telling too, especially in our country, church, and day. Many people are confused about real justice, what it is, and just who is responsible for establishing or maintaining it.

If you are an agnostic or a secular humanist, who doesn't believe

God matters, you are responsible for deciding the definition of justice and how to establish and maintain justice yourself. You're acting as your own god. Or you will say that human government or consensus is responsible for this determination, definition, and execution.

If you are a Bible-believing Christian, you will have a high view of God and an experiential relationship with Him and realize that He defines, establishes, and maintains justice from on high, just as He says in the Bible and as history demonstrates. I think all humans have an innate understanding of justice, perhaps because we are created in His image. In case you haven't looked at the definition lately, with all the hubbub about social justice, maybe a definition is in order. Then let's reflect on a few things the Bible says about justice.

jus·tice/noun (from Oxford Languages)
1. just behavior or treatment, a concern for justice, peace, and genuine respect for people
2. a judge or magistrate, in particular a judge of the Supreme Court of a country or state

"Clouds and thick darkness surround Him; righteousness and justice are the foundation of His throne"

(Psalm 97:2).

"The Lord is in His holy temple; the Lord's throne is in heaven; His eyes behold, His eyelids test the sons of men"

(Psalm 11:4).

"For the Lord loves justice and does not forsake His godly ones; they are preserved forever, but the descendants of the wicked will be cut off"

(Psalm 37:28).

"Vengeance is Mine, and retribution, in due time their foot will slip; for the day of their calamity is near, and the impending things are hastening upon them"

(Deuteronomy 32:35).

"For these are days of vengeance [of rendering full justice or satisfaction], so that all things which are written will be fulfilled"

(Luke 21:22, AMP).

"For we know Him who said, 'Vengeance is Mine, I will repay.' And again, 'The Lord will judge His people'"

(Hebrews 10:30).

"He has told you, O man, what is good; and what does the Lord require of you but to do justice, to love kindness, and to walk humbly with your God?"

(Micah 6:8).

PUZZLING CHAPTER 8

Fault Lines of Social Justice

"I AM NOT AN AFRICAN. I am not an African American. I am an American, and I wouldn't want to be anything else. America doesn't owe me anything. America has blessed me beyond measure. If anything, I owe America." These words are from *Fault Lines* written by Voddie Baucham Jr., a man's man raised by a single mom in Watts. He provides us with a complete look at the current issues of "social justice," Black Lives Matter, "critical race theory," "intersectionality," etc., which are part and parcel of the same world view. He has read their background material carefully and quotes it accurately to show how it distorts the truth, history, and the Bible. He does all this with a very kind but prophet-like, child-like honesty.

The most important book I read in 2020, *Fault Lines*, deals with these issues thoroughly, leaving no stone unturned. Critical race theory is a deception that needs to be exposed and addressed, so you can take a stand or understand what's being said, why it's being said, and what's at stake. Do your research, of course, and this book is an excellent place to start. The 20/20 men's reading and friendship group that meets in our home recently spent four sessions discussing it, and we all feel the same way.

Parts of the book are a bit academic, but that's because the author is a college president and an academic himself. Also, the terms and their meanings must be defined and understood before they can be discussed. Rest assured, however, his storytelling, personal history, and Spirit-led sharpness shine throughout and certainly in the end.

It's hard-hitting, factual, and informative. Baucham addresses the things you've wondered about, as the media have promoted the worldview of the radical dissidents in reporting the violence and looting of the protesters. In the end, it's also an excellent segue to understanding "lies and deception," the worldwide delusion impacting our world today. This has been an interest and study of mine for some time, and something the Spirit continually points out to me as the main answer to, "How can these things be happening?" In the church of Jesus Christ, no less!

If you're puzzled by this topic and the events of 2020 - 2022, this book is an excellent place to start your search for truth and what to do about it. Godspeed as you journey.

PUZZLING CHAPTER 9

Epiphany 2021

JANUARY 6, 2021, WAS EPIPHANY in the Christian Church around the globe and the USA. It's the day celebrated for centuries, if not millennia, as the day gentiles, Magi from the East, first saw Jesus, knowing Him to be God, the Messiah, the promised King of Kings — an epiphany.

I thought it ironic and telling, a synchronicity of sorts, that it was also the appointed day for the next king, or president, of the United States to be declared after the votes were counted and confirmed valid by Congress. Votes were cast in record numbers despite the pandemic with its confusing uncertainty. According to the US Census Bureau, Americans cast seventeen million more votes than in the 2016 election. 73% of the eligible population was registered to vote, and 67% did vote. It was a highly contested and emotionally charged election, with the media doing its part to portray the choices. According to many, the options in candidates were not all that different, yet the many were polarized and galvanized. The choices in platforms could not have been more clear, distinct, or stark.

I don't think it too strong to say if you voted conservatively, you voted for the platform that more closely resembled God's Word and God's rule in the affairs of man. If you voted liberally, you voted for secular humanism, man being his own god and making his own rules, trusting the government to take care of the people, and ignoring or rebuffing God's law and governance.

During and after the large turnout of voters, there were accusations of election fraud in several places, including many of the critical states determining the election's outcome. The evidence was handled in predictable ways by the media and by politicians. But IF there was sufficient evidence of fraud and IF politicians had the backbone to stand up, investigate, and say so, legally, the election results could have yet been changed by law to favor a platform more conforming to God's Word than opposing God's Word. That did not happen. So perhaps that was not the case? Or maybe it was? At any rate, the people, and their leaders, stated their preferences loudly and clearly by votes and action, or inaction. Let the record show, and let the people know, their choice was clear. It was shouted from the rooftops by the media, who apparently couldn't be more pleased with the result.

I believe while many were celebrating Epiphany quietly, worshipfully, acknowledging and giving thanks to God for Jesus the Savior and soon-coming King, that the USA had its own epiphany. It was an epiphany of rejecting this King and acknowledging another. It seems as if God was saying, "I want to make it clear to you what you are asking for, so you will know it was by your choice that My judgment begins."

And so it was. And so it will be.

I felt what many are feeling and saying now. The USA has gone over a waterfall into a cascading decline and sequence of events that looks like judgment. God is removing His favor or turning away His face from the USA due to apostasy and unfaithfulness, what the prophets called "whoring after idols."

Once I saw this was the people's decision and that God was letting it go this way, I had a deep peace about it. I was sad for the church who helped it happen and for my country. I was concerned for the world, which has long looked up to her. I knew the darkness would increase, and the blessings we have known would decrease and be given to others and taken away by foreign powers, according to the will and word of the Lord — the just rewards for sin, rebellion, and injustice.

But I also know God to be full of mercy and grace. I saw that in times of sin, rebellion, and apostasy in ancient Israel and Judah, the prophets who saw it coming prayed to God, "In wrath remember mercy," knowing that discipline was necessary to awaken the people and allow them to change their hearts and their ways. These prophets, like the Israelite Priest Eli, on a day when he received some terrible news about the Lord's judgment coming on his family for sin, but knowing the goodness of God, and His mercy, said: "Let the LORD do what seems good to Him" (1 Samuel 3:18).

I also saw the LORD saying through His servants the prophets during these dark times that He would take note of those who fear Him, protect them and care for them. He would do so even as He chastised those who were doing wrong and in open rebellion to Him and His ways. "But for those who fear My name, the sun of righteousness will arise with healing in its wings" (Malachi 4:2a). "I will be a wall of fire around her, and I will be the glory in her midst" (Zechariah 2:5b).

This judgment or correction will be painful to watch. I feel the Lord has impressed me not to watch it that much but instead dwell on the good things in life, the gifts of God, experience Him more and more intimately, and look for His grace to be on the move, letting it move through me. He says in His Word, "Where sin abounds, grace much more abounds" (Romans 5:20).

That's my position and worldview, given the situation and circumstances. I believe it to be Biblical and what the Spirit is saying to the churches, therefore worthy of your consideration. Godspeed on your journey! Stay awake and ready to join the battle. Rest in Him—His peace to you and yours.

PUZZLING CHAPTER 10

A Word for a Wilderness

THE APOSTLE PAUL TELLS US that "we are not to be conformed to the world but to be transformed by the renewing of our minds" (Romans 12:1). The Word of God transforms us as we read it, meditate upon it, memorize it, pray it, sing it, share it, and fellowship with the One Who wrote it. Our minds are renewed, our hearts are strengthened, and our behavior is changed; not by an external force, but by internal transformation.

I borrow that from Charles Simpson's excellent pastoral letter published each month at csmpublishing.org. I've been in a spiritual wilderness of late, experiencing both the isolation, cleansing, and terrible beauty of that wilderness, disorienting as it is, and I've been in the Word experiencing its beauty, purification, and reorientation.

Against the mostly hidden enemy of our souls, there is no substitute nor defense like the Word. Christ used the Word of God when attacked in the wilderness by Satan.

Words from Luther's most famous hymn, "A Mighty Fortress," come to mind: "…one little Word shall fell him."

"The Prince of Darkness grim, we tremble not for him;
His rage we can endure, for lo, his doom is sure,
One little word shall fell him.
That word above all earthly powers, no thanks to them abideth;
The Spirit and the gifts are ours, through Him Who with us sideth;
Let goods and kindred go, this mortal life also;
The body they may kill: God's truth abideth still,
His kingdom is forever."

So we see the Word can silence our enemy and put him to flight. Scripture is essential and provides examples to help us in our earthly journey in the seen and unseen realms. Words of God seen in Scripture also have power for the "transformation and the renewing of our minds." It's beautiful. It's relational. It's mystical. It's joyful. It's reorienting. It's life and light. It's hard to describe but beautiful to experience.

Our Catholic brothers have a saying that goes like this, "We don't read the Word of God; the Word of God reads us." While both are true at the same time, the latter is observable and accurate. "The word of God is living and active … piercing as far as the division of soul and spirit, … and able to judge the thoughts and intentions of the heart" (Hebrews 4:12).

I have a very high view of Scripture. Surprisingly I once felt the Lord impress me, "I didn't give the Word for you to serve it; but for it to serve you." That's at once humbling and essential to know if it is accurate. It's an important distinction, even if both are true at the same time. Think about it. God doesn't need the Bible. It describes Who He is and how He acts with nature, angels, and men. He knows all that. We need it to know and learn so we can better relate to Him and our environment. He gave us the Word as a map to help us along our way in the world and help us know Him if we wish.

Jesus in His wilderness experience quoted Deuteronomy 8:3: "It is written, 'Man shall not live by bread alone, but by every word of

God.'" We need food every day, in the natural and in the spiritual.

And we need to practice good hygiene every day to stay healthy. Ephesians 5:26 tells us Jesus "washes us with water through the word."

We need healthy relationships each day to thrive. Our Father meets us when we read and meditate on His Word to illuminate us, love us, and be with us as a friend.

Please excuse me. I'm taking a break from this puzzle to wash up and have breakfast with a Friend. I suggest you do the same today and every day! You'll be glad you did, and so will those around you.

"For the word of God is living and active and sharper than any two-edged sword, and piercing as far as the division of soul and spirit, of both joints and marrow, and able to judge the thoughts and intentions of the heart"

(Hebrews 4:12).

"You are my hiding place and my shield; I wait for Your word"

(Psalm 119:118).

"Thy word have I hid in mine heart, that I might not sin against thee"

(Psalm 119:11 KJV).

"Your word is a lamp to my feet and a light to my path."

(Psalm 119:105 NASB).

"Be careful to listen to all these words which I command you, so that it may be well with you and your sons after you forever, for you will be doing what is good and right in the sight of the Lord your God"

(Deuteronomy 12:28).

"Forever, O Lord, Your word is settled in heaven"

(Psalm 119:89).

"To know wisdom and instruction,
To discern the sayings of understanding,
To receive instruction in wise behavior,
Righteousness, justice and equity;
To give prudence to the naive,
To the youth knowledge and discretion,
A wise man will hear and increase in learning,
And a man of understanding will acquire wise counsel,
To understand a proverb and a figure,
The words of the wise and their riddles. The fear of the Lord is the beginning of knowledge;
Fools despise wisdom and instruction"

(Proverbs 1:2-7).

"The Spirit gives life; the flesh counts for nothing. The words I have spoken to you are spirit and they are life"

(John 6:63).

PUZZLING CHAPTER 11

Race

TREAT EVERYONE THE SAME WAY and stay far away from any blame game. Treat everyone as you would want to be treated yourself. That's all! Be especially wary of anyone trying to divide people based on race. It's been too common and attempted throughout history to cause turmoil and seize power by unscrupulous demagogues or would-be demagogues.

Jesus would have no part of it. He created all races and all people and considers us the same — sacred. We bear His image, and He made us the way we are. Each one of us is capable of being a temple of his Holy Spirit if we desire. That's the clear teaching of Scripture and the experience of millions of His followers, who regularly meet together. They pray, worship, and fellowship with each other around this shared experience and revelation. They enjoy His presence being part of His global family as the Scriptures say, "…men from every tribe and tongue and people and nation" (Revelation 5:9).

Any discrimination based on race is wrong, period. I can say that because it's plainly what the Scriptures say from beginning to end and what Jesus and the Apostles taught and practiced. Reverse discrimination is wrong and unjust, as unfair as discrimination. Both are discrimination based on race. Pastor Martin Luther King, I believe, would say the same thing. He was a very spiritual man and was led and helped by God to accomplish one of the most unique reformations or revolutions in history. The civil rights movement did more to disclose and dispose of widespread discrimination based on race than is possible without supernatural help. He did this with little bloodshed, although every life is precious, compared to similar social movements in history. Praise be to God.

But then, some in the movement, or some in the government, or both have tried to push our government, our country, and our people into the other ditch – reverse discrimination. I never liked it when bureaucratic government forms, seemingly printed as fast as money these days, ask us to mark a square indicating our race or ethnicity. Why? God doesn't care about ethnicity, so why should the government? I knew it was to help blacks or those formerly oppressed get a step up. So, who wouldn't have a heart and comply? I figured it would last for a limited time, and it might be God's will in the matter or His doing.

I don't mark those boxes any longer. It's now clear the government won't stop and they have another agenda. It's none of the government's business. They use the information for race discrimination, and I want no part of it. It's hurtful, unjust, and unfair to all parties concerned.

Just say no to discrimination. Say no to humanism. Say no to socialism, which is a government based on secular humanism, man trying to be his own god. Just say no. Say this to yourself and others, "I won't be a part of it. I want nothing to do with it, and I'll call it out when I see it. It's hurtful, and it's harmful. It's not just. It's not social, and it's not social justice."

When you speak out about this issue, be kind and loving. Trust God to sort it out and go on to other more healthy and productive pursuits. Let the truth speak for itself.

Jesus would have nothing to do with racial discrimination. Read the Gospels, noting every related thing He said and did. The Pharisees, the most influential religious leaders of Jesus' day with considerable political clout, approached him publicly and asked, "Isn't it true that you are a Samaritan and have a demon?" (John 8:48). It was a loaded question meant to challenge or cast doubt on his spiritual authority and to divide his followers based on race.

The Samaritans were a mixed-race people from 722 BC when the ten tribes of Israel were carried away into captivity by Assyria due to their idolatry and apostasy before God. Assyria forced them to intermarry and live in different parts of the empire. Many captives moved back to settle again in northern Israel or Samaria, their native homeland, when it became possible.

Racial division and man's nature to exalt himself or his people raised its ugly head again. These two people groups Samaria and Judah now rejected their half brothers and began to despise and discriminate against each other. They were continually exalting themselves and putting the other side down. This feud was quite heated and often accompanied by violence. They generally would not welcome each other or travel in each other's territory.

Jesus' answer to the Pharisees was telling, insightful, and instructive – brilliant. "I don't have a demon." That's all he said, the simple truth about the demon issue, then let the people decide what they would. Jesus didn't even address the Jew's attempt to be racially divisive. He didn't think it was a question worth answering or entertaining. We shouldn't either.

He probably knew the Pharisees' intent. He was as wise as a serpent and gentle as a dove in his answer, not allowing even a truthful answer to be divisive based on race. He could've put them down and exalted himself in their sight with an honest answer like, "Both my father and my mother are from the lineage of David, from the tribe of Judah. I am not a Samaritan."

But the reality of how God sees all people was more profound than that. We are all his image-bearers, created in his image, and potentially the temple of his Holy Spirit. None are better than others.

How Jesus felt about Samaria and race division is further shown by the fact that He walked through Samaria with his disciples when almost no Jew would, indeed not the religious. The first person He told He was the Messiah was a Samaritan woman at Jacob's well. He even stayed in her village for a few days, with many coming to faith in Him.

Remember the story Jesus told in response to a question from a religious lawyer publicly testing him asking, "And who is my neighbor?" (Luke 10:29). Jesus made the hero of the story a Samaritan. We now call it "The Parable of the Good Samaritan." Today international ministries have sprung up from this story Jesus told. One such ministry is "Samaritan's Purse," which has distributed millions of dollars in gifts and needed supplies to children without regard to ethnic or racial lines globally. Little is much when God is in it; when his Spirit leads and infuses it with power. It also shows His heart. And it shows the truth about the matter of race.

A good definition of wisdom is: seeing things as God sees them because that's how they are. Read your Bible. Learn how God sees things and people. Don't be deceived into believing something else. Be wise, not foolish.

"Indeed He says, 'It is too small a thing that You should be My Servant to raise up the tribes of Jacob, and to restore the preserved ones of Israel; I will also give You as a light to the Gentiles, that You should be My salvation to the ends of the earth'"

(Isaiah 49:6 NKJV).

"A light to bring revelation to the Gentiles, and the glory of Your people Israel"

(Luke 2:32).

"The people walking in darkness have seen a great light; on those living in the land of deep darkness a light has dawned"

(Isaiah 9:2 NIV).

"And they sang a new song, saying: 'You are worthy to take the scroll and to open its seals, because you were slain, and with your blood you purchased for God persons from every tribe and language and people and nation'"

(Revelation 5:9).

PUZZLING CHAPTER 12

Grace to See

MATTHEW 28 TELLS US THERE were three hours of darkness as Jesus hung on the cross. Then the light dawned on a new creation — new life. On the third day after his crucifixion, the Spirit of God raised Jesus from the dead. A few days later, Jesus appeared to his disciples, breathed on them, and said to them, "Receive the Holy Spirit" (John 20:22b). Subsequently, Jesus told them to wait in Jerusalem until they were clothed with power from on high. They did so, and fifty days after Passover, on the day of Pentecost, about one hundred twenty of Jesus' disciples experienced the Holy Spirit in a new way. Peter preached to a large group who saw this happening, and three thousand people came to faith in Christ. The church was born. And the last days began, according to the prophet Joel.

The kingdom of God came then, too, in the hearts of men and women, if we have eyes to see. And it's still coming, or continuing, to this day as more people put their faith in Christ and submit to His Lordship, living it out by the power of the Holy Spirit. Wherever the laws or wishes of the king are upheld, is one definition of a kingdom.

Obeying and honoring the King is what Christians commit to doing out of love and devotion for his sacrifice and kindness. Indeed, by revelation, they see He is the King, the promised Christ of God.

Jesus' first coming is not the final coming of His kingdom. That will be ushered in by His second advent — a kingdom reality indicated by verses such as these: "The kingdom of the world has become the kingdom of our Lord and of his Christ, and he shall reign forever and ever" (Rev. 11:15). "And the twenty-four elders who sit on their thrones before God fell on their faces and worshiped God, saying, 'We give thanks to you, Lord God Almighty, who is and who was, for you have taken your great power and begun to reign'" (Revelation 11:16-17). "Then the sovereignty, the dominion and the greatness of all the kingdoms under the whole heaven will be given to the people of the saints of the Highest One; His kingdom will be an everlasting kingdom, and all the dominions will serve and obey Him" (Daniel 7:27).

Nonetheless, in Jesus' view, His kingdom came with Him at His first coming. He made statements like this: "…and heal those in it who are sick, and say to them, 'The kingdom of God has come near to you'" (Luke 10:9). "But if I cast out demons by the finger of God, then the kingdom of God has come upon you" (Luke 11:20). "Nor will they say, 'Look, here it is!' or, 'There it is!' For behold, the kingdom of God is in your midst" (Luke 17:21).

So we see from the Bible that we are not experiencing the Kingdom of God as it will eventually be, but we are experiencing it in some measure, with the seal and the power of the Holy Spirit working in believers. The Kingdom of God is both "now and not yet," a present and future reality.

To whom and how does the Kingdom of God come? By revelation and faith is the answer, one person at a time, by revelation and believing apparently. Let's take a closer look at this piece of the puzzle.

It's incredible and insightful how slow Jesus' disciples were to believe in him. Most will remember how Peter boldly proclaimed that if everyone else deserted him, that he would not, but that he would die with him. If you read the Gospels closely, you'll notice that Thomas said the same thing as Jesus prepared to go up to Jerusalem, the center of a corrupted religion that had become very dangerous for Him. "Therefore Thomas, who is called Didymus, said to his fellow disciples, 'Let us also go, so that we may die with Him'" (John 11:16).

Jesus told his disciples several times in the days leading up to His last Passover in Jerusalem that He would die. However, His sheep would not die but be scattered. Instead, they would lead many other sheep into his fold. They didn't get it like we don't get it. They needed spiritual illumination, spiritual help, to see — beyond the natural. They couldn't get past their paradigm, what they were taught, and what they had imagined. Overlooking the suffering servant prophecies in Isaiah and the Psalms, they could only imagine Christ as a conquering King. Undoubtedly one who was compassionate and good and had the authority to raise the dead, heal the sick, and calm the forces of nature could overthrow Rome, end oppression, and usher in the eternal kingdom. That was the scenario disclosed by the prophet Daniel and others. This conquering Messiah-King is all they could see. We would have been no different.

So how did it play out in the lives of those who knew Jesus best in the natural, after He was offered up by God, just as He told them He would be? Have you ever noticed or marveled at their lack of faith in what He told them? It appears they couldn't fathom or accept it! Notable, isn't it? Have you ever noticed how kind, gentle, and understanding Jesus was with them — how He continued to help them understand and see what was happening in the spiritual realm and the natural realm? It's both touching and insightful into the King's nature, our faith, and spiritual life.

Back to the Future

This past Easter season, I noticed for the first time how many times Jesus told his disciples the week before his crucifixion and then after his resurrection to meet Him in Galilee. He sent them back to that intimate setting and quiet place where they first met Him by the sea. They are fishing in the early morning, and they see Him on the bank fixing breakfast. I think you will recall the scene. He must have looked slightly different in His resurrected body or in the early morning mist because Peter looked at John, the disciple who seemingly knew Him best, with a question in his eyes. John says, "It is the Lord" (John 21:7).

How beautiful, kind, and gentle — how personal and non-judgmental of our Lord to meet them at the place of their first meeting, perform a similar or identical miracle, and be with them eating, fellowshipping, and spending time with them. That's the way faith comes sometimes and how it's enjoyed. It's not always like a mighty rushing wind or earthquake but like a gentle mist that makes you wonder if what you're seeing is real. It's more like a spring of fresh water, refreshing, soothing, sure — beautiful, desirable, and most valuable — life-giving and life sustaining, coming from someplace you can't see.

Memories surely flooded the disciples' hearts and minds of their three years with the Master in the surrounding mountains, valleys, and villages of the Galilee and beyond. They had been eyewitnesses to healings, deliverances, food miracles, weather miracles, and more. They had heard the words of God, from God Himself. They had felt His touch, enjoyed His fellowship, and now they were with Him again, just like before.

That's one way faith comes, again and again. It's like a Christian reading the Psalms daily, rehearsing their poetry, beauty, and reality in their own lives, hearts, and minds. It's like reading the Bible in general, but especially where God deals with individuals intimately.

I want to go back to the first time faith comes and during

vision-crushing times like the crucifixion. How did it come to the disciples then? How did it return to them? Seeing those circumstances may help us see how faith can or does come to us - spoiler alert - it involves much grace and initiated activity on God's part.

What about our part? I don't have a spoiler alert for that. I'm not sure I understand that part or the first part, for that matter. It's a mystery, a beautiful mystery. Maybe it's akin to the mystery that tantalized Solomon, as recorded in Proverbs, "the way of a man with a maid" (Proverbs 30:19d). The fact is that faith does come and is observable. Faith being experienced is the testimony of myriads of peaceful, happy people.

This book is a puzzle about puzzles, so let me share a few scriptures describing faith and things happening around Jesus' resurrection and let you stitch them together or puzzle them out. Ask yourself, "How are these related?" Or, "What do I see happening here in the spiritual realm?" "How does it apply to me and my situation?"

"As the women were terrified and bowed their faces to the ground, the men said to them, 'Why do you seek the living One among the dead?'"
(Luke 24:5).

"So the other disciple who had first come to the tomb then also entered, and he saw and believed"
(John 20:8).

"But Thomas, one of the twelve, called Didymus, was not with them when Jesus came. So the other disciples were saying to him, 'We have seen the Lord!' But he said to them, 'Unless I see in His hands the imprint of the nails, and put my finger into the place of the nails, and put my hand into His side, I will not believe'"
(John 20:24-25).

Read the chaos and crisis of faith in John 20, Luke 24, and the other Gospels. It's all genuine and very personal. Read how Jesus kindly dealt with two disciples on the road to Emmaus (Luke 24:13-35). He was helping with everyone's faith personally, and he still does today.

So what's our part? If I had to guess, I would say it's to be childlike, humble, trusting, and believing when Jesus or his Holy Spirit comes to call. If you sense by grace or revelation that Jesus is the son of God, the promised Savior, believe it and invite Him to be your Lord. Trust him with your present and your future. Then enjoy the relationship that comes, as well as the journey. "Believe in the Lord Jesus Christ, and you will be saved" (Acts 16:31). The most famous chapter in the Bible and one of the most beautiful is the three-thousand-year-old Psalm 23. It will begin to describe your life and journey after you do.

Repentance

You may ask or be wondering, "What if He doesn't come for me?" Two things come quickly to mind: "The Lord is not slow about His promise, as some count slowness, but is patient toward you, not wishing for any to perish but for all to come to repentance" (2 Peter 3:9). "You will seek Me and find Me when you search for Me with all your heart" (Jeremiah 29:13). So the Lord doesn't wish that any should perish, and He promises if you seek Him sincerely with your heart, you'll find him.

And if you think you've messed up too much, or your mistakes loom too large for Him to have a relationship with you, you might hear Him say, "'Yet even now,' declares the Lord, 'return to Me with all your heart, and with fasting, weeping and mourning; and rend your heart and not your garments.' Now return to the Lord your God, for He is gracious and compassionate, slow to anger, abounding in lovingkindness and relenting of evil. Who knows whether He will not turn and relent and leave a blessing behind Him" (Joel 2:12-14a). "'Come now, and let us reason together,' says the Lord, 'though your sins are as scarlet, they will be as white as snow; though they are red like crimson, they will be like wool'" (Isaiah 1:18). The ground is level at the foot of the cross. That's where we all must come if we are to have a relationship with God. It's not about the grotesqueness of your sin but the magnitude of His grace, His magnanimous heart, and the enormity of His sacrifice. He can and does forgive sin. None is too gross. Nor is any too small in light of His holiness. Believe Jesus is the Christ, and believe His promise to forgive your sins. You may feel the burden of your sin lift right away. You certainly will over time because it is a fact.

I didn't intend to walk far down this road, but I would be remiss and not true to the whole counsel of Scripture if I left out this tiny word, concept, and act — repentance. It's significant. It's actually essential but not often preached or taught in our churches today. John the Baptist came preaching repentance for the forgiveness of sins. When Jesus learned that Herod had executed John, He started preaching repentance for the forgiveness of sins. "I have not come to call the righteous but sinners to repentance" (Luke 5:32). Similarly, the Apostle Paul declared "both to those of Damascus first, and also at Jerusalem and then throughout all the region of Judea, and even to the Gentiles, that they should repent and turn to God, performing deeds appropriate to repentance" (Acts 26:20).

These last verses are a small sample of many, many verses. Do a Google search on repenting and repentance, or in one of the excellent online Bible apps if you wish. You'll be wiser, freer, and walking down the right path if you do. In a nutshell, to repent means to be sorry or remorseful for your moral or relational failures, then with a firm decision, change your actions. Expect the Holy Spirit to come beside you and help you. He promised to do so. Christianity is not a do-it-yourself project, but do your part to demonstrate your commitment to the process and sincerity. Don't try to play games with God. It doesn't work! You won't deceive anyone but yourself.

Summary

Repent and believe. That's what Jesus taught, along with the prophets and apostles. Those two directives involve a change of heart and mind and an act of your will. And those two directives require action — different actions on your part. He will do His part when you do your part, perhaps before and after. Faith comes, so enjoy the grace. Godspeed on your journey and adventure!

"Then Jesus said, "Did I not tell you that if you believe, you will see the glory of God?"

(John 11:40 NIV).

"Faith is to believe what you do not see; the reward of this faith is to see what you believe."

(Augustine)

"For understanding is the reward of faith. Therefore, do not seek to understand in order to believe, but believe so that you may understand."

(Augustine)

"For we walk by faith, not by sight"

(2 Corinthians 5:7).

"So then faith comes by hearing, and hearing by the word of God"

(Romans 10:17 NKJV).

"And without faith it is impossible to please Him, for he who comes to God must believe that He is and that He is a rewarder of those who seek Him"

(Hebrews 11:6 NASB).

"Jesus said to him, 'Because you have seen Me, have you believed? Blessed are they who did not see, and yet believed'"

(John 20:29).

"And he said: 'Truly I tell you, unless you change and become like little children, you will never enter the kingdom of heaven'"

(John 18:3 NIV).

"Peter replied, 'Repent and be baptized, every one of you, in the name of Jesus Christ for the forgiveness of your sins. And you will receive the gift of the Holy Spirit'"

(Acts 2:38).

PUZZLING CHAPTER 13

A Gentle Breeze

I RECENTLY RECEIVED A PHOTO of a Bible text from a friend in a men's group with some verses circled in red. Below that, he asked the question, "Do you think this is possible today?"

"And they devoted themselves to the apostles' teaching and the fellowship, to the breaking of bread and the prayers. And awe came upon every soul, and many wonders and signs were being done through the apostles. And all who believed were together and had all things in common. And they were selling their possessions and belongings and distributing the proceeds to all, as any had need. And day by day, attending the temple together and breaking bread in their homes, they received their food with glad and generous hearts, praising God and having favor with all the people. And the Lord added to their number day by day those who were being saved"
(Acts 2:42-47 ESV).

I gave it some thought then replied with what came to my mind. "Yes, I don't see why not. God is the same, yesterday, today, and forever.

It's possible. It's happening in places around the earth, I believe." He was asking if what was happening in the early church should be happening in our churches today.

I awoke this morning with that question on my mind, and a couple of verses came quickly to me, followed by other thoughts as I got up and journaled. I'll share the verses first, then the thoughts.

The Verses

"Those who cling to vain idols leave behind the gracious love that could have been theirs"

(Jonah 2:8 ISV).

"The wind blows where it wants to. You hear its sound, but you don't know where it comes from or where it is going. That's the way it is with everyone who is born of the Spirit"

(John 3:8).

The Thoughts

The Spirit moves where He wants to move. Those born of the Spirit and those born by the Spirit sense where He's moving and are carried along by His power in that direction. These people include sailors, pilots, army scouts, accountants, teachers, business people, laborers — spiritual adventurers. They are those who exercise faith in God and risk following his Spirit, those who become adept and practice doing so, who make it their lifestyle and passion.

These are people like David, the shepherd boy and king, who the Bible says "… served the purpose of God in his own generation" (Acts 13:36a). Is it possible to live a life like his? Or like Amos, the fig grower? Or like Elijah the prophet? Or Esther the orphan? Or Ruth the Moabitess? Or Abigail, caught up in a bad marriage — or rather perhaps a good marriage to a bad person? Where is the wind of the Spirit blowing in each of these person's lives and in their times? Ask yourself that.

Someone has said that wisdom begins with asking the right question. We may not be asking the right question in this case. Do we look at the church in Acts and try to mimic it? Is that a reasonable approach or course of action in our day?

I say, "yes and no." Yes, in that it's a valid expression of what a church or people flowing in the Spirit of God can look like, just as the lives of the Bible characters listed above are examples. I say no, in that our job is not to take one of these demonstrations of life in the Spirit and try to replicate it precisely in the flesh or in our power.

We read about the Spirit wind blowing in the lives of individuals and groups of people. We get insights into the actions of the Spirit in their lives, watching them act differently. We see the Spirit's peace and power flow in people's lives and in their times, like the wind moving leaves on trees.

Men love to emulate a model to take credit for accomplishing a similar success. "But we have this treasure in jars of clay to show that this all-surpassing power is from God and not from us" (2 Corinthians 4:7 NIV). Or, as explained by an Old Testament prophet, real spiritual progress is accomplished in humans: "'Not by might nor by power, but by My Spirit,' says the LORD of hosts" (Zechariah 4:6b).

It's good to look at the examples in Scripture to learn about the Spirit of God moving and working among people. We also learn about the people God chooses, blesses with His presence, and entrusts with His power. So, it's best to ask what the Spirit is doing in our day and how we can function as a son or daughter of the gentle breeze — the Holy Spirit.

In Acts, we see the Spirit of God moving in power to birth the church and establish the kingdom of God in some measure with the first advent of the King. In the times of the prophets of Judah and Israel, we see the Spirit moving in judgment and redemption to save people from idols and themselves and turn their hearts back to their Creator Redeemer. In Esther and Daniel, we see the Spirit, boldly but in His hidden, understated way, moving in the lives of chosen people to effect righteousness and peace in two gentile, world-ruling kingdoms. In Ruth, it's about two people, or a few people, in a backward time and place, knowing their God, walking in faith, being empowered by the Spirit to give birth to a king, and eventually, godly direction and leadership for a chosen but impoverished nation.

"What is the Spirit doing in your day and life?" is the best question to ask. The next best question might be: "How do I hear Him? How do I know Him? How do I learn to flow in His power, presence, and leading?"

It's possible because He's always on the move to save, redeem, and call needy people and lost sheep out of darkness and into His marvelous light. Seek Him. Ask Him to show you how to become and stay a son or daughter of the gentle breeze — the Holy Spirit.

I get that phrase from the life of Elijah, one of the most powerful prophets in the Bible sent to the idol-ridden, northern kingdom of Israel. They were in a deceived and spiritually dark time like ours. The Bible tells us that "Elijah was a person just like us" (James 5:17a ISV), not some made-up superhero. He was spiritually sensitive, as we can come to be. Yet, he had his ups and downs on his spiritual journey, which should give us insight and encouragement.

One time on Mount Carmel, he heard the Spirit and moved in power, calling down fire on a sacrifice to God in the presence of the people and the king. Then he prayed for rain ending a three-year drought. Immediately after that, he experienced a very low point. In fear for his life due to a death threat from an evil queen, he ran to Horeb, the mountain of God. There he hid in a cave, praying for God to take his life because he was "no better than his fathers," apparently at hearing God's voice and moving in the Spirit, exercising courage and faith.

A mighty wind came upon the mountain, and an earthquake, followed by fire, but none of these moved Elijah. "Then there was a fire, but the Lord was not in the fire. Finally, there was a gentle breeze" (I Kings 19:12 CEV), which Elijah recognized to be the Spirit of God. At the coming of the "gentle breeze," Elijah came out of hiding to hear God provide revelation, restore vision, and instruct him to continue his journey.

That's my prayer for you and myself — that we simply, humbly become and remain sons and daughters of the gentle breeze — the voice and leading of God's Spirit. May we be moved by that gentle breeze whether we live in a time of correcting judgment, or the birth of something new, or both—Godspeed as you journey.

PUZZLING CHAPTER 14

The Spirit Without Measure

"...for He gives the Spirit without measure"
(John 3:34b).

ISN'T THAT AN INTRIGUING VERSE and thought? It's a beautiful thought that Father God gave to Jesus His Son, "the Spirit without measure," for His earthly sojourn. Then if you read John 3, the whole book of John, or really the whole New Testament, looking at what Jesus said about the Holy Spirit, you can't help but see that Jesus sent to His disciples, His bride, those who believe in Him, the same "Spirit without measure." Incredible.

Am I sure we believe it? If we do, we don't act like it!

I was recently in a men's Bible study and discipleship group for nine months, called "The Journey." It focused around a single verse: "I am the vine; you are the branches. If you remain in me and I in you, you will bear much fruit; apart from me you can do nothing" (John 15:5 NIV). Toward the end, we looked afresh at what the Bible says about the Holy Spirit and His place in the Christian life.

The ten of us were from different denominational backgrounds, which required us to look at the material anew. We considered what we had been taught and what the Bible clearly says with a fresh look, discarding doctrinal baggage that might not be as accurate as we believed. No one seemed threatened by this. Instead, all seemed strangely encouraged and leaning into the new light shining upon the Scriptures and the possibility of experiencing a different life with the Holy Spirit. We felt the class coming together was orchestrated by the Spirit and at His invitation as we met, especially as our time together concluded. It didn't feel like our group was exclusive, but we also felt we were there by invitation.

That brings us back to John chapter 3, which must be the most important, insightful, and instructive teaching about the Holy Spirit in the Bible. Here you see Jesus, "a teacher sent from God," meeting with Nicodemus, "the teacher of Israel," sharing about God and spiritual truth. I think it's safe to infer from Scripture that Nicodemus was humble, loved truth, feared the Lord, and had perhaps a better understanding of the Bible and its revelation of God than anyone else in his day.

These teachers coming together is a fascinating setup! The Spirit Who gave the Word meets the best disciple and teacher of the Word in his day. The result must surely give revelation and insight into God and the spiritual nature of life on earth — the reality of how things are and how they work. If you look at John 3 through this lens, you will see far into the vastness of God and also His nearness and intimacy. There is nothing more intimate than birth and caring for a young child's life.

Nicodemus begins: "We know you are a teacher sent from God, because no one can do the miracles you do unless God is with him" (John 3:2 NCV). Almost as if to say, "I know why you're here, and the answers you seek," Jesus answers him: "Truly, truly, I say to you, unless one is born again he cannot see the kingdom of God" (John 3:3). Then shortly after that, Jesus adds to His first statement: "Truly, truly, I say to you, unless one is born of water and the Spirit he cannot enter into the kingdom of God" (John 3:5).

In the same context and almost in the same breath, Jesus tells him in verse seven: "Don't be amazed by this." This spirit life is as different from the natural life as these many miracles you have called to mind. And the Spirit's activity is as hard to grasp and understand as how the wind operates, yet it's as easy to feel and hear as is the wind once you're born of the Spirit. Isn't this the clear teaching of Jesus? Are you amazed at its simplicity and clarity? Is it what you've been taught?

Don't feel too bad if you haven't heard. Nicodemus wasn't aware either, nor had he been taught this truth obviously, until now. Then, Jesus said something that seems a bit out of place on the surface: "As Moses lifted up the serpent in the wilderness, even so must the Son of Man be lifted up; so that whoever believes will in Him have eternal life" (John 3:14-15). I've often wondered if that might have been one of Nicodemus' favorite Bible stories or about a time in Israel's history that he had received some special revelation? By Jesus bringing it up, did Nicodemus realize that Jesus was looking into his mind, personal history, and heart? Or was it that in the days ahead, Jesus' crucifixion to be exact, Nicodemus would see what was happening, realize Jesus had predicted it, then connect the dots with the serpent being lifted up in the wilderness, and believe Jesus to be the Son of Man, just as He said? It could be either or both. We have evidence that Nicodemus gave up his position and career to become a follower of Jesus. He was with Joseph of Arimathea, asking Pilate for Jesus' body and giving Him a proper burial.

"A Teacher Sent From God"

Let's go back to John 3 — the most explicit, most concise teaching on the Person and purpose of the Holy Spirit in the Bible, from "a Teacher sent from God" to "the teacher of Israel." This teaching is more than a convergence of the Word and the Spirit. It's more like the Spirit Who gave the Word, giving more insight into the Word and Himself speaking through Jesus. The Holy Spirit was about to be sent to function more intimately in the affairs of God and man. I can't think of anything more important to know and experience. The book of Acts would lend validity to this fact.

In twenty-one short verses, Jesus lays out the necessity and operation of the Spirit to one who knew the Word well and had many revelations about God. Also mixed in is a brief glimpse of Jesus' sacrifice on the cross, and then a few verses about the gift of eternal life — the redemption plan of God for the whole world, experienced by those who want eternal life and believe Jesus to be the Christ of God. Then, for Nicodemus' questioning or our understanding, Jesus ended the discussion with the psychology of belief and non belief, practicing evil or truth, and loving light rather than darkness. These issues revolve around free will and the motives of the heart. This text records one of the most profound and enlightening conversations in the whole of Scripture. It would all hinge on the Spirit, giving eyes to see and giving a different type of birth and subsequent new life. Do you see that? Do you want that? Ask God in prayer to help you if you do. It's His to proffer and His to effect.

John's Final Testimony About Jesus and the Spirit

In the final verses of John chapter 3, we see John the Baptist's disciples asking him questions and making observations about Jesus. John gives credence to the fact that Jesus came from above, and everything He says is valid with the proper perspective. It's a miniature or reflection of Jesus' conversation with Nicodemus, but this time with those who believe in part and know in part — followers of the prophet John. The conversations are not visibly connected by space and time, yet they seem associated with many similar elements, like a reflection of an image in a pool of water.

The last four things John says are fascinating and telling, as he mentions the Father, Son, and the Holy Spirit in context with each other. He also speaks about "belief" and "eternal life," just as Jesus did in the conversation with Nicodemus. Here are the four last words: (1) "He who has received His testimony has set his seal to this, that God is true" (John 3:33). (2) "For He whom God has sent speaks the words of God; for He gives the Spirit without measure" (John 3:34). (3) "The Father loves the Son and has given all things into His hand" (John 3:35). (4) "He who believes in the Son has eternal life; but he who does not obey the Son will not see life, but the wrath of God abides on him" (John 3:36).

These are the last recorded words we have from the prophet John the Baptist: "a man sent from God" (John 1:6 NIV). He was: "A voice of one calling 'In the wilderness prepare the way for the LORD; make straight in the desert a highway for our God'" (Isaiah 40:3 NIV). Jesus added to John's credentials: "Truly I say to you, among those born of women there has not arisen anyone greater than John the Baptist!" (Matthew 11:11a). Jesus also says of John the Baptizer that: "He himself is Elijah who is to come" (Matthew 11:14, Malachi 4:5-6). Do you think that the last recorded words of someone so spiritually sensitive and devoted to God might be valid? Could they be some of the most distilled truth from someone who lived his life apart, who lived his life with God? Could they be important to you? Indeed they are foundation stones on which you can build your life and your afterlife. Ask God in prayer to help you see, to give you His Spirit without measure. Prepare yourself for grace and a new way of life — in fact, a new life.

Correct but not Politically Correct

In Jesus' conversation with Nicodemus, we see these words: "Are you the teacher of Israel and do not understand these things? Truly, truly, I say to you, we speak of what we know and testify of what we have seen, and you do not accept our testimony. If I told you earthly things and you do not believe, how will you believe if I tell you heavenly things? No one has ascended into heaven, but He who descended from heaven: the Son of Man" (John 3:10-13).

The same thoughts are repeated at the end of John 3: "The one who comes from above is above all; the one who is from the earth belongs to the earth, and speaks as one from the earth. The one who comes from heaven is above all. He testifies to what He has seen and heard, but no one accepts His testimony" (John 3:31-32). It's not clear if these are the words of John the Baptist, just quoted by John the Apostle who wrote the Gospel, or are the words of John the Apostle, but it's beautiful how this point of contention is clearly stated again, like reflections in a mirror or a pool of water. These thoughts are insightful and beautiful.

What do they tell us? Without being born of the Spirit, we cannot see the things of God or know God Himself. If Nicodemus, the Bible scholar, and teacher of Israel, couldn't apprehend God with just his mind, why do we think we can? Or that it's our job to make the issue more clear for others than Jesus made it and left it. It is God's job by His Holy Spirit. Thankfully to those who believe Jesus' testimony: "He gives the Holy Spirit without measure."

"I am the door; if anyone enters through Me, he will be saved, and will go in and out and find pasture. The thief comes only to steal and kill and destroy; I came that they may have life, and have it abundantly"

(John 10:9-10).

"I am the way, and the truth, and the life; no one comes to the Father but through Me. If you had known Me, you would have known My

Father also; from now on you know Him, and have seen Him"

(John 14:6-7).

"But I tell you the truth, it is to your advantage that I go away; for if I do not go away, the Helper will not come to you; but if I go, I will send Him to you"

(John 16:7).

"But the Helper, the Holy Spirit, whom the Father will send in My name, He will teach you all things, and bring to your remembrance all that I said to you. Peace I leave with you; My peace I give to you; not as the world gives do I give to you. Do not let your heart be troubled, nor let it be fearful"

(John 14:26-27).

"If you then, being evil, know how to give good gifts to your children, how much more will your heavenly Father give the Holy Spirit to those who ask Him?"

(Luke 11:13).

PUZZLING CHAPTER 15

Christmas Puzzle

I TOOK MY WIFE ON a Christmas date to see *Christmas with the Chosen*. It was inspiring and wonderful, like Christmas is, especially for the chosen — those who have, or are given, eyes to see and ears to hear the story of the King. This year it's in theaters nationwide for ten days for those who want to enjoy it there and show their support for *The Chosen*. Soon it will be free on the web.

Here's a quick sidebar for those who haven't heard: *The Chosen* is a wildly popular and highly acclaimed film series about the life of Jesus Christ. It's crowd-funded and has produced two seasons of eight episodes each, with something like 318 million views, as of today, in every country of the world. It's viewable free, thanks to supporters, on YouTube, FaceBook, and on The Chosen app. This film series is beautiful and fresh—inspired, and inspiring.

As a dark cloud seemingly descends on our country and world during these past two years, this film series is a good reminder that it was that way when the King came the first time, to humble parents and humble people, in a place we know as Bethlehem Judea, within tiny Israel. It's encouraging to remember also something the Scriptures say: "But as people sinned more and more, God's wonderful grace became more abundant. So just as sin ruled over all people and brought them to death, now God's wonderful grace rules instead, giving us right standing with God and resulting in eternal life through Jesus Christ our Lord" (Romans 5:20-21 NLT).

Recently in conversation, a quote about Christmas came up, "Christmas is not a time nor a season, but a state of mind. To cherish peace and goodwill, to be plenteous in mercy, is to have the real spirit of Christmas" (Calvin Coolidge). Indeed, everyone should cherish peace and goodwill. Certainly, everyone should be plenteous in mercy. And those things are rightly celebrated at Christmas. However, *Christmas is a time and a season*, and perhaps a state of mind, to focus on the King whose advent makes these things possible on a wide scale in a dark world at spiritual war. *Christmas is about Christ* more than about his rule and reign, his attributes, or even His kingdom. It's about the gem of creation — God becomes a man. A Son of Man to tell us about God, His kingdom, His rule, His purpose, His Person, and then to send us His power in the form of His Spirit to live this life and make peace, goodwill, and mercy possible on the earth and in our realm of family and friends. He came to dwell with us.

Some might ask, "Isn't the point of Christmas love, peace, mercy, truth, goodness?" I'd say yes, of course, these are the things we celebrate which are made possible by the King and are descriptive of the King. But I would add that many people think and act as if they can bring these qualities to bear on the earth on their own. History would demonstrate that we can't in any widespread measure or lasting degree. We need a righteous, kind, powerful king to effect what we celebrate at Christmas and desire year-round and lifelong.

Christmas is a time and a season to be still, to be quiet, and focus on this gift from above — a baby, a gift of power and love. A king is born — beautiful, personal, good, enabling. He is mighty to reign and enforces justice in the middle of His enemies all around. His rule ensures "the wrong shall fail, the right prevail, with peace on earth and goodwill to men" (Longfellow).

Worship and give thanks — honor and celebrate Jesus the King.

"Now to the King eternal, immortal, invisible, the only God, be honor and glory forever and ever. Amen"
(I Timothy 1:17 NASB).

> "But as for you, Bethlehem Ephrathah,
> Too little to be among the clans of Judah,
> From you One will go forth for Me to be ruler in Israel.
> His goings forth are from long ago,
> From the days of eternity.
> Therefore He will give them up until the time
> When she who is in labor has borne a child.
> Then the remainder of His brethren
> Will return to the sons of Israel.
> And He will arise and shepherd His flock
> In the strength of the Lord,
> In the majesty of the name of the Lord His God.
> And they will remain,
> Because at that time He will be great
> To the ends of the earth.
> This One will be our peace"
>
> (Micah 5:2-5a).

"'She will bear a Son; and you shall call His name Jesus, for He will save His people from their sins.' Now all this took place to fulfill what was spoken by the Lord through the prophet: 'Behold, the virgin shall be with child and shall bear a Son, and they shall call His name Immanuel,' which translated means, 'God with us'"

(Matthew 1:21-23).

PUZZLING CHAPTER 16

Epiphany 2022

IN A FUNNY LITTLE BATTLE of wills with my wife, who would like to take down all our Christmas decorations the day after Christmas, and myself, who would prefer to keep them up the Twelve Days of Christmas, our outside angel came down today. Our tree made it until the Eleventh day of Christmas this year. It was the only thing left besides the angel until today. My wife is still winning, but I'm gaining a little ground.

Today is January 6th, Epiphany in Christendom, celebrating the arrival of the Magi from the east as recorded in Matthew chapter two. They came to King Herod's court in Jerusalem, then on to Bethlehem, becoming the first gentiles to have an epiphany — the realization and revelation that Jesus was the promised Messiah, God in human flesh, the prophesied King of the Jews.

I attended a men's Bible study this morning on the Book of Revelation. Our teacher noted the difference in appearance between angels coming from the presence of God and those fallen angels released for a time from the bottomless pit. That got us thinking about how life-changing it is to behold God.

I immediately thought of the Aaronic blessing, where the LORD told Moses to instruct Aaron, the High Priest, how to bless the sons of Israel. It's a blessing repeated over believers for more than three thousand five hundred years now: "The Lord bless you and keep you; the Lord make his face shine on you and be gracious to you; the Lord turn his face toward you and give you peace" (Numbers 6:24-26).

Similar verses came from men in the class. "Beloved, now we are children of God; and it has not yet been revealed what we shall be, but we know that when He is revealed, we shall be like Him, for we shall see Him as He is" (I John 3:2 NKJV).

We are told in the Bible that no man can look upon God's face: "You cannot see My face, for no man can see Me and live!" (Exodus 33:20). But we can look upon Jesus, as the Magi did, and start to live differently. Jesus said that's why He came, to show us the Father.

I also think that every time a believer, with the help of the Holy Spirit, catches a glimpse of God while reading the Bible or by a revelation elsewhere, they become a little more like Him. "And we all, who with unveiled faces contemplate the Lord's glory, are being transformed into his image with ever-increasing glory, which comes from the Lord, who is the Spirit" (II Corinthians 3:18).

"For our light and momentary troubles are achieving for us an eternal glory that far outweighs them all. So we fix our eyes not on what is seen, but on what is unseen, since what is seen is temporary, but what is unseen is eternal" (II Corinthians 4:17-18).

Happy Epiphany! And may you have many more epiphanies in 2022 and beyond. Godspeed and *shalom*.

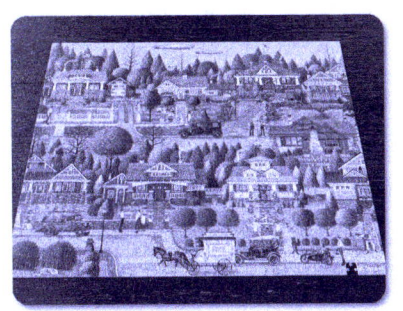

PUZZLING CHAPTER 17

Trust Is The Key

THIS IS FROM MY JOURNAL on July 8, 2020 — Pieces of the puzzle.

There is irrational hate of young people for our country, their own country right now. Puzzling!

Black Lives Matter is a banner over racial tensions. In this instance, it excuses the proponents to place undue blame on humans and human nature. It also shows the need for God's redemption. And it shows the need for Christ's forgiveness.

I hear the Old Testament prophets speak into the fray: "Those from among you will rebuild the ancient ruins; You will raise up the age-old foundations; And you will be called the repairer of the breach, the restorer of the streets in which to dwell" (Isaiah 58:12). There is supposed to be a spiritual awakening during our times. How does it happen? And when? I don't know. Stay tuned.

When does the light shine through? Usually, when there are cracks exposed — when what is trusted starts to crumble.

Don't curse the darkness — pray for, expect, and reflect the light.

In first, second, and third John, we see the phrases "little children" and "to the special lady and her children." One verse reads: "The elder to the chosen lady and her children, whom I love in truth; and not only I, but also all who know the truth" (2 John 1:1-2). How can you know for yourself and others to a certain extent that you have power over sin and death and are walking in truth? How can you become light walkers and love talkers?

Scholars tell us John recorded the Apocalypse, "The Revelation of Jesus Christ," around 95 AD. That's only sixty-two years after Jesus' death and resurrection. It's only twenty-nine years after Paul's home-going at the hands of Rome, after establishing powerful churches in Asia and Europe that changed and continue to change world history.

Yet in this very short period, thirty to sixty years, the powerful churches in modern-day Turkey, once ancient Rome, were slipping spiritually and fighting for their lives against dark spiritual and cultural forces. In Revelation chapters two and three, we see this as Jesus Himself graciously speaks to seven of them through His servant, disciple, friend, prophet, and apostle, John. He both encourages these churches and admonishes them to continue in the truth and Spirit, or else He would remove the Spirit due to the direction they were headed — toward apostasy and unfaithfulness.

Does this surprise you? That strong churches could disintegrate spiritually in such a short time? Many times it has happened this way in history. It doesn't shock or surprise the Holy One. He knows what to do and has indeed done the essential part.

He has sent the Holy Spirit in power. It's the same power that raised Jesus from the dead. He can raise the church from being deaf and lifeless too. And He wants to give you new life if you are spiritually dry and desire life — to live and not die.

Be thankful for the political schism. It's not the issue, but brings the issue into sharper focus and sheds much light on the most critical matters. It demonstrates the problem and shows us how we arrived here.

Who is to be obeyed, loved, and honored as ruler and sovereign of the planet and the nations? Humans, ourselves, idols, or Yahweh, and His Son, the Christ, the King of Kings? Who is to be trusted?

The Bible gives a clear answer. History would confirm that answer. But what do Americans and the American church know of the Bible? Or of history? Not as much as we thought, it would seem.

Enter deception. Enter the deceiver. Enter American education. Enter unfaithfulness in the western church. Put it together, and it affects us all very much, like delusion, deception, and a massive lie or false paradigm always does.

Enter *Patterns of Evidence, the Exodus*, by Timothy P. Mahoney, one of the best documentaries I've seen on Egyptology, archeology, evidence, and faith. What do you believe? Will you look at new evidence? Do you wish to know the truth even if it's not what you think or have been taught? Or is your mind closed?

Are you influenced by the majority and what the culture of our day hold as truth? Are you affected by a paradigm flawed in its foundation — the omission of the Creator, the rightful sovereign and legitimate, active, Judge and Ruler of all? Have you tried to make Him in your image and likeness?

If you have or you are, this omission is to your own hurt — destruction actually — by a patient, benevolent, sovereign God, Creator, King, and Judge. One Who so honors humans with a free will that He limits Himself in displaying His limitless power and awesome presence when He could. He has displayed it occasionally, just enough for thinking, searching people to see, to help them to believe.

This mysterious free-will plan is His system. The Creator, Sovereign, All-Powerful One loves faith. You can read Hebrews 11 for confirmation and demonstration of this quality called faith. Some have called Hebrews 11 "The Great Cloud of Witnesses." Others have called it "The Faith Hall of Fame." I have a feeling God might call it "child-like, gut level, truthful and absolute trust." Maybe something akin to your young child jumping into your arms from some height because you promised you'd catch them and keep them from harm. Trust displayed in that simple act is a supreme compliment at that moment, from the child to the catcher.

Hebrews 11 starts like this with a definition and commendation of faith's worth to God: "Now faith is the assurance of things hoped for, the conviction of things not seen. For by it the men of old gained approval" (Hebrews 11:1-2). Two verses above that, we're told: "But My righteous one shall live by faith; and if he shrinks back, My soul has no pleasure in him" (Hebrews 10:38). Paul stresses faith's importance in the very first chapter of his most famous letter: "For in it the righteousness of God is revealed from faith to faith; as it is written, 'But the righteous man shall live by faith'" (Romans 1:17).

I've been intrigued that this phrase, "The just shall live by faith," has cropped up at three critical times in human history. We first see it around 600 BC written by a Hebrew prophet in the culturally dark time before Judah was conquered and carried captive into Babylon, "Behold, as for the proud one, His soul is not right within him; but the righteous will live by his faith" (Habakkuk 2:4). Then we see it again around 50 AD in a culturally dark time with the world being oppressed by Rome echoed by Paul the Apostle in several texts, including this one: "Now that no one is justified by the Law before God is evident; for, 'The righteous man shall live by faith'" (Galatians 3:11). And then, around 1500 AD, in a dark time culturally and spiritually, a Catholic monk named Martin Luther rediscovered this truth. It became the cry and creed of the Reformation, turning people from a corrupted faith in religion to a living faith in God.

There is an even more ancient insight into this truth about faith and its value. It's from the life of Abraham about 2000 BC. It's very simple, and we see it lived out in his life, family, and times. Abraham comes to be called "The Father of the Faith." Here is the insight: "Then he believed in the Lord; and He reckoned it to him as righteousness"

(Genesis 15:6). It doesn't say Abraham believed in his ability to hear God, what he thought about God, or anything like that. It simply says that Abraham trusted God. Period.

Another verse comes to mind: "And without faith, it is impossible to please Him, for he who comes to God must believe that He is and that He is a rewarder of those who seek Him" (Hebrews 11:6). With my mathematically oriented brain, I immediately think, "If without faith it's impossible to please God; then with faith it's possible to please God." God is pleased by the faith we place in Him. Always be ready to jump into His arms, and rest there.

Faith or trust is an unlikely key to unlock all of His grace, but it does. "For by grace you have been saved through faith; and that not of yourselves, it is the gift of God; not as a result of works, so that no one may boast" (Ephesians 2:8-9). Grace can be defined as divine power and favor gifted and available to humans for their good and to restore relationship with their Father and Creator — forever.

Trust in idols, humankind, or oneself results in loneliness, sin, and death. That's what the Bible says.

It would seem that the Creator, sovereign King of all, has been pleased to make faith or trust a key — the only key — to all of human destiny.

Whether you understand it clearly or not, you're born into a family by God's good pleasure and ingenious design. The most important thing to you from the earliest times is: who do you trust and mistrust. That simple, single key shapes all of your life, all lives, and all destinies.

You can argue about it if you like, even be a bit like The Preacher and theorize or believe that life is meaningless. You can live like that if you choose. You can also argue that breathing, breath, oxygen, lungs aren't vital until you no longer breathe. Then people carry you away. Besides, "meaningless" in Solomon's Ecclesiastes means "like smoke, a vapor, not eternal," and not that it has no meaning.

Faith matters. Trust matters. They are the same thing. Be wise, be searching, be discerning about whom you trust. Then trust Him or them. It is the main issue of life.

This verse comes to mind from the life and times of Joshua after the Lord brought Israel out of slavery and gave them the promised land against all odds. They were about to experience rest and prosperity. It was time to decide! "But if serving the Lord seems undesirable to you, then choose for yourselves this day whom you will serve, whether the gods your ancestors served beyond the Euphrates, or the gods of the Amorites, in whose land you are living. But as for me and my household, we will serve the Lord" (Joshua 24:15). I hope that Joshua's decision is your decision for your sake and those around you. It is time to decide.

The phrase "choose you this day" from that passage jumped out at me recently. Maybe it is not only a one-time decision but also an everyday decision? Choose again today, and every day, whom you will serve. It's just a thought. He will help you.

"Today is the day of salvation" (2 Corinthians 6:2). I recently heard Francis Chan talk about that concept and why "today" is critical. His mother died in childbirth. His stepmother died when he was eight. And his father died when he was twelve. Maybe more than most, he knows the truth, that today is all we have. Someone has said that's why we call today "the present." It's also said: "Today if you hear His voice, do not harden your hearts" (Hebrews 3:15a). It's His invitation to faith.

Can you hear? The Scripture tells us: "The hearing ear and the seeing eye, the Lord has made them both" (Proverbs 20:12). So you, and all we humans, have the capacity, ability, and functionality to hear and see, but do we hear and see? Do we listen? Do we catch what the Creator says to us? Do we see what He is doing? Are we spiritually aware?

Do we hear what the Spirit is saying to the churches? Do we listen to the voice of our Creator and rightful, benevolent King? Do we hear His most Holy Spirit sent by Christ from the Father to help us and dwell within us, Immanuel? God sent Him to help us and endue us with divine power for living and loving on earth. Those who believe and receive God's grace by faith will experience His presence and power throughout eternity, where there is no end to our existence with Him and others who exercised this key of faith.

Paul saw this beautiful truth when he penned: "I have been crucified with Christ; and it is no longer I who live, but Christ lives in me; and the life which I now live in the flesh I live by faith in the Son of God, who loved me and gave Himself up for me" (Galatians 2:20). It's by trust, faith, and believing until faith becomes sight.

Has your faith become sight? Do you see, feel, and experience the Lord's presence in your life and his goodness along your journey? Can you identify with the song "Amazing Grace" experientially? Can you read Psalms 23 and see its reality in your life?

Many do experience it today and have through the ages. I certainly have. We have a great cloud of witnesses that this life is possible and actual. We have a fantastic book, the Bible, that testifies to all this and explains how it works. It tells us about the sovereign Creator and his Messiah, Christ the King. We have The Law, a moral code from God for man and man's good. We have The Prophets, men who heard from the Spirit of God and told us what they heard. We have the words of God for peoples and nations at specific times, and for all times. The Law and The Prophets bear witness to His majesty, His benevolence, and His good intentions toward people.

It is His way to honor us with free will and not overpower us with His presence and Person. We can choose to experience His grace and mercy because we want to do so, and we want to know Him. Trust is the key to it. It is in His power to do it this way, and He chose to do it this way. The wise and hearing will take the key of faith and exercise it — put it into the keyhole of life by grace, and turn it. Trust, believe, and walk into a different life. You will continue to walk with that key into your future and forever. You have now entered a new realm, "by a new and living way" (Hebrews 10:20a), with the faithful One, loving, living, all-powerful, and True.

His Name be praised for life unimaginable and life eternal. Amen.

"And I saw heaven opened, and behold, a white horse, and He who sat on it is called Faithful and True, and in righteousness He judges and wages war"

(Revelation 19:11).

"Now to Him who is able to do far more abundantly beyond all that we ask or think, according to the power that works within us, to Him be the glory in the church and in Christ Jesus to all generations forever and ever. Amen"

(Ephesians 3:20-21).

"But God, being rich in mercy, because of His great love with which He loved us, even when we were dead in our transgressions, made us alive together with Christ (by grace you have been saved), and raised us up with Him, and seated us with Him in the heavenly places in Christ Jesus, so that in the ages to come He might show the surpassing riches of His grace in kindness toward us in Christ Jesus. For by grace you have been saved through faith; and that not of yourselves, it is the gift of God; not as a result of works, so that no one may boast"

(Ephesians 2:4-9).

"But now in Christ Jesus you who formerly were far off have been brought near by the blood of Christ. For He Himself is our peace, who made both groups into one and broke down the barrier of the dividing wall, by abolishing in His flesh the enmity, which is the Law of commandments contained in ordinances, so that in Himself He might make the two [Gentiles and Jews] into one new man, thus establishing peace, and might reconcile them both in one body to God through the cross, by it having put to death the enmity. 'And He came and preached peace to you who were far away, and peace to those who were near;' for through Him we both have our access in one Spirit to the Father. So then you are no longer strangers and aliens, but you are fellow citizens with the saints, and are of God's household, having been built on the foundation of the apostles and prophets, Christ Jesus Himself being the corner stone, in whom the whole building, being fitted together, is growing into a holy temple in the Lord, in whom you also are being built together into a dwelling of God in the Spirit"

(Ephesians 2:13-22).

"For this reason it says, 'Awake, sleeper, and arise from the dead, and Christ will shine on you'"

(Ephesians 5:14).

PUZZLING CHAPTER 18

Two Witnesses

I'M NOT TALKING ABOUT THE two witnesses in Revelation 11. I am the curious type and would love to see them, but upon thinking that through, maybe not. They appear in the end-times, great tribulation.

I'm talking about the Bible verses and concept that say, "… on the basis of two or three witnesses, let a matter be decided." At least seven places in the Bible espouse that method for getting at the truth of a matter. Perhaps the most succinct is "on the evidence of two or three witnesses a matter shall be confirmed" (Deuteronomy 19:15b).

The matter I want you to think about briefly with me is origins, creation vs. evolution. Why is this a part of the puzzle of our times? It's tied to deception and delusion.

Charles Darwin's book *On the Origin of Species*, published in 1859, first put forth the theory of evolution by natural selection. If you've been asleep or part of the blind following the blind, you might have assumed that idea is valid and that life on this planet has evolved. To be fair, it made some sense at the time, but evidence in recent years overwhelmingly shows it to be wrong. The baffling part is that many people and institutions still cling to this outdated theory being true or plausible ignoring the evidence.

I want to be kind, and I do not want to spend much time on this. But I do like to point out that it is a vast deception, birthed about the same time our Civil War started and has been blindly accepted as fact until our day by many who are happy to believe in a world without God. Or who have not taken the time to look at current evidence and the mathematical probabilities involved in that notion?

Instead of "two or three witnesses," I want to point you to fifty witnesses and a book entitled *In Six Days*, edited by John F. Ashton, Ph.D. It's not that this book is unique or conclusive on the matter. There are a plethora of similar books in book stores and available online written by a rapidly increasing number of truth-seeking scientists. They debunk evolution and tout the Biblical account of creation, with Noah's yearlong flood being the most plausible account of how we got here based on our scientific method and evidence.

The preface of *In Six Days, Why Fifty Scientists Choose to Believe in Creation* states: "during the past century, the biblical story of Genesis was relegated to the status of a religious myth and it was widely held that only those uneducated in science or scientific methods would seriously believe such a myth." The author continues, "…there are a growing number of highly educated critically thinking scientists who have serious doubts about evidence for Darwinian evolution and who have chosen to believe in the biblical version of creation."

He goes on to say: "The 50 scientists who contributed to this effort gave their response to the question, 'Why do you believe in a literal six-day biblical creation as the origin of life on earth?' No other requirements were specified. I think you will find their insights and thinking very enlightening and insightful. Although they are some of the most educated and intelligent people on the planet, they speak in human terms with the freedom to roam in answering the question. They principally answer the question through the lens of their scientific discipline and address matters personally, through the lens of other evidence, truth, experience, and their life's journey.

To give you the book's flavor and yet be brief, I'll share that my two favorite contributors are Andrew Mcintosh, Ph.D., and Dr. Andrew Snelling (chapters 17 and 34). Dr. Mcintosh writes from the perspective of mathematics, while Dr. Snelling is a geologist.

Mcintosh started with "world view" and wrote a book on the philosophy behind science called *Genesis for Today*. World view is essential for linear thinking and proper evaluation of the positions. The beginning words of his chapter summarize his answer to the question asked: "As a scientist, I look at the world around me, and observe engineering mechanisms of such remarkable complexity that I am drawn to the conclusion of intelligent design being behind such complex order." His awe at the complexity and brilliance of this design is on full display as he describes the science involved and intricate construction of wings and flight in birds, insects, and mammals. His post-graduate and research work has been mainly in combustion theory, where he has authored chapters in ten textbooks and published over eighty research papers.

In his chapter, he includes a short blurb on "combustion and the bombardier beetle." He states: "Even the combustion chamber of the latest Rolls-Royce Trent Gas Turbine would not reach the complexity of this little creature." And: "For the creature to function, everything must all be in place together – as a good Rolls Royce engineer knows – for aircraft gas turbines to work!" You can see why a pilot like me, with twenty years of jet fighter experience, twenty-five years of airline experience, and now eight years of backcountry flying experience – still in awe of flight and creation, would be drawn to this chapter.

But Mcintosh also addresses in beautiful, simple ways (1) the second law of thermodynamics, (2) irreducible complexity, and (3) the fossil record. These three are daggers in the heart of the theory of evolution, a belief system still taught in universities and held by many as an actual rendering of science. This belief in evolution is reminiscent of the flat earth society. In our day of reason, research, information, science, sensors, computers, and computer models, it seems that to believe in the theory of evolution is to think that the earth is flat. I can think of only one word to describe this quandary — delusion.

The second law of thermodynamics is a fundamental law in the universe to which there is no known exception. We observe this law in every field of science. Simply stated, everything left to itself tends to decay and disorder. You can see how this would fly in the face of an evolutionary theory that proposes things become more and more orderly by themselves over time. Nothing like this has been observed in nature or science. In fact, it's more like some invisible force is continually fine-tuning things for life and order to continue on earth, something akin to: "And He is the radiance of His glory and the exact representation of His nature, and **upholds all things by the word of His power** [emphasis mine]" (Hebrews 1:3).

I seldom read the Amplified Version of the Bible. But my eyes fell on this translation as I was looking for the verse above, so I'll share it here for your reading pleasure and contemplation: "The Son is the radiance and only expression of the glory of [our awesome] God [reflecting God's Shekinah glory, the Light-being, the brilliant light of the divine], and the exact representation and perfect imprint of His [Father's] essence, and **upholding and maintaining and propelling all things [the entire physical and spiritual universe] by His powerful word [carrying the universe along to its predetermined goal]**. When He [Himself and no other] had [by offering Himself on the cross as a sacrifice for sin] accomplished purification from sins and established our freedom from guilt, He sat down [revealing His completed work] at the right hand of the Majesty on high [revealing His Divine authority] [emphasis mine]" (Hebrews 1:3 AMP). That's strong, isn't it, and makes a point.

"Irreducible complexity" in simple terms says that for something to work, all the parts must be present and assembled simultaneously. This is true whether it's a mousetrap, a mechanical watch, or a bat flying skillfully with skin stretched over bones navigating by incredible sonar. Mcintosh mentions the 1996 book *Darwin's Black Box: The Biochemical Challenge to Evolution* by Michael Behe, and it deserves a shout-out all its own. It was the first book I ever read about intelligent design, where a credentialed scientist of the highest rank boldly stated that he was a bit angry that evolution had been taught to him as fact his whole life, and then he had come to see that the facts don't support it. His book became a firestorm in the evolutionist community. Recently a movie appeared about this event and his life. Search for it! It's a part of the very human battle for truth against delusion. But as you will see, a battle for truth still rages.

The fossil record doesn't support evolution but points to design with the two daggers mentioned above. Dr. Andrew Snelling, an Australian geologist in chapter 34 of the book, points this out and talks about the evidence for the Biblical flood matching what we observe today. He notes: "Perhaps my favorite example [of intelligent design] is the trilobites, arthropods (invertebrates with jointed legs) that are extinct and only found as fossils worldwide. They occur among the earliest fossils in the so-called Cambrian rocks, and are the lower most multicellular fossils with hard parts found in the Grand Canyon, for example. Often regarded as primitive creatures, their anatomy reveals that they are, perhaps, the most complex of all invertebrate creatures. They are thought to have been marine creatures, because their fossils are commonly found with the remains of creatures that still live in the ocean today. Furthermore, they appear to have a set of gills associated with every leg. The animal shell is usually divisible into three sections or lobes – the head, thorax, and tail. Hence, the animal's name (tri for three, and lobite for lobes). Because of their jointed legs and antenna, the trilobites are classified with lobsters, crabs, scorpions, spiders, and insects. The legs require them to have had complex muscle systems, and because of their similarities to modern arthropods, trilobites are thought to have had a circulation system, including a heart. They also had a very complex nervous system, as indicated by antennae, which probably had a sensor function, and the presence of eyes on many species."

"Indeed, some scientists believe that the aggregate (schizochroal) eyes of some trilobites were the most sophisticated optical systems ever utilized by any organism. The schizochroal eye is a compound eye, made up of many single lenses, each specifically designed to correct for spherical aberration, thus allowing the trilobites to see an undistorted image under water. The elegant physical design of trilobite eyes also employs Fermat's principle, Abbe's sine law, Snell's laws of refraction, and compensates for the optics of birefringent crystals. Such a vision system has all the evidence of being constructed by an exceedingly brilliant designer!

"The trilobite's extraordinary complexity hardly warrants the creature being called 'primitive,' but herein lies the dilemma for evolutionists. There are no possible evolutionary ancestors to the trilobites in the rock layers beneath where the trilobites are found, for example, in the Grand Canyon. In fact, the trilobites appear in the geological record suddenly, fully formed and complexly integrated creatures with the most sophisticated optical systems ever utilized by any organism, without any hint or trace of an ancestor in the many rock layers beneath. There is absolutely no clue as to how the amazing complexity of trilobites arose, and thus they quite clearly argue for design and fiat creation, just as we would predict from the Biblical account in Genesis. Evidence like that of the trilobites shows that remarkable design and complexity abound in nature today and as far back in the fossil record as we've been able to peer. All this while the missing links in Darwin's theory are, well, still missing."

Let me go back to Mcintosh's chapter a moment for an Einstein quote about humility when looking at creation. Mcintosh says: "In my view we need to get back to the attitude of Einstein who, though he himself did not believe in an anthropomorphic deity, had a deep awe for the harmony of the universe." Einstein said in an interview in 1929:

> "We are in the position of a little child entering a huge library filled with books in many different languages. The child knows someone must have written those books. It does not know how. It does not understand the languages in which they are written. The child dimly suspects a mysterious order in the arrangement of the books but doesn't know what it is. That it seems to me, is the attitude of even the most intelligent being toward God. We see a universe marvelously arranged and obeying certain laws, but only dimly understand those laws. Our limited minds cannot grasp the mysterious force that moves the constellations."

Mcintosh goes on to say: "Such humility has been all but lost in our scientific world today. Many hold tenaciously to a strange view that theism is by definition excluded by science. Such a position is not logical, since theism or atheism is a product of one's assumptions. I unashamedly start not only from a theist position (which rather than be contradicted by my scientific inquiries, is confirmed by them), but also recognize that God can reveal himself to us – this I believe he has done in Jesus Christ."

It's worth noting *In Six Days* was first published in 2001 (the 10th edition published in 2013), and how fast knowledge is increasing globally. One can only imagine what might be available on the subject now. David Russell Schilling published an article in 2013 entitled "Knowledge Doubling Every 12 Months, Soon to be Every 12 Hours." In that article, he states: "Until 1900, human knowledge doubled approximately every century. By the end of World War II, knowledge was doubling every 25 years. Now on average human knowledge is doubling every 13 months. According to IBM, the build out of the 'internet of things' will lead to the doubling of knowledge every 12 hours.'"

In Six Days was recently loaned to me by a relatively new friend and a very good one. He's an octogenarian, fun-loving, life-living, outdoorsman, and adventurer. I consider him a savant. He's a retired lawyer, and his friends tell me he sailed through law school without reading much of anything, just attending the lectures. He is successful and has a wide range of interests, knowledge, and a good mind facilitating the joining of the two. His favorite genre of books is those on natural science, design, and creation. He's also very simple in his faith, focus, and approach to life. I once asked him: "John, why do you read so many of these types of books or think them so important?"

I was surprised that his answer was not based on science or intellect but upon spiritual matters. Oh, the first two are essential to him, don't get me wrong, and you would know that within five minutes of meeting him. But his telling answer was: "Because evolution is such an easily disproved myth, yet so commonly accepted that many of our young people accept it as fact and then easily turn away from God." In other words, it's a delusion. It's an easy path to walk in our day, our culture, and our lukewarm churches, all of which are walking away from the Creator, Who gave them life, Who saves, Who offers a knowledge of truth, and Who offers eternal life.

This acceptance of evolution illustrates that a significant number of people are deluded and living a lie. Could this be possible? In our day of mass communication and knowledge? Some ancient texts have predicted it.

A major Hebrew prophet who lived about 600 BC writes: "**Those who have insight will shine brightly like the brightness of the expanse of heaven, and those who lead the many to righteousness**, like the stars forever and ever. But as for you, Daniel, conceal these words and seal up the book until **the end of time; many will go back and forth, and knowledge will increase** [emphasis mine]" (Daniel 9:3-4).

The Apostle Paul, in 51 AD, writes to one of the early churches some detailed teaching on the last days and concludes: "**Let no one in any way deceive you, for it will not come unless the apostasy comes first… with all the deception of wickedness for those who perish, because they did not receive the love of the truth** so as to be saved. For this reason **God will send upon them a deluding influence so that they will believe what is false, in order that they all may be judged who did not believe the truth**, but took pleasure in wickedness [emphasis mine]" (2 Thessalonians 2: 3a,11-12).

I will suggest one more book and then leave the subject. I haven't read it myself yet, but I ordered it yesterday as a birthday gift for my friend John Harris. We live in different cities but have cabins on the same remote mountain top and see each other and share books fairly regularly. The book is *Animal Algorithms: Evolution and the Mysterious Origin of Ingenious Instincts* by Eric Cassell. A quote from the cover reads: "How do some birds, turtles, and insects possess navigational abilities that rival the best manmade navigational technologies? Who or what taught the honey bee its dance, or its hive mates how to read the complex message of the dance? How do blind mound-building termites master passive heating and cooling strategies that dazzle skilled human architects? In *The Origin of Species*, Charles Darwin conceded that "**such instincts are 'so wonderful' that the mystery of their origin would strike many as a difficulty sufficient to overthrow my whole theory** [emphasis mine]."

In making this gift selection, I consulted Joe, another dear friend and the most intellectual, best-educated person I know with extensive knowledge of the search for origins and many other fields of human endeavor. He is exceptionally well-read. He replied, "I think it's a good choice. I haven't read it myself. It's pretty recent, I think. It's a good publisher."

Joe and John are two good witnesses. I'm thankful they are my friends. We need good witnesses, and we need to be good witnesses. All a witness is required to do is to say what they see or what they believe to be true.

I can hear Jesus as He tells the disciples: "...you shall be My witnesses both in Jerusalem, and in all Judea and Samaria, and even to the remotest part of the earth" (Acts 1:8b).

"'You are My witnesses,' declares the Lord,
'And My servant whom I have chosen,
So that you may know and believe Me
And understand that I am He.
Before Me there was no God formed,
And there will be none after Me'"

(Isaiah 43:10).

"Thus says the Lord, 'Let not a wise man boast of his wisdom, and let not the mighty man boast of his might, let not a rich man boast of his riches; but let him who boasts boast of this, that he understands and knows Me, that I am the Lord who exercises lovingkindness, justice and righteousness on earth; for I delight in these things,' declares the Lord"

(Jeremiah 9:23-24).

"**Let no one in any way deceive you**, for it [the coming of the Lord Jesus Christ] will not come unless **the apostasy comes first**." "... **with all the deception** of wickedness for those who perish, **because they did not receive the love of the truth** so as to be saved. For this reason **God will send upon them a deluding influence so that they will believe what is false**, in order that they all may be judged who did not believe the truth, but took pleasure in wickedness [emphasis mine]"

(2 Thessalonians 2: 3a,11-12).

PUZZLING CHAPTER 19

What We Carry

CALL US WHAT WE CARRY is a book of poems by Amanda Gorman, a young black woman who spoke at the recent presidential inauguration. That title, or that phrase, came to me over and over in my early morning sleeping hours. So I'll ask you, "What do you carry?"

Do you carry the worries and cares of the world? Do you carry the coronavirus? Do you carry a personal sickness or one that can spread? Do you carry sin? Do you carry fear? Or do you carry the Holy Spirit? The Spirit of the living God? The Spirit of God Almighty?

Do you carry Christ? Then, does Christ by his Spirit carry you? Are you a Christian? Or are you a secular humanist? Either way, you are human. One way, your sins are forgiven once for all times. Yet you often take the Lord's supper and celebrate communion. You also pray and practice communion. Like Peter, Jesus' disciple, you've had a bath and are clean, yet you need Jesus to wash your feet from the contamination you pick up along your journey. It's God's plan.

Christ gives you victory over sin and death, but you've not realized it yet. You can walk in it to some large or small degree during your earth life according to your faith.

Remember, Jesus often said things like: "…your faith has made you well; go in peace and be healed of your affliction" (Mark 5:34). "'Do you believe that I am able to do this?' They said to Him, 'Yes, Lord.' Then He touched their eyes, saying, 'It shall be done to you according to your faith'" (Matthew 9:28b-29). And: "When the Son of Man comes, will He find faith on the earth?" (Luke 18:8).

Paul echoed the truth about faith many times with phrases like: "The righteous shall live by faith" (Galatians 3:11). And Jude added: "But you, beloved, building yourselves up on your most holy faith, praying in the Holy Spirit" (Jude 1:20).

Faith is powerful, and it is a precious commodity to God. When you trust Him, He moves to help, bless, heal, cleanse, and minister to others through you. You could never do these things on your own. You can only do this because of the truth expressed in Revelation 5:5: "The Lion of the tribe of Judah has triumphed." He triumphed over sin, death, and the grave. He has earned the power to forgive all your sins and gift you eternal life, a life that starts now, or whenever you believe, and has no end.

The key is your faith — your trust in Him. It opens the door to eternity and eternal life for you as it did for the thief on the cross (Luke 23:43). Then as long as you're in a human body, faith invites the communion and the activity of the Holy One by His Spirit.

Do you believe you carry the Spirit of God? Do you believe the prophecy about Jesus, "God is salvation?" And about Immanuel, "God with us?" See Matthew 1:21-23, Isaiah 66:1-2, Ephesians 3:20, Colossians 1:27, John 15:5.

Do you commune with him by faith? In your conduct? In your daily living? In reading His Word? In prayer? And in living in a Christian community? According to your faith, be it unto you. Be building yourself up in your most holy faith.

Be walking in humility. Be confessing your sins to one another, so

God will honor His Word and be faithful to forgive those sins and cleanse you from all unrighteousness. Be faithful to be tenderhearted and forgive one another from your heart, even as Christ forgave you. Forgiving frees the other person, but just as importantly, it frees you.

People will call you what you carry. You should travel light. You should also call yourself what you carry. In truth, that's what you are.

Be Careful What You Eat

Be careful what you eat. And where you eat. Don't eat junk food. You'll get fat and become unhealthy. Also, you crave or want more of what you eat. Many experts say, "You are what you eat." And soon you will carry what you eat! You'll carry it either way — for better or worse, for good or bad.

Also, be careful where you eat, the Lord's table or the table of demons: "You cannot drink the cup of the Lord and the cup of demons; you cannot partake of the table of the Lord and the table of demons" (I Corinthians 10:21). One table leads to life and healthy living, and the other leads to sickness and death. You carry what you eat. We all do. You can call us what we carry.

Be Careful What You Look At

Be careful what you see! You will come to resemble what you look at most of the time. You will come to look like the world or look like Christ.

Remember what the Scriptures say over and over about idols. They are the work of man's hands, and those who worship them will become like them. They will have eyes but can't see. They will have ears but can't hear. They will have a mouth but can't speak. They will have legs but can't walk. Instead, gaze upon the Living One. You will either carry your idols around on your back, or God's presence, and God's Spirit will carry you.

Are you a Christian or idolater, Christian or pagan, Christian or secular humanist? Call us what we eat. Call us what we gaze upon. Call us what we carry. That is who we are.

"His delight is not in the strength of the horse, nor his pleasure in the legs of a man, but the Lord takes pleasure in those who fear him, in those who hope in his steadfast love"

(Psalm 147:10-11 ESV).

"Some trust in chariots and some in horses, but we trust in the name of the Lord our God"

(Psalm 20:7).

"Stop regarding man in whose nostrils is breath, for of what account is he?"

(Isaiah 2:22).

"But whoever listens to me will dwell secure and will be at ease, without dread of disaster"

(Proverbs 1:33).

"Those who are in the flesh cannot please God. You, however, are not in the flesh but in the Spirit, if in fact the Spirit of God dwells in you. Anyone who does not have the Spirit of Christ does not belong to him"

(Romans 8:8-9).

"But we all, with unveiled face, beholding as in a mirror the glory of the Lord, are being transformed into the same image from glory to glory, just as from the Lord, the Spirit"

(2 Corinthians 3:18 NASB).

PUZZLING CHAPTER 20

Sex and Marriage

SEX IS A WONDERFUL SERVANT and a terrible master.

God created and gave it for procreation and fostering ever-increasing intimacy between a man and a woman. Sex is intended to be enjoyed within the boundaries of God's decrees. These decrees He gives out of His love and goodwill toward all, especially those who believe.

It's a beautiful way to bring children and grandchildren into the world. It's a way and gift from God to have a part in gifting and enjoying a new life, then to experience the wonder of life anew with children as they grow and journey through their time of discovering creation. *Selah*. (Hebrew for "Stop and think about that.")

Sex is a legitimate need placed within us by our creator. Sex gives mountainous enjoyment within the boundaries, but eventual pain, grief, and emptiness outside God's borders. These boundaries are for our good. They keep us from evil, and keep evil from us. You can trust God and the limits He sets for exercising and enjoying His gift in His Word.

To do otherwise is to go out on your own, to decide you don't or can't trust God and His ways with this part of your life. You'll end up being self-absorbed, incredibly selfish, easily hurt, and always with similarly minded people. Choosing your own way results in a vacuum of unfulfilled expectations and conflict.

Sex experienced inside a boundary of love and commitment brings joy, fulfillment, and peace to husband and wife, indeed to the whole family. It's a way of ever-increasing intimacy. It's a haven and respite amid life's journey with its struggles. Sex fosters the support and commitment we all need. It's a good gift from a good God.

That loving, giving, sharing, authentic intimacy is a partial picture of how Christ loves his bride the church. Paul says as much clearly, while not dismissing the mystery: "For this reason a man shall leave his father and mother and shall be joined to his wife, and the two shall become one flesh. This mystery is great; but I am speaking with reference to Christ and the church" (Ephesians 5:31-32).

The mystery is as great as it is beautiful! It is great to see and to experience.

Of course, I'm writing from the perspective of a man who is sixty-nine years into his earth journey, forty-seven years married to one woman, and being informed by the Bible. It's an incredibly ancient and complete book that says about itself: "All Scripture is God-breathed and is useful for teaching, rebuking, correcting and training in righteousness" (2 Timothy 3:16 NIV). And, "'For my thoughts are not your thoughts, neither are your ways my ways,' declares the Lord. 'As the heavens are higher than the earth, so are my ways higher than your ways and my thoughts than your thoughts'" (Isaiah 55:8-9). Perhaps most directly, Paul by the Spirit writes: "Let God be true, and every human being a liar" (Romans 3:4a NIV).

I have many friends and acquaintances who have different experiences, inside and outside God's boundaries, and hearing their stories has informed and confirmed my perspective that God's ways are highest and best.

I believe the vast majority would say God's ways are best, even among those marriages which have failed. We all have failed in some areas of our lives or another. Someone said, "God can work with failures, but not quitters." He's the God of the second chance. That is clear if you read His Word and notice how He interacts with people.

It's by grace every one of us is saved or delivered, not by our strength or works, lest any of us should be prideful and boast (Ephesians 2:8-9). What about divorce and remarriage? It's been an issue throughout all times of human history. Moses wrote about it 3500 years ago. Teachers of the law asked Jesus about it in the first century. The Bible mentions divorce, and some guidance is given, but not much, probably for a reason. Men and women would try to lawyer the issue to death, trying to figure out ways to justify getting into or out of a marriage.

The guidance given may surprise you. It's probably not what you think it says exactly. It's not what our churches usually teach. But that's another piece of the puzzle. You'll find it eventually. It's lying on the table, along with an adjoining puzzle piece: how to deal with failure. Puzzle on toward the finished image and see how to live in our day within God's good plan and boundaries.

Enjoy God's gift of sex within God's boundaries for the same, and you will be blessed!

Godspeed as you puzzle and journey.

"For this reason a man shall leave his father and his mother, and be joined to his wife; and they shall become one flesh"

(Genesis 2:24).

"As a loving hind and a graceful doe, Let her breasts satisfy you at all times; be exhilarated always with her love"

(Proverbs 5:19).

"For the lips of an adulteress drip honey and smoother than oil is her speech; but in the end she is bitter as wormwood, sharp as a two-edged sword. Keep your way far from her and do not go near the door of her house, or you will give your vigor to others and your years to the cruel one; and strangers will be filled with your strength and your hard-earned goods will go to the house of an alien; and you groan at your final end, when your flesh and your body are consumed; ... Drink water from your own cistern and fresh water from your own well. Should your springs be dispersed abroad, streams of water in the streets? Let them be yours alone and not for strangers with you. Let your fountain be blessed, and rejoice in the wife of your youth"

(Proverbs 5:3-4, 8-11,15-18).

"Let there be no sexual immorality, impurity, or greed among you. Such sins have no place among God's people"

(Ephesians 5:3 NLT).

"'For this reason a man will leave his father and mother and be united to his wife, and the two will become one flesh.' This is a profound mystery"

(Ephesians 5:31-32a NIV).

"There are three things which are too wonderful for me,
Four which I do not understand:
The way of an eagle in the sky,
The way of a serpent on a rock,
The way of a ship in the middle of the sea,
And the way of a man with a maid"

(Proverbs 30:18-19).

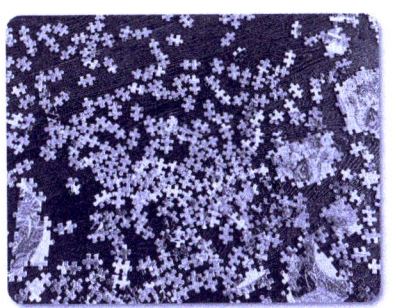

PUZZLING CHAPTER 21

Marriage Failure

SEX IS A BEAUTIFUL SERVANT and a terrible master.

Why would I even address sex and marriage in a book like this? And I intend to do it simply and directly: (1) God's design and plan for sex and marriage. (2) Failures and mistakes along our way. (3) How do we press on from where we are with the best chance of happiness and fulfillment?

I address marriage and sexual needs because they are foundational to who we are and what makes us happy or miserable on our earth journey. The family — a man and a woman with the children God may give them — is God's basic building block for cultures and life on the planet. It's where love is best experienced and expressed. It's where children can grow, live, and love while being loved in security and safety.

Where there are strong loving families, there are strong people, cultures, and countries. The opposite is also true, as history bears witness, and as individual stories of heartbreak and loneliness attest.

For reasons primary and nuclear, living in a family is the essential endeavor in human life for promoting joy of the individual and the family. Yet like life in general, missteps and failures abound because we are flawed, selfish creatures. And we have a spiritual enemy. All the while, we have an incredibly gracious God Who gives us free will to roam and decide what we believe for ourselves.

We have a Father in heaven who knows us better than anyone, including ourselves. He is wise and has given us His counsel in the Scriptures for living happy and fulfilled lives. He also stays involved during our journey and nurtures us through others and by His Spirit.

He extends this grace to everyone but especially to those who believe. By faith, they enter a portal into a different reality and relationship with the Spirit of God and with others.

What are some of the guidelines God gives us about sex and marriage? I shouldn't assume the reader has read the Scriptures. So based on Scripture, I'll also suggest two books among the myriads available about sex and marriage. I picked one because my friends chose it to teach pastors and their wives on a recent trip to Honduras, *The Four Laws of Love* by Jimmy Evans. The second is *Holy Sexuality and the Gospel: Sex, Desire, and Relationships Shaped by God's Grand Story* by Christopher Yuan.

Then I want to address failures in marriages or sexual relationships. It will be a simplistic overview at best, but you'll get the message. What should you do or believe? Where do you go from where you are? What help is there for one who believes God is to be trusted and His ways are much superior to our ways?

To form this puzzle piece, I will tell three true stories shared publicly in church meetings in Honduras in the first month of 2022. I will abbreviate them to make the points desired, and I will change the names, although the courageous, truth-speaking people involved haven't asked me to do so and likely wouldn't care if I used their actual names.

Let me set the stage. A ten-person team from Louisiana with a couple of members from Arkansas and California traveled to a remote location in the mountainous jungles of Honduras to teach a pastor's conference on faith and marriage. Another part of the team finished a water well project in a distant village.

In the evenings, after the American and Honduran believers shared a meal cooked over an open fire together, there were times of sharing testimonies and worship before retiring for a night's rest.

One particular evening after dinner, and after two of our teachers had taught about marriage from the Bible and *The Four Laws of Love* by Jimmy Evans all day, a time for sharing arrived. A young worship team of Honduran musicians led us. Then Pastor Dario, the pastor of a church in the largest town in the area and a pastor to the pastors in the surrounding mountain villages, invited our team to speak. Surprisingly, the team members who ministered in the village for two days, praying for people, sharing the gospel, and finishing plumbing on the water well led the charge in sharing, and not the teachers.

Freedom In Christ

First, a beautiful young woman with braided blonde hair and piercing blue eyes boldly stepped to the podium. Lydia, a single mom, probably in her early 30s, shared that as a teen and into her early 20s, she had lived a life of sexual promiscuity and drug abuse. But she came to know Jesus through faith a few years ago, and He delivered her from those hurtful behaviors. Now she lives to experience "real love," "the Holy Ghost," and to "pray for women in prison and other dark places to experience the same deliverance and freedom."

Her calm, pleasant, unemotional, confident, sincere telling of her story was something to hear and beautiful to behold. It was brief and accompanied by such a presence that the surprised crowd of pastors and team members wanted to hear more of anything she wanted to share. However, she was finished, standing as beautiful and free as a bird and as pure as the wind-driven snow. She turned and walked back to her chair.

I Have Failed

Pastor Dario then spoke, "Maggie, do you have something to share?" The petite middle-aged woman with graying brown hair and discerning brown eyes, a nurse practitioner, experiencing her first trip with our team, stepped forward toward the podium at his invitation, a bit reluctantly but boldly.

Her first words struck the hearers hard and pierced the heavens with her courage, faith, and gut-level honesty. "I don't really feel like I have any business speaking at a marriage conference because my marriage of 36 1/2 years failed."

The reasonably recent dissolution of her painful marriage was told through some tears, but very clearly with some invisible power seemingly holding her up. She recounted how her husband, the son of a Baptist seminary professor, became a drug addict, very angry, verbally and finally physically threatening. Then she described the moment he told her his fist would be the last thing she would ever see. He ordered her to drive him to the bank and withdraw some money. When they returned home, he left, probably to buy drugs, and she felt the Lord tell her, "It's time to go." So she "ran away from home." And she's been on a hopeful, healing path during the months ever since.

She shared that part of her healing has been the truthful sharing of her story with others. She ended with a strong message: "Find someone you can trust and share your struggle with them. Don't let Satan isolate you." And she shared some strong words about "shame" and what a strong chain it is to keep people in bondage. "Don't let this happen to you," was her warning.

In the end, her story was like Lydia's, one of deliverance from bondage and hope for the future. One of living in Christ, His presence, and His ways. She now enjoys a daily relationship in this reality and help with the problematic issues of forgiveness and hope for the future.

My eyes just noticed the Bob Goff thought for the day on my desk, "Failure is just part of the process, and it's not just okay; it's better than okay." Back to the story.

Honestly, I don't remember a lot after Maggie's testimony. It put us all in a sober peaceful attitude of truth, reality, and awareness that deliverance, help, and peace come from God. I remember that following her testimony, the meeting was over. Everyone was milling around peacefully, happy, quietly sharing laughter and hugs.

The Honduran pastors wanted to pray for our team. So we got in the middle of their circle, and they began to pray with hands extended toward us or touching us. I felt a tremendous amount of spiritual power coursing through me as they prayed. I don't understand Spanish well enough to know what they prayed, but I know that my body was shaking at times or quivering at the sound of their words and touch. And I recall the peace and a stillness that's hard to describe, with quiet joy, while standing there, seemingly under a waterfall of the Lord's presence. Soon afterward, the meeting broke up, and we all retired for a night's rest. That feeling was still with me as my head lay on my pillow, unaware of the spiritual earthquake the Spirit was planning for the following day.

Only God Can Forgive Sins

These testimonies were powerful punctuation marks ending a day learning about God's ways and wisdom for sex and marriage. But I don't think anything could have prepared our hearts and minds better for what we would hear in church the following day. Along with these testimonies, the next day's activities would fall under the heading of "only God can forgive sins."

You may recognize that phrase. It was spoken to Jesus by scribes, the most learned and religious Jewish leaders of His day (Mark 2:5-9). They were right about this! Yet they were blind to Who was standing in front of them, as He walked among the people, healed diseases, and forgave sins.

Amazing blindness! Amazing Grace!

Sunday — The Lord's Day

On the porch of the mission house after breakfast, it was Maggie's appointed day to lead our devotional. It's a favorite time for the team as we gather with our journals, a cup of coffee, a guitar, and hearts ready to hear from God in the stillness and beauty of a jungle morning, tucked between mountains by a clearwater stream, with toucans and parrots flying tree to tree. We also share our thoughts, hearts, and lives as the leader shares. Maggie asked us to turn to Mark chapter two, and then she set the stage.

It was the Lord's day in Capernaum on the Sea of Galilee. Jesus taught in the synagogue there, then went to Peter's home where He healed people brought to Him until well after dark. After a short night of rest, Jesus' disciples arose from their sleep and couldn't find Jesus. When they did, they learned that He had been by the sea in prayer with His Father and it was time for them to visit other villages with the good news and healing power. This they did, and now they returned to Capernaum, which came to be known as "Jesus' Town" because He centered his Galilean ministry there. In Hebrew, the name means "covering of mercy."

When the people knew He was back in town, they brought so many people to him for healing no one could get near the door. Four friends desperate to help their paralyzed friend saw this dilemma and determined to take their friend up on the roof, take tiles off the roof, and let their friend down by ropes on a pallet into the presence of Jesus. Two things from the story stood out to me that morning like never before. "And **Jesus seeing their faith** said to the paralytic, '**Son, your sins are forgiven** [emphasis added]'" (Mark 2:5). And "'But so **that you may**

know that the Son of Man has authority on earth to forgive sins'—He said to the paralytic, 'I say to you, get up, pick up your pallet and go home [emphasis added]'" (Mark 2:10-11).

Soon we were loaded in two pickup trucks, in the cabs, and in the beds, heading down twenty minutes of dirt road along a beautiful river, then joining another river with ten minutes of paved road into town and the church.

Church

The Honduran youth worship team lead us in a beautiful and spiritual worship time in Spanish. Pastor Dario introduced our team to the congregation and invited us to speak to the people. Our team leader responded quickly and first with strong, beautiful, gracious words about our week with the Holy Spirit, their people, and the warm and hospitable community of faith that invited us to speak into their lives about faith and marriage. He also thanked them for graciously hosting us.

I mused in amazement that I was with this brother five short years ago on his first mission trip when he had just been released from prison for drug abuse. But I digress. Besides being the team leader this year, he was one of the teachers about faith at the conference, and he is a pastor in his local church. Amazing. Grace.

Next, Gary, another pastor associated with the same church, spoke a short word urging the people to share their faith and hope continually, as they are doing. He shared a few insights about faith and then expressed the team's gratitude for the hospitality and warm friendship of the Honduran community of believers.

Spiritual Tremor

Then the spiritual tremors giving rise to a possible earthquake were felt. There was a short, pregnant pause as if to ask, "Is anyone else going to speak?" Then, the least likely person on our team shot up to the pulpit. It was the young blonde-haired woman with the braids.

I say "least likely" because, as I've gotten to know Lydia on these trips, she has a very gentle and quiet spirit. She's confident and bold when responding to the Spirit's prompting but also a little bit shy. She never puts herself forward to be seen. Because she often sees things in the Spirit and has a keen spiritual sensitivity, I've asked her at times, "What are you sensing or seeing in the Spirit?" If she isn't seeing or sensing anything, she smiles at me and humbly says, "Nothing." Maybe that says something about the people God chooses? And about the people God uses to represent Him, trusting them with His words, prayers, and impressions. He chooses obedient, humble ones.

Lydia shot up to the front rather unexpectedly and briefly shared what was on her heart and in her spirit. She shared about forgiveness and asked the Spirit to reveal to the people any person in their life that they needed to forgive. She said, "You will have a breakthrough if you forgive this person." Then she asked, "Are you willing to forgive them right now?" She then led the congregation in a short prayer, "I forgive that person, Lord. Forgive me for holding the unforgiveness, in light of what You have forgiven me. Amen." Lydia was brief, confident, beautifully sincere, and transparent as she spoke. Her words added to the expectancy and mounting spiritual tremors and became catalysts for what would happen next.

Major Tremor

Like the night before, Maggie followed Lydia and stepped from her chair to the pulpit. Unlike the night before, she did so even more boldly, confidently, and purposefully. Maggie had something to say, and in a way that she hadn't said it before. Lydia had encouraged her to share again what she shared the night before, only with more details about the final days of her thirty-six-year marriage that failed.

She shared that the last ten years of her marriage were very abusive. There were times when her husband's fist crashed through the wall inches from her face. Soundbites from her sharing would include, "Find a Christian prayer partner you can pray with and confide in." "Shame causes us not to ask for help." "You are the church. Look for problems and go to them." "Most people in abusive relationships will not ask for help." "Be the church. Be the light. If you sense something, say something to the person." About pornography, she said, "Porn, from a woman's point of view, is extremely degrading. I remember my husband saying, 'You would look great like this.'" The petite dynamo said, "I reminded him I was a nurse and knew how to use a scalpel to remove body parts."

It was a stirring, stilling, gut-level honest testimony that shocked us at the misery and ruinous power of sin. We were also in awe at the courage of the woman addressing us and the power of God by His Spirit to change things, giving hope to the hopeless, deliverance to those bound, and freedom to the captive for life – a life lived with God at a new level and in a new way.

If possible, her address was even more impactful than the evening before at the pastor's conference. She was able to tell her story without any, or many, tears succinctly, factually, courageously, sharing even more detail to drive home the validity of the pain and suffering, as well as the magnitude of the deliverance into a new life and circumstance.

She ended by sharing that the last time her husband forced her to go to the bank and get money, then drove off, she felt she heard God say: "'It's time to go.' So I ran away from home. I felt a lot of shame involved with this marriage failure. One Scripture that burned on my heart during the days that followed was, 'As for you, you meant evil against me, but God meant it for good in order to bring about this present result, to preserve many people alive'" (Genesis 50:20).

Finally: "I don't like to remember the pain of those times, but if I can help anybody find help, I want to do it. 2019 was a tough year, a time of healing and restoration. I drew closer and closer to God. He's never far away. At times I was engrossed in the Word. At times the cover was too heavy for me to open. I could pray only, 'God help me.'"

Maggie's last two sentences said with a pensive but beautiful smile, were, "There can be no healing if you don't bring the problem to God. He is the God of the second chance." She walked back to her chair to the hugs of her team members who had come to love this spiritual warrioress and lover of people.

Her words had ripped some spiritual veils. Some powerful truth had pierced the darkness. Some people under her voice were beginning to be set free. Hope for life and living, and freedom was being restored. In short, they heard the gospel of Jesus Christ in an old but new and living way.

There was a good size tremor in the spiritual crust of the region and in the souls listening to her Spirit-empowered words. An earthquake immediately followed. Titus, a beloved brother and several-year participant with this team came to the pulpit, slightly off to the left side, and began to speak.

Earthquake

"I stand before you a broken man. I have been living in sexual sin, in adultery, in fornication, and in pornography. I have relapsed into using marijuana and alcohol. The Bible says that we're supposed to confess such sins to our brothers and sisters in the church. So that's what I'm doing."

That may not be word for word or in the exact order, but it's close. Wow! He calmly walked to the back of the church, where he stood with some tears and a heart of repentance accompanying such a confession. He had expressed a destitute-like need for God's help and His power to deliver.

The spiritual earthquake had come and rocked the place, and it was over almost as suddenly as it had begun.

In the tremors that followed, one of the team members moved quickly to the pulpit. Daryl quoted the Scriptures, "If we confess our sins, He is faithful and righteous to forgive us our sins and to cleanse us from all unrighteousness" (1 John 1:9). And "…confess your sins to one another, and pray for one another so that you may be healed" (James 5:16a). Daryl ended by stating, "The Word of the Lord," and expressed his gratitude to God that he had his brother back before walking quickly to embrace Titus in a long, loving, strong, bear hug.

Other team members surrounded Titus, too, with hugs, words of love, affirmation for what we just witnessed, and words of encouragement and commitment.

What courage! What raw, bold courage to come out of the darkness and risk walking into God's marvelous light. It is a risk. He took a chance opening himself to ridicule or rejection, justice, and judgment. But instead, the Spirit-led team received him back, in mercy, as a brother, as the Scriptures tell us to do. As the soft aftershocks of the confession continued, Pastor Dario spoke from the pulpit to the church about what had just happened, in Spanish, with Laura interpreting for our team in English. The verses he shared over brother Titus were from the prophet Isaiah:

"Surely our griefs He Himself bore,
And our sorrows He carried;
Yet we ourselves esteemed Him stricken,
Smitten of God, and afflicted.
But He was pierced through for our transgressions,
He was crushed for our iniquities;
The chastening for our well-being fell upon Him,
And by His scourging we are healed.
All of us like sheep have gone astray,
Each of us has turned to his own way;

But the Lord has caused the iniquity of us all
To fall on Him"

(Isaiah 53:4-6).

"Seek the Lord while He may be found;
Call upon Him while He is near.
Let the wicked forsake his way
And the unrighteous man his thoughts;
And let him return to the Lord,
And He will have compassion on him,
And to our God,
For He will abundantly pardon"

(Isaiah 55:6-7).

    The pastor brought brother Titus back to the front, where he embraced him and prayed for him privately. The congregation and team started worshiping again, led spontaneously by the youth, flowing with the Spirit. And people came and stood at the front of the church, seemingly on their own accord. It was a holy moment, one in which everyone felt the tangible presence of the Holy Spirit.

    After the pastor finished praying for Titus with the people worshiping, Titus sat down on the front row. Some of the Honduran youth he had mentored came to Titus and embraced him with their hugs, words, and prayers.

    If you are a churchman or a churchwoman in the western church reading this, you might be thinking, "That was a bit of a copout and an easy place for him to come clean, confess his sins and unburden himself, in a foreign place and foreign culture."

    Nothing could be further from the truth and reality. Titus has known this community of faith for ten years or more. He confessed in front of the team, possibly his closest spiritual friends. He confessed in front of the Honduran youth, who I call guerrilla spiritual warriors due to their devotion, tenacity, and selfless service to the kingdom of

God and his Christ. These young men and women Titus has known for years. He was a good role model, even championing the cause of sending some of them to college. No! It was as hard a place as possible to make such a confession, one that I have not seen the likes of for candor and gut-level honesty with God, and before a church, for a very long time.

Besides, I might ask you, "When was the last time you heard such a confession in your church? Or heard a sermon where this type of confession is encouraged, with the subsequent freedom it brings?"

Perhaps you should find a "Celebrate Recovery" expression of the church and get involved if you want to see it and experience the power of The Holy mixed with His mercy and His cleansing ways. It's normal, historical Christianity from the earliest days of the church as recorded in the gospels, the acts of the apostles, and the epistles. Repentance like this was prescribed and experienced in the law and the prophets. Also, in the early days of the kings of Israel, as noted in David's repentance and confession in the Psalms (Psalm 51). It's the Lord's way.

Back Story

You should know the backstory to this confession. Titus was in a dysfunctional, codependent marriage without much intimacy for years. His pastor and spiritual brothers had gathered around him in counsel and prayer for a very long time.

Finally, these brothers, who I know to have a great fear of the Lord, knowledge of the Scriptures, and a track record of hearing and obeying the Holy Spirit, advised Titus that he should seek a divorce. Recommending divorce is almost unheard of in church circles, but apparently, there comes a time when God, who knows the heart and doesn't just look at outward appearances, knows that a person will not repent or change their thoughts and actions. In mercy for both parties, He declares the relationship over and a new beginning for each, committing themselves and the other person into God's caring hands, hopefully in forgiveness for wrongs suffered and wishing the other the best, which requires God's help — grace.

This point of failure is known only to God and the person or persons involved. It's a very intimate acknowledgment of faith in God instead of oneself. It's an acknowledgment of failure and great need as well.

Titus' marriage was dysfunctional for a long time, and the temptation and sin took place during the divorce decision and process. I'm not making excuses for the evil, and neither did Titus. It was wrong, harmful, and hurtful. And it is now forgiven by God.

Our heavenly Father forgives sin. He has the power and goodness of heart to do so. He desires to receive His sons and daughters back home and into the family.

The story of the prodigal or lost son (Luke 15:11-32) is the story of us all. God can work with or rescue failures, but not quitters. Failures are all He has to work with because that describes us all. Quitters only hasten their demise because our Creator God has chosen to honor us all with free will. CS Lewis has famously said: "Free will, though it makes evil possible, is also the only thing that makes possible any love or goodness or joy worth having."

To continue the backstory, the brothers and sisters knew Titus hadn't been himself and struggled mightily with something. They were praying, often and much.

Titus didn't plan this confession. I don't think anyone does. By his admission later to the team, he said, "I came to Honduras hiding like a dog under the porch." But the Spirit of God was drawing him. The Spirit of God helped him express his needs, sin, and request for forgiveness.

The week's script was like the wind blowing where it wills (John 3:8), among the leaves of the jungle and the sons and daughters in Honduras. No man could have scripted that day. But the team said this display of God's kindness, leading Titus to repentance and the power of God displayed in his confession and forgiveness, was the highlight of their week and the trip.

Even more so than getting clean running water to a school in the village. Even more than teaching pastors and wives about faith and marriage. Even more than all the prayers prayed and lives touched.

To see one of our own valued, sought after, and rescued by God's Spirit was a prominent faith builder in the faithful One and a reminder of the power of love and God's own Son.

Yes, the scribes in Jesus' day had it right when they told Jesus: "Only God can forgive sins." But they had it wrong by saying He was blaspheming for forgiving them. He was God, God in the flesh, doing what only God can do, forgiving sins. He still is forgiving sins! Do you hear Him saying anything to you? Perhaps He's about to tell you: "Take up your bed and walk" (Mark 2:9).

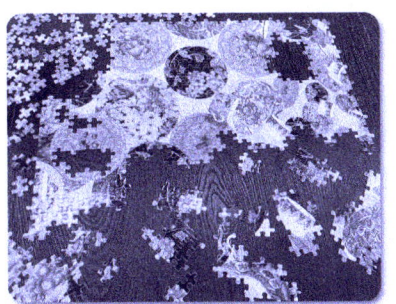

PUZZLING CHAPTER 22

Divorce and Remarriage

God Redeems

Failures happen. Divorce happens. It happens more and more frequently in decaying cultures. It's a sign of decay, the weakening, and the breakdown of the family, from people going their own way and ignoring God's way without the help of His Holy Spirit.

But it's not the end of hope or life. While dashing some dreams, it can become the beginning of others. God is in the business of redeeming people from their mistakes and failures, of giving people their lives back anew and full of hope and promise. It's His way. It's His plan. He is gracious, full of compassion, mercy, and love.

Consider reading the book of Ruth in the Old Testament. It's my favorite book in the Bible. God shows himself to be a kinsman redeemer. And we see in a true-life story, what redemption means, and what God can do with horrible situations.

Read the Gospels, the first four books of the New Testament, and watch what Jesus did, hear what He said, note how He related to sinners — people who had missed the mark in life in some form or fashion. We all do. "Sin" is an archery term meaning "to miss the mark."

Jesus was God in the flesh. That's what He said. That's what the Bible says about Him, revealed in the Law, the Prophets, the Gospels, and in the Apostles' lives and teaching. His many acts of love and demonstrations of miracles and power testify to that. So does His sacrifice on a Roman cross, and rising from the dead to new life, spending forty days with His disciples, then ten days later sending His Holy Spirit back into the world to seal, help, and dwell with and in those who will come to faith in Him. "But we have this treasure in earthen vessels, so that the surpassing greatness of the power will be of God and not from ourselves" (2 Corinthians 4:7).

A good friend who meets with a small men's group next door recently shared about some trauma and attack on his teenage daughters. The Spirit provided some wisdom, prayers, and counsel from the brothers. Yesterday, one of them shared from Scripture, "The thief comes only to steal and kill and destroy; **I have come** that they may have life, and have it to the full [emphasis added]" (John 10:10 NIV). When we read this passage, we often focus on Satan, his attack, and his evil intent. But this time, "*I [Jesus] have come*" stood out to us all. The point is He came to purchase us, help us, and deliver us from evil. And He stayed in the Person and power of His Holy Spirit. He rescues people, restoring hope and life yet today, every day, to the end of the age. This is our God.

A Painful Failure

Divorce is a painful failure. Only those who experience it or its effects know the depth of the pain. It's emotionally damaging to the family involved, especially to the husband and wife, but it also sends shock waves of failure, shame, betrayal, hopelessness to the children and the extended family. It would seem almost to the level of our DNA. Vows were broken, and trust betrayed. Hope for happiness that an intact family promises seem gone and far away. Family members start to doubt their self-worth and value. They might wonder if there is a curse on their lives and ask, "Why is this happening to me?" They have experienced one of life's most painful failures. A failure that strikes at the core of who they are and who they will become.

Is it worse than lying, stealing, blaspheming, gossip, slander, sexual sin, drug abuse, or murder? All these behaviors are missing the mark, damaging, and destructive. All take away life and the beauty in which life can be lived. So the answer is "no," in a sense. God paid a very high price to redeem any person ensnared or practicing these behaviors. The Lord plans to help people walk away from those behaviors into a new life. And He helps people to recover from family failure, like divorce, which strikes at our core.

Shame seems to be the biggest core issue for divorced people and their children. It may be more spiritual than rational, but it comes. Shame is so widespread, critical, and deep-seated it affects the subject of "living free" and will be a separate piece of the puzzle.

The Bible on Divorce

For the moment, let's look at what the Bible says about divorce. This discussion will point to the fact that Christians in our day are not as knowledgeable about their Bibles as they should be. Our churches have set a low bar in teaching the Word, as well as teaching us how to study it for ourselves.

A couple of caveats before I begin. [1] This subject seems a bit ambiguous, probably for a reason known only to the Spirit that inspired the sacred writing. That said, I'm not claiming I understand the Lord's position perfectly. And if He wants it somewhat obscured for a reason, what business do I have trying to clear it up? That said, I feel He's given me some insight into what the Scriptures say and the encouragement to write about it here. [2] This discussion will not be exhaustive by any means. I will only introduce the premise and discuss it enough for you to reach a conclusion or launch your research. I first heard these truths in some teaching sessions taught by a Church of Christ minister about ten years ago. I then did my study based on his insights.

I need quickly say this probably was not the accepted or understood teaching of his denomination. From how he conducted the meetings and the Q & A sessions, I could tell that he expected a lot of flack and opposition. He asked the hearers to wait with their questions until the end of each session so he could get through the material. The questions that followed were lively, contentious, and passionate.

I think most of us were taught in our US denominational churches that according to our English translations of the Bible, if a person is divorced and remarries, they are now living in adultery. Even with this belief, and I grew up in church never hearing anything different, there was a pause when it was taught as if to say, "This is what the Bible says, so we believe and teach it, but it sounds a little harsh for these types of deep-reaching, personally-painful failures, in light of the God Who forgives sin and the God of the second chance portrayed elsewhere in the Bible."

As it turns out, it may be too harsh and not what the Bible teaches or what God says or thinks about divorce. Let's see what you think.

I must insert a quick word about hermeneutics, the theological science of interpreting Scripture. You can look up the definition and discussion of the methods if you like, but the best Bible teacher I ever sat under gave us three questions that pretty much cover it. When you read Scripture, ask yourself: (1) What did it mean then? (2) What does it mean now? And, (3) What does it mean to me?

The two most significant areas in the science of interpretation are looking at the original languages of the Bible, mostly Hebrew for the Old Testament and Greek for the New Testament, and then looking at what we know about the times, customs, and cultures in which the passage was written or lived out.

Surprisingly little is said in the Bible about divorce. That's surprising considering how helpful marriage is and harmful divorce is in the human experience. I must deduce that an all-powerful and all-knowing God, full of love, wisdom, compassion, and goodwill toward humanity, must limit what He says for good reason. Maybe so we'll search hard for the answers ourselves and seek Him personally in prayer, counsel, and study.

It might surprise you that there is only one divorce recorded in the Bible. Shockingly, it is God Himself, Who grants Israel a divorce certificate: "I gave faithless Israel her certificate of divorce and sent her away because of all her adulteries. Yet I saw that her unfaithful sister Judah had no fear; she also went out and committed adultery" (Jeremiah 3:8 NIV).

Do you want to know briefly what the Lord thinks about divorce? "'For **I hate divorce,' says the Lord, the God of Israel**, 'and him who covers his garment with wrong,' says the Lord of hosts. 'So **take heed to your spirit, that you do not deal treacherously** [emphasis added]'" (Malachi 2:16).

The LORD knew it was bound to happen, so when He initially gave the Law and moral code to Israel through Moses about 1500 BC, He included a law of divorce: "When a man takes a wife and marries her, and it happens that she finds no favor in his eyes because he has found some indecency in her, and he writes her a certificate of divorce and puts it in her hand and sends her out from his house" (Deuteronomy 24:1).

Fast forward to Jesus' time around 30 AD in the Roman Empire, and we find the experts in the law, the Pharisees, questioning Jesus about this vital matter. They were very jealous of Him and His popularity with the people, so they were trying to trip Him up and find some reason to discredit Him, more than to get at the truth of God's heart and counsel about divorce.

Jesus said in the Sermon on the Mount: "It was said, 'Whoever sends his wife away, let him give her a certificate of divorce; but I say to you that everyone who divorces his wife, except for the reason of unchastity [adultery], makes her commit adultery; and whoever marries a divorced woman commits adultery" (Matthew 5:31-32).

Later we see the lawyers testing Jesus on the subject. He gives them an insightful answer, and to us all, for all ages and all times. "Some Pharisees came to Jesus, testing Him and asking, 'Is it lawful for a man to divorce his wife for any reason at all?' And He answered and said: **'Have you not read that He who created them from the beginning made them male and female, and said, 'For this reason a man shall leave his father and mother and be joined to his wife, and the two shall become one flesh'? So they are no longer two, but one flesh. What therefore God has joined together, let no man separate.'** They said to Him, 'Why then did Moses command to give her a certificate of divorce and send her away?' He said to them, **'Because of your hardness of heart** Moses permitted you to divorce your wives; but from the beginning it has not been this way. And I say to you, whoever divorces his wife, except for immorality, and marries another woman commits adultery [emphasis added]'" (Matthew 19: 3-9).

So we see in Scripture that God hates divorce. His original intent was for one man to wed one woman for life until separated by death. And that it was because of "hardness of heart" in humankind that God permitted divorce when He first gave Israel their moral code, a code serving them and all humanity for millennia.

But is divorce, when it does happen, to be the end of one's hope and future, for remarriage and happy family life? Jesus taught and showed us God's heart in the matter. It's essential to look at the culture in Jesus' day and some words in the original language to understand it accurately.

In Jesus' day, there were two influential rabbis, Hillel and Shammai, who each had large schools of followers. One taught that a man could divorce his wife based on "some indecency in her." The other school held that only for adultery could one divorce his wife. They each wanted Jesus to side with them, to divide His followers, and hopefully for Him to endorse their view. He did neither.

Instead, Jesus focused on their hypocrisy and hard hearts, and pointed out, if you look at the original language, that it was their practice of putting their wives away without a certificate of divorce that God hated even more than the divorce. This act would result in both husband and wife being in adultery if they remarried.

Set Her Free

There is an earlier mention of divorce in Deuteronomy that may hint at God's heart in the matter. "And it shall be, if you have no delight in her, then **you shall set her free**, but you certainly shall not sell her for money; **you shall not treat her brutally**, because you have humbled her [emphasis added]" (Deuteronomy 21:14 NJKV). The Hebrew word translated 'set her free' is *shalach*. It's used 800 times in the OT and translated as divorce in the nine instances that divorce is mentioned. There is another Hebrew word mentioned in some of those instances with it, *kĕriythuwth*, which means bill/ certificate/ writ of divorce.

The use of two distinctly different words in the OT for a divorce sets the stage for what happened in Jesus' day when two different Greek words were used denoting different circumstances. Unfortunately, they are both translated as "divorce," in English adding ambiguity and confusion. The Greek word *apoluo* means "put away." This word is used for the husband orally dismissing and sending away his wife without giving her a divorce certificate. She must return to her family or fend for herself, dishonored and not free to remarry because she's still legally married with no divorce decree. If she lived with a man as husband and wife, they would both be in adultery — the practice Jesus spoke against in the Sermon on the Mount.

The Greek word *apostasion* meant that the husband wrote and handed a divorce certificate to the wife. In this case, the divorced wife could legally remarry and have hope for a new future, a family, and a better outcome. This is what Jesus said must happen if, because of hard hearts, you can't make the marriage work. God is a God of redemption and the second chance. It's why He came as a man—to show the way and help us go the way by His Word and His indwelling Spirit in those who believe.

So get a Strong's concordance, or search on the web. Look at the Greek word used for "divorce" in each instance, and I think you'll see two types of divorces in Jesus's day. Although God hates the thought and act of divorce for all the pain and shame it brings on people and families, He would not abide only "putting away." There had to be a certificate of divorce, so the injured person could have hope and start anew — be set free.

I Can't Believe That!

You might say, "I can't believe that! I can only believe what my church teaches." If this is you, you have a lot of company. But you and your company ought to think about what you're saying. Aren't you possibly saying that you trust what your church teaches more than what God might say? Or what the Bible says? You may have misplaced your trust. That's what the Pharisees of Jesus' day did.

Jesus told those experts in the law and religion, "You search the Scriptures because you think that in them you have eternal life; it is these that testify about Me; and you are unwilling to come to Me so that you may have life" (John 5:39-40). And Paul, an Apostle of Jesus Christ, commended an early church in Greece because they checked out what he was teaching them to see if it was in the Scriptures. "Now the Berean Jews were of more noble character than those in Thessalonica, for they received the message with great eagerness and examined the Scriptures every day to see if what Paul said was true" (Acts 17:11 NIV).

So this discussion is as much about how you approach the Bible as the divorce and remarriage issue. Remember, what you think about God is the most important thing about you. Getting to know Him is a dance during your earth life and the most important one. Probably 90% of what we think about God comes from what we hear in church, and I'm just making that percentage up. Shouldn't most of what you know about Him come from reading the Bible? It's the inspired and ancient authority. You can trust the Holy Spirit to reveal the Holy Scriptures to you as you read. The most important thing is to show your sincere desire to know Him by reading, studying, discussing, and sharing the Word yourself with others. This dialogue and dance is the everyday Christian life, the life of Jesus' disciples and followers.

Does that Sound Like God?

Never be threatened by what others believe. Trust in God's unfailing love for you and your sealed destiny in Him. But discuss anything and be a humble learner with those of like mind. He'll take responsibility for helping you know the truth if that's your goal. It honors Him that you want to know Him and are seeking for truth.

This discussion of divorce and remarriage hasn't been exhaustive. But I hope you get the point, and it whets your appetite for studying some more Bible topics or issues that interest you. Too many of us don't explore or read for ourselves. We settle and expect our churches to spoon-feed us.

It's an accepted fact that the Bible is the best commentary on the Bible. So compare what you read there with every other similar passage or verse. You'll be amazed at the clear picture that starts to form. And you'll be amazed that some beautiful mystery remains still.

The Bible says things like, "See, **I have inscribed you on the palms** of My hands; your walls are continually before Me [emphasis added]" (Isaiah 49:16, NKJV). Also, "**You keep track of all my sorrows. You have collected all my tears in your bottle**. You have recorded each one in your book [emphasis added]" (Psalm 56:8, NLT). And most poignantly perhaps, "**Surely our griefs He Himself bore, and our sorrows He carried**; yet we ourselves esteemed Him stricken, smitten of God, and afflicted. But **He was pierced through for our transgressions**, He was crushed for our iniquities; **the chastening for our well-being fell upon Him, and by His scourging we are healed** [emphasis added]" (Isaiah 53:4-5, NASB).

I knew what my church taught about divorce didn't sound like what the rest of the Bible said about our redeemer God. So when new evidence came my way, I studied it in light of other Bible passages and discovered something plausible that sounded precisely like our Redeemer God. And that's what I've shared briefly with you.

I have always accepted it as accurate because it's taught widely by the church that the unsaved burn forever in hell. Granted, hell is a little fuzzy in the Bible, probably for a reason, as the subject of divorce and remarriage. But the teaching I've grown up with, handed down by most of the church, doesn't sound like the God portrayed in the rest of Scripture. Recently some new evidence on that subject came my way, and after much study, starting as a doubter, I came away with a different view. That view will be an adjoining but separate piece of the puzzle, one that will hopefully drive you toward the same point. Where is your trust? Religion? Or the Bible and the God of the Bible? And, what do you think about God? Draw near and continue to puzzle. Enjoy learning. Enjoy the dance. Enjoy God. *Shalom* as you puzzle.

I have a good friend, Dwayne Russell, who lives in another city about an hour away. A couple of days ago, he sent a missive that summarizes what I've said above and adds a little more perspective. I'll share it with you here.

"Worthy are you, our Lord and God, to receive glory and honor and power, for you created all things, and by your will they existed and were created"

(Revelation 4:11 ESV).

"By Your will they exist! All that we see with our eyes and all that we can't see was created by a limitless God, and there is nothing He can't see and didn't prepare before hand! When we read the Book of Revelation we read what is going to happen! We may not understand all that we read in this book, but there is a promised blessing if we read it. Yet so many shy away from it! Why? Open the book and read it. You are not going to understand it all, but God will give you highlights that will stand out, and you can build your faith on that" (Dwayne Russell).

"So Jesus was saying to those Jews who had believed Him, '*If you continue in My word, then you are truly disciples of Mine*; **and you will know the truth, and** *the truth will make you free* [emphasis added]'"

(John 8:31-32).

"This is what the Lord says: "*Stand* at the crossroads and **look; ask for the ancient paths, ask where the good way is, and walk in it**, and you will find rest for your souls [emphasis added]'"

(Jeremiah 6:16a NIV).

"**Study** to shew thyself approved unto God, a workman that needeth not to be ashamed, **rightly dividing the word of truth** [emphasis added]"

(2 Timothy 2:15 KJV).

PUZZLING CHAPTER 23

Hell and Mr. Fudge

Introduction

Yes, this piece of the puzzle certainly needs an introduction. While its name sounds funny, the subject is far from funny. The truth about hell is truth, and it is sobering. Yet the facts may not be what you learned in church.

I don't say this to disparage the church in any way. The church has been, through the ages, the guardian of truth. She has taught people about God and His ways. The church provides a family environment or community for practicing faith while discovering and living out the truth. The church is God's plan and Christ's bride. We'll discuss the church later as another piece of the puzzle.

And I am not trying to be controversial. That's the last thing I want to do. The Scripture speaks to that in instructive and insightful ways: "But avoid foolish controversies and genealogies and strife and disputes about the Law, for they are unprofitable and worthless" (Titus 3:9). These days, I run from controversy for controversy's sake, as the Scripture encourages us to do: "Don't have anything to do with foolish and stupid arguments, because you know they produce quarrels" (2 Timothy 2:23 NIV). "Remind them of these things, and solemnly charge them in the presence of God not to wrangle about words, which is useless and leads to the ruin of the hearers" (2Timothy 2:14 NSAB).

Not arguing, but discussing the facts that one can know, I want to point out that what we have heard about hell may not be entirely accurate. While most of it is, recent scholarship and theological research with accompanying book publications have revealed there may be a small but essential aspect about hell that we have gotten wrong.

If this threatens you, consider that your faith may be in your faith and not in God or the Bible or truth. Wouldn't this be important to know? I think we all might need a spiritual wake up call to put our minds back on reality and the God of the Bible. We do not need to defend Him or the truth. The opposite is true. Let God speak for Himself through His Word and by His Spirit. We need only talk about the truth in love, humbly as we understand it. The Bible instructs us to be witnesses, make disciples, and seek the truth. The heavy lifting is God's to do.

Also, consider that we might have become so Biblically illiterate from not reading or studying the Bible for ourselves that we can't quickly evaluate the truth of a Biblical matter. We don't know our Bibles well enough to know what it says elsewhere and throughout. Remember that the Bible is the best commentary on the Bible and the only infallible one. The Bible is a gift and a window to knowing God and truth, aided by revelation from the same Spirit Who gave it.

So what about hell? Hell is a reality referred to many times in the Bible. Jesus spoke of it more often than heaven but never used it as a scare tactic. Do people who do not accept the Gospel of Jesus Christ and choose to live their own lives their way, in essence being their king, rejecting Jesus' kingship, spend eternity tormented in the flames of hell? That, in essence, is what the church has taught for a very long time, since the days of Augustine, Bishop of Hippo, around 400 AD. He was the most influential theologian in the first 1000 years of church history.

The subject of hell is ambiguous, and it is easy to come away with the above conclusion. But it never really sounded to me like something the God of the Bible would desire or decree.

Yet, I believe God to be true, that His ways are high above our ways, and that His judgments are true and altogether righteous, as the Scriptures attest. So I thought, "Maybe in light of Jesus' enormous sacrifice, it might be a fair and just judgment or recompense for people's sins not covered by Jesus' blood." Still, in my heart of hearts, it just didn't sound like the God of the Bible, One trusted and loved, One so good, gracious, full of mercy, and kind — albeit He is also the righteous Judge and King of the whole earth.

I reasoned that there are more essential tenets of the faith than heaven and hell for my focus. Yet those are crucial, and a reality discussed in Scripture. I chose to major in the parts more clearly understood and more important to day-to-day living, like pleasing God and serving others. I decided to leave the truth about hell to God. It's totally in His realm anyway — like everything else!

A.W. Tozer's words often ring in my ears: "What you believe about God is the most important thing about you." I believe he's correct. And once you catch a glimpse of God, you are consumed with Him. I want to know Him better and better, and all I can, until I see Him face to face and know Him as He Is, by His grace and good pleasure. I can identify with Paul at the end of his life, saying: "That I may know Him and the power of His resurrection and the fellowship of His sufferings, being conformed to His death" (Philippians 3:10). Or, as David penned a thousand years earlier, "As the deer pants for the water brooks, so my soul pants for You, O God. My soul thirsts for God, for the living God; when shall I come and appear before God?" (Psalm 42:1-2).

The truth about hell would reflect a truth about God, the God I want to know. It also affects how we should be living our daily lives.

I awakened this morning with the lyrics of a hymn playing in my head, one I hadn't sung or thought about in years: "This is my Father's world, and to my listening ears, all nature sings, and round me rings, the music of the spheres." Then I heard, "the church of the firstborn." That's all. I knew that phrase was in Hebrews but couldn't remember the context or where it was, so I looked it up. It's in Hebrews 12, a fascinating chapter, with several synchronicities for me, that I will journal and meditate upon at length during upcoming quiet times.

The phrase is in this section: "For you have not come to a mountain that can be touched and to a blazing fire, and to darkness and gloom and whirlwind, and to the blast of a trumpet and the sound of words which sound was such that those who heard begged that no further word be spoken to them. For they could not bear the command, 'If even a beast touches the mountain, it will be stoned.' And so terrible was the sight, that Moses said, 'I am full of fear and trembling.' But you have come to Mount Zion and to the city of the living God, the heavenly Jerusalem, and to myriads of angels, to the general assembly and **church of the firstborn** who are enrolled in heaven, and to God, the Judge of all, and to the spirits of the righteous made perfect, and to Jesus, the mediator of a new covenant, and to the sprinkled blood, which speaks better than the blood of Abel [emphasis added]" (Hebrews 12: 18-24).

Chapter 12 ends: "…for our God is a consuming fire" (Hebrews 12:29).

Hell and Mr. Fudge

Six or seven years ago, a new friend, Tom, and I went to a coffee shop after an early morning men's group at a local Methodist church. Out of the blue, he asked me, "What do you think about hell? Do you believe that people who do not know Jesus are judged for their unforgiven sins and spend eternity there in torment?" I replied, "I suppose I do. That's the teaching of Scripture, the position of the church, and what I have always been taught." He then smiled and said, "You should watch the movie *Hell and Mr. Fudge*."

Yes, there is a movie by that name! And I would suggest you watch it if you're interested in the truth of this matter or just curious. It's well done, with good actors and a great storyline. Advertisements describe it as: "A 2012 American drama film directed by Jeff Wood and written by Donald Davenport. Based on a true story, the film stars Mackenzie Astin as Edward Fudge, an Alabama preacher who has been hired to determine the nature of hell."

It turns out Mr. Fudge is real. Edward Fudge lived much of his life as a lawyer in Houston, Texas. He was also a Bible student and scholar with a classical education in theology, the study of God. The movie gives a good account of his life and history so I won't recount it here.

I was so intrigued by the movie, Edward Fudge himself, his approach to the Scriptures, and what happened to him I decided to read further. I was also intrigued by his proposition and his Biblical research. In short:

1. There is a literal hell prepared for Satan and his demons, and their lot is torment there forever.
2. God will judge humans for their sins at a great end-times judgment.
3. Those without their sins forgiven will be cast into that hell, suffer its torment, then be totally, utterly consumed, never to be heard from or thought of again.

Wow! That was different, at least on one crucial point. And something that would take a little study, thought, and investigation. It turns out Mr. Fudge published the findings of his years of research in a rather large, academic book entitled, *The Fire That Consumes: A Biblical and Historical Study of the Doctrine of Final Punishment, 3rd edition.*

Wikipedia says about the book and Mr. Fudge: "Edward William Fudge (July 13, 1944 – November 25, 2017) was an American Christian theologian and lawyer, best known for his book 'The Fire that Consumes,' in which he argues against traditionalist Christian interpretations of Hell. He has been called 'one of the foremost scholars on hell' by The Christian Post.'"

Some well-known British theologians were convinced Fudge's position is correct and lined up better with their knowledge of Scripture. I also learned that some influential theologians throughout church history read the whole Bible and questioned whether eternal punishment in hell was really what the Bible taught. But it was hard to stand against Augustine on any matter.

I decided to read a smaller version of the 500-page book written by Fudge, *Hell: A Final Word*. Then I would look closely at the Scriptures he cited and explained in light of other Scriptures and make up my mind, asking the Spirit for insight on the issue as I journeyed. Speaking of this smaller book, Fudge said the name reflected that this was the last thing he would write about hell, and that hell is final for humans. Clever, and it speaks volumes about what became his life's work and contribution to theology, the church, and truth in our day.

The Debate

Shortly after I had dealt with this material and the subject, the wife of a good friend said to me, "You're just changing your mind because you can't bear the thought of Edward's young friend burning forever in hell." I replied, "No, I changed my mind because after reading the book and looking at all the Scriptures cited, I think this is what the Bible says about hell." She then added, "What if it keeps people from fearing hell and therefore not coming to salvation in Christ?" I replied, "What if it is the truth? And what if flawed teaching about hell has portrayed God inaccurately?"

One side of me sees that the flawed teaching would be wrong and tragic in a way. Another side of me considers that a vast and powerful God could have made it clearer if He wanted to do so. It may have served His purposes to state the information as He did, truth revealed in a time-release form to accomplish His objectives in many different generations. I like to say He made it a bit fuzzy for a reason, like the issue of divorce and remarriage. At any rate, it's a truth worth seeking out and truth worth knowing if God is worth knowing. That's why I write, to awaken sleeping Christians and a sleeping church that has lost touch with the Person and object of their worship — the God Who created them and then redeemed them out of His great love and magnificent grace.

Allow me one more word about the debate and my inquiry into the issue. After watching the movie a few times and reading *Hell: A Final Word*, I became aware of another book on the subject where a leading theologian espousing the traditional view of hell and Edward Fudge had a debate in book form. A well-known publisher invited each to present their case in a certain number of pages, and then each was allowed to read the position of the other and respond, adding two more chapters to make a four-chapter book on the subject. Here's the publisher's description of that book: *Two Views of Hell: A Biblical & Theological Dialogue.*

"Hell is real and terrible. It is the fate of those who reject God. Evangelicals agree about this unhappy truth. Yet on some questions about hell disagreements arise. Some evangelicals believe the wicked will experience perpetual, conscious torment after death. Others argue that the wicked will experience a limited period of conscious punishment and then they will cease to exist. In this book you will find an irenic yet frank debate between two evangelical theologians who present strong scriptural and theological evidence for and against each view. Both make a case that their view is more consistent with Scripture and with the holy and just nature of a loving God. Robert Peterson defends the traditional view that those who do not have faith in Christ will suffer eternally in hell. Edward Fudge advocates the conditionalist perspective that after a period of suffering, the unfaithful will experience a complete extinguishing, or annihilation, of existence. In addition, each author presents a rebuttal to the viewpoint of the other. Here is a dialogue that will inform and challenge those on both sides, while impressing on all the need for faithful proclamation of the gospel of deliverance from sin and death."

For me, Edward Fudge won this debate hands down, by his facts, conclusions, and his kind demeanor. But read it for yourself and search the Scriptures they each point out. If you're still with me and looking to know the truth about this matter, what the Bible says, and what it says about God, I will recommend a video that recently came to my attention. It's one of the last talks Mr. Fudge made on the subject. Here you can hear the facts and experience his gentle, kind spirit for yourself in spoken form. Do a web search on The Lanier Library Lecture Series, Edward Fudge, 2011.

The debate says something about the state of our churches, our Bible knowledge, our culture, and maybe you — where does your faith lie? Hopefully our faith is in God, and in Truth, and not wholly in what we have been taught. God give you grace and light as you read and listen.

PUZZLING CHAPTER 24

Sex In Perspective

Introduction

Okay! Here is a disclaimer. I never intended to write about sex in the first place. I don't like to talk about it. I seldom even think about it outside the context of my own marriage and my life with my wife. And now it seems the Spirit is leading me to address it once more, starting with thoughts that came to me as I was taking my truck to the mechanic for an oil change. I remembered something a copilot friend once told me about sex being a problem for men, as we were flying across the Pacific. Then, a good friend who picked me up from the mechanic's shop and brought me back home began talking to me about some sexual issues affecting some of the men in our men's group. That was confirmation enough. Maybe this discussion, with its brief thoughts from the Bible and life, will help some men and women to find their way and navigate this area of their lives in more happy and healthy ways.

Sex is a mysterious servant and a malicious master.

I flew my airplane to Monroe, Louisiana, in the spring of 2021 with a close friend to attend a church conference with Charles Simpson. Before one of the meetings, a woman named Sheila came up to me and asked: "Are you writing another book?" I was a bit incredulous because I didn't know her personally, just by reputation, and I had no idea she knew I had written a book. I smiled at her and replied, "Yes." She then looked deep into my eyes and said: "Don't be afraid to write about the hard things." It was like the Lord wrote that on my heart. And I have thought about it several times as I worked on the manuscript for this book. It came to me again just now. So I feel it's the Spirit's leading and invitation to write.

Sex seems so mysterious, private, intimate, and wonderful that to discuss it or experience it outside God's boundaries seems to degrade it or make it less valuable than it is — maybe we dishonor the gift. It's a little bit like giving pearls to pigs — the gift, though precious, will never be used for its intended purpose or be appreciated for its rare value but trampled in the mud.

At the real heart of it, I think, sex is intended for us to know someone completely and to be completely known. To be loved and accepted for who you are at your very core — open, honest, bare. And to enjoy the journey and exploration that is an earth life with someone of like mind, spirit, and heart — someone you trust and who trusts you, to see the whole process through to the end. To take risks, journey, and adventure together is a very meaningful experience. Sex is a mysterious and beautiful part of "knowing" someone. You give yourself to another, expressing trust in the other person — their character, their heart, their faithfulness, their love for you to the point of laying down their lives in sacrifice for you and you for them. Sex is to be experienced more than understood, with our hearts, not our heads.

The idea of sex being a means of knowing someone comes from the first mention of sex in the Bible: "And **Adam knew Eve his wife; and she conceived,** and bare Cain, and said, I have gotten a man from the

Lord [emphasis mine]" (Genesis 4:1). So God gives us a hint from the very first mention of sex in the Bible, close to the source and at the beginning of humankind, that **sex is not only for procreation but for deeply knowing someone.**

That said, we've seen a lot of use and abuse of the gift since that time. Both are a testament to how powerful and unique the gift is. Its strength, a bit like nuclear energy, can wield its enormous power for good or evil, help or harm. Let's have a quick look at a few of the issues this presents to us.

You'll Need to Talk About Sex

I piloted a Boeing 777 from Japan to the United States a few years ago. On such long flights over hours and hours of the Pacific Ocean, you have a lot of time to talk and think. Because of computers and automation, the colossal airliner only requires two pilots on the flight deck. But due to the lengthy 12-13 hour flight, we carried four pilots so each set of two crews could take rest breaks. It was on one of those three-hour stretches of flying, monitoring the airplane systems and plotting its navigational accuracy, that I had a fascinating conversation with a copilot. He was a Christian and had been married twenty plus years. He asked me a typical question, "What are you gonna do this weekend?" I told him that I was to speak at a men's retreat in the Ozark mountains near our home and that I was struggling because nothing had come to me as subject matter. His immediate reply was: "Well if it's a men's meeting, you'll need to talk about sex."

I probably looked at him like he was from Mars as if to say: "Where did that come from?" After a pause, I did say to him: "That never entered my mind. Why do you say that?" I will never forget his answer. He said sex is such a strong impulse and force among men that most struggle. He went on to say: **"Sex was a problem for the strongest man who ever lived, Samson, and the wisest man who ever lived,**

Solomon, and the guy with the best heart, David." If you read the Bible, you know that this problem is well-stated, illustrated, and his point well-made.

He went on to say: "Sex is the glue that holds my marriage together." I knew he had a good marriage with intimacy and joy, but this point was also well-made and well-taken.

Sex Is the Glue

I am already in mystery over my head. So let me just state that the Bible teaches that a husband and wife should enjoy each other sexually and not keep themselves from each other: "**The wife does not have authority over her own body, but the husband does; and likewise also the husband does not have authority over his own body, but the wife does. Stop depriving one another,** except by agreement for a time, so that you may devote yourselves to prayer, and come together again **so that Satan will not tempt you** because of your lack of self-control [emphasis added]" (I Corinthians 7:4-5).

The Bible teaches that sex is a legitimate need that makes a married couple dependent on each other. This dependency is a good thing. Withholding oneself from the other is a bad thing and gets into the area of control and co-dependency, which are harmful behaviors, even destructive to a relationship. Of course, you can be playful with sex within the boundaries; that's a big part of what sex is for, but not for controlling each other. Instead, give freely, work out whatever problems there might be, and trust God for the results. When you show you trust Him by adherence to His ways, He will send answers and help you in this crucial relationship. He wants the best for you and desires your happiness and joy. It was His idea in the first place and His creation.

These words about sex from the Word are true, beautiful, and positive. But did you notice the warning at the end? "… come together again so that Satan will not tempt you because of your lack of self-control." The Creator knew how powerful He made this force and attraction for joy and good. And like all His good gifts, they can become idols if not used as directed and intended.

Malicious Master

"For this is **the will of God**, your sanctification; that is, **that you abstain from sexual immorality** [emphasis mine]" (1 Thessalonians 4:3). This verse is one verse typical of many in the Scriptures. The Spirit of God speaks to an early church in Greece and the church through the ages. God is straightforward about this and very understated, as always. It's almost as if He is saying throughout His Word, "This is my plan and path for your sexual fulfillment and enjoyment, but it's a gift, and you may use it as you choose." **In His plan, faithfulness and boundaries are mysterious and hidden parts of His formula for maximum enjoyment of the gift.**

To go your own way, or to follow the course of the world, in this matter, is like shooting yourself in the foot. In the end, only you and God will know the truth of it, what it was, wasn't, or could have been. While we don't get "do-overs" in this area or most areas of our earthly life, we do get "start-overs." **We confess our wrongdoings to Him and others in sorrow, experience His gracious forgiveness, and start using our free will to abstain from immorality.** We receive help from His promised Helper, the Holy Spirit, trusting the best will happen. As He says elsewhere, "Then **I will make up to you for the years that the swarming locust has eaten**, the creeping locust, the stripping locust and the gnawing locust, **My great army which I sent among you** [emphasis mine]" (Joel 2:25).

It seems at times in human history, sexual idolatry or sexual sin was at rampant levels in countries, cultures, even the world, more than at other times. Need I say more?

We have some very ancient warnings about this: "Watch yourself that you make no covenant with the inhabitants of the land into which you are going, or it will become a snare in your midst. But rather, you are to tear down their altars and smash their sacred pillars and cut down their Asherim —for you shall not worship any other god, for the Lord, whose name is Jealous, is a jealous God" (Exodus 34:12-16). You can read the last chapters of Judges to see what can happen if a culture accepts homosexuality as normative.

Sure it's disappointing to God and, in fact, infidelity toward Him if you know Him and practice immorality. It's also very harmful and destructive for you. It's as if God metes out some judgment or justice for this disobedient behavior and transgression of His ways. It's mysterious and slow-growing, like cancer. You don't usually know it's there until you are very sick. Unless He graciously shines His light on the matter so that you may deal with it, you will probably die in this condition.

"Shame" almost always accompanies sexual sin. Isn't that interesting? Why? Could it be because it's shameful? We see it first in the Garden: "Then the eyes of both of them were opened, and they knew that they were naked; and they sewed fig leaves together and made themselves loin coverings" (Genesis 3:7). Shame is not a sin but seemingly always an unseen result of sexual sin, making one want to hide it and hide, period. Whether it's spiritual, psychological, emotional, or who knows, it seems to become an unwelcome guest causing emotional pain, regret, turmoil, paranoia, insecurity, and unhealthy reactions, as well as toxic behavior among members of the human family. Oddly, shame has the characteristic that it can deceive a person into thinking it's an ally or friend and should be carried and kept in debilitating darkness.

Last week a good friend said to me, **"Shame is like sin, in that it must be dealt with in the light of day. It must be brought into God's light of forgiveness and washed away."** Do you think he's on to something? That means telling God how you feel, asking for His help in prayer, and sharing it with some trusted spiritual friends — into the light it goes, soon to disappear, by His Grace.

Back to the malicious master, here is a word or two about pornography and masturbation. I was once in a men's seminar talking about wholesome living and what the Bible teaches about God's ways. In a break-out, small-group session, one of my friends called masturbation "self sex." Enough said. That's not the purpose of sex from the Garden until now, is it? It's a shortcut to a dead end and probably not healthy. But let's be honest, it's bound to happen on some scale based on the power of the gift in the normal maturing process of life and exploration.

There is little mention of it in the Bible, and no prohibition, probably for a reason. Yet when I've heard it discussed, many report feeling ashamed or shameful about it. Has some boundary been crossed. Are you cheating on yourself or your spouse? Or your future spouse? Is your self-effort short-circuiting what otherwise would be a gift to enjoy rightfully? Be wise. I knew a guy in his thirties who shared with me he made a quality decision in his shower one day when struggling with this issue, to trust God and his wife with his sexual fulfillment and permanently give up any other behavior. He reported back in his fifties, pleased with that decision.

A similar or related dance with the malicious and merciless master is pornography. Much discussion isn't needed. People who dabble or are addicted to it know the feelings of shame that accompany viewing it and then acting out some fantasy by masturbation, or self-sex. What does it say about you, or how you value the misguided people in the pictures? Or how do you love others in general? It's not the truth about enjoying sex, and you know it in your heart of hearts. But eventually, you can sear your conscience a good bit and lose touch with reality and the path back. It leads to a place of being controlled, in torment, no satisfaction, no joy, no peace — a lonely place of no return, except by the grace of God.

Flee! Run from it. As a young man reading the Bible, I noticed that there were many "do nots" or "thou shalt nots." Since then, I've seen the wisdom in those commands. God gave them for our protection, well-being, and enjoyment of life. I also noticed that when it came to sexual sin, the injunction was different: "**Flee sexual immorality**. Every sin that a man does is outside the body, but he who commits sexual immorality sins against his own body [emphasis added]" (1 Corinthians 6:18 KJV). Per how strong God made the gift, the command is "flee." Paul, by the Spirit, was writing to the church in Corinth who had plenty of experience and problems with immoral sexual practices in their culture and in the young church. Paul later said the same thing to Timothy, his best-known mentee-pastor, elder, and a leader of the early church: "**Now flee from youthful lusts and pursue righteousness**, faith, love and peace, with those who call on the Lord from a pure heart [emphasis added]" (2 Timothy 2:22 NASB). The traits are opposites, "flee **lusts** and pursue **righteousness**" but are undoubtedly connected — and mutually exclusive. So, who do you trust? Who do you believe in these matters of the heart and body — sexual conduct? I encourage you to trust God and show it by doing what He says. There is plenty of information that this is His way, and the promise is that He will provide power to help the sincere, repentant heart change their thoughts, actions, and habits. Go with God!

Babylon and Our Culture

Babylon? I know you're probably thinking, "What does Babylon have to do with sex or anything in the modern world?" Well, on Thursday mornings between 6:00 AM and 7:30 AM, I meet with about thirty guys doing a year-long study of Revelation, the last book of the Bible, which reveals much about Jesus Christ, and end-times events on the earth. Many believe we are in the end times, the end of this age, as predicted and described in considerable detail in the books of Daniel and Revelation, with many snippets scattered like puzzle pieces throughout the Old and New Testaments. Yesterday we were discussing chapter 14 and the verse that says: "And another angel, a second one, followed, saying, 'Fallen, fallen is **Babylon the great, she who has made all the nations drink of the wine of the passion of her immorality** [emphasis added]'" (Revelation 14:8).

A brother to my left, Mark, piped up and said: "But the Scripture says that **Babylon made them do it — be immoral.**" That didn't sound right or correct given the rest of Scripture to me, so I went quickly to a free app on my phone, Strong's Concordance and KJV Bible, by Kairos, to see what the original Greek word translated "made" in English meant. According to Strong's definitions, the word *potizo* means "to furnish drink, irrigate, give (make) to drink, feed, water." Thayer's Lexicon has it: "to furnish drink, **to water, irrigate, (plants, fields, etc.), metaphorically to imbue, saturate one's mind** [emphasis added]." To my right, Bill, a brother, leaned over and said to me, "**That sounds like pornography.**" It did! Does that sound like pornography to you? Does that sound like pushing for sexual freedom, and anything goes? Does that look like the myriads of billboards and TV advertisements with images flooding the eyes and mind with sexual images? **Babylon then and now is about the exaltation of sex to an idol or god.** Do you go with the mores and guidelines of secular humanism, man being his own god, or do you go with the moral code prescribed by God? Scripture speaks again; those who worship idols become like them, **dysfunctional and lifeless.** "**They [idols] have ears, but do not hear, nor is there any breath in their mouths. Those who make them become like them, so do all who trust in them!** [emphasis added]" (Psalm 135:17-18). "Every goldsmith is **put to shame by his idols, for his images are false, and there is no breath in them** [emphasis added]" (Jeremiah 10:14b).

Speaking about irrigating or flooding the fields of the mind and the similarity to pornography, I remember reading twenty years ago that only 3% of the internet comprised porn sites. Still, those sites accounted for about 30% of internet traffic. Wanting to see if I could find any updated, credible information or recent research on that statistic, I found a credible article written by Katharina Buchhloz for the website *Statista*, February 11, 2019. She cites two studies between 2005 and 2014 by Boston University and by Google and Columbia University that suggest: "Only 4% of websites are estimated to be porn," but "web and mobile searches show the web traffic to be 13% and 20% respectively on those sites." That might sound like a small number on the surface, but if you ponder how many websites there are today, it's a huge number!

The same article goes on to say: "87% of US men, 18-35, watch porn at least weekly, along with 28.5% of US women the same ages." So is there a problem? Do we have an epidemic? Have there been unusual rises in human sex trafficking, suicide, depression, sexually transmitted diseases, and related maladies? Have we pushed men and women farther apart instead of closer together? Have we left the gates open and are now experiencing a flood of escalating problems due to immorality and not choosing God and His plan for sex?

Another Way to Look at Porn

Here's a bonus for reading this chapter. My sweet wife loves to read. She has a Master's Degree in Education and Reading. She especially loves the genre of Christian fiction, where people use their literary skills and imagination to take readers on adventures in matters of the heart. For example, she and some of her friends read many of Francine Rivers' books. Recently an intellectual friend who seldom reads fiction recommended another author, Charles Martin, and his book *When Crickets Cry* as an introduction to his writing. I got her the book as a gift. She read a third of it aloud to me in two sittings and now has absconded with the book to the cabin with a friend while I attend a men's retreat with our new church this weekend.

If you are this type of reader, and you already know if you are, read this book and get to know this author. You will thank me.

These writers use little religious verbiage or any expressed intent at morality to point people toward God. Yet they lead people to consider truth, relationships, philosophy, chance, destiny, and many beautiful facets that make up our earth journey. Their writing reminds me of the verse: "Finally, brothers and sisters, whatever is true, whatever is noble, whatever is right, whatever is pure, whatever is lovely, whatever is admirable—if anything is excellent or praiseworthy—think about such things" (Philippians 4:8).

Notice with me how this author in one little snippet addressed pornography, after clearly describing his first love of a beautiful young girl, Emma:

"One day, a kid in my class brought his dad's playboy to school and passed it around during recess. I took one look, and it struck me as completely wrong. It made me feel dirty, like I wanted to take a shower. Deep down, I knew that whoever had done that to those girls, taking all those pictures, must be a pretty sick person. My heart told me that.

"I handed it back. 'That could be Emma,' I thought.

"Don't let me sound like some saint. Of course I wanted to see naked women, but beneath a part of me that was intrigued was another part, the part that knew better, the part that knew I was here to fix Emma. That part of me, where my soul lives, convulsed, vomited, and spewed disgust across the glossy centerfold.

"Walking home that day, I was quiet. Even embarrassed. When Emma asked me what was wrong, I told her. When we got to her steps and I had finished my story, she pulled me close and kissed me on the cheek — one heart speaking to another in a language that only the two of them speak.

"Emma had [physically] the sickest heart of any human I've ever met, but out of it flowed more love than from any other 10 hearts put together."

What Are We Doing to Ourselves

I have addressed the malicious master to the point that I am way over my head, yet I feel led to share some reality that recently came to our men's group about rape and molestation.

Two guys in our group have an excellent friend who has some baseball-loving sons and beautiful daughters, all near their teen years. The parents have thriving businesses, the kids do well in school and are active in their church.

Recently one of the older daughters went to a large city with a friend to visit friends, and they were invited to a party. While there, a young man, a sexual predator, executed a well-orchestrated scheme, spiked her drink, and attempted to rape her. A month earlier, a cousin molested the youngest daughter while on a family vacation. Amid a season and flurry of counselors, lawyers, and private investigators, these precious young women dealt with the trauma and shame of these occurrences. It also came to light that another sister, the mother, and grandmother had been molested — five women in the same family!

Someone has left some gates open, or the walls are broken down in our culture and churches, not necessarily in that order. We are suffering from a sexual flood that is highly harmful and hurtful to people and wars against the enjoyment of our lives on earth.

The flood of sexual images in TV advertising, billboards, and internet porn sites has emboldened sin-laden, sexually-perverted folks to push their agendas until they have found favor enough to legalize sexual immorality. The laws of the land reflect these mores in direct opposition to God's moral code, which are His decrees for peace, joy, and love.

Homosexuality

I must say something about this crucial issue because it is at the forefront or epicenter of the tension between God's ways and those of secular humanists. I needn't say much because most people have their minds firmly made up. It's a volatile issue with passions high on both sides, especially among the proponents of homosexuality, advocating it as a lifestyle, human right, and genetic predisposition.

One of my friends, a Greek scholar, Bible teacher, and Russian pastor, says homosexuality is the "line in the sand" today between God's ways and man's ways. He also says it's one of the primary pieces of evidence that we live in the last days because it's delusional. People are confused today about whether they are male or female? Isn't that about as delusional as it gets? He cites the Scripture: "**Let no one in any way deceive you**, for it [Christ's return] will not come unless **the apostasy comes first** [emphasis added]" (2 Thessalonians 2:3a). The same passage also says: "For this reason, **God will send upon them a deluding influence so that they will believe what is false** [emphasis added]" (2 Thessalonians 2:11).

God made the gift of sex strong enough that this temptation has been around a long time, at the fringes of cultures and nations. God addressed it clearly in the first moral code given Moses for Israel and all His creation 3500 years ago: "**You shall not lie with a male as one lies with a female; it is an abomination**" (Leviticus 18:22). Or in stronger language: "**If there is a man who lies with a male as those who lie with a woman, both of them have committed a detestable act; they shall surely be put to death** [emphasis added]" (Leviticus 20:13a-b).

Paul by the Spirit wrote to the church in Rome 1500 years later, 2000 years ago the same guidance with more information about how it works, or doesn't, in God's view: "**Therefore God gave them over in the lusts of their hearts to impurity, so that their bodies would be dishonored among them.** For they exchanged the truth of God for a lie, and worshiped and served the creature rather than the Creator, who is blessed forever. Amen. **For this reason God gave them over to degrading passions; for their women exchanged the natural function for that which is unnatural, and in the same way also the men abandoned**

the natural function of the woman and burned in their desire toward one another, men with men committing indecent acts and receiving in their own persons the due penalty of their error. And just as they did not see fit to acknowledge God any longer, God gave them over to a depraved mind, to do those things which are not proper, being filled with all unrighteousness, wickedness, greed, evil; full of envy, murder, strife, deceit, malice; they are gossips, slanderers, haters of God, insolent, arrogant, boastful, inventors of evil, disobedient to parents, without understanding, untrustworthy, unloving, unmerciful; and although they know the ordinance of God, that **those who practice such things are worthy of death, they not only do the same, but also give hearty approval to those who practice them** [emphasis added]" (Romans 1:26-32).

The moral code is the same, recorded in the Old and New Testaments, and the language couldn't be more precise or more robust, even spelling out motives and rationale for the indecency. **Please consider this, those of you who have entertained the lie that homosexuality is genetic and a person doesn't have free will in the matter.** What do you think about God? Is He good as the Bible attests? He is. Those of you who know Him by the Spirit, which is the only way to know Him according to John 3, and the rest of Scripture, certainly know that He is good, loving, and merciful toward all He has made. **Would a loving, good-hearted God create someone with a bent toward homosexuality they couldn't overcome and then declare they would receive a death sentence** if they lived it out? No, certainly not. It's a choice.

Dr. James Dobson, a nationally known family health expert, often pointed out that like boys, girls are also: "at risk because of many 21st-century cultural influences such as violence, **hyper-sexuality**, and spiritual impoverishment."

What are we doing to ourselves? This is a question for our culture and our churches. There are glaring deficiencies in both places. But I am addressing individuals, and it's a personal question first and foremost. It's among the most intimate of questions. How do you see it right now, in light of this discussion and these Scriptures? I think it is wise not to curse the darkness or have anything to do with it, but light a candle of truth, being very honest with yourself and others.

David, who had some problems and made mistakes in the sexual area of his life, said it this way: "Your word is a lamp to my feet and a light to my path (Psalm 119:105). And, "How can a young man keep his way pure? By guarding it according to your word" (Psalm 119:9).

How are you living your life sexually, or going to live going forward? It's important to God, but it's more important for you. Take the high road with His help and your firm decision, and you'll find it trending upward always to new heights and endless days filled with more and more joy. Godspeed! And Bon Voyage.

"How can a young man keep his way pure?
By guarding it according to your word.
With my whole heart I seek you;
let me not wander from your commandments!
I have stored up your word in my heart,
that I might not sin against you.
Blessed are you, O Lord;
teach me your statutes!
With my lips I declare
all the rules of your mouth.
In the way of your testimonies I delight
as much as in all riches.
I will meditate on your precepts
and fix my eyes on your ways.
I will delight in your statutes;
I will not forget your word [emphasis added]"
(Psalm 119:9-16).

"My son, pay attention to my wisdom, Incline your ear to my understanding, so that you may maintain discretion And your lips may comply with knowledge. For **the lips of an adulteress drip honey, and her speech is smoother than oil; but in the end she is bitter as wormwood, sharp as a two-edged sword. Her feet go down to death, her steps take hold of Sheol. She does not ponder the path of life; her ways are unstable, she does not know it.** Now then, my sons, listen to me and do not turn away from the words of my mouth. **Keep your way far from her, And do not go near the door of her house, otherwise you will give your vigor to others, and your years to the cruel one; and strangers will be filled with your strength, and your hard-earned possessions will go to the house of a foreigner; and you will groan in the end, when your flesh and your body are consumed**; and you say, 'How I hated instruction! And my heart disdainfully rejected rebuke! I did not listen to the voice of my teachers, Nor incline my ear to my instructors! I was almost in total ruin in the midst of the assembly and congregation. '**Drink water from your own cistern, and fresh water from your own well. Should your springs overflow into the street, streams of water in the public squares? Let them be yours alone, and not for strangers with you. Let your fountain be blessed, and rejoice in the wife of your youth** [emphasis added]"

(Proverbs 5:1-18).

"For on account of a harlot one is reduced to a loaf of bread, and **an adulteress hunts for the precious life** [emphasis added]"

(Proverbs 6:26).

Mysterious Servant

Here's another Charles Martin quote from *A Life Intercepted*, a different book than mentioned earlier. It says exactly what I'm trying to convey about the beautiful relationship God intends for us via sex and marriage. It is a self-sacrificing commitment, with resultant joy in the journey. Here's the quote:

> "I stood there, staring at her. Flickering candlelight. The slight upturn of her lips. The small of her back. The beauty that's her, the part she only shared with me, the part of us that was just our secret, hidden from everyone but me. Whatever it is that God hard-wired into the heart of man, into our very DNA, which is satisfied only in and by knowing the mystery and wonder that is a woman's heart wrapped in the layers of her external beauty — I'd found it in my wife."

Solomon, reportedly the wisest man who ever lived, after giving the warning about the adulteress as quoted above, gives men this advice about valuing and appreciating their wives in a long-lived relationship: "As a loving hind and a graceful doe, let her breasts satisfy you at all times; **be exhilarated always with her love** [emphasis added]" (Proverbs 5:19).

> "While the king was at his table,
> My perfume gave forth its fragrance.
> My beloved is to me a pouch of myrrh
> Which lies all night between my breasts.
> My beloved is to me a cluster of henna blossoms
> In the vineyards of Engedi.
> How beautiful you are, my darling,
> How beautiful you are!
> Your eyes are like doves.
> How handsome you are, my beloved,
> And so pleasant!
> Indeed, our couch is luxuriant!"
>
> (Song of Solomon 1:12-16).

"**There are three things which are too wonderful for me**,
Four which I do not understand: The way of an eagle in the sky,
The way of a serpent on a rock,
The way of a ship in the middle of the sea,
And **the way of a man with a maid** [emphasis added]"

(Proverbs 30:18-19).

Chapter Epilogue or Summary Reflection

I awakened this morning at the cabin with a March snow on the ground thinking about this chapter and what I've learned writing it. After nearly a half century being married, I can speak with some objectivity and from experience about sex and marriage. And not just me: the Lord has blessed me with many close friends who are real about their life experiences, successes, failures, and lessons learned. Many share their stories with me.

Next year I'll become a septuagenarian, something I never saw coming. I'm so thankful, and couldn't be more pleased that I've stayed the course of Scriptural counsel in marriage and I can't imagine being at this stage without the wife of my youth, who is also my faithful, fun, life-giving, life-sharing, best friend.

You will recall a main purpose of marriage is friendship and knowing another person by risking being bare, faithful, real, honest, trusting, sacrificial, and loving.

My early morning thoughts turned to how I've come to know God, and continue to do so. In the last ten years since I retired, He's really shown me grace upon grace: "For of His fullness we have all received, and grace upon grace" (John 1:16). It's a side of Him I really never knew experientially like I'm coming to know it now. Maybe this only comes with wearing out shoe leather. We're told in the oldest book in the Bible: "Wisdom is with aged men, with long life is understanding" (Job 12:12).

If this is you, enjoying the benefits of a long marriage, rejoice and be glad. If you've made some mistakes and things have turned out differently, remember that God is the God of the second chance, and can do miraculous things of the redeeming and restorative nature. Someone has wisely said, "The best time to plant a tree was forty years ago. The next best time is today." Trust Him and walk in His ways from where you are. As the prophet exhorts us from his ancient time: "Thus says the Lord, 'Stand by the ways and see and ask for the ancient paths, where the good way is, and walk in it; and you will find rest for your souls'" (Jeremiah 6:16). If you do, you will fare well.

I'm just saying there is a beautiful connection between marriage and knowing God, also between knowing a mate and knowing God, for life. I pray you live to see it and enjoy it. His *shalom* (peace) to you and yours.

"Grow old along with me! The best is yet to be, the last of life, for which the first was made. Our times are in his hand who saith, 'A whole I planned, youth shows but half; Trust God: See all, nor be afraid!'"

(Robert Browning).

PUZZLING CHAPTER 25

Holy Spirit Perspective

Christ In Us

We are walking cathedrals of God's presence. Isn't that what the Bible teaches? Look with me at verses like: "To whom God willed to make known what is the riches of the glory of this mystery among the Gentiles, which is **Christ in you, the hope of glory** [emphasis added]" (Colossians 1:27). "'Heaven is My throne and the earth is My footstool. **Where then is a house you could build for Me?** And where is a place that I may rest? For My hand made all these things, thus all these things came into being,' declares the Lord. '**But to this one I will look, to him who is humble and contrite of spirit, and who trembles at My word** [emphasis added]'" (Isaiah 66:1-2).

The Gospel of Matthew quoting the Prophet Isaiah (7:14) says it this way: "'Behold, the virgin shall be with child and shall bear a Son, and they shall call His name **Immanuel**,' which translated means, '**God with us** [emphasis added]'" (Matthew 1:23). Paul perhaps expresses the living mystery better than anyone: "But **we have this treasure in earthen**

vessels, so **that the surpassing greatness of the power will be of God and not from ourselves** [emphasis added]" (2 Corinthians 4:7).

During the forty days after His resurrection, Jesus spent time with his disciples encouraging them and giving them a few instructions. In what would come ten days later, unknown to them, Jesus declared, "And behold, I am sending forth the promise of My Father upon you; but you are to **stay in the city until you are clothed with power from on high** [emphasis added]" (Luke 24:49).

Spiritual Power

I wonder what happened on the 9th day? Nothing! I would venture a guess.

But on the 10th day after Jesus' ascension, the 50th day from Passover and Jesus' crucifixion, the day of Pentecost on the Jewish calendar, Jesus sent the Holy Spirit, and the church of Jesus Christ was born. She is coming up on her 2000th birthday!

The Greek word *enduo* translated "clothed" above and "endued" in other translations; according to Rick Renner, a Greek scholar, means "to be clothed," "with power like a Roman army," and "comfortable in that power—those clothes."

Rick Renner goes on to say: "Salvation of the Holy Spirit brings peace." And: "Baptism in the Holy Spirit brings power."

"Now He said to them, 'These are My words which I spoke to you while I was still with you, that **all things which are written about Me in the Law of Moses and the Prophets and the Psalms must be fulfilled.' Then He opened their minds to understand the Scriptures**, and He said to them, 'Thus it is written, that the Christ would suffer and rise again from the dead the third day, and that repentance for forgiveness of sins would be proclaimed in His name to all the nations, beginning from Jerusalem. You are witnesses of these things. And behold, **I am sending forth the promise of My Father upon you; but you are to stay in the city until you are clothed with power from on high.**' And He led them out as far as Bethany, and He lifted up His hands and blessed them. While He was blessing them, He parted from them and was carried up into heaven. And they, after worshiping Him, returned to Jerusalem with great joy, and were continually in the temple praising God [emphasis added]"

(Luke 24:44-53).

"When the day of Pentecost had come, they were all together in one place. And suddenly **there came from heaven a noise like a violent rushing wind,** and it filled the whole house where they were sitting. And there appeared to them tongues as of fire distributing themselves, and they rested on each one of them. And **they were all filled with the Holy Spirit and began to speak** with other tongues, **as the Spirit was giving them utterance** [emphasis added]"

(Acts 2:1-3).

"Jesus answered and said to him, 'Truly, truly, I say to you, **unless one is born again he cannot see the kingdom of God.**' Nicodemus said to Him, 'How can a man be born when he is old? He cannot enter a second time into his mother's womb and be born, can he?' Jesus answered, '**Truly, truly, I say to you, unless one is born of water and the Spirit he cannot enter into the kingdom of God.** That which is born of the flesh is flesh, and that which is born of the Spirit is spirit. Do not be amazed that I said to you, 'You must be born again.' **The wind blows where it wishes and you hear the sound of it, but do not know where it comes from and where it is going; so is everyone who is born of the Spirit** [emphasis added]'"

(John 3:3-8).

Roman Christians

I'm presently attending a semester long study of Romans with about fifty men from a different community of faith in an adjoining city. One morning after the study, Bruce, a new friend and recently retired CEO of a large inner-city, parachurch ministry sent me a text: "Hey one question, 'When the circumcision is by the spirit [Romans 2:28-29], is that the Holy Spirit? Because what do these people know about the Holy Spirit? Paul is writing this to Christians and Jews that are in Rome. Has the Holy Spirit been introduced to to these people? What does that mean to these people back in Rome? Just asking.'"

I texted back: "Yes, I would say the Holy Spirit. One might as easily ask, 'What do any of us know about the Holy Spirit?' Jesus told us the Spirit would come to help us, but 'The wind blows where it wills' (John 3:8). We only learn to sense Him, and be moved by Him. I think it was no different then. We have a lot to learn, and may be a few things to unlearn, about the Holy Spirit. Maybe starting with what Jesus told us about Him, then without our theological grid, praying and listening. After all, He too is God, and 'Who has known the mind of God?'" (Isaiah 40:13, Romans 11:34, 1Corinthians 2:16).

The question is a good and a telling question. It's good because we need to know the answer to understand God's grace, plan, and how things work in the Spirit. It's telling because it betrays the fact a large faction of the western church in our day teaches or implies an intellectual understanding of the faith is all important, and how we come into relationship with the Holy One.

This apparently isn't true and actually leads us into some spiritual blindness, pride, and along an unfruitful path toward Him Who calls us, gives us spiritual birth, and circumcises our hearts. This faulty paradigm is contrary to the Word, stunts our growth, and inhibits the carefree joy that could be ours, if we didn't contend that so much of spiritual life and growth depends on us — a deception. It appeals to us, because we like to take a little more credit than we should — pride.

In the natural, your brain and intellect has nothing or little to do with your conception or embryonic development. Rather your cells divide mysteriously and feverishly as they apparently are programed to do. Once you are a living being, upright, and walking — gazing at the yellow sun, blue skies, and green leaves of your awe-inspiring home, you start to put things together with your mind. You begin to ponder your purpose, the mystery of life, and enjoy your being. Life in the spirit is probably more like that. You hear Jesus say to Nicodemus: "Truly, truly, I say to you, unless one is born of water and the Spirit he cannot enter into the kingdom of God. That which is born of the flesh is flesh, and that which is born of the Spirit is spirit" (John 3:5-6).

"Both Testaments focus on the need for repentance and inward change in order to be right with God. In Jesus, the Law has been fulfilled (Matthew 5:17). Through Him, a person can be made right with God and receive eternal life (John 3:16; Ephesians 2:8-9). As Paul said, true circumcision is a matter of the heart, performed by the Spirit of God" (gotquestions.org).

About the Spirit, the elderly apostle John tells us: "I write these things to you **about those who are trying to deceive you**. But the anointing that you received from him [Holy Spirit] **abides in you, and you have no need that anyone should teach you**. But as his anointing teaches you about everything, and is true, and is no lie—just as it has taught you, **abide in him** [emphasis added]" (1 John 2:26-27 ESV).

PUZZLING CHAPTER 26

Signs Before Jesus Comes

Sign Posts

I just finished reading Rick Renner's book *Signs You'll See Just Before Jesus Comes*. Even in the title, you see insights and emphasis on what Jesus said when his disciples asked Him about the end times.

A summary of his observations follow:

1. All of the signs Jesus mentioned will be happening simultaneously.
2. Like "signposts" on modern highways and ancient highways, they alert us to how far we are from the destination or city center.
3. As in such signage, the markers often get more numerous and closer together approaching the destination.
4. Before the big event, you can say the same about birth pangs and labor. The closer the pangs of pregnancy, the closer the revealing new life and some new life events. Something that began in obscurity sometime ago is about to spring forth.

The plague and pandemic chapter was a good refresher on HIV/AIDS and pertinent to a theme of this book, the COVID-19 pandemic. The author points out the hidden time bomb HIV/AIDS is and how it spreads exponentially and has no known cure. Rick Renner wrote this book in 2018 before the 2020 COVID-19 outbreak.

By coincidence, my wife and I read Mark 13 in our daily Bible reading this morning — the last day's predictions of Jesus, which mirror the record of Matthew 24.

Jesus starts with a prophecy no one could see coming and coming soon. It began with his disciples pointing out the beautiful temple, and we pick it up there: "As He was going out of the temple, one of His disciples said to Him, 'Teacher, behold what wonderful stones and what wonderful buildings!' **And Jesus said to him, 'Do you see these great buildings? Not one stone will be left upon another which will not be torn down** [emphasis added]'" (Mark 13:1-2). From 33 AD to 70 AD was 37 short years, and then it happened according to His word.

Solomon's Temple, built about 1000 BC, was one of the wonders of the ancient world. Babylonian armies destroyed it in 586 BC, and a Jewish remnant rebuilt it about 500 BC as the Second Temple on the same foundation. Then it was completely refurbished and updated by Herod the Great, one of the world's greatest architects, just before the time of Christ (2 BC-33 AD).

No one standing there, knowing the longevity of the Jews, the 1000-year history of the Temple, and the stability of the mighty Roman empire, would have believed the Temple might be destroyed. The thought that these ancient, massive, beautifully-restored buildings would be destroyed, decimated, thrown down in their lifetime, or anytime soon, or ever, seemed incredible. But that is what Jesus said, and that's what happened.

I've traveled to Israel six times. My favorite thing to do when visiting Jerusalem is to approach the western wall of the Temple Mount, where people are praying night and day and look around. One can't help but be in awe of the size and symmetry of those stones, many laid by Solomon 3000 years ago. They form the foundation of the Temple Mount. It's the holiest place in Judaism. It's the closest Jews can get to where the ark of the covenant, and the very presence of God dwelling with man, last was located.

After taking it all in with those thoughts tumbling through my mind, I fix my gaze on the pile of large stones strewn in front of the Western Wall toward the south end. They are to me a significant, silent witness to the words of Jesus and the Word of God, which is forever settled in heaven, recorded for us as the Holy Bible. Those huge stones are a 2000-year-old witness to the faithfulness of God to do what He says and to work out His plan for humankind. According to His goodwill, He accomplishes this with justice, mercy, and patience.

God often announces significant events of His plan before they happen through His servants, the prophets. Prophecy is one element that sets Judaism and Christianity apart from all the world's religions — the volume and accuracy of these predictions or foretelling of the future. **"Surely the Lord GOD does nothing unless He reveals His secret counsel To His servants the prophets** [emphasis added]" (Amos 3:7).

The prophet Isaiah summarizes this fact as well as it can be said: **"Remember the former things long past, for I am God, and there is no other; I am God, and there is no one like Me, declaring the end from the beginning, and from ancient times things which have not been done, saying, 'My purpose will be established, and I will accomplish all My good pleasure** [emphasis added]'" (Isaiah 46:9-10).

I have read the biblical accounts of the Assyrian and Babylonian conquest of Israel, the destruction of the Temple, and the 70-year captivity many times. I just read again *The Jewish War* by Josephus, recounting all the gruesome details of the Roman destruction of the Temple and the razing of Jerusalem in 70 AD.

What Does This Mean to Me

What should today's Christians take away from these prophesied and historical facts? God is to be feared, His ways should be known, and His rule over humankind appreciated for what it is. Especially noteworthy is how He deals with his covenant people — Israel, and the church of Jesus Christ.

A well-known verse speaking to this subject is: "**For it is time for judgment to begin with the household of God**; and if it begins with us first, **what will be the outcome for those who do not obey the gospel of God?** [emphasis added]" (1 Peter 4:17). The verse and its truth are known to anyone who reads the Bible and knows something of history.

Another example is the book of Hebrews addressed to both groups, Jews who became Christians, in the first century? There are many salient truths in its thirteen chapters, but two verses come to mind in this context: "**How will we escape if we neglect so great a salvation?** [emphasis added]" (Hebrews 2:3a). And "…for **our God is a consuming fire** [emphasis added]" (Hebrews 12:29).

You might say, "Those are examples of God dealing with the Jews and Israel, not the church." You should read chapters two and three of *The Revelation of Jesus Christ*. It's the last book in the Bible. These chapters address **similar issues in the seven prominent gentile churches in Asia Minor**, modern-day Turkey, during the middle days of the Roman Empire.

A good summary of those letters is what Paul wrote to the church in Rome reminding them of how God deals with His own: "**Behold then the kindness and severity of God; to those who fell, severity, but to you, God's kindness, if you continue in His kindness**; otherwise you also will be cut off [emphasis added]" (Romans 11:22). And from the writer of Hebrews, we read: "**For those whom the Lord loves He

disciplines, And He scourges every son whom He receives [emphasis added]" (Hebrews 12:6).

Another Signpost

May 14, 1948. Israel became a nation again after being displaced from her native soil for almost 2000 years. After two millennia of wandering and being dispersed throughout the countries of the world suffering persecution, pogroms, and a holocaust in Europe, the Jewish people retained their language, culture, and religion. They became a nation again on that day. "**Who has ever heard of such things? Who has ever seen things like this? Can a country be born in a day or a nation be brought forth in a moment? Yet no sooner is Zion in labor than she gives birth to her children** [emphasis added]" (Isaiah 66:8).

There is nothing to parallel this in history. No other nation, culture, or people can make this claim or have this distinction in humankind's 4000 years of recorded history. Mark Twain, one of America's greatest minds, said it this way: "The Egyptian, the Babylonian, and the Persian rose, filled the planet with sound and splendor, then faded to dream-stuff and passed away; the Greek and the Roman followed; and made a vast noise, and they are gone; other people have sprung up and held their torch high for a time, but it burned out, and they sit in twilight now, or have vanished. The Jew saw them all, beat them all, and is now what he always was, exhibiting no decadence, no infirmities of age, no weakening of his parts, no slowing of his energies, no dulling of his alert and aggressive mind. All things are mortal but the Jew; all other forces pass, but he remains. What is the secret of his immortality?"

The obvious answer to his questioning mind in a word is "**God!**" The Jew's preservation is miraculous and powered by Someone outside the natural realm Who does what He pleases, establishing His purpose and accomplishing His good pleasure. The Same said: "then **I will** remember My covenant with Jacob, and I will remember also My covenant with Isaac, and My covenant with Abraham as well, and I will remember the land** [emphasis added]" (Leviticus 26:42).

Jesus is the Great Prophet spoken of by Moses: "**The LORD your God will raise up for you a Prophet like me from your midst, from your brethren. Him you shall hear** [emphasis added]" (Deuteronomy 18:15 NKJV). Besides predicting the destruction of the Temple thirty-seven years before it happened, He had something else to say about His return and the nation of His birth, Israel.

For another of Jesus' prophecies concerning the end times and His imminent return, let's look at Matthew's record of what Jesus told His disciples in the same Temple setting quoted above: "Now learn the parable from **the fig tree: when its branch has already become tender and puts forth its leaves**, you know that summer is near; so, you too, **when you see all these things, recognize that He is near**, **right at the door**. Truly I say to you, **this generation will not pass away until all these things take place** [emphasis added]" (Matthew 24:32-34).

Many times in Scripture, a fig tree represents the nation of Israel. So many believe Jesus was saying, "When you see Israel as a young or newly budding nation, My return is near. In fact the generation that sees that event will see My return, and the end of all these things." A good friend next door and I were talking about this prophecy of Jesus, and he said to me: "I was born in April 1948, and all my generation has not passed away!"

That's a lot to ponder and apply to the church and the nation of Israel in our day. Seek God. Watch and listen with spiritual eyes and ears. Godspeed as you journey to more intimacy with Him by His Spirit.

"**When it is My desire, I will chastise them**; and the peoples will be gathered against them when they are bound for their double guilt [emphasis added]"

(Hosea 10:10).

"**Sow with a view to righteousness, reap in accordance with kindness; break up your fallow ground, for it is time to seek the Lord** until He comes to rain righteousness on you [emphasis added]"

(Hosea 10:12).

"'**Then I will draw near to you for judgment; and I will be a swift witness against the sorcerers and against the adulterers and against those who swear falsely, and against those who oppress the wage earner in his wages, the widow and the orphan, and those who turn aside the alien and do not fear Me**,' says the Lord of hosts. '**For I, the Lord, do not change; therefore you, O sons of Jacob, are not consumed** [emphasis added]'"

(Malachi 3:5-6).

"Then those who feared the Lord spoke to one another, and the Lord gave attention and heard it, and **a book of remembrance was written before Him for those who fear the Lord and who esteem His name. 'They will be Mine,' says the Lord of hosts, on the day that I prepare My own possession, and I will spare them as a man spares his own son who serves him.' So you will again distinguish between the righteous and the wicked, between one who serves God and one who does not serve Him** [emphasis added]'"

(Malachi 3:15-18).

"Never be afraid to trust an unknown future to a known God"

(Corrie Ten Boom, Holocaust Survivor).

"Be on your guard and stay alert! For you do not know when the appointed time will come"

(Mark 13:33).

"And what I say to you, I say to everyone: Keep watch!"

(Mark 13:37).

PUZZLING CHAPTER 27

With Eyes Wide Open

Pagan Worship

Pagan Worship was what I intended to entitle this chapter or piece of the puzzle. I thought about the fact that a pagan king of Babylon, emperor of the entire known world in his time, and a pagan prophet a thousand years earlier, a contemporary of Moses, uttered some of the most worshipful truths about God, His creation, and His ways ever spoken by humans. I find this fascinating.

Nebuchadnezzar II

I'm speaking about Nebuchadnezzar, king of Babylon, and Balaam son of Beor, near the Euphrates River, a prophet, seer, and a contemporary of Moses. Moses was leading the covenant children of Israel, some two million strong, out of Egypt and through the wilderness where their paths crossed, though not directly, toward the land promised by God to Abraham and his descendants, Canaan.

Nebuchadnezzar was often afflicted with pride, and understandably so, because he was human and because "power tends to corrupt, and absolute power corrupts absolutely" (English historian Lord Acton). He did, however, have a very spiritual Jewish prime minister who also functioned to him as a prophet, priest, and personal advisor.

Several times this absolute monarch lapsed into blinding pride, and each time Daniel prayed for him, spoke the truth to him, and counseled him on how to stay in right standing with the Almighty and walk in wisdom, preserving his position and the kingdom.

At the end of some of these lapses, the monarch humbles himself after experiencing God's grace through Daniel's counsel and prayers. Then with eyes wide open or spiritual sight restored, he uttered things amazingly accurate and powerfully expressed:

"Nebuchadnezzar the king to all the peoples, nations, and men of every language that live in all the earth: 'May your peace abound! It has seemed good to me to declare the signs and wonders which the Most High God has done for me. How great are His signs and how mighty are His wonders! His kingdom is an everlasting kingdom and His dominion is from generation to generation'" (Daniel 4:1-3).

"But at the end of that period, I, Nebuchadnezzar, **raised my eyes toward heaven and my reason returned to me**, and I blessed the Most High and praised and **honored Him who lives forever**; for **His dominion is an everlasting dominion, and His kingdom endures from generation to generation. All the inhabitants of the earth are accounted as nothing, but He does according to His will in the host of heaven and among the inhabitants of earth**; and no one can ward off His hand or say to Him, 'What have You done?' At that time my reason returned to me. And my majesty and splendor were restored to me for the glory of my kingdom, and my counselors and my nobles began seeking me out; so I was reestablished in my sovereignty, and surpassing greatness was added to me. **Now I, Nebuchadnezzar, praise, exalt and honor the King of heaven, for all His works are**

true and His ways just, and He is able to humble those who walk in pride [emphasis added]" (Daniel 4:34-37).

Balaam Son of Beor

The story of Balaam recorded in Numbers 22 through 24 intrigues me even more, especially the oracles, proclamations, or prophecies that he receives from God and repeats to Balak king of Moab under very trying circumstances. The prophecies are impressive, to be sure, and I'll share a few of them. But almost as intriguing is how he begins the last of these oracles or insights from God, "He took up his discourse and said:

> "The utterance of Balaam the son of Beor, the utterance of the man whose eyes are opened, the utterance of him who hears the words of God, who sees the vision of the Almighty, who falls down, with eyes wide open"
> (Numbers 24:3-4 NKJV).

Balaam had knowledge of the Holy One. He even exhibited a strong fear of the Lord as the supreme spiritual superpower in every realm. In his declarations to King Balak, who hired him to curse Israel, you can see this: "Balaam replied to the servants of Balak, 'Though Balak were to give me his house full of silver and gold, I could not do anything, either small or great, contrary to the command of the Lord my God'" (Numbers 22:18).

Yet, at the same time, or after some time, he became deceived and deceiving.

It all ended very poorly for him. He was run through with a sword at the hands of Israel when Joshua's army came through the region (Joshua 13:22). But worse, I wonder what his life was like after that encounter with Israel and Israel's God? After that, I predict that he experienced darkness — no spiritual light, no relationship with the Holy due to his calculated decision and actions to misuse his prophecy gift and spiritual position. Balaam was motivated by the desire for wealth, which was demonstrated by his aiding Balak and plotting a sexual-sin trap among God's people.

Knowing what God said about His holy people, Balaam said the right things by the Spirit, using God's gift and repeating what he heard. But then, on the sly, he told Balak how he could trip up Israel and have some chance of prevailing against them.

Sexual sin — Balaam told King Balak to tempt them with some of the women of the land. If they sinned, Balaam knew the hand of their holy God would be against them for judgment and purification. God will judge sin and the people involved, removing the blemish or cancer to preserve and purify His holy people.

Israel's fidelity and morally healthy relationships with each other and with God were due to His great mercy and grace extended to them through the law, the covenants, and His very presence traveling in the midst of them abiding on the mercy seat of the Ark of the Covenant housed in the Tabernacle. This relationship was a treasure for God and Israel, His holy, covenant people.

What Balaam said to Balak is not recorded in the Old Testament account. But the Holy Spirit gives insight into Balaam's error — his actions and motives — toward the end of the New Testament. His motivation for going was money — financial gain for exercising his spiritual gift: "Forsaking the right way, they have gone astray, having followed the way of Balaam, the son of Beor, who loved the wages of unrighteousness" (2 Peter 2:15). And: "for pay they have rushed headlong into the error of Balaam" (Jude 1:11b).

When Balaam's error almost cost him his life and that of his donkey, he relented and went at God's command, instructed to say only what God told him to say. He did this making the king angry and causing him to receive no compensation: "Then Balak's anger burned against

Balaam, and he struck his hands together; and Balak said to Balaam, 'I called you to curse my enemies, but behold, you have persisted in blessing them these three times! Therefore, flee to your place now. I said I would honor you greatly, but behold, the Lord has held you back from honor'" (Numbers 24:10-11).

Then for reasons not stated, Balaam did help Balak, telling the King if he could entice the Israelites to sexual immorality with the women of the land, he might have a chance of prevailing against them. We read in the last book of the Bible a letter to a church giving this insight: "But I have a few things against you, because you have there some who hold the teaching of Balaam, who kept teaching Balak to put a stumbling block before the sons of Israel, to eat things sacrificed to idols and to commit acts of immorality" (Revelation 2:14).

Prophecy with Eyes Wide Open

This piece of the puzzle is as puzzling as puzzles can get. We can learn a lot from Balaam about spiritual life and hearing from God. We will address those insights as other pieces of the puzzle. Were it not for glimpses of Balaam by the Spirit at the end of the New Testament, the story would be most confusing and without resolution—an image unclear. But this piece of the puzzle you're reading will end with the prophet speaking the words of God — beautiful words, truthful words, words 3500 years old — as accurate now and relevant as they were then.

"Balaam said to Balak, 'Did I not tell your messengers whom you had sent to me, saying, Though Balak were to give me his house full of silver and gold, I could not do anything contrary to the command of the Lord, either good or bad, of my own accord. What the Lord speaks, that I will speak'? And now, behold, I am going to my people; come, and I will advise you what this people will do to your people in the days to come'" (Numbers 24:12-14).

The Oracle of Balaam

"**The Spirit of God came upon him.** He took up his discourse and said,

'The oracle of Balaam the son of Beor, and **the oracle of the man whose eye is opened; the oracle of him who hears the words of God, who sees the vision of the Almighty**, falling down, yet having his eyes uncovered, **how fair are your tents, O Jacob, your dwellings, O Israel!** Like valleys that stretch out, **like gardens beside the river**, like aloes **planted by the Lord**, like cedars beside the waters. Water will flow from his buckets, and **his seed will be by many waters, and his king shall be higher** than Agag, and **his kingdom shall be exalted. God brings him out of Egypt**, He is for him like the horns of the wild ox. **He will devour the nations who are his adversaries**, and will crush their bones in pieces, and shatter them with his arrows. He couches, he lies down as a lion, and **as a lion, who dares rouse him? Blessed is everyone who blesses you, and cursed is everyone who curses you** [emphasis added]'" (Numbers 24:2b-9).

"He took up his discourse and said, 'The oracle of Balaam the son of Beor, and **the oracle of the man whose eye is opened, the oracle of him who hears the words of God, and knows the knowledge of the Most High, who sees the vision of the Almighty**, falling down, yet having his eyes uncovered. **I see him, but not now; I behold him, but not near; a star shall come forth from Jacob, a scepter shall rise from Israel,** and shall crush through the forehead of Moab, and tear down all the sons of Sheth. Edom shall be a possession, Seir, its **enemies, also will be a possession, while Israel performs valiantly. One from Jacob shall have dominion**, and will destroy the remnant from the city [emphasis added]'" (Numbers 24:15-19).

"**Remember the former things long past, for I am God, and there is no other; I am God, and there is no one like Me, declaring the end from the beginning, and from ancient times things which have not been done, saying, 'My purpose will be established, and I will accomplish all My good pleasure** [emphasis added]'"

(Isaiah 46:9-10).

"**There is no wisdom and no understanding and no counsel against the Lord** [emphasis added]"

(Proverbs 21:30).

"'**Incline your ear and come to Me. Listen, that you may live**; and I will make an everlasting covenant with you, according to the faithful mercies shown to David. Behold, I have made him a witness to the peoples, a leader and commander for the peoples. Behold, you will call a nation you do not know, and a nation which knows you not will run to you, because of the Lord your God, even the Holy One of Israel; for He has glorified you. **Seek the Lord while He may be found; call upon Him while He is near. Let the wicked forsake his way and the unrighteous man his thoughts; and let him return to the Lord, and He will have compassion on him, and to our God, for He will abundantly pardon.** For My thoughts are not your thoughts, nor are your ways My ways,' **declares the Lord. 'For as the heavens are higher than the earth, so are My ways higher than your ways and My thoughts than your thoughts** [emphasis added]'"

(Isaiah 55:3-9).

"**So will My word be which goes forth from My mouth; it will not return to Me empty, without accomplishing what I desire, and without succeeding in the matter for which I sent it** [emphasis added]"

(Isaiah 55:11).

PUZZLING CHAPTER 28

Did God Say?

Did God Say?

I awakened recently with some simple thoughts. As I made coffee and moved to the chair in front of the fire, I prayed the Spirit would bring back to me those thoughts as I journaled.

Who has the final say in your life and the life of nations? Whose word counts? Who knew the reality of this truth better than Daniel, whose very name means "God is my judge."

In Daniel's case, the king of Babylon, even if he was the reigning monarch of the world's superpower, was not Daniel's judge. He was his master in the earthly realm by God's decree, as Daniel was carried as a slave into Babylon and reeducated to serve the king. Nebuchadnezzar possessed splendor, riches, and power unknown today, becoming the essence of fables and the dreams of rulers since ancient times.

While driving to an appointment I heard on the radio: "If you fear God, you fear nothing else. If you don't fear God, you fear everything else." This truth played out in Daniel's life, the lives of his three best friends, and many others in the Bible throughout history.

A Daniel-type person can function and live in any realm. Indeed he was called, gifted, and lived on his path by the Lord's decree, just as we are led on our paths today. Some of my favorite verses from Acts come to mind. The Spirit gave them to Paul as he spoke to the intelligentsia of his day on Mars Hill in Athens: "He [God] marked out their [our] appointed times in history and [where we would live] the boundaries of their [our] lands… He [God] is not far from any one of us. For in him we live and move and have our being" (Acts 17:26,27b-28a).

Daniel knew all of this or figured it out as he went. He saw into the spiritual realm and lived a life apart (holy) to God. He was in the world, but not of the world. We get that last phrase and thought from Jesus' prayer to God before His sacrifice. Listen as God prays to God: "**They are not of the world, even as I am not of the world. Sanctify them in the truth**; Your word is truth. As You sent Me into the world, **I also have sent them into the world** [emphasis added]" (John 17:17-18).

Daniel did not have Acts 17 because it was given to Paul by the Spirit 600 years later and published for our benefit — the benefit of the church, the *ecclesia*, the "called out ones," for their spiritual insight and encouragement during their 2000-year walk toward Christ the King's second appearance. But it describes Daniel's walk, mission, and life perfectly, as it does all of the heroes in the Biblical record.

Daniel did have in his time the 400-year-old Psalms of David. God-fearing Jews and Christians since David have regarded David as the best, highest, most holy king of Israel, except for the One he prophesied would come. Daniel prophesied about this King too in great detail.

The Psalms of David, and a few anointed contemporaries in his court like Asaph, are beautiful, life-sustaining, and life-giving to those who have spiritual insight — eyes to see revelation by the Spirit of God.

That Hebrew poetry, like the 3000-years-old Psalms, could be translated into English and the languages of the earth, retaining their life-giving, life-sustaining, spiritually-enlightening messages about life on our planet, and life with God, is beyond words and comprehension. They even maintain their poetic quality in vastly different languages. I did mention they are 3000 years old! And they are readily available to humans all over the globe at this moment. This reality takes my mind away to places I want to go, but know I probably cannot without spiritual revelation and insight.

I read a Psalm almost every day of my life and aloud with my wife for the past few years. We also read a chapter in Proverbs for our minds — wisdom, and instruction in matters of life and conduct. And we read a chapter from the New Testament, most often from the Gospels. Lately, we've re-discovered the Apostle's writings are very rich too, and add them into the mix.

I'm trying to bring this back to Psalms, especially chapters 1 and 2. But before I do, I want to say two things I'm unable to get off my mind. One is the beauty of the Psalms and the Word of God in general. Two, prophecy: God speaks to humans about the future, truth, relationship, Himself, and His coming King, the Christ.

I often sit in solitude and silence and read large portions of the Psalms, or smaller portions, two or three chapters. It's like breathing in deep breaths of fresh air and looking out over a beautiful landscape. It makes one feel alive, cared for, a part of God's vast plan, aware of his goodness and eternity. It's life-enriching, life-sustaining, life-enabling. It's joy unspeakable and full of glory (I Peter 1:8), as the Spirit opens your eyes and takes you there. He wants to do so, and He will. Make time and start reading. Beautiful insight will come to you if it hasn't already — Godspeed on that journey.

Early yesterday morning, I sat in a men's group, part of a nine-month study of *The Revelation of Jesus Christ*, known simply as The Revelation. We read: "For the testimony of Jesus is the spirit of prophecy" (Revelation 19:10b). I love this inspired statement! I love prophecy, which is broad and bizarre – childlike and simple. I am fascinated by prophets, their lives and times, but mainly what they say. Because prophecy's most simple, all-encompassing definition might be: "God speaking through men and women to men and women." People hear from God as a thought, picture, or vision, or in a dream and report under His leading what they saw or heard.

Oddly, or maybe not so much, there are also accounts of false prophets. These people didn't hear from God but another source and thought it was from God. Then they share the thought, vision, or dream and act following what they saw or heard as if it were true.

Of course, you can see this figures into deception and delusion, which are significant pieces to the puzzle you are assembling. You will find the other pieces in due time if you haven't already. But for this piece, simply said, all prophecy from God points to Jesus His Son, the soon coming King, and the absolute truth. You may recall Jesus said truthfully about himself, "I am the way, and the truth, and the life; no one comes to the Father but through Me" (John 14:6). So: "The testimony of Jesus is the spirit of prophecy" (Revelation 19:10b).

In his letter to us, God can be poetic, mysterious, and at times, ambiguous. This ambiguity is on purpose, of course. It's not that He lacks power or the ability to communicate clearly. He apparently doesn't want to blow anyone away or overly influence them toward faith, the key to the kingdom, if they are unwilling or would rather go their own way. Their own way ends up being the way of Balaam and Babylon, driven or enticed by deceiving dark spirits of wealth and immorality to their destruction.

Only God is wise, powerful, and all-knowing enough to preside over such a system and do it justly, sprinkled with grace and mercy. This designed, planned, purposeful ambiguity is another piece of the puzzle you will find on the table if you haven't already. It's puzzling, I know.

That said, God can be very direct and straightforward too! I see him being so in times of great sin and error, spiritual darkness, and apostasy. These were the times, and this was the situation in Israel (the ten northern tribes) before Assyria carried them away into captivity in 722 BC, distributing those not destroyed into captivity among the nations. The same was the case in Judah (the two southern tribes) before 586 BC when Babylon captured and carried them into captivity. After seventy years, a holy, refined remnant returned to Israel to carry on with the purposes of God.

In these sinful times, God sent some of the best, most courageous, most spiritually-sensitive prophets to tell his covenant people the truth about themselves, Himself, and what He was about to do. Prophets like Elijah, Elisha, Isaiah, Jeremiah, Ezekiel, Daniel, and the twelve we call the minor prophets due to the brevity of their books or messages from God. Their messages were brief but to the point, with God doing exactly what He said He would do in the messages they delivered to the people.

This was Grace. This was mercy. This time in their land and lives was about to become a refiners fire. Judgment from God's hand would come in the form of foreign armies and peoples. Read the short prophecy of Habakkuk. The land, culture, and people would be purified by fire and sword — it would be cleansed. The people were told the truth and given time to change their minds or continue in their wayward ways. Those who listened became holy to the Lord. When the fire came, they became purified further and more holy to Him and their peers. Those who would not change, not believe God or His prophets, having lost the ability or desire to hear, were consumed by the fire, slain by the sword, or lived out their lives in slavery to dark forces and cruel people. God cut them out like malignancy or cancer threatening the people as a whole.

As stated before, only God can orchestrate and preside over a mass judgment like this. He does it after long patience and plenty of warning, but then it comes swiftly like a surgeon's knife for preserving healthy life and for healing life that is headed in the right direction — away from the ways of death.

Psalms and Revelation seem connected to me, as they haven't been before. In both places, we're told: "The judgments of the Lord are true; they are righteous altogether" (Psalm 19:9b). And: "His judgments are true and righteous; for He has judged the great harlot who was corrupting the earth with her immorality" (Revelation 19:2a).

The God of Israel, God of the church, God of creation can be this precise and righteous when He judges or purifies a person, church, or nation because He can look at the very hearts of men and women — not only their actions. As God told one of his most famous prophets, Samuel, sending him to find and anoint a good leader and king for Israel: "For **God sees not as man sees, for man looks at the outward appearance, but the Lord looks at the heart** [emphasis added]" (I Samuel 17:6b). Paul the Apostle would add a millennium later by the Spirit: "He raised up David to be their king, concerning whom He also testified and said, 'I have found David the son of Jesse, a man after My heart, who will do all My will" (Acts 13:22). This confirms where and what God can see and how deeply He can know us. Plus, it adds a little more spiritual truth and insight if you have eyes to see — an obedient heart is God-like.

The Point

The point of it all, in simplicity and laid bare is this: "Who has the right to rule and reign?"

This question seems to be the issue in all 66 books of the Bible. It's stated in different ways and dated on different days, yet it is the constant theme. It stretches from: "Did God say?" in Genesis (Genesis 3:1b) to the wedding supper of the Lamb, where "the Spirit and the Bride say come" in Revelation (Revelation 22:17). It stretches from Genesis: "He [Christ] will crush your head, while you only bruise his heel" (Genesis 3:15) to Revelation: "And I saw heaven opened, and behold, a white horse, and He who sat on it is called Faithful and True, and in righteousness He judges and wages war" (Revelation 19:11).

For Nations and Rulers

Perhaps God communicates his truth about who has the right to reign most clearly and succinctly in Psalm Two.

> *"**Why are the nations in an uproar and the peoples devising a vain thing?** The **kings of the earth take their stand and the rulers take counsel together against the Lord and against His Anointed**, saying, 'Let us tear their fetters apart and cast away their cords from us!' **He who sits in the heavens laughs, the Lord scoffs at them. Then He will speak to them in His anger and terrify them in His fury, saying, 'But as for Me, I have installed My King upon Zion, My holy mountain.'** I will surely tell of the decree of the Lord: He said to Me, '**You are My Son, today I have begotten You. Ask of Me, and I will surely give the nations as Your inheritance, and the very ends of the earth as Your possession.** You shall break them with a rod of iron, You shall shatter them like earthenware.' Now therefore, O kings, **show discernment; take warning, O judges of the earth. Worship the Lord with reverence and rejoice with trembling. Do homage to the Son,** that He not become angry, and you perish in the way, for His wrath may soon be kindled. **How blessed are all who take refuge in Him!** [emphasis added]"*
>
> (Psalm 2).

Psalm 2 addresses the people God allows to exercise authority on the earth, kings and rulers. But it speaks powerfully to individuals, too, those of us who suffer if our rulers do not act wisely before God. It's weighty and most significant as addressed and written, but takes on even more meaning and proper perspective when we learn from the prophet Isaiah: "Behold, the nations are like a drop from a bucket, and are regarded as a speck of dust on the scales"

(Isaiah 40:15a).

For Individuals

Psalm 2 addresses the main point and most succinct answer to nations answering the question: "Who has the right to rule and reign?" Psalm 1 may be the most elegant, poetic, succinct address to us as individuals:

> "*How **blessed is the man who does not walk in the counsel of the wicked, nor stand in the path of sinners, nor sit in the seat of scoffers!** But his delight is in the law of the Lord, and in His law he meditates day and night. **He will be like a tree firmly planted by streams of water, which yields its fruit in its season and its leaf does not wither; and in whatever he does, he prospers**. The wicked are not so, but they are like chaff which the wind drives away. Therefore the wicked will not stand in the judgment, nor sinners in the assembly of the righteous. For **the Lord knows the way of the righteous, but the way of the wicked will perish** [emphasis added]*"

(Psalm 1).

It's not harsh or coercive in any way. It's a matter of fact, beautiful and trustworthy. It's almost like a summary of Proverbs, in one short Psalm. Life and death are laid out before you in honesty and spoken with a loving Father's kindness, gentleness, and firmness, who honors you with free will to choose. Whichever path you choose, He will honor your decision. After you decide, He will honor His promise to see it happens as He says.

Choose wisely and enjoy a fruitful, well-watered life. Here's a little secret. As you meditate on His Word, you become more and more like Him and a good choice as a friend or bride for His Son, the King. Go in peace. Walk in wisdom, obeying His Word. *Shalom*, God's peace to you as your journey.

"The fear of the Lord is the beginning of wisdom, and the knowledge of the Holy One is understanding. For by me your days will be multiplied, and years of life will be added to you. If you are wise, you are wise for yourself, and if you scoff, you alone will bear it"

(Proverbs 9:10-12).

"The conclusion, when all has been heard, is: fear God and keep His commandments, because this applies to every person. For God will bring every act to judgment, everything which is hidden, whether it is good or evil"

(Ecclesiastes 12:13-14).

PUZZLING CHAPTER 29

Hearing God

Hearing God

The incredible thing about Balaam's life is that he could hear God's voice.

This was widely known about him, making him unique and famous. That would point to Balaam's relationship with God, that they knew something of each other and valued each other.

Hearing God and knowing God are connected. It seems God made it that way. I can't think of a single instance in the Bible where God spoke through a person He didn't know and who didn't know Him. That's important to your story and an essential piece to this puzzle.

I can think of a time God spoke through an animal, and we'll get to that soon. God's ways are many. The scope of his power and creativity is boundless.

The Bible tells us that God's ways are hidden and past finding out. The Bible also tells us we can know Him through Jesus and whom the Spirit chooses to reveal Him.

It's a mystery, and a bit of a puzzle, designed that way on purpose to separate the sheep from the goats—those who would see costly grace and shun cheap grace.

Prophets

What do you know about prophets? Most in the lukewarm, biblically-illiterate, 21st-century church in the west know very little.

Fairly simply stated a prophet is someone who hears from God and tells what they hear or see in a vision or a dream. They communicate something for God, from God to others.

For the most part, these are ordinary people with a call from God and gifting to hear him in the spiritual realm. They all have a fear of the Lord and a relationship with him.

These are traits evidenced in the life of Balaam. I respect the man. We can learn a lot from what he did right and wrong, and maybe by comparing him with Moses, his contemporary prophet.

To learn would be the wise and humble approach, not to throw stones. Who among us is without sin or knows what you would have done in this setting, in this ancient culture and time?

We benefit from the Scriptures spanning millennia and from many prophets and their stories to search for answers and truth. The Scriptures say about themselves: "All Scripture is inspired by God and profitable for teaching, for reproof, for correction, for training in righteousness; so that the man of God may be adequate, equipped for every good work" (2 Timothy 3:16-17). If you doubt this applies to our times, read the first five verses of this chapter.

Why Is This Important?

Why is this important, you might ask. Do people still hear from God today? Of course, they do. I have a neighbor next door, Ron, who is as spiritually sensitive as anyone I know and constantly hears from the Lord. Following what he hears, he can be found praying for the sick in the neighborhood (with good results, I might add), taking food to someone in need, mentoring three young men in his home weekly, or making someone's house payment on a spiritual leading. I haven't scratched the surface of his hearing, followed by obedience. These are a fraction of things I know to be true about him in recent weeks.

To further illustrate this point, sometimes he's heard weird sounding things but was obedient to say what he heard and see what would happen next or what the Spirit might do. We have a common neighbor, a successful businessman, and a cradle Catholic. This man has significant trouble sleeping and some significant back pain at times. Ron prayed for him with his concurrence and at his request as they got to know each other. The man experienced substantial help. One day Ron heard in the Spirit the verse about the woman with a demonized daughter who asked Jesus for help. The Canaanite woman beseeched Jesus on behalf of her demon-possessed daughter, and the Lord replied to her: "It is not good to take the children's bread and throw it to the dogs" (Matthew 15:26). Well, that could have been offensive when Jesus said it, and it could be offensive now! But on a spiritual leading, Ron just quoted the verse to his neighbor, then asked him, "Do you think you're one of God's children?" The man answered, "I don't think so. Will you pray with me?" So Ron led him in a prayer accepting the Lord's grace by the Spirit and has been meeting with him weekly ever since, disciplining him in the Bible and the ways of God.

So in one way, you may not know anyone like Balaam, Moses, Elijah, Daniel, or Malachi. They may be out there in places like Africa, China, or Argentina. Or, in our times and culture, the way God speaks to and through people might be a little different? But He still talks to people intimately by His Spirit — Spirit to spirit. God is the same yesterday, today, and forever. He still invites people into His kingdom and His family, meeting their needs and getting to know them better as they journey together.

Learn To Hear

Maybe this will change your perspective or paradigm. Perhaps you haven't been taught you can hear the Lord speak. You can. I think it wise to learn from those who do or have. I love the prophets and what they teach us about hearing from God. Start to study them in the Bible. Find someone like Ron, and ask them to pray for you and lead you in this pursuit. It will result in the most incredible adventure of your life and the most satisfying one.

The lives you will touch, the things you will see, and the stories you will tell will be unique, rewarding, and fulfilling. But the greatest blessing is the One you get to know along the way. As God told Abraham, known as the Father of the Faith: "Do not be afraid, Abram. I am your shield, your exceedingly great reward" (Genesis 15:1).

Moses and Balaam

One of the strengths God gifted me at birth and built into me is attention to detail. I am a noticer. I think of the little book *The Noticer* by Andy Andrews, which I heartily recommend. One of the weaknesses associated with this gift is that I feel I must describe or communicate everything I see or notice to people at times.

Thankfully, I heard two things from the Spirit as I was beginning this book that are helpful for you and me: (1) Don't try to lawyer or explain everything to death. People will either get it or they won't. Be short. (2) Have fun with it.

In short, these are a few of the things one can learn about hearing God from the life of Moses and Balaam:

(1) Moses—was more spiritual than worldly. Balaam ended up being more worldly than spiritual. Who had God's interest at heart?

(2) Moses — If you don't go with us, I don't want to go. I don't want it to be said that You couldn't deliver Your people.
Balaam — Can I go and use the gift You've given me for worldly blessing? Who was most interested in God's people?

(3) Moses — seemingly loved God's people like God loved them and risked his life for them. One could even say he laid down his life or sacrificed it for them. To be fair, they were his people, but God gave him opportunities to make Moses great and destroy the Israelites.
Balaam — consorted with Balak on how to lay a trap and perhaps cause God to destroy Israel, even after knowing God favored these people and intended to bless them.

Upon hearing God well and once, they both knew or should have known that God is not a man that He should change His mind. Balaam asked God again the same question, "Can I go with them?" after God had spoken on the issue. Did Balaam know God as well as he thought?

I will leave that to you. Balaam did say to every emissary and king Balak himself, "I must say what God says and nothing else." But what he did later in secret showed his heart and allegiance. Balaam counseled king Balak to entice the people of Israel into sexual sin with the women of Moab so God Himself would rise against them to punish evil and remove its cancerous effects. And to judge His people according to His word and their covenant.

On the contrary, we see a time in Moses' experience with the Israelites when God was going to judge them for their rebellion, sin, and apostasy. God told Moses as much: "The Lord said to Moses, 'I have seen this people, and behold, they are an obstinate people. Now then let Me alone, that My anger may burn against them and that I may destroy them; and I will make of you a great nation'" (Exodus 32:9-10).

But Moses interceded for the people, praying for God to have mercy and extend forgiveness and grace, which God agreed to do at Moses' request, and in keeping with His nature: "Then Moses entreated the Lord his God, and said, 'O Lord, why does Your anger burn against Your people whom You have brought out from the land of Egypt with great power and with a mighty hand? Why should the Egyptians speak, saying, 'With evil intent He brought them out to kill them in the mountains and to destroy them from the face of the earth'? Turn from Your burning anger and change Your mind about doing harm to Your people. Remember Abraham, Isaac, and Israel, Your servants to whom You swore by Yourself, and said to them, 'I will multiply your descendants as the stars of the heavens, and all this land of which I have spoken I will give to your descendants, and they shall inherit it forever.' So the Lord changed His mind about the harm which He said He would do to His people'" (Exodus 32:11-14).

God's People Are Close To God's Heart

So, who knew God better? Who had God's heart about His people? Who was God's friend? Who was the most humble man on the earth? It seems a conundrum, but the Spirit of God told Moses to write this: "Now the man Moses was very humble, more than any man who was on the face of the earth" (Exodus 12:3). What can we learn from the man God chooses? And from the man God uses? Much! Humility may be at the top of that list. It may be the thing about God's character that He likes most about Himself. Read Philippians chapter 2, written about His Son.

The most important thing about the prophet or human that God chooses is character. I think the Bible will bear that out.

But aside from that personal, intimate relationship that the prophet has with God, the most important thing to God and the prophet, are the words of God delivered to humankind. What did God say? What is God saying or thinking about a situation? About the future? About his decisions to bless or curse people? These are incredibly valuable things to know, are they not?

People want to know! Most especially if they know by faith, history, and the Bible that God has a plan and rules on earth as He pleases. We hear this from the prophet David: "The kings of the earth take their stand and the rulers take counsel together against the LORD and against His Anointed, saying, 'Let us tear their fetters apart and cast away their cords from us!' He who sits in the heavens laughs, the Lord scoffs at them'" (Psalm 2:2-4). We hear it from the prophet Isaiah: "Remember the former things long past, for I am God, and there is no other; I am God, and there is no one like Me, declaring the end from the beginning, and from ancient times things which have not been done, saying, 'My purpose will be established, and I will accomplish all My good pleasure'" (Isaiah 46:9-10). We hear it from the prophet Daniel and see it worked out in his life and hundreds of other instances in the Bible and history: "And no one can ward off His hand or say to Him, 'What have You done?'" (Daniel 4:35b).

Balaam's Oracles

So what did God say? It was valuable information for Balak in the short term! And it would prove to be valuable information through the ages, for the long term. A good part of it has proved true, some of it is still coming true, and it will be shown true in the end.

The short oracles concerning Israel are as beautiful and poetic as eternal and true. Listen with me to the words of the Lord, spoken by Balaam, son of Beor, from the banks of the Euphrates river in ancient Mesopotamia — the birthplace of humankind, the cradle of civilization, what would become Babylon the great. This area also is the birthplace of Abram, called out of there by God five hundred years earlier to dwell apart in the land of Canaan, receiving it as a gift from the Lord.

Then five hundred years later, just as God promised Abraham: "Know for certain that your descendants will be strangers in a land that is not theirs, where they will be enslaved and oppressed for four hundred years. But I will also judge the nation whom they will serve, and afterward they will come out with many possessions" (Genesis 15:13-14). Abraham's descendants were approaching the gifted land to take possession of it according to the word of the Lord, and in the power of the Lord.

Five hundred years is a long time. We have no idea what Balaam knew of all this. Or, for that fact, what Moses knew about this. But they were prophets, acquainted with God and his ways. And they could hear his voice. They lived in a particular time with Him who knows no time, except the times He marks out for us, like today.

Let's look at what He said. Oracle one goes like this:

"From Aram Balak has brought me, Moab's king from the mountains of the East, 'Come curse Jacob for me, and come, denounce Israel!' **How shall I curse whom God has not cursed?** And how can I denounce whom the Lord has not denounced? As I see him from the top of the rocks, and I look at him from the hills; **behold, a people who dwells apart, and will not be reckoned among the nations. Who can count the dust of Jacob, or number the fourth part of Israel? Let me die the death of the upright, and let my end be like his** [emphasis added]!" (Numbers 23: 7-10).

Oracle two goes like this:

"Arise, O **Balak**, and hear; **give ear** to me, O son of Zippor! '**God is not a man, that He should lie, nor a son of man, that He should repent; has He said, and will He not do it?** Or has He spoken, and will He not make it good?'

Behold, **I have received a command to bless; when He has blessed, then I cannot revoke it.** He has not observed misfortune in Jacob; nor has He seen trouble in Israel; **the Lord his God is with him, and the shout of a king is among them. God brings them out of Egypt**, He is for them like the horns of the wild ox. For **there is no omen against Jacob, nor is there any divination against Israel**; at the proper time **it shall be said to Jacob and to Israel, what God has done!** Behold, a people rises like a lioness, and as a lion it lifts itself; it will not lie down until it devours the prey, and drinks the blood of the slain [emphasis added]"

(Numbers 23: 18-24).

"The oracle of Balaam the son of Beor, and the oracle of the man whose eye is opened; the oracle of him who hears the words of God, who sees the vision of the Almighty...."

(Numbers 24:3-4).

"Falling down, yet having his eyes wide open"

(Numbers 24:4b).

The story of Balaam speaks volumes to our day and every era of human experience and history, for those "whose eye is opened, hears the word of God, and sees the vision of the Almighty." Let's ask the Lord in prayer for that ability and learn from the stories of those who do.

PUZZLING CHAPTER 30

An Ass

A Donkey Saves the Day

As you can tell, I became rather engrossed in the story of Balaam the prophet and how his life and times speak to our life and times. Like visions and dreams or thoughts that didn't originate with me, the Spirit sometimes speaks to me in "synchronicities." These are coincidences or instances of related things happening that couldn't or shouldn't happen, statistically speaking. It's like God saying to me, "You should pay attention to this, or I want to point this out to you." Synchronicities also carry the humorous connotation: "So you thought that was hard for Me?" The chances of them happening are remote, if not nil.

I will give you a recent and pertinent example. Two weeks ago, on a Thursday morning, I walked out of an early morning Bible study where about thirty guys discuss the Book of Revelation. I had spent the previous two days reading and rereading the story of Balaam and meditating on it for pertinent truth about our times, but that was unknown to the two friends walking with me to our cars. Out of the blue, one of the friends began to speak, "I had a teacher in graduate school who had a Ph.D. in physics, then became a Christian after looking into the case for intelligent design. He went back to school and got a Ph.D. in theology. His favorite Bible story was Balaam."

See what I mean? Out of all the things he could have said, in those sixty seconds and all the Bible stories that might have come up, what are the chances he would mention to me the relatively obscure name Balaam? Of course, it immediately spoke to me something like, "You're on to something. Keep looking and journaling — there is some insight for you here."

My friend went on to say that his teacher's favorite thing to point out from the story of Balaam was: "Others are so focused on their personal mission that they can't hear God. And even a jackass can hear from God." His inference was that a prophet or spiritual human should easily be able to do so. Balaam's spiritual vision had already started to dim. We will pick up his story again in a moment.

The next thing my friend said before we got into our cars was just as incredible or credible, for different, puzzling reasons. I have no idea why he said it. Maybe the same physics teacher said it: "He [God] makes the sun come up in east, and set in the west every day and every night for millennia. The earth rotates 1,000 miles per hour in one direction orbits 10,000 miles per hour around the sun in the opposite direction and every 365 1/4 days comes back to the exact same spot, every year. And we can't balance the tires on our car. Maybe we should listen to a being that can balance the universe and handle the details!"

Let's get back to Balaam and our story. The following week after church, we had lunch with some friends. While our three wives were busy talking at the other end of the table, I asked the guys what they knew about Balaam. One friend is reading through the Bible in a year and recently read how Balaam died. The other friend mentioned the donkey. That's what people usually remember if they remember anything at all about Balaam. So let's look at the donkey part of the happening.

There are many takeaways from this part of the story, though I haven't focused on it too much. Some of them are exploding in my spirit that I hadn't even thought about or noticed before. The donkey might be the essential part of the story, after all. From here, it all goes downhill or starts to hang in the balance. You feel that Balaam is too casual about his close relationship with God. Not to honor God enough, fear God enough, or know God well enough after having the type of relationship indicated is the beginning of the end. Balaam thought it trivial to ask the God of the universe to change His mind after He had graced him with speaking to him once. Don't take grace for granted or God for granted, especially if you have a somewhat intimate relationship, or have had at any time.

Balaam did, and you can see God's mercy mixed with judgment starting to work itself out. We can see that God holds prophets and people who know him well to a higher standard. You can see what happens next, and you can reference what happened to Moses when God instructed him to speak to the rock in the desert to bring forth water. In his anger at the people, he struck the rock instead. His punishment from God would be that he would see the promised land from Mount Nebo but not be allowed to enter with the people. This judgment might seem harsh to us but look at Moses' position and all the miracles God empowered him to do — all the honor shown him. It should be our great honor to honor God with our obedience to His word and heart as best we can.

God decided to end Balaam's life for disobedience and for opposing his purposes if something didn't change in the prophet's heart. For Balaam, the morning started well. He had permission to go, and off he went with: "...other officials, more numerous and more distinguished than the first [time]" (Numbers 22:15). He had two of his servants with him too. The donkey was the first to notice things were not as they seemed. Apparently it was the only member of the entourage that could see the angel of the Lord standing in front of them with a drawn sword. To avoid the angel, the donkey turned off the path and was beaten for his transgression by Balaam. The second time to keep from getting too close, the donkey pinned Balaam's leg against a stone wall by the path, resulting in another beating. The donkey had nowhere to turn the third time and just lay down with Balaam on its back, incurring a third beating. The anger, more like rage, that Balaam was exhibiting due to his damaged pride was becoming evident to everyone, and lastly to himself, as is often the case. That's when the prophet's vision started to clear, but not immediately.

A Donkey Speaks

I'm as mystified by the miracle that happened next as anyone else. It raises the question, was God doing it this way for a reason or to be creative? He intended to get His point across to the prophet so he could clearly understand the situation and the gravity of the situation. The donkey spoke: "Then the Lord opened the donkey's mouth, and it said to Balaam, 'What have I done to you to make you beat me these three times?'" Oddly, a conversation ensued between a prophet and a donkey. The prophet didn't seem aware due to his blinding pride and rage, that he was conversing with a donkey.

Balaam: "Balaam answered the donkey, 'You have made a fool of me! If only I had a sword in my hand, I would kill you right now.'" [Isn't that interesting? Considering there was a sword close by, in someone else's hand.]

Donkey: "The donkey said to Balaam, 'Am I not your own donkey, which you have always ridden, to this day? Have I been in the habit of doing this to you?'"

Balaam: "No" (Numbers 22:29-30).

His rage subsided, and reason and vision returned as he realized this wasn't normal. It's not clear when in this debacle he saw the angel. One thing striking about the donkey is how calm and rational it is. After all, it was trying to save its master's life and was the one who endured the wrongful beatings, beatings from one who should have known better than to be there and should have seen the angel himself.

There are a lot of ironies here. The seer cannot see—his donkey can. The one who should be beaten for disobedience is beating a faithful servant trying to save his life. I'm not sure Balaam gets all this and how it relates to the gracious God he calls "the LORD my God" early in the story (Numbers 22:18) and simply "the LORD" after that (Numbers 24:13). Balaam has started to believe his plans for Balaam are better than God's plans and let his heart drift away toward the world. But he has an immediate concern and epiphany — a rather dangerous one.

The Angel of the LORD Speaks

We've seen a remarkable miracle already and a lot of centering wisdom shared by an ass. That's nothing compared to what happens next: "Then the Lord opened Balaam's eyes, and he saw the angel of the Lord standing in the road with his sword drawn. So he bowed low and fell facedown" (Numbers 22:31). He is experiencing Grace and Mercy, an epiphany indeed for one in need.

If there is any question about what's on God's mind and His position with the whole situation, it's answered clearly here: "The angel of the Lord asked him, 'Why have you beaten your donkey these three times? I have come here to oppose you because your path is a reckless one before me. The donkey saw me and turned away from me these three times. If it had not turned away, I would certainly have killed you by now, but I would have spared it'" (Numbers 22:32-33).

The first words out of the angel's mouth are unexpected, insightful, and telling. It seems the Lord is concerned about the donkey (His last words indicate this care, too) and the unjust treatment by the prophet. And then the more profound meaning comes to light. Why were you beating it? Did you think it was being disobedient? Was it not going the way you wanted it to go? Did that make you angry? I'm much higher above you, than you are above your donkey. So now, you see the situation and how it feels to be so dishonored by a servant.

His following statement seemed to indicate to Balaam: "I don't know if I can trust your ability to hear and obey me. Do you?" It's as if the Lord told him: "I've invested you with a lot of authority and spiritual power, and I see your path as a reckless one. Do you see it?"

The killing part was clear enough, and it seems obvious Balaam got the message, and a fear of the Lord returned. He faithfully carried out his prophet duties to speak only the word of the Lord after that. But in his heart, he was in a slow fade due to injured pride, pride in general, the love of money, and the love of the world. It all culminated in him opposing God's people and God himself. This fade happened after God showed him plenty of mercy and gave him time to change. Sound familiar?

French writer Jean-Baptiste Alphonse Karr said: "The more things change, the more they stay the same."

Solomon said: "That which has been is that which will be, and that which has been done is that which will be done. So there is nothing new under the sun" (Ecclesiastes 1:9).

Winston Churchill said: "The farther back you can look, the farther forward you are likely to see."

So it is with the 3500-year-old story of Balaam. It's the story of God's manifold goodness and people who end up loving the world more. He made a beautiful world. And He gave us beautiful, sometimes challenging, choices. It's about the heart, and it's about trust. It's about love.

A Quaker Writes

One of my favorite books is *The Celebration of Discipline* by Richard Foster. It's about the path to spiritual life and falling in love with God, and living that love in truth through everyday decisions and habits. It's beautifully written and has become a Christian classic in Foster's lifetime.

He authored another book that I find shockingly peculiar given the nature of his famous book. Its title is *Money, Sex, and Power*. I've not read it, but I think I must, as time allows and the Spirit leads. These two books seem to be polar opposites and the antithesis of each other in subject and scope. Maybe that's why he wrote the second to warn about its warring against the first. And warring against the Greatest Commandment as quoted by Jesus: "Love the Lord your God with all your heart and with all your soul and with all your mind" (Matthew 22:37).

The Apostle John

The elder disciple addressed the issue in his Epistle: "Do not love the world or anything in the world. **If anyone loves the world, love for the Father is not in them. For everything in the world—the lust of the flesh, the lust of the eyes, and the pride of life—comes not from the Father but from the world.** The world and its desires pass away, but **whoever does the will of God lives forever** [emphasis added]" (1 John 2:15-16).

Moses and Balaam

We see Balaam's path after having a genuine fear of the Lord, a knowledge of the Holy, and even a vibrant relationship with Him. And we read about the path Moses took in the same Book.

I've compared similarities and differences between these two ancient, contemporary prophets in another piece of the puzzle so I won't replicate that. I would only add on this issue of choosing the world or God, that the Scriptures have some high commendations for Moses.

First: "By faith Moses, when he had grown up, refused to be called the son of Pharaoh's daughter, **choosing rather to endure ill-treatment with the people of God than to enjoy the passing pleasures of sin**" (Hebrews 11:24-25). Secondly: "**considering** the reproach of **Christ greater riches than the treasures of Egypt;** for he [Moses] was looking to the reward [emphasis added]" (Hebrews 11:26).

Encyclopaedia Britannica

"Balaam, non-Israelite prophet described in chapter 22-24 of the Book of Numbers, the fourth book of the Hebrew Bible (Old Testament), as a diviner who is importuned by Balak, King of Moab, to place a malediction on the people of Israel, who are camping ominously on the planes of Moab" (Encyclopaedia Britannica).

That's a summary and a reasonably good one. But we know in the spiritual realm, which is the more significant reality, there is much more to this story. More than one would expect an encyclopedia to record.

Motives of the Heart Matter

Balaam, a contemporary of Moses and a prophet was a great man. We typically read through the story and the New Testament references for further insights, and we tend to vilify him. This I do not intend nor wish to do. He was known to kings in his day as having a relationship with God, spiritual authority, and the ability to hear God and to speak about future and practical matters.

While we read about this real-life drama and how it played out after the fact, he didn't know how it would. He lived it amid relationships and in real-time. What would you have done if a wealthy king had invited you with the promise of honor and money if you only came and used your gift to help him? Oh, and by the way, the king might have been a distant relative. Their ancestors hailed from the same area, so they were friendly, and related by culture, if not by blood. He may have introduced him to some of the women of Moab or his harem? What would you do?

Stay humble. Stay obedient. Keep good habits. They are your friends. Stay away from the love of money. Stay away from sexual sin. Keep good friends. Wash with the water of the Word. Pray that you do not enter into temptation: "Keep watching and praying that you may not enter into temptation; the spirit is willing, but the flesh is weak" (Matthew 16:41). Stay in the Christian community: "not giving up meeting together, as some are in the habit of doing, but encouraging one another—and all the more as you see the Day approaching" (Hebrews 10:25). Godspeed as you journey with Him Who called you and loves you, and sent you His Spirit.

Spiritually Sighted

I have a friend who has known God well but has fallen into sexual sin. I had a beautiful and really straight talk with him this week. The Spirit helped me press in on the urgency of the issue, and the onset of spiritual blindness. It happened in Israel because of Balaam's counsel. Because of spiritual blindness and immoral sexual activity among God's people, twenty-four thousand people died before a courageous, God-fearing man named Phinehas stopped the flaunting of sexual sin with a spear (Numbers 25:1-9).

That made me think later about how serious this is and some hard words Jesus said about it: "You have heard that it was said, 'You shall not commit adultery'; but I say to you that everyone who looks at a woman with lust for her has already committed adultery with her in his heart. If your right eye makes you stumble, tear it out and throw it from you; for it is better for you to lose one of the parts of your body, than for your whole body to be thrown into hell. If your right hand makes you stumble, cut it off and throw it from you; for it is better for you to lose one of the parts of your body, than for your whole body to go into hell'" (Matthew 5:27-30). I don't think He was kidding about this.

I told my friend, "Cut it off! Your very life is in the balance." He knows I'm not trying to guilt him. I'm just being straight up with him, because I love him. We've always talked truthfully, man to man.

Then I felt led to pray and journal a simple prayer: "Father, have mercy and extend grace for righteous living to my friend, I pray. Amen." Then, like Mary with Jesus at the wedding in Cana, I walked away feeling sure He would act, with His big heart and powerful arm.

It's safe to say, if you have a problem with the love of money or sexual sin, you are not going to be able to see clearly in the spirit or hear much from God, if anything. The further you go down those roads, the closer you are to blindness, confusion, and destruction.

Balaam teaches us that!

"If it is disagreeable in your sight to serve the Lord, **choose for yourselves today whom you will serve: whether the gods which your fathers served which were beyond the River,** or the gods of the Amorites in whose land you are living; but **as for me and my house, we will serve the Lord** [emphasis added]"

(Joshua 24:15).

"I call heaven and earth to witness against you today, that I have set before you life and death, the blessing and the curse. So **choose life in order that you may live, you and your descendants, by loving the Lord your God, by obeying His voice, and by holding fast to Him** [emphasis added]"

(Deuteronomy 30:19-20a).

And Jesus famously said: "**No one can serve two masters**. Either you will hate the one and love the other, or you will be devoted to the one and despise the other. **You cannot serve both God and money** [emphasis added]"

(Matthew 6:24 NIV).

"For he **[Abraham] was looking for the city which has foundations**, whose **architect and builder is God** [emphasis added]"

(Hebrews 11:10).

"If **the righteous receive their due on earth**, how **much more the ungodly and the sinner!** [emphasis added]"

(Proverbs 11:31).

"For by these **He has granted to us His precious and magnificent promises**, so that **by them you may become partakers of the divine nature**, having **escaped the corruption that is in the world by lust** [emphasis added]"

(1Peter 1:4).

"Therefore, brethren, be all the more diligent to make certain about His calling and choosing you; for **as long as you practice these things, you will never stumble**; for in **this way the entrance into the eternal kingdom of our Lord and Savior Jesus Christ will be abundantly supplied to you** [emphasis added]"

(1Peter 1:10-11).

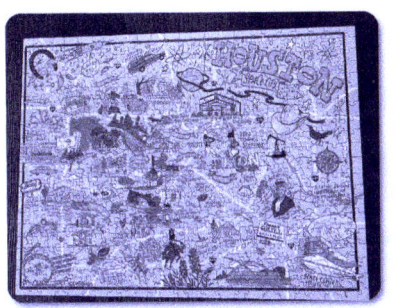

PUZZLING CHAPTER 31

An Apology

Does Anyone Owe Anyone an Apology

My journal entry for April 4, 2022, started like this: "Well, I'm a mathematician, so I must stop and ponder whether 4–4–22 means anything? It seems like it should and possibly does, but it probably means I'm easily distracted and need to get back on task.

"It's 7:30 AM and I'm up by the fire starting chapter 20 in *Is Atheism Dead?* by Eric Metaxas. It's a very enjoyable, insightful, stimulating read. I am 66% through the book, reading it with highlights and notes, on an iPad."

Why I am enjoying it:

1. I still enjoy learning about life, nature, history, and things in the world as they are while we march through time to what will be. I think that is in us as humans. We are wired that way. Discovery gives joy, fulfillment, peace, humility, direction, and

meaning to our lives — a sense that all this beauty and mystery matters, and we do too.

2. I suppose this book is so enjoyable and compelling for me because Metaxas, in layman's terms and thoughts (excusing his lofty vocabulary, which somehow adds value to the book), tells the Christian, "You needn't fight the war against atheism — it's been won."

I've been given permission or the opportunity for a moment to celebrate and enjoy the science, archaeology, and philosophy that puts the notion of atheism to rest or points to the fact that it is indeed dead.

If you want to continue to "contend for the faith," it will probably continue in the area of "deception." People who are deceived don't know it. Suppose the Spirit leads you to cross someone's path who has a heart to know the truth but has been deceived by some of atheism's dead and dying arguments. In that case, the facts and framework of this book will serve as an excellent place to start helping them step out of the darkness of lies and deception into the light of truth and life.

Prayer will be the best and primary tool to help your friend, relative, or acquaintance because truth is spiritual in nature and requires revelation from above. But the discovery also involves reason because of God's gift — free will. One must be willing to open the door to truth in their heart and mind. It's His design.

Because I grew up when faith and Christianity were under attack by worldly forces using reason and science as bludgeons, the apology of the church handed to me was "evidence that demands a verdict."

Apology and apologetics are funny words to me for "defense of the faith." This apology has nothing to do with being wrong or offensive to another and acknowledging such with regret and an implied or stated request for forgiveness. Instead, it comes from the name of a book, *Apology for the Christian Faith*, written by Aristides, an Athenian philosopher in the second century.

The book was addressed to the Roman emperor, probably Hadrian, giving his reasons why Christianity is a system of belief and faith and truth superior to the Egyptians, Babylonians, Greeks, and even the Jews. However, he held that the Jews religion and practices had merit. It is well worth your time to read a summary of Arístides' thoughts from this letter as recorded in the Encyclopedia Britannica, easily found with a Google search.

If you consult a dictionary, you will find three definitions of "apology." While only one is well known to most of us, the second is insightful and curious. One could say, "The church in the USA and the west is an apology for true Christianity." But that will be a discussion in another piece of the puzzle.

A third definition for an apology is the one we're talking about here: "a reasoned argument or writings in justification of something, typically a theory or religious doctrine" (dictionary.com).

An Apology!

With that as background information, I'll share what I learned a few years ago in Bible college for the first time. Since the late 1700s, the latter days of the Enlightenment in Europe, the apology (defense) of the church or Christianity has been *Evidence That Demands a Verdict*. This apology is summed up pretty well in a book with that same title by Josh McDowell, Ph.D. The subtitle of the latest edition (2017) of the book, co-authored with his son Sean McDowell, Ph.D., reads: *Life changing truth for a skeptical world*.

That line of thinking was all I knew until Bible College, when in a lecture by the president, I learned that wasn't the church's apology for the first 1700 years of her existence. Do you know what it was? Simply, **"The Presence of God with His People."** People inside the church knew it and enjoyed it; that is, the Presence. People outside the church observed it from afar and noticed Christians were peculiar people. They seemed happy, vital, loving, caring for people inside their community and those outside. They cared for the elderly, the sick, and the poor, established hospitals, took in orphans and established orphanages. They built schools so people could read the Bible and colleges to train young preachers. Christians founded the Ivy League schools in the US for this purpose. They sent missionaries around the globe to follow the Spirit in the same activities. These activities were the kind of fruit people on the outside could observe about Christians. You might recall that Jesus said: "So then, you will know them by their fruits" (Matthew 7:20).

In individual Christians, the light of the indwelling Christ by his Spirit could be seen too, transforming them from whatever state of corruption and decay they presently found themselves to beacons of light — bearing fruit different from before. This fruit was described by Paul to the Galatian church 2000 years ago: "The fruit of the Spirit is love, joy, peace, patience, kindness, goodness, faithfulness, gentleness, self-control" (Galatians 5:22-23a).

The apostle John said the same thing in recording Jesus' words to Nicodemus: "That which is born of the flesh is flesh, and that which is born of the Spirit is spirit" (John 3:6). Then recording Jesus' words to his disciples: "I am the vine, you are the branches; he who abides in Me and I in him, he bears much fruit, for apart from Me you can do nothing" (John 15:5).

And then, just before He was to leave his disciples and the earth for a season, Jesus told them: "But I tell you the truth, it is to your advantage that I go away; for if I do not go away, the Helper will not come to you; but if I go, I will send Him to you" (John 16:7). **The Holy Spirit, Emmanuel, "God with us," is that reality.**

"The presence of God with his people" was the church's apology for seventeen centuries. Then was added to the apology, "evidence that demands a verdict," for the past three centuries.

I think the older, longer-lived apology is the better of the two. It's the ancient path. It's more akin to: "This is the Lord's doing; it is marvelous in our eyes" (Psalm 118:23). The newer apology seems to rely on us more than the Lord. But it doesn't have to do so. And it never really did nor does depend on us. Perhaps we have let ourselves be duped into entering the fray, defending the faith using the enemy's tools instead of relying more on God. It tends to draw one into Christian humanism, which should be an oxymoron, but it's a reality of our day — thinking we need to defend God. Delusional. It speaks of faith too small, ill-informed, or deception in a Christian.

I recall reading about the life and exploits of David, where he would defeat a powerful enemy, then burn their chariots and hamstring their horses, making them unfit for warfare but still useful for agriculture. From my military training and common sense, I wondered, "Why?" His armed forces could have used them to make them stronger! Then I read the rules of "the King" in the books of Moses (Deuteronomy 17:14-20), written 500 years before there even was a king in Israel. God told Moses the prophet, there would come a time when there would be a king, and this is how I want him to act. Among other things, I don't want him to multiply horses and chariots for himself so that he would start depending on himself (humanism) and not upon God: "Moreover, he shall not multiply horses for himself, nor shall he cause the people to return to Egypt to multiply horses since the Lord has said to you, 'You shall never again return that way'" (Deuteronomy 17:16). Evidently, David read it too and obeyed, trusting God to be God and love and protect the king and His people, Israel.

The most compelling example I've read about "God's presence with His people" in the Old Testament is also from the life and times of Moses. God, it seems, had lost patience, as bizarre as that may sound depending on your view of God, with Israel after providing for them with miracle after miracle in the desert. These miracles were followed by their continual disobedience and complaining. After one such episode, God told Moses to go on into the promised land with the people, and He would send a strong angel before them to see that they made it. But He would not go lest He destroy them for their wayward capers.

What was Moses' answer to this offer or directive from God? It was unique, insightful, and telling for all ages: "Then he [Moses] said to Him [God], 'If Your presence does not go with us, do not lead us up from here. For how then can it be known that I have found favor in Your sight, I and Your people? **Is it not by Your going with us, so that we, I and Your people, may be distinguished from all the other people who are upon the face of the earth?** [emphasis added]'" (Exodus 33:15-16).

"It's God's presence with His people" that distinguishes us from all the peoples of the earth. Since 1500 BC for 3500 years, that's been the oldest, tried, genuine, best apology of God's people. It was true of Abraham, Isaac, and Jacob around 2000 BC. God keeps his word. God loves to dwell with His people, His bride.

You can read the following Bible verses to get a sense of the truth and reality of God dwelling with His people as being central to His plan. (Colossians 1:27, Isaiah 66:1-2, Ephesians 3:20, 2 Corinthians 4:7, Isaiah 7:14, Matthew 1:23, John 15:4-5). It's just a small sampling of verses scattered throughout the Bible. It could be said: "The whole Biblical narrative is the story of a King and his Bride, God and Israel, Christ and the Church." One takes a bride to dwell with her, does he not?

Let the nations rage. Let them do what they are going to do. Read the Psalms and Gospels to see how God feels about you. You can begin with Psalms 2 and 32.

Apology Ended

So, is it "**evidence that demands a verdict?**" Or "**God's presence with his people?**" I suppose it's not either/or, but instead, **both/and**.

In his short, potent book of the Bible, just before *The Revelation of Jesus Christ*, Jude tells us he was about to write to us about our shared, glorious faith. Then unexpectedly, the Spirit told him to write about contending for the faith and to be aware of false teachers in the church — with deception their craft and motive. He writes: "Beloved, while I was making every effort to write you about our common salvation, I felt the necessity to write to you appealing that you **contend earnestly for the faith** which was once for all handed down to the saints [emphasis added]" (Jude 3).

Therefore, "contend for the faith" where, when, and how the Spirit leads. Be honest, courageous, kind, loving, and humble. Your contending will probably be with believers and those seeking the truth — not antagonists in the world or outsiders.

That said, it's not always with people in the church that we are to contend for the faith. I would be remiss if I didn't mention the example of Paul on Mars Hill (Acts 17), or one of the most foundational admonitions on the subject from Peter: "Sanctify Christ as Lord in your hearts, always being ready to make a defense to everyone who asks you to give an account for the hope that is in you, yet with gentleness and reverence" (1Peter 3:15).

Never argue for argument's sake. The apostle Paul who spent most of his life contending for the faith, wrote: "The Lord's bond-servant must not be quarrelsome, but be kind to all, able to teach, patient when wronged" (2 Timothy 2:24). Paul also wrote: "Stay away from foolish and stupid arguments, because you know they grow into quarrels" (2 Timothy 2:23 NCV).

So then: "Make every effort to give yourself to God as the kind of person he will approve. Be a worker who is not ashamed and who uses the true teaching in the right way. Stay away from foolish, useless talk, because that will lead people further away from God" (2Timothy 2:15-16 NCV). Study the scriptures and know them well. Also, learn what you can from science, history, philosophy, any field that interests you, and the natural order of things.

But remember, it doesn't depend that much on you to defend or contend for your faith. You hopefully have had experiences with God.

And as one of my favorite mentors, Charles Simpson, says: "A person with an experience is never at the mercy of a person with an argument." Just be confident in who you are and whose you are. Remember, the best apology for the faith is the presence of God with His people. Keep drawing and living close to Him, and that will be on full display. As the Lord told Gideon: "Go in the strength you have and save Israel out of Midian's hand. Am I not sending you?" (Judges 6:14 NIV).

Whether it be in science, theology, or any number of earthly pursuits, this T.S. Elliot quote comes to mind: "We shall not cease from exploration and the end of all our exploring will be to arrive where we started and know the place for the first time." Keep exploring and keep learning fearlessly. There is no conflict between science and the Bible or faith in God. You will come to know this harmony the further you go and the older you grow. Metaxas describes it beautifully.

I started this diatribe by reading and discussing *Is Atheism Dead?* by Eric Metaxas. So now I'll end precisely where I began by saying you would enjoy reading this book, becoming up-to-date with discoveries in science, archaeology, and philosophy. The facts are enjoyable to discover and know. And his framework for those facts might provide a foundation to help you grow — in the knowledge of The Holy One Who needs no apology — forever, amen.

"There is no wisdom and no understanding and no counsel against the Lord"

(Proverbs 21:30).

"Deep calls to deep at the sound of Your waterfalls; all Your breakers and Your waves have rolled over me"

(Psalm 42:7).

"If I take the wings of the dawn, if I dwell in the remotest part of the sea, even there Your hand will lead me, and Your right hand will lay hold of me"

(Psalm 139:9-10).

"I will give thanks to You, for I am fearfully and wonderfully made; wonderful are Your works, and my soul knows it very well"

(Psalm 139:15).

"The fool has said in his heart, 'There is no God'"

(Psalm 14:1a).

"The heavens declare the glory of God, and the skies announce what his hands have made. Day after day they tell the story; night after night they tell it again. They have no speech or words; they have no voice to be heard. But their message goes out through all the world; their words go everywhere on earth."

(Psalm 19:1-3 NCV).

"Where were you when I laid the earth's foundation? Tell me, if you understand. Who marked off its dimensions? Surely you know! Who stretched a measuring line across it? On what were its footings set, or who laid its cornerstone—while the morning stars sang together and all the angels shouted for joy?"

(Job 38:4-7 NIV).

"Because that which is known about God is evident within them; for God made it evident to them. For since the creation of the world His invisible attributes, His eternal power and divine nature, have been clearly seen, being understood through what has been made, so that they are without excuse"

(Romans 1:19-20).

PUZZLING CHAPTER 32

Pause for Revelation

Wrapping Up

I was awakened by the Spirit early this morning thinking about how to wrap up this puzzling book. It seems too much for me — quite a bit more needs to be said to make even this simple puzzle a relatively complete image of the Christian life in our times. I know it's to be more of an impressionist image than a photographic image, but there's still work to do.

My vision for the book may be too lofty, it may be too broad or too encompassing. I'm asking the Spirit to help me find the part I need to address, and bring that perspective into focus.

Even my close friends who are becoming more aware of the book are starting to ask questions. What's going to be the book's title? What is the desired purpose of the book? Then they thoughtfully make some suggestions, saying they will pray for an expeditious completion, and that it reaches its intended audience, the lives and hearts of those in the family of God whom it would benefit.

I desire it to be an encouragement to solid, mature believers who already have a robust relationship with Jesus, those who are leading and discipling others. We all need to be reminded to adventure with the Holy Spirit who guides and befriends us. There is much more to learn about our Father in heaven. There are more people to help, people to rescue, and friendships to forge enabling the journey and making it more enjoyable and meaningful.

Do you know Jesus? Do you know who you are in Him? Have you heard him call your name? And started your spiritual adventure under His guidance and in His power?

If you have, you're still looking along with Abraham, and all those gone before us, for "a city whose builder and maker is God" (Hebrews 11:10). Like Paul, your overriding passion is to know Jesus, and the power of his Spirit, continually raising you to new life (Philippians 3:10).

My hope, goal, and prayer is that this book will find its way to all truth seekers who might find it helpful on their journey amid the smoke, confusion, and rubble of our day. The book is intended to give direction, hope, and a heading, to use an aviation analogy, to fly your way out of the smoke to clear skies, so you can see the situation more clearly from above. Then you can live a life above the fray. You will be called and led by the Spirit on missions back into the fray to help and rescue those in the war zone, probably often and much, but you will dwell apart, on the mountain of God. This way you can maintain perspective, peace, the ability to hear, and the availability of power to act.

So, dear reader, puzzler, truth seeker, adventurer, friend — by describing the intended audience and goal of this humble, thoughtful book, it starts to express itself. And when I consider the goal, it seems too much for me.

Elijah — "A Man Like You"

I feel like Elijah, with the high and low points of his life separated by only a few days. I'm running toward Horeb, the mountain of God, for some answers because my paradigm and perspective of life has imploded or changed drastically from what I envisioned and expected. My foundations are shaking and causing me to wonder if the building will stand, or the life I had imagined can be lived. My dreams seem crushed. The vision I had for my future now seem unattainable.

Truthfully, I don't feel this way now. But I have in times past. And I think many have during these puzzling COVID-19 times. Like Elijah, I've run through the wilderness toward God, hoping He would meet me. On the way, I've fallen, exhausted, then collapsed into a deep sleep.

And like Elijah, I felt the angel of the Lord awaken me, strengthen me with food and drink, and say: "Get up and eat, for **the journey is too much for you** [emphasis added]" (1 Kings 19:7).

Is this you? Have you felt this way during the long, confusing COVID-19 years, 2020-2022, that seem to be dragging on even as I write and we breathe breaths a little more uncertain than before COVID-19?

I must laugh and smile a hundred internal smiles at what just happened as I penned that last paragraph. A good friend in another state who has had a lot of life and faith struggles in the past months just texted me a song at 6:25 AM. The title of the amazing song, one I haven't heard before is "Behold God is Great" by Jake Hamilton. You must listen or read the lyrics to see how perfectly it fits with the story of Elijah that I am recounting, and asking you to consider with me.

The answer for our confusion, brokenness, disillusion, despair, self-pity — a multitude of ills and evils — is a fresh encounter with God. We need a new awareness of the One who sits above the circle of the earth and stretches out the heavens like a curtain (Isaiah 40:22). We need to lift up our eyes to the heavens and behold our God (Isaiah 40:26).

He is so much bigger than any image you have of him. The ancient Job who apparently knew God better than anyone else in his day said: "Behold, God is great and we do not know Him" (Job 36:26).

Elijah, whose name means "Yahweh is my God," was about to have a new encounter with this God. He desperately needed some new spiritual life, power, and some questions answered — a paradigm change. This was the case in the middle of his life — a life solidly lived with God.

Elijah was strong physically — a wilderness, locust-and-wild-honey type prophet like John the Baptist. He was an Ethiopian-type runner, known for long, fast jaunts on feet and legs through remote desert areas. Being strong and self-reliant is sometimes part of the problem. I'm reminded of the verse: **"He gives strength to the weary and increases the power of the weak**. Even youths grow tired and weary, and young men stumble and fall; but those who hope in the Lord will renew their strength. They will soar on wings like eagles; they will run and not grow weary, they will walk and not be faint [emphasis added]" (Isaiah 40: 28b-31 NIV). This verse starts, if you're weak, He makes you strong. I sometimes wonder if the opposite might not be true? If you're strong, He might have to make you weak? Or show you your weakness.

Anyway this happened to Elijah. God sent him an angel to tell him the journey was too much for him, and to help him with the strength to continue his run to the remote mountain of God. God met him there, as I've related in another piece of the puzzle or you can read for yourself in 1 Kings 19.

The Message and The Method

It seems to me that the message was very important. It cleared up a lie that Elijah had believed, one that made him very discouraged, and caused him to wallow in self pity. The method God used in speaking to Elijah was just as important as the message, actually more so. But let's consider the message first.

God spoke first: **"What are you doing here, Elijah?"** (1 Kings 19:13b). That might be the first indication he wasn't where he should be? Or it may have been God's way of drawing him out and getting quickly to the heart of the matter. Elijah speaks next: "**I have been very zealous for the Lord, the God of hosts**; for **the sons of Israel have forsaken Your covenant, torn down Your altars and killed Your prophets** with the sword. And **I alone am left; and they seek my life, to take it away** [emphasis added]" (1 Kings 19:14).

I want to be kind here because Elijah was a servant of the Lord. He also was a much greater man than I could ever be. Yet at the same time we're told in Scripture: "Elijah was a man with a nature like ours" (James 5:17a). He was a man like us. This is a little bit hard for us to grasp because at the same time he was the best known prophet in Israel, and had a track record of hearing God accurately, even calling down fire on occasions (2 Kings 1). But seasoned Christians, prophets, any of us can be deceived, believe a lie, and wallow in self-pity because of it. I believe that's a big part of what Elijah's very short speech to God tells us and shows us. Doesn't it almost seem like Elijah is telling God something that Elijah thinks God does not know? For one who has exhibited so much faith and spiritual sensitivity in the past, it seems like his head is a little cloudy, and his vision is not clear. He ends his talk with God something like this: "I've done everything I can for You. I'm all alone. And they're trying to kill me."

What do you make of this? It seems like his faith level is low. His fear level is high. Maybe he feels like God hasn't taken care of him, or won't? Certainly, things have not turned out the way he envisioned to this point. And I think I hear self-pity about the whole situation, don't you?

This wouldn't be rare. In fact it's common to prophets and to the human condition. Prophets suffer a lot of rejection, and can start to feel sorry for themselves. Christians can too. In fact, it's a part of the normal Christian life: "Indeed, **all who desire to live godly in Christ Jesus will be persecuted** [emphasis added]" (2 Timothy 3:12). Charles Simpson said once upon reading this verse, there was a pause, then he heard the Spirit say: "Where's yours?"

So expect persecution, it's part of the job description. And beware of self pity — it's spiritually blinding. It's living a lie — that God doesn't know your situation and that's He's unwilling or unable to help you, care for you, and see you through.

Look at the beauty and brevity of God's message to Elijah in reply: "The Lord said to him, '**Go, return on your way** to the wilderness of Damascus, and when you have arrived, you shall **anoint Hazael king over Aram;** and **Jehu** the son of Nimshi **you shall anoint king over Israel;** and **Elisha** the son of Shaphat of Abel-meholah **you shall anoint as prophet in your place** [emphasis added]'" (1 Kings 19:15-16).

God did not address Elijah's zeal for God, the sons of Israel's rebellious and covenant breaking infractions, or the murder of God's prophets — none of it. His brilliant and only reply was to recommission Elijah, telling him to "go back through the wilderness," and anoint two kings and a prophet. And God corrected one flaw in Elijah's thinking. There was no shaming Elijah for being there, no speaking to his lack of faith or addressing his self pity. There was the all important second part of the message that perhaps said all that needed to be said: "Yet I will leave **7,000 in Israel, all the knees that have not bowed to Baal and every mouth that has not kissed him** [emphasis added]" (1 Kings 19:18). Elijah wasn't alone as he had believed. God was on the the move as He had been all along. Only Elijah was sidetracked by losing sight of that and believing a lie, when his well-being was threatened.

Sidetracked seems to be a bit of an understatement. It's interesting to note that Elijah ran from Mt. Carmel in northern Israel to the southern border of Israel, Beersheba, where he left his servant, a distance of 120 miles. Then he ran 40 days and 40 nights to Mt Horeb (the same as Mt Sinai), a distance of 240 miles. This is the location where God spoke to Moses from the burning bush, where God met Moses again when the Israelites came out of Egypt and received The Ten Commandments, and where Paul would go to seek God after his conversion near Damascus hundreds of years later.

I think it's safe to say Elijah was desperate to hear God, as well as flee from his troubles, both real and imagined. When you consider the brevity of the conversation, six sentences, one might wonder if it was worth the trip. But what price do you put on an audience with God? What's it worth to have your spiritual vision restored, and to be back flowing in the purposes of God, versus wallowing in self pity and believing a lie? It was worth it! And it's worth it today, whatever it takes or cost!

The Moses Method

As important as the message was, it seems the method might be more so. There is something about having God come near! I recently read in Exodus that God came near to Moses on Horeb some eight hundred years earlier. I hope to include a little of that experience in another piece of the puzzle. You can read about it Exodus 19. It's chilling. Here's a glimpse: "Now Mount Sinai was all in smoke because the Lord descended upon it in fire; and its smoke ascended like the smoke of a furnace, and the whole mountain quaked violently. When the sound of the trumpet grew louder and louder, Moses spoke and God answered him with thunder. The Lord came down on Mount Sinai, to the top of the mountain; and the Lord called Moses to the top of the mountain, and Moses went up. Then the Lord spoke to Moses, 'Go down, warn the people, so that they do not break through to the Lord to gaze, and many of them perish.'" (Exodus 19:18-21).

So here is another humble man, Elijah, a man like us, seeking some answers from God, in the wilderness, alone in a place he might hear from God. Then after some time inside a cave on the mountain waiting, praying, and listening for God — God comes near: " So He [God] said, 'Go forth and stand on the mountain before the Lord.' And behold, **the Lord was passing by! And a great and strong wind was rending the mountains and breaking in pieces the rocks before the Lord;**

but the Lord was not in the wind. And after the wind **an earthquake**, but the Lord was not in the earthquake. **After the earthquake a fire**, but the Lord was not in the fire; and after the fire a sound of a gentle blowing [emphasis added]" (1 Kings 19:11-12).

If you know the story, you know Elijah doesn't come out immediately, because spiritual sensitivity is being restored to him. I think I'd have come out during the earthquake! Most would have and probably died in the earthquake or subsequent fire. But in this slowly developing, brief, powerful, intimate encounter with the LORD, a lot changed in Elijah's psyche and heart. Spiritual sensitivity was restored, and God came near, very near: "And after the fire a sound of a gentle blowing. When Elijah heard it, he wrapped his face in his mantle and went out and stood in the entrance of the cave" (1 Kings 19:12b-13).

Six sentences later, after a proximate experience with the Almighty, Elijah had a new direction and a renewed sense of mission — new faith and new fire in his soul. This brings new meaning to the verse: "The fear of the Lord is the beginning of wisdom, and the knowledge of the Holy One is understanding" (Proverbs 9:10). As stated before, "If you fear God, you fear nothing else. If you don't fear God you fear everything else." We often need a fresh encounter with the LORD — for reality to be restored.

A month or so earlier, after a great victory over idolatry and the cult worship of Baal on Mount Carmel, God had answered Elijah by fire from heaven. Then immediately, Elijah prayed for rain and God ended a three year drought with a torrent. Then Elijah thought things would turn around quickly for good in Israel, but they went unexpectedly badly. The evil queen issued a "Wanted Dead or Alive" edict for Elijah expected to take no more than twenty-four hours, with the wealth and power of the kingdom behind her. Actually it was a "Wanted Dead" edict.

Now, after a fresh vision of God, none of that mattered. He went back to Israel, to do the bidding of the Lord, with joy, purpose, and even more resolution and faith than before. That's what happens to a person who has a fresh encounter or vision of the Almighty. Reality is restored with an accurate perspective, and then they're back on an adventure with God. As God told Gideon a few centuries earlier after he had a similar encounter with the LORD: "**Go in the strength you have. Am I not sending you** [paraphrase]" (Judges 6:14).

Somehow I don't think you'll get this vision or live this reality watching TV or reading the newspaper or spending a lot of time on social media. If you listen to the world, you'll end up living in a different, false reality, and functioning out of the same. "Living a lie" one could call it, not living the truth that God is real and really Who He says He Is — One continually doing the things He does. You can feed your faith or feed your fears. Those seem to be the main two choices we have. And then we also have the Wind, the Spirit of God, mysteriously blowing where It wills, with grace, mercy, and help in time of need among humankind with the motive of great love — observable but in ways past finding out.

Isaiah Illustration

The life of Isaiah also demonstrates this truth and reality.

A.W. Tozer raises our awareness of who God is in his beautiful, short book *The Knowledge of the Holy*. He writes a systematic summary of insights the Bible gives us about God. He also tells us this is not for the intellect primarily, or to be a collection of facts about God, but for worshipers, people who want to experience God.

Tozer ends up saying knowing the Holy is the most important thing about us. He says it isn't theoretical, but experiential. Then he points us to Isaiah, and Isaiah chapter six as an example for us all. We must experience God in some similar way.

We need to get a vision, our own vision of God like Isaiah experienced in the year King Uzziah died. It was a time of cultural and spiritual shaking and progressing toward darkness like he could not have anticipated. Sound familiar?

Time in the Temple

For Isaiah it wasn't on the top of the wilderness mountain Horeb where Moses and Elijah experienced an encounter with God. But it was in the wilderness of the city, the capital, the king's court, and in the temple of God where he had duties as priest, amid the hubbub of life, that Isaiah experienced a visit and fresh vision of God.

The vision God gave him recorded in Isaiah chapter six changed him and his paradigm, even though things were growing gloriously dark around him. The leadership and culture of God's people were in a moral slide toward apostasy, injustice, and judgment. But Isaiah experienced a fresh vision of God in splendor, knew that his sin had been forgiven and taken away, and that he was now sent by God to speak His words to the people. This enabled him to be a force for good, and for God, no matter what was going on around him. And he was!

That is God's will for us. Where sin abounds, God's grace (His power and favor — unmerited and freely given), abounds more for his sovereign activity and purposes in the world. We get to experience the exhilaration of knowing Him better, adventuring with His Spirit and with others in worthwhile purposes, and to experience a life well-lived.

Run

What could be better than this? Run to the mountain of God through your wilderness, asking God for an epiphany. Share your heart and hurts with him. He's not threatened. He understands, and He will help you run to Him. But don't be surprised if He corrects your thinking and changes your paradigm before sending you back out in His strength, with His authority, to do His bidding — with His blessing.

He has your best interest at heart! He knows what makes you tick, and your best destiny. His plans for you are better than your plans for you. How can you not love such a good and powerful God? Trust Him, and run to Him! Find your Horeb, the Mountain of God, and listen to what He tells you there.

PUZZLING CHAPTER 33

Atheism Postmortem

Is Atheism Dead?

Factually yes! I think Eric Metaxas makes a beautiful, readable, enjoyable, incredible case for that in his book, *Is Atheism Dead?* He is a biographer and historian of the first rank. He gives us the facts surrounding the debate. He puts them in historical perspective so we can understand the propositions of materialistic atheism and why those facts are no longer accurate or relevant.

But what if the facts don't matter? What if people have their minds made up as is commonly heard: "Don't confuse me with the facts."

I'm thrilled to know about the book and feel enriched by reading it. It blows away a lot of smoke and sheds a lot of light on where we are as humankind and have been. It also shines a lot of light on lies and deception — delusion.

So, I'd have to say that atheism isn't completely dead as long as delusion lives. This brings up a central theme of this book and a significant explanation for the puzzles of our day — lies and deception, deception and delusion.

Lies and Deception

The truth is that you believe what you want to think. You accept the sum of all the truth and lies you've been told. Then you evaluate how they interacted with your hurts and joys. It's how you make sense of what your eyes see and your heart feels. You love your eye's ability to see things and your brain's ability to process and retain the facts as you interpret them. That's sort of how it works.

Then there are junctions. Paths often split on significant issues, and you must go one way or another. You start to build on the truth or lie you've believed, which sets the course of your life. And who can know the difference? Who can see the truth?

Many rely on their heart to cast the final vote. They decide with their heart what matters most — what the truth of a matter is to be for them. But can that beautifully functioning heart, or soul, be deceived? Should we rely on our brain or our heart? I don't know? I'm asking.

I suppose we rely on both. Maybe one more than the other? It's how we are wired. It's also how we decide what will be our course and our way of making future decisions. Maybe we flip-flop, between using our brain or heart, depending on our phase of life. Or when we have really important decisions. But it seems our hearts determine the truth we believe. Our brain serves the heart in processing information, facts, and feelings in reaching that decision, then records our decision as permanent or temporary awaiting future inputs.

The ancients tell us:

> "Watch over your heart with all diligence,
> For from it flow the springs of life"
>
> (Proverbs 4:23 NASB).

Bible Translations

One of the most basic Bible study techniques is to look at a verse or passage in different translations. So let's do that here:

> "Above all else, guard your heart, for everything you do flows from it"
>
> (Proverbs 4:23 NIV).

> "Keep your heart with all vigilance, for from it flow the springs of life"
>
> (Proverbs 4:23 ESV).

> "Keep your heart with all diligence, For out of it spring the issues of life"
>
> (Proverbs 4:23 NKJV).

While I generally read the word-for-word oriented translations like the NASB, ESV, and NKJV above, some of the thought-for-thought translations like the NIV and the more modern translations bring scholarly thought and more modern language to the table and provide insights. Let's keep going with a few of those. The translation isn't as important as reading it when it comes to the Bible. Just pick one and read it! Then compare passages occasionally in other translations as we do here, relying on your mind and the Spirit for insight.

"Guard your heart above all else, for it determines the course of your life"

(Proverbs 4:23 NLT).

"Above everything else, guard your heart. Everything you do comes from it"

(Proverbs 4:23 NIRV).

"Be careful what you think, because your thoughts run your life"

(Proverbs 4:23 NCV).

"Keep vigilant watch over your heart; that's where life starts. Don't talk out of both sides of your mouth; avoid careless banter, white lies, and gossip. Keep your eyes straight ahead; ignore all sideshow distractions. Watch your step, and the road will stretch out smooth before you. Look neither right nor left; leave evil in the dust"

(Proverbs 4:23 MSG).

Context

It's conventional wisdom that the Bible is the best commentary on the Bible, so we always look at the context of verses we're trying to understand to get the whole meaning. The context is the verses immediately around the central verse. There you consider the audience, the speaker, the subject matter, the times, etc. In the end, you ask yourself three questions (and listen for answers): (1) What did it mean then? (2) What does it mean now? and (3) What does it mean to me?

Here's the context of our central verse — with the verse above and the verse below it. Consider those, and then you can spread out your contextual observation above or below from there as you like:

"For they are life to those who find them and health to all their body. **Watch over your heart with all diligence, for from it flow the springs of life.** Put away from you a deceitful mouth and put devious speech far from you [emphasis added]" (Proverbs 4:22-24 NASB).

That's insightful, right away. The verse numbers help find and reference the text but weren't in the original, so I've omitted them. They sometimes distract a bit from hearing the meaning.

You can see from the context that something above our verse is "life to the finder" and "health to their whole body." Then we learn from the verse immediately following that a "deceitful mouth" and "devious speech" connect to "watching over the heart." I would suggest your mouth has a large part in programming your heart, for better or worse, for lies or truth, deceit or wisdom.

From reading the Word repeatedly, I can think of several passages that confirm that proposition. And that's what you can do as well — see if any related Scripture comes to mind, or you can search for related words and thoughts in the Bible. Google is a helpful tool.

Getting back to the heart and the subject of deception, a few verses I've noted through the years on the subject come to mind:

"The heart is deceitful above all things, and desperately wicked; who can know it" (Jeremiah 17:9 NKJV). That's disturbing. And it shouts that we need help guarding our hearts. Maybe a moral code for guidance, like the Bible. And a guide in life, like the Holy Spirit. And friends who will tell us the truth about the things they hear us saying and see us doing.

How to Kill Eleven Million People

After giving us facts from science that refute what atheists have believed and taught, Metaxas gives us facts from archeology that point to the validity and veracity of the Bible, the book atheists claim isn't reliable or accurate. Then he broaches the most intriguing of his three proofs that atheism is dead — philosophy.

That's right; it's the search for truth. It is "the rational investigation of the truths and the principles of being," if you want to use the first definition of Dictionary.com. Most simply said, perhaps, philosophy the search for truth and the meaning of life.

The truth wouldn't be such a big issue if it weren't for lies. Truth gives life, and lies produce death — joy and well-being, or hurt and destruction. I'm going to finish this piece of the puzzle with some things the Bible says about truth. And then some things Eric Metaxas and Andy Andrews point out about lies and the resulting delusion. That's more than enough for one simple but hugely important puzzle piece.

Truth

"If any of you lacks wisdom, let him ask God, who gives generously to all without reproach, and it will be given him"

(James 1:5 ESV).

"Always learning and never able to arrive at a knowledge of the truth"

(2 Timothy 3:7).

"But the wisdom from above is first pure, then peaceable, gentle, open to reason, full of mercy and good fruits, impartial and sincere"

(James 3:17).

"And the Lord's servant must not be quarrelsome but kind to everyone, able to teach, patiently enduring evil, correcting his opponents with gentleness. God may perhaps grant them repentance leading to a knowledge of the truth, and they may come to their senses and escape from the snare of the devil, after being captured by him to do his will"

(2 Timothy 2:24-26).

"Behold, you delight in truth in the inward being, and you teach me wisdom in the secret heart"

(Psalm 51:6).

"Send out your light and your truth; let them lead me; let them bring me to your holy hill and to your dwelling!"
(Psalm 43:3).

"Who desires all people to be saved and to come to the knowledge of the truth"
(1 Timothy 2:4).

"So Jesus said to the Jews who had believed in him, "If you abide in my word, you are truly my disciples, and you will know the truth, and the truth will set you free"
(John 8:31-32).

"The sum of your word is truth, and every one of your righteous rules endures forever"
(Psalm 119:160).

"Teach me your way, O Lord, that I may walk in your truth; unite my heart to fear your name"
(Psalm 86:11).

"For if we go on sinning deliberately after receiving the knowledge of the truth, there no longer remains a sacrifice for sins"
(Hebrew 10:26).

"Correcting his opponents with gentleness. God may perhaps grant them repentance leading to a knowledge of the truth"
(2 Timothy 2:25).

"Do your best to present yourself to God as one approved, a worker who has no need to be ashamed, rightly handling the word of truth"
(2 Timothy 2:15).

"Therefore, having put away falsehood, let each one of you speak the truth with his neighbor, for we are members one of another"

(Ephesians 4:25).

"Where is the one who is wise? Where is the scribe? Where is the debater of this age? Has not God made foolish the wisdom of the world?"

(1 Corinthians 1:20).

"Sanctify them in the truth; your word is truth"

(John 17:17).

"These are the things that you shall do: Speak the truth to one another; render in your gates judgments that are true and make for peace"

(Zechariah 8:16).

"Whoever speaks the truth gives honest evidence, but a false witness utters deceit"

(Proverbs 12:17).

Deceit and Lies

"Repeat a lie often enough, and it becomes the truth," is a law of propaganda often attributed to the Nazi Joseph Goebbels.

Lest you think telling the truth is trivial, consider the Holocaust. *How Do You Kill 11 Million People?: Why the Truth Matters More Than You Think* is a compelling little book by Andy Andrews that makes a case for lies, more than anything else, accounting for the mass murder of 6 million Jews and 5 million Christians and other undesirable people during the Holocaust. He makes a rational and easily understood case that the people of Germany lying to themselves was the single most significant factor enabling that horror to come to pass.

You may say that's extreme, and granted, it is. But it came to pass with thousands of photos, articles, and eyewitness accounts of its reality, and extreme horror. This happened only eight decades ago, during the lifetime of many of our parents.

So even if the Holocaust is on the extreme end of the lying scale, it's on the scale and the result of lies. People deceive themselves and others by knowingly telling and promoting lies.

In the philosophy section of *Is Atheism Dead?* Eric Metaxas starts to discuss lies and deception in insightful ways. About the Holocaust, he writes:

> *"One problem with this line of thinking is that it is precisely the same as that embraced by the Nazis. There's no way around that. The Nazis cynically gave public lip service to God [lying to the people] but were grimly calculating atheists in practice, and the moment they had power they put all the serious Christians in concentration camps or on the front lines of the war, the sooner to die — and then did precisely as they had always wanted to do, without any backward religious people [a lie] to carp at them.*
>
> *"For example, everyone considered mentally ill was thought a drain on the National Socialist state and logically ought not to be fed and cared for with valuable resources that could otherwise be employed in winning the war. Under the gruesome T4 Program, innumerable hospitalized handicapped people were murdered, or rather "euthanized" via injection. Their corpses were delivered to crematoria, and their parents received a package containing their ashes and a letter claiming that they had died of natural causes [lies built on previous lies]. They were declared to be "life unworthy of life." The Nazis had the power to say as much and act on it, and did."*

If you still think this is extreme or far-fetched, you should recall the German civilization of Hitler's day was one of the most advanced, intelligent, civilized of all time. If you'd like an inside look at their mindset and civilization, read Eric Mataxas' excellent book *Bonhoeffer: Pastor, Martyr, Prophet, Spy.* Germany had reached this pinnacle by some natural gifting, but more so by the love of the truth, hard work, and a strong church teaching and preaching the realities of the Bible.

That the German people could be led down the road to deception and destruction in a couple of generations by lies and lying leaders, defies natural explanation and points to the spiritual dimension of deceit and delusion. As with truth, we'll look at a few things the Bible says about lies and deception. Then we'll pick up lies and deception again as other essential pieces of the puzzle with different twists or appearances.

Lies

"**You shall not** steal, nor deal falsely, nor **lie to one another** [emphasis added]"

(Leviticus 19:11).

"There are six things which **the Lord hates**, yes, seven which are an abomination to Him: Haughty eyes, **a lying tongue**, and hands that shed innocent blood, a heart that devises wicked plans, feet that run rapidly to evil, **a false witness who utters lies**, and one who spreads strife among brothers [emphasis added]"

(Proverbs 6:16-19).

"**A false witness will not go unpunished**, and **he who tells lies will perish** [emphasis added]"

(Proverbs 19:9).

"**Do not lie to one another,** since you laid aside the old self with its evil practices, and have put on the new self who is being renewed to a true knowledge according to the image of the One who created him [emphasis added]"

(Colossians 3:9-10).

"You are of **your father the devil**, and you want to do the desires of your father. He was a murderer from the beginning, and does not stand in the truth because **there is no truth in him. Whenever he speaks a lie, he speaks from his own nature, for he is a liar and the father of lies** [emphasis added]"

(John 8:44).

"so that by two unchangeable things in which **it is impossible for God to lie** [emphasis added]"

(Hebrews 6:18a).

"**Lying lips are an abomination to the Lord**, but those who deal faithfully are His delight [emphasis added]"

(Proverbs 12:22).

"Therefore, **laying aside falsehood**, speak truth each one of you with his neighbor, for we are members of one another [emphasis added]"

(Ephesians 4:25).

"The **remnant of Israel will** do no wrong and **tell no lies, nor will a deceitful tongue be found in their mouths**; for they will feed and lie down with no one to make them tremble [emphasis added]"

(Zephaniah 3:13).

"But for the cowardly and unbelieving and abominable and murderers and immoral persons and sorcerers and idolaters and **all liars, their**

part will be in the lake that burns with fire and brimstone, which is the second death [emphasis added]"

(Revelation 21:8).

"But the things that proceed out of the mouth come from the heart, and those defile the man. For **out of the heart come** evil thoughts, murders, adulteries, fornications, thefts, **false witness,** slanders. These are the things which defile the man [emphasis added]"

(Matthew 15:18-20).

"realizing the fact that **law is not made for a righteous person, but** for those who are lawless and rebellious, for the ungodly and sinners, for the unholy and profane, for those who kill their fathers or mothers, for murderers and immoral men and homosexuals and kidnappers and **liars and perjurers, and whatever else is contrary to sound teaching** [emphasis added]"

(1 Timothy 1:9-10).

"But Peter said, 'Ananias, why has **Satan filled your heart to lie to the Holy Spirit** and to keep back some of the price of the land? While it remained unsold, did it not remain your own? And after it was sold, was it not under your control? Why is it that you have conceived this deed in your heart? **You have not lied to men but to God** [emphasis added]'"

(Acts 5:3-4).

PUZZLING CHAPTER 34

Easter in Emmaus

Easter 2022

Easter is such a special time, because spring and new life are evident everywhere and coming forth with a ferocity that one can't ignore. One looks at brown soil one day and a green-grass carpet the next. Trees without a single leaf yesterday now flutter in the wind by thousands or millions, and colorful flowers pop out of the ground from seemingly nowhere. It's as if Someone commanded them to come forth. It seems mystical, magical, and beautiful. It makes our hearts sing with hope and expectation of warmer seasons, longer days, and more light to work and play.

That's fitting and apropos, but not the real meaning of Easter per se. New spiritual life has been made possible and commanded to come forth from the original passion week culminating in Christ's resurrection — life from death. It's hard to put into words even for those who see, yet it makes our hearts swell and feel alive, with hope for better days in this life and then for eternity with the One whose sacrifice made it possible. Amen.

Something changes in response to the light of the sun and the tilt of the earth. Something changes in response to the light of the Son and the inclination of a human heart and head. That's the spirit and truth about Easter. It's not that simple, and it's not that complicated. Maybe it isn't elementary to explain precisely or in detail, but simple to experience because the grace and revelation are there, awaiting the key of faith.

The Road

The road to Emmaus provides many insights into its complexity and simplicity. And why our hearts are full of joy and excitement at Easter's realization. Our pastor preached on this today, and most of the insights I share here are from his sermon. It's beautiful synchronicity to me that I wrote a chapter in my upcoming book *Puzzling 2020* over the weekend saying that the vision or dreams of many had been altered or crushed by the COVID-19 pandemic, and the cure for crushed dreams and blurred vision is a fresh encounter with God. I used Elijah and Isaiah as examples. Then in a Good Friday blog, I cited this same Emmaus incident.

Maybe the dashed dreams of his disciples and those who believed Jesus to be the Son of God (as He claimed and His miracles attested), the promised Jewish Messiah and King, are summed up by two of his disciples walking to their hometown, Emmaus. They said to a Stranger walking with them: "Are you the only one visiting Jerusalem who does not know the things that have happened there in these days? ... About Jesus of Nazareth, He was a prophet, powerful in word and deed before God and all the people. The chief priests and our rulers handed him over to be sentenced to death, and they crucified him; but we had hoped that he was the one who was going to redeem Israel" (Luke 24:18b-21a NIV).

The Luminary

Their answer describes the rather hopeless state of two friends walking home, their vision and dreams crushed. They were about to have a God encounter. But it took a while for the light to dawn. That the light did dawn is the most beautiful part of the story for all of us. But fascinating too is that it took a while for its truth to light upon them. Let's look at Luke 24 for what it might teach us.

I will take some liberties and assume that most of you have read or heard the story many times and have gleaned many of its insights. So I'll move quickly and trust your familiarity will help you appreciate these insights and apprehend them quickly. They speak to our day and age of doubt and skepticism. They speak to the need for revelation and illumination. It's a beautiful mystery that is more easily caught than taught, as this story illustrates. Let's dive in.

These two travelers are on the dark road of doubt. Are you in a dark place? Are you having a debate or an argument about your faith? Are you slow of heart to believe — foolish? Are you walking away from your faith? Do you think Jesus let you down? Jesus himself met these two on the road in this very situation.

Many of us ascribe to the saying, "Seeing is believing." But these guys have the resurrection staring them in the face, and they're not believing. Jesus starts to draw them into a conversation: "What are you talking about?" They answer him with their gloomy and doubting assessment that I recorded above. It's ironic that Cleopas speaking a bit rudely, says: "Are you the only one visiting Jerusalem who does not know the things that have happened there in these days?" (Luke 24:18). It's ironic because he's the one who isn't aware of what happened in Jerusalem during these days.

They had hoped for what they did not see. How can they reconcile this in their mind? They saw Jesus suffering and then dying. Our suffering can drive us to moments of doubt. Do you have your vision of a king? A savior? What will he look like? Obviously, this is not what they expected of Jesus.

But now we see the Stranger (Jesus) rebuke them a little bit: "'**How foolish you are, and how slow to believe all that the prophets have spoken! Did not the Messiah have to suffer these things and then enter his glory?' And beginning with Moses and all the Prophets, he explained to them what was said in all the Scriptures concerning himself** [emphasis added]" (Luke 24:25-27 NIV).

What about us?! They should know because of what He told them during 3 1/2 years together. They also knew the Scriptures they had pretty well. Then what about us? Indeed, we have more of the story, more evidence, and more proof to understand the happenings that day and believe Jesus and everything He told us. So we should quickly and easily move into His life by faith. Isn't this a reasonable expectation? Isn't this His expectation? You decide. But there are some tricky parts to the story we've not addressed yet.

Let's back up toward the beginning of the story: "As they talked and discussed these things with each other, Jesus himself came up and walked along with them; but **they were kept from recognizing him** [emphasis added]" (Luke 24:15). They were kept from recognizing him! What do we make of this, especially in light of the rest of the story? On the surface, it seems that it takes God's action for people to recognize Jesus, at least in part. Let's go on with the story, remembering they just received one last Bible lesson.

Breaking Bread

Will they get it? The suspense grows as they reach their home, and Jesus continues to travel onward: "As they approached the village to which they were going, Jesus continued as if he were going farther. But they urged him strongly, 'Stay with us, for it is nearly evening; the day is almost over.' So he went in to stay with them" (Luke 24:28-29).

Then what? They sat down to eat: "When he was at the table with them, **he took bread, gave thanks, broke it and began to give it to them. Then their eyes were opened and they recognized him** [emphasis added]" (Luke 24:30-31a). So it is; your eyes must be opened to see Him as He is. So it is, if He breaks the bread of revelation for you Himself, you know it. And you're never the same! You don't live by bread alone any longer, but by every word or revelation that proceeds from God.

It's fascinating what happened next: "and he disappeared from their sight" (Luke 24:31b). While He was with them, they didn't recognize Him. When they recognized Him, He vanished. Apparently, after you see the Son, from then on, you relate to Him mainly by His Spirit. It's not merely semantics, and it doesn't matter either. You know it's Him, and He can teach you how it works by walking, or by revelation from His Word, or revelation period. You've seen the resurrected Lord, and you can trust Him and live with Him in a new way on a new day. That's the Gospel, and that's a fact.

Burning Hearts

How do we know? Burning hearts demonstrated what they saw and experienced — the living, resurrected Lord. He disappeared from their sight in bodily form, and all of a sudden, they doubted no more and spoke of it: "They asked each other, 'Were not our hearts burning within us while he talked with us on the road and opened the Scriptures to us?'" (Luke 24:32).

Not only that, with their sorrow turned to joy, they hurried back into Jerusalem, but not in the same spirit they had departed. They were delighted with the new reality and couldn't wait to share it with their brothers. Travel wasn't that safe at night, and they didn't have street lights, but off they went on the seven-mile trek to tell their friends what they had seen, heard, and experienced with great joy. It couldn't wait!

Their actions are more evidence of their burning hearts: "They got up and returned at once to Jerusalem. There they found the Eleven and those with them, assembled together and saying, 'It is true! The Lord has risen and has appeared to Simon.' Then the two told what had happened on the way, and how Jesus was recognized by them when he broke the bread" (Luke 24:33-35).

What Happens Next

It gets better! And it's more of the same. Humans are sometimes dull, hard to convince, and slow to believe. The Lord Himself shows up immediately after these two tell their story to the disciples! You'd think this timing and this appearance would do a great deal for them and put all doubt aside about what had happened. Wouldn't you?

Let's take a glimpse: "While they were still talking about this, Jesus himself stood among them and said to them, '**Peace be with you.**' They were startled and frightened, thinking they saw a ghost. He said to them, '**Why are you troubled, and why do doubts rise in your minds? Look at my hands and my feet. It is I myself! Touch me and see; a ghost does not have flesh and bones, as you see I have.**' When he had said this, he showed them his hands and feet. And **while they still did not believe it because of joy and amazement**, he asked them, 'Do you have anything here to eat?' They gave him a piece of broiled fish, and he took it and ate it in their presence [emphasis added]" (Luke 24:36-43).

I'm sure Jesus enjoyed the fish and the beautiful reunion moment with His followers and friends, but He had to shake His head at their continuing disbelief! At first, they didn't believe because of fear and disillusionment. Now they don't believe because of joy and amazement!

I will choose to believe the best and step out on a limb a bit and say they couldn't be rational or use their hearts and minds to believe or process because of all the joy at His surprise visit. He was alive! With them! Just like before the crucifixion and burial. It was like being surprised by a dear old friend who's come knocking at your door late at night, and you say, "I can't believe it's you!" Or, "I can't believe you're standing here!" But multiply that feeling times a quad zillion. They had been separated by death!

That said, I still find this a bit puzzling and disconcerting. Maybe you can't process things with all that flood of emotion, but you still know Who is standing there, and it shouldn't take anything else to believe. Well, let's move on to what happens next. It does add a little bit of clarity.

Jesus went on: "He said to them, 'This is what I told you while I was still with you: Everything must be fulfilled that is written about me in the Law of Moses, the Prophets and the Psalms'" (Luke 24:44). This reminder was helpful and got them to piece the puzzles of Scripture together again with what they had just seen happen. But what happens next seems to be the rest of the story and the part we usually don't notice or understand.

What did Jesus do next: **"Then he opened their minds so they could understand the Scriptures** [emphasis added]" (Luke 24:45).

Is this the same as breaking bread for them and with them? Maybe so. At any rate, what they didn't believe before, they understood and believed now. Again, there appears to be an unseen God part in moving from doubt to belief. Because we have grown up in a secular, materialist culture and church many times, we have trouble with the unseen. But it's central to the Bible, and we must be schizophrenic not to realize it and function in that realm. Jesus told the woman at the well: "God is spirit, and those who worship Him must worship in spirit and truth" (John 4:24). And Jesus told Nicodemus in John chapter 3 that being born of the Spirit and operating in the Spirit is the key and secret (an open secret) to life in the Spirit and life in the Kingdom.

What A Day!

Jesus was now telling His disciples something for the last time. I think He had their attention: "He told them, '**This is what is written: The Messiah will suffer and rise from the dead on the third day, and repentance for the forgiveness of sins will be preached in his name to all nations, beginning at Jerusalem. You are witnesses of these things. I am going to send you what my Father has promised**; but **stay in the city until you have been clothed with power** from on high [emphasis added]'" (Luke 24:46-49).

So Jesus finished this welcome surprise and exhilarating visit with a charge and a promise to them. Wow! What a day! Easter, April 7, 33 AD! They know again they are accepted by God, their sins are forgiven, taken away by His sacrifice, and now they receive new directions and vision for the future — a future not devoid of Him. What could be better?! They could now sleep in peace! Or maybe they couldn't sleep at all? Because He told them He would do something else for them not many days from now.

Then He led them out to Bethany, a place they had often enjoyed with Him, blessed them, and left them — but not for long. He would come to them ten days later in a different way, on Pentecost.

Addendum

What we see in Emmaus that first Easter day is a picture of total transformation. Early on, the eyes of the two travelers were "kept from recognizing Him." Isn't this a big clue into how things work in the spiritual realm?

He had told them, and then told them again what He had told them, about going to Jerusalem to die and be raised the third day before it happened. The specifics of the details, and the number of times he told his disciples is mind-boggling. But they didn't get it.

The Scriptures and the Supper

In the end, what they saw in the Scriptures, and what they saw at the table when He broke the bread changed things for them. They saw it as it was, and is, and finally believed. The disciples came to faith in the whole narrative, and the One who lived and lives the narrative, Jesus Christ, the prophesied and now risen Lord, the Messiah, King of heaven and earth.

It was the Scriptures and the supper! It was the word of God given and preserved through the ages telling the true story of God and man. And it was the God of scripture, sitting down with them at the table, breaking the bread of life for them so they could and would understand. The somewhat mystical proposition apparently takes both activities. The faith, the love, the hope, apparently does not come without communion with the King, in person or by his Spirit.

Not Alone

Don't isolate yourself. Don't walk down the road of doubt alone. Be honest about your doubt and He will come to you.

Scripture, and the community of those who see Him, can help you work through your doubts and get you back to Jesus, and the Truth. You will experience communion, a life of communion, and the power and pleasure of prayer. Godspeed as you travel to your own Emmaus, by way of Jerusalem, and on your way home.

"He is not here, for He has risen, just as He said. Come, see the place where He was lying"

(Matthew 28:6).

PUZZLING CHAPTER 35

Fault Lines and Deception

SPEAKING OF DECEPTION VERSUS TRUTH, the title of Voddie Baucham's book on race and CRT, *Fault Lines,* is remarkable. It deserves a few remarks. Fault lines or faults in the earth's crust cause earthquakes, one of the most potent forces in nature. They usually are dormant, lying unnoticed for long periods, with people oblivious to them. Then what is not seen, known but ignored, explodes, resulting in death, destruction, and chaos. This analogy is telling and prophetic of our lives as we willingly dwell with these known lies, faults, or danger zones. We think they are not dangerous and that nothing will happen in our life — until it does. If we read and believed our Bibles, we would be aware.

Ask the business owners and residents of downtown Minneapolis, Portland, or Seattle if they now consider the delusion of Black Lives Matter or critical race theory harmless. They experienced blatant lawlessness and injustice in the (false) name of justice. If they have eyes to see, they would say "fault line or earthquake" isn't language too strong for what they experienced. But the chances are that most don't have eyes to see, and that's what got them there or caused them to stay, ignoring the warning signs of an active fault.

The name *Fault Lines* is significant because the seismic shift with resultant destruction comes from casting blame, finding fault, or accusing others of being at fault. I'm not sure if Baucham intended this, but it fits. All critical theories base themselves on criticizing and fault-finding and a blame game bent on dividing people groups for their purposes, usually to seize for themselves power or money.

If you believe the foundational lies and deception over time, you will reap what you sow and suffer the consequences of a shaky or fault-ridden foundation, with eventual destruction and loss. We can see where it led for the businesses, economy, homes, and governments – the loss of loveliness and desirability of these formerly beautiful cities. But did they see it coming? Did any of us? It happened all at once, unexpectedly, like an earthquake.

Fault Lines is a book, like this one, written primarily to Christians: individuals and families who believe the Bible is true, inspired, and given to humanity by God. We are people who believe Jesus is the Son of God, the prophesied Messiah King as foretold in the Hebrew Bible, the Christian Old Testament, and then as told by the Gospel writers and Apostles as His story unfolded in the New Testament. The Holy Spirit then came to birth and sustain the church of Jesus Christ miraculously and established Jesus' kingdom from His first appearing until the final consummation of his reign at His second appearing, which could occur any day now.

Could these fault lines appearing in cities and regions of our nation and culture also be found in our churches — the church of Jesus Christ in the United States of America? Voddie Baucham says "yes," and after reading the evidence in his book, I agree.

The Southern Baptist Convention is the largest protestant denomination in the United States and the last place I would suspect to see wokeness presented as compatible with the Bible. Baucham shows us it's there, with some leaders who embrace the deception and promote it as truth. It is, in fact, another gospel, and a much inferior one, as Baucham's book points out.

It's troubling that church people who reportedly or supposedly read their Bibles don't see this deception. Accurately, Voddie attributes this to "Biblical illiteracy." He should know because he's a pastor and has been one for decades. It's a likely answer to why many Christians fall for this flawed belief system founded on someone's imagination and proven lies.

Wokeness fails miserably if you hold it up to the Bible or the Gospel of Jesus Christ for comparison or a validity check. So it must be that people are not comparing CRT, BLM, etc., with the truth revealed in their Bible, or they don't know their Bible well enough to do so.

The fact that some Christian leaders espouse wokeness is far more telling and troubling! They have studied the Bible and personally have a relationship with Christ and are presumably led by his Spirit. So this suggests a much more severe problem and a clear and present danger for the sheep.

Deception and Delusion

Only a powerful deception or delusion can account for once-solid leaders being carried away into error. Wokeness is a severe error, seeing what these fault lines can produce.

Wokeness raises the question of who is deceived or deluded. That's a valid question. Could it be me? Could it be them? Could it be you? That's a question each of you has to answer for yourself. And we may be getting at the very crux and purpose of the virus pandemic and the race pandemic, as some have called it.

We are not in Kansas anymore, spiritually, culturally, individually, or as a church. It's as though we are waking from a bad dream, and everything good and stable, or so we thought, has changed. Is it possible God is rescuing us from a rut of self-confidence, lukewarm faith, materialism, secular humanism, Christian humanism — trust in ourselves to fulfill ourselves apart from God? Have we come to trust in our government and idols to provide for us, entertain us, and save us? Christian humanism should be an oxymoron, but sadly it is not. It's precisely why these things are happening.

We trust these idols to sustain us – something we've made with our own hands. At the same time, we ignore the God of creation, who created us and sustains us and all creation by the power of His word. He's the king of the universe, the king at Calvary, and the king of the Apocalypse. He's the one who rules in the affairs of men. He is merciful and just. He is putting some to sleep, it seems, and awakening others. It's getting interesting out there!

It's time to move. We must move away from fault lines and into the shadow of the Almighty. We must ask him for help, leading, and spiritual sight. Ask him for protection from the coming storms. Yes, but more so, ask him for grace for abundant living – to know and be filled with his Spirit for the days ahead, days He's planned for you. Ask Him to teach you and help you sail in the storms of this age. Please make sure you are one of His sheep. Then remember His words recorded in John for all people and all times: "My sheep hear My voice, and I know them, and they follow Me, and I give them eternal life" (John 10:27).

You should be in a flock (local church) with under-shepherds who hear God's voice, and you resonate with his voice. It's God's plan and directive. It's past time to move away from false and dead religion and fault lines into his marvelous light. The Spirit could lead you to stay where you are and be an agent for reformation and change. But don't stay just because you want to or are comfortable. Deception is real, dangerous, and rampant in the church and culture. This may call for a move – to get you out on the water, walking again by faith with the Faithful One you committed to at the beginning of your spiritual journey and adventure.

To be continued or connected to other pieces of the puzzle…

"My sheep hear My voice, and I know them, and they follow Me"

(John 10:27a).

"For this reason God will send upon them a deluding influence so that they will believe what is false"

(2 Thessalonians 2:11).

"For false Christs and false prophets will arise and will show great signs and wonders, so as to mislead, if possible, even the elect"

(Matthew 24:24).

"The idols of the nations are silver and gold, made by human hands. They have mouths, but cannot speak, eyes, but cannot see. They have ears, but cannot hear, nor is there breath in their mouths. Those who make them will be like them, and so will all who trust in them"

(Psalm 135:15-18).

"To the angel of the church in Laodicea write: "… But you do not realize that you are wretched, pitiful, poor, blind and naked. I counsel you to buy from me gold refined in the fire, so you can become rich; and white clothes to wear, so you can cover your shameful nakedness; and salve to put on your eyes, so you can see. Those whom I love I rebuke and discipline. So be earnest and repent"

(Revelation 3:14-19).

"But at the end of that period, I, Nebuchadnezzar, raised my eyes toward heaven and my reason returned to me, and I blessed the Most High and praised and honored Him who lives forever; for His dominion is an everlasting dominion, and His kingdom endures from generation to generation"

(Daniel 4:34).

PUZZLING CHAPTER 36

Spiritual Vision & Deception

I DEBATED ABOUT THE TITLE of this piece of the puzzle. It could be called *spiritual vision* and deception. It could be called *spiritual hearing* and deception. We primarily make our way in the natural world through and by these two senses. It's the same in the spiritual realm.

With our ears and hearts, we hear what to make of the things we see, beginning with our parents teaching us and guiding us from our earliest days. Listening and processing what we hear determines how we make our way, enjoying valuable and good things while avoiding obstacles or traps that might harm us. It is easy to see that it works this way with these two essential senses in the natural.

That brings up an interesting question. Which is more important, hearing or seeing? Considering how we start, as infants and toddlers, I think you might say hearing. Seeing is more stimulating with its lights, shadows, colors, and movement. Maybe we value it a little more because of its pop, dazzle, and ease of processing. The things we see seem more concrete, objective, and straightforward than what we hear.

This is certainly true as we mature and learn the significant differences between the things that are helpful and harmful.

We march into maturity to explore creation and the world around us on our own, hearing now from peers, bosses, cultures, churches, companies, and the media how to interpret what we see with our eyes. We're not threatened as much by what we see as in the days of our early youth, but we still sense some paths are better than others. Some courses of action in dealing with inanimate objects, and animate ones, are better than others. We must make our way. To whom do you listen to make sense of what you see? Yourself? Others? Which others? God? You must decide because you don't live in a static world. It's the natural order of things and the creation into which we are born. It's our personal journey. We base our actions on what we hear and see. Those actions determine the joy or sorrow we experience along the way.

Wrestling with those thoughts now, I conclude that hearing may be the most important. Indeed it is early in life. And it is in the last chapters of life. But the middle chapters are no less critical and, in many ways, determine the joy or pain of the later chapters of life — really all along the way.

The Hearing Ear and Seeing Eye

A couple of Scriptures come to mind: "The hearing ear and the seeing eye, the Lord has made both of them" (Proverbs 20:12). The second has puzzled me for years, yet I accept it as accurate, like all of Scripture: "However, the spiritual is not first, but the natural; then the spiritual" (1 Corinthians 15:46).

Doesn't that seem like it should be the other way around? After all: "The Spirit gives life; the flesh counts for nothing" (John 6:63a). In introducing this subject above, we started as toddlers, hearing and seeing and making sense of the world. So in that sense, "the natural first, then the spiritual," does make perfect sense. We're born in the natural first. Then if we choose, we're born in the Spirit and start to appraise all things spiritually, with eyes that see and ears that hear. Note Jesus' discussion with Nicodemus recorded in John chapter 3.

Also, note this Scripture: "But a natural man does not accept the things of the Spirit of God, for they are foolishness to him; and he cannot understand them, because they are spiritually appraised. But he who is spiritual appraises all things, yet he himself is appraised by no one. For who has known the mind of the Lord, that he will instruct Him? But we have the mind of Christ" (1 Corinthians 2:14-16). God gives spiritual hearing and seeing, which is hearing and seeing indeed — things as they really are. Spiritual seeing and hearing are a gift, a reality, and a necessity for life in our dark days. They are also requirements for living life with God, which is life indeed.

I ran across this insightful quote while researching "natural first" on the web: "What is this idea of first the natural, then the spiritual? To understand this fully, I believe we must view it prophetically. The Bible says God's people are to be prophetic. That is, since we have the Holy Spirit living on the inside of us, we have the ability to look at events and know from these events signs of things to come. The Bible says, however, that we know in part and we prophesy in part. That is, no one person has all the answers; if we did, we would be like God. So it takes all of the body of Christ with its different gifts to help discern what God is saying to us" (The Rev. Mike Taylor, Baltimore Sun, 2014). This quote gives the same gist with a slightly different slant to the issue of seeing and hearing in the spiritual realm, the natural first, with some hints about how and why we hear.

Deceived in Hearing and Seeing

Seeing isn't as simple as our brains assume. There are two competing voices ready to help us understand what we see — one true and one a lie.

We probably take seeing and hearing for granted because they've been with us and our reality since our earliest days. Our eyes are still better than the best camera, and science points to them as one of the most amazing mechanisms in nature. Our brains are better at processing and storing information than the fastest computers. That both eyes and brains (ears and hearts) work so well in helping us determine reality is a fantastic miracle if you think about it. The complexity of how they work boggles the mind if you look into it. But we don't — we simply focus these extraordinary powers in search of truth, meaning, and reality. We want to do so, we seemingly must continually, we're wired that way.

This natural phenomenon carries over into the spiritual realm. Spiritual hearing and seeing connect, and we're usually unaware if we have not been born a second time by the Spirit. The Bible tells us that the spiritual realm is more real, lasting, and meaningful than the natural realm. So it follows that seeing and hearing in the spiritual realm is more important than with our natural ears and eyes.

The point in the comparison is that seeing in the spirit may not be as straightforward as it appears on the surface, even though we do see and hear and are used to it if born of the Spirit. If you think this is completely straightforward, let me give you a bizarre case of spiritual sight and blindness in the Bible. The instance involves prophets, people gifted and called to hear in the spiritual realm. And it involves lies and deception.

The reason for pointing this out is not to confuse you or confuse the matter. But it demonstrates that hearing in the spiritual realm is real and really important. It's also something that cannot be tied up nicely with a bow by any denomination or theology. It is tied to a relationship with the Creator and how well you know Him. Let's look.

We typically fear what we don't understand or can't be explained or has resulted in harm to humankind on occasion. Learning to hear in the spirit and to practice the same can be compared to lightning. We don't understand lightning. We observe it in awe and know its mysterious power is helpful to our atmosphere but devastatingly harmful if not respected, with precautions taken when it comes near. Similarly, hearing and seeing in the spirit shouldn't be and can't be totally avoided, just respected. The more you know about it, the less likely you will suffer harm, injury, or death.

It's a normal part of life. Observe the mystery, trust God for your safety, and avoid deception while embracing the truth. We have instructions and clues in the Bible for how to do this.

Young Prophet — Old Prophet

In my second book, *God Came Near*, I share the story of being fired from a job where I was doing well and prospering by every typical metric. During that event, I felt the Spirit say something that wasn't my thought, "Your family has been under a spiritual attack, and you didn't even know it or see it coming." The inference was the Lord was about to show me something about spiritual warfare — lies, and deception. I call it "Lies and Deception Training 101" or "The Story of Two Prophets." It's recorded in 1 Kings 13.

The story is of a young prophet and an old prophet from two different but related kingdoms. One would think that two of God's prophets would hear the same thing from God, wouldn't you? They did, to a point, and then they didn't. It cost the younger, seemingly more noble prophet his life. Let's look at the story briefly for what we can learn about hearing God and the reality of a lightning strike or a lion attack ending a life. "Be of sober spirit, be on the alert. Your adversary, the devil, prowls around like a roaring lion, seeking someone to devour" (1 Peter 5:8).

The Young Prophet

One cannot tell this story more succinctly than the Bible does for its truth and profundity, so here it is:

> "At the Lord's command, a man of God from Judah went to Bethel, arriving there just as Jeroboam [the king] was approaching the altar to burn incense. Then at the Lord's command, he shouted, 'O altar, altar! This is what the Lord says: A child named Josiah will be born into the dynasty of David. On you he will sacrifice the priests from the pagan shrines who come here to burn incense, and human bones will be burned on you.' That same day the man of God gave a sign to prove his message. He said, 'The Lord has promised to give this sign: This altar will split apart, and its ashes will be poured out on the ground.'
>
> When King Jeroboam heard the man of God speaking against the altar at Bethel, he pointed at him and shouted, 'Seize that man!' But instantly the king's hand became paralyzed in that position, and he couldn't pull it back. At the same time a wide crack appeared in the altar, and the ashes poured out, just as the man of God had predicted in his message from the Lord.
>
> The king cried out to the man of God, 'Please ask the Lord your God to restore my hand again!' So the man of God prayed to the Lord, and the king's hand was restored and he could move it again.
>
> Then the king said to the man of God, 'Come to the palace with me and have something to eat, and I will give you a gift.'
>
> But the man of God said to the king, 'Even if you gave me half of everything you own, I would not go with you. I would not eat or drink anything in this place. For the Lord gave me this command: 'You must not eat or drink anything while you are there, and do not return to Judah by the same way you

came.' So he left Bethel and went home another way"
(1Kings 13:1-10 NLT).

So far, so good. Now for the rest of the enigmatic, insightful story.

The Old Prophet

"As it happened, there was an old prophet living in Bethel, and his sons came home and told him what the man of God had done in Bethel that day. They also told their father what the man had said to the king. The old prophet asked them, 'Which way did he go?' So they showed their father which road the man of God had taken. 'Quick, saddle the donkey,' the old man said. So they saddled the donkey for him, and he mounted it.

Then he rode after the man of God and found him sitting under a great tree. The old prophet asked him, 'Are you the man of God who came from Judah?'

'Yes, I am,' he replied.

Then he said to the man of God, 'Come home with me and eat some food.'

'No, I cannot,' he replied. 'I am not allowed to eat or drink anything here in this place. For the Lord gave me this command: 'You must not eat or drink anything while you are there, and do not return to Judah by the same way you came.'

But the old prophet answered, 'I am a prophet, too, just as you are. And an angel gave me this command from the Lord: 'Bring him home with you so he can have something to eat and drink.' But the old man was lying to him. So they went back together, and the man of God ate and drank at the prophet's home.

Then while they were sitting at the table, a command from the Lord came to the old prophet. He cried out to the man of God from Judah, 'This is what the Lord says: You have defied the word of the Lord and have disobeyed the command the Lord your God gave you. You came back to this place and ate and drank where he told you not to eat or drink. Because of this, your body will not be buried in the grave of your ancestors.'

After the man of God had finished eating and drinking, the old prophet saddled his own donkey for him, and the man of God started off again. But as he was traveling along, a lion came out and killed him. His body lay there on the road, with the donkey and the lion standing beside it. People who passed by saw the body lying in the road and the lion standing beside it, and they went and reported it in Bethel, where the old prophet lived.

When the prophet heard the report, he said, 'It is the man of God who disobeyed the Lord's command. The Lord has fulfilled his word by causing the lion to attack and kill him.'

Then the prophet said to his sons, 'Saddle a donkey for me.' So they saddled a donkey, and he went out and found the body lying in the road. The donkey and lion were still standing there beside it, for the lion had not eaten the body nor attacked the donkey. So the prophet laid the body of the man of God on the donkey and took it back to the town to mourn over him and bury him. He laid the body in his own grave, crying out in grief, 'Oh, my brother!'

Afterward the prophet said to his sons, 'When I die, bury me in the grave where the man of God is buried. Lay my bones beside his bones. For the message the Lord told him to proclaim against the altar in Bethel and against the pagan shrines in the towns of Samaria will certainly come true'" (1 Kings 13:11-32 NLT).

WOW?

Where do you start? How can this be understood? Only in the light of the whole counsel of Scripture, for one thing. And realizing God included it in the Bible for a reason, for our benefit.

This story provides deep insight into the nature of life on the planet for humans as we relate to God and dark or lying spirits. This is not pasted this clearly on every page of the Bible, but it's there, concisely and consistently. So what are our immediate takeaways about spiritual hearing?

Here are some of mine. You may have received your own as you read the story or now after meditating on it. Let's not forget the context. These men are prophets of God with a different calling and level of experience than most of us. Yet hearing from the spiritual realm is common to all of us, and we can learn some valuable lessons from what happened. Even if we can't distinguish spiritual voices always from our thoughts, we do hear and must decide what we will do.

Well, it's safe to say that the young prophet was clear on what he heard because he repeated it several times to the king and then to the old prophet. He intended to obey entirely and did a pretty good job, even being enticed by the king to do otherwise. It's also noteworthy that God confirmed the young prophet's spiritual authority and mission by the miracle of splitting the altar at his command and healing the king's arm and hand when he prayed.

So when did things go wrong? When another prophet, whom God and the people recognized, told him something contrary or slightly different from what he had heard initially from God. Does this story sound a little familiar, like the Balaam story or Moses striking the rock? Anyway, some say, "It takes one to know one." This young prophet recognized the person and gifting of the old prophet standing before him. But then the old prophet lied to him! It seems unthinkable, but the way the story reads, it looks intentional. Maybe the older prophet, living among the idolatry of the northern kingdom, had lost some of his fear of God or actual knowledge of the Holy? Perhaps he thought it would be okay and not that harmful. He just wanted to spend time with a young, fiery prophet who heard and valued the word of the LORD and whose obedience brought God's hand to bear, even on the king.

Whatever his motive, lying was wrong. It was a boundary he should have known, and no doubt formerly did know, but crossed. Now God moved on him to prophesy to the young prophet that his end was near for not obeying what he heard from God and that he wouldn't be buried with his family in his native land. This prophecy is the most shocking moment in the story and the most insightful. Two prophets realize the preciousness of hearing from God and the high cost of disobedience to what's heard. The lie of the old prophet becomes known, but too late for the young prophet.

On his way back to his land after his last supper, unknown perhaps to him, a lion meets him on the road and kills him. People walk by and see a strange sight. A donkey and a lion are resting beside a dead man, killed by the lion but not eaten or mauled and not threatening for some supernatural reason to the donkey. The people report it in the city. The old prophet hears and orders his sons to bury the young prophet in his tomb and to bury him there when he dies. God honored the young prophet, really, in the way God called him home. And the old prophet honored the young prophet and his memory as the LORD's anointed.

We all learn that it's important to hear clearly in the spiritual realm. It's a matter of life and death. We understand deception is at work there, even among God's people — beware. If God speaks something clearly to you, don't expect He will change His mind. Be suspicious of anyone who says He has, especially someone spiritual. The young prophet was more susceptible to deceit from the old prophet than the wealth and power of the king. In this context, let's remember the verse: "No wonder, for even Satan disguises himself as an angel of light" (2 Corinthians 11:14). Yet we are to trust God. He is so much greater, compassionate, and rich in mercy. But we must honor Him with obedience, remembering partial obedience is disobedience. We must be even more careful to do so; the better we get to know Him. He is Holy. Obedience is a boundary, as well as a path to power.

Chaucer said: "Familiarity breeds contempt." It's a seven hundred-year-old adage implying that extensive knowledge of or close association with someone leads to a loss of respect for them. Of course, this must never happen with God because He can never be fully known in this realm, and there is nothing to disrespect about Him. That delusion, if that should happen, might be the beginning of evil and trouble for you. "The fear of the LORD is the beginning of wisdom; a good understanding have all those who do His commandments" (Psalm 111:10).

This story is for old prophets in our realm as a warning, as well as instruction for young prophets in our day. This story speaks to all those becoming aware of hearing spiritually and those who aspire to do so. Hearing from God is rewarding, and it is risky. Faith involves risk. Just remain aware that deceit is lurking, then go boldly in faith and friendship with the Holy. It's the adventure of adventures! It's normal Christianity.

What Happened to the King and the Kingdom?

This question or part of the story is not germane to our purpose of learning about spiritual hearing and the roles lying and deception play in the process. But it's very brief and pertinent to lies and deception and what happens to kings, kingdoms, and cultures who refuse to listen to what God says through His prophets. So I include it here; as Paul Harvey used to say: "Now for the rest of the story":

> *"But even after this, Jeroboam did not turn from his evil ways. He continued to choose priests from the common people. He appointed anyone who wanted to become a priest for the pagan shrines. This became a great sin and resulted in the utter destruction of Jeroboam's dynasty from the face of the earth"*
> (1 Kings 13: 33-34 NLT).

Delusion! These bad things happened to the king after the altar split before him; God paralyzed his hand, and then healed his hand as the prophet prayed. He was deluded and delusional. The deception cost him his life and kingdom.

Old Testament or New Testament

"Well, that was the Old Testament," some will say. It seems to come up from time to time in religious circles. But in reality, it's One Testament. It's the same God relating to people during their various times in human history. And it seems that as we go, He is revealing more of Himself and His activities in history, moving toward some preplanned conclusion — the return of the King.

In discussing religious deception, consider that Paul was writing several centuries later in the first century, about the same topic — lies, and deception. He wrote to the church in Corinth that deceivers were present. He described them as religious and spelled out some of their deceitful tactics.

His principal counsel was for the church to be aware, to focus on the simplicity of the Gospel of Jesus, and judge these false ones by the fruit in their lives. He writes: "But I am afraid that, as the serpent deceived Eve by his craftiness, your minds will be led astray from the simplicity and purity of devotion to Christ" (2 Corinthians 11:3).

Then Paul says: "For such men are false apostles, deceitful workers, disguising themselves as apostles of Christ. No wonder, for even Satan disguises himself as an angel of light. Therefore it is not surprising if his servants also disguise themselves as servants of righteousness, whose end will be according to their deeds" (2 Corinthians 11:12-14).

"The more things change, the more they remain the same"
(Jean-Baptiste Alphonse Karr).

PUZZLING CHAPTER 37

Hopenots and the Song of the King

WE ENJOYED A SIBLINGS' WEEKEND at the mountain cabin a few weeks ago, and my sister told me about a delightful, insightful, and charming book by Max Lucado *The Song of the King*. It's a favorite of her granddaughters, and she reads it to them often. It's short, beautifully illustrated, and full of hidden truth and deep insights for adults too.

I awakened this morning thinking about the "Hopenots." They are "small, sly creatures with yellow eyes." Perhaps they were fellow travelers who lost their way in the dark forest. Now they choose to live there without hope, singing their deceitful, menacing songs, trying to allure other travelers to their hopeless lifestyle away from the King and toward their delusion and destruction.

Some analogies you can draw immediately. The Hopenots are trying to replicate the song of the King to confuse and draw many away to their death in the darkness of idols, idol worship, sports, entertainment, immoral sex, false religion, secular humanist government, apostasy, rebellion, lawlessness, money, greed, and power. The media of our day promotes, spreads, and empowers the deceiving spirits of the Hopenots in our age. All the while, the King plays his beautiful song several times a day from the castle walls. All who know the music, and have the right guide, find their way through the dark forest to the safety of the King.

As one of my favorite pastors, Bill Bennett Ph.D., said in the 1980s, "It's growing gloriously dark." Forty years later, if you look at the media and the world around us (as portrayed by the media) compared to the moral standard of the Bible, it seems to be midnight. And the darkness is increasingly made worse by thick clouds, dust, haze, and the smoke of the battlefield.

It's the absence of God's grace — the light of God's countenance and His presence shining upon our world and in our hearts that makes it so dark. Darkness is defined as the absence of light, and so it is.

Darkness, the absence of light, can be national, cultural, or personal. We are talking about spiritual light here — truth. Vision is seeing things as God sees them, which is how they really are.

The darkness makes us stumble over things, bump into things, or even walk over a cliff. Sight is life in a genuine sense. It preserves living and adds quality to life.

Choose to walk in the light, seek the light, and live in the light. You can then make your path straight and help others do the same.

Personal spiritual darkness is like blindness in the natural. If faced with the choice to keep only one of my five senses, perish the thought, I would choose sight. The world would not be nearly as alive to me as it now is without taste, touch, hearing, and smell. But I could make my way through it without running into things, tripping over things, and falling over cliffs or off of buildings.

Even in a silent, odorless, tasteless, and unfeeling world, left only with sight and my thoughts, I could observe the movement of the spheres. I could see birds, animals, leaves, and the hues of sunsets and sunrises on the rest of creation. I could gaze at the azure blue of the sky, the aqua green of limestone lakes and streams, the myriad of colors in flowers, plants, and animal's fur, skins, and wings — the beauty of sight is enough to make the soul sing.

Spiritual sight is that and more. It opens up the earth, its fabulous beauty to explore, with eyes to see what science sees, then additional, breathtaking beauty galore. It transports the soul on endless flights in the light of high noon or the darkness of night. The other senses pale, as a soul alive to God senses His approach or where His feet have passed. The nearness of the Creator, His creatures discover anew, beautiful and refreshing like the sun-lit dew. Full of promise, hope, and love — things the five senses only dimly apprehend shine brightly from above. Spiritual eyes only can see the Father, Son, and Spirit — these Three. It is mystical, magical, a gift from God's Son. He paid the price to make it so, then asked His Father to send us His Spirit to help us know, grow, and glow with the likeness of Him — so we are full of light and seldom dim.

So how about light? And how about sight? How about darkness? How about the night? If you are desperate to see and want light more, tell Jesus what you want, then see what's in store.

A blind guy named Bartimaeus, who lived in a low and lonely place called Jericho, one day heard that Jesus of Nazareth was passing his way. He cried out in desperation with what faith he had. Jesus heard above the din and made his way in front of him. "What do you want me to do for you?" was the simple question asked. "I want to see," was Bart's reply, and his sight returned fast.

Jesus is still in that business, yesterday and today. It only takes the faith to ask, and the confidence to pray.

There's some desperation as you sense your plight. Your soul says, "I have no spiritual vision. I'm walking blindly at night." But even now, you feel the Son of David is near. Say your prayer, or shout your plea, and Jesus will give ear.

Which is more important, natural vision or spiritual vision? I wonder what Hellen Keller would say? Or Joni Eareckson Tada? Or any number of people with some natural, sensual disability but with keen spiritual sight? "Life is a daring adventure or nothing at all," is my favorite Hellen Keller quote.

It's time to do everything you can to get your spiritual vision restored and operating as intended. It's foundational for relationships and getting along in life. As the days grow colder and darker, you will need it to stand. And to navigate the battlefield that's coming upon the land.

Einstein said: "Adversity introduces a man to himself." Spiritual vision is a part of that same puzzle—Godspeed as you journey.

"Then Jesus again spoke to them, saying, 'I am the Light of the world; he who follows Me will not walk in the darkness, but will have the Light of life'"

(John 8:12).

"The people who walk in darkness will see a great light; those who live in a dark land, the light will shine on them"

(Isaiah 9:2).

"This is the judgment, that the Light has come into the world, and men loved the darkness rather than the Light, for their deeds were evil"

(John 3:19).

"For even though they knew God, they did not honor Him as God or give thanks, but they became futile in their speculations, and their foolish heart was darkened"

(Romans 1:21).

"God saw that the light was good; and God separated the light from the darkness"

(Genesis 1:4).

"They did not see one another, nor did anyone rise from his place for three days, but all the sons of Israel had light in their dwellings"

(Exodus 10:23).

"Your word is a lamp to my feet And a light to my path"

(Psalm 119:105).

"'What do you want Me to do for you?' And he said, 'Lord, I want to regain my sight!' And Jesus said to him, 'Receive your sight; your faith has made you well'"

(Luke 18:41-42).

"So we have the prophetic word made more sure, to which you do well to pay attention as to a lamp shining in a dark place, until the day dawns and the morning star arises in your hearts"

(2 Peter 1:19).

PUZZLING CHAPTER 38

The Man of God

I ATTENDED A MEN'S MEETING at our new church Saturday at 7:00 a.m. I wasn't sure what to expect, but the excitement of our new church and getting to know men whose hearts pant after God was enough to keep me from going to the cabin as usual and get up early on a Saturday morning.

There were twenty to thirty men in attendance. Most were in their 20s, 30s, or 40s, but there were also a few guys with gray hair like me in their 60s. To my surprise, Clark, a friend of mine who has attended our church for only a short time, was the speaker.

The leader of the men's group introduced him, saying the church hadn't had many gray-haired guys around until recently and our coming to join them was a welcome development. They wanted to learn from us and hear what wisdom we might impart to them as they raised their families, navigated their careers, and made sense of a world more and more upside down. After these remarks, the leader said, "Clark, we want to hear your story, and what you would say to us. Then in the coming weeks we'll hear from others."

On the flip side of the coin, the older guys joining this younger group of men delight in finding young men with this attitude, a love of the Bible, and devotion to Jesus. We are only too happy to support these younger, humble, serious believers and contribute what we can.

Clark was up, and we weren't prepared for what happened next. He recounted his early life, with his father dying in a horrific oil field explosion when he was young, then life with his second dad and the father wounds he experienced from both. Thankfully his mom was a saint, making sure her fatherless boys were churched. She eventually remarried, and Clark became close to his second dad, although he wasn't very spiritual on the surface. He appreciated the good things this "Uncle Daddy" sowed into his life.

Do the Right Thing

He recounted his uncle daddy took him and his two brothers fishing on the Mississippi in August of 2000. "It was work and extremely hot and dangerous. We never fished again like that again." He rode back with his Uncle Daddy and got the best advice ever. Clark said: "He never quoted or used the Bible as a reference, but after sharing my struggles with my wife being an alcoholic he said, 'Do the right thing.' I stayed in the battle the next fourteen years, until I found one morning that she had passed in her sleep."

After some healing time, Clark was ready to entertain the idea of marriage again and called a lady who a friend recommended he get to know. Their first date was a meeting on the town square under Christmas lights, and a year later, they were married at the same spot. That was about seven years ago. He delightfully shared how beautiful this woman is and the immense joy of being married to a charming, caring, loving woman and some humorous and captivating stories about their courtship and lives together.

More Drama and Trauma

Heart attack! Three heart attacks! Life can be hard and rewarding — bitter and sweet. Sometimes it's close together that these circumstances meet. Clark told us he worked for thirty-plus years for a large food company as an outside salesman, which he described as: "The easiest job in the world — people love to eat." One day at his office, he experienced a widow-maker heart attack, which only 5% of people survive. A woman coworker in the next cubical realized the gravity of the situation and got him on a service elevator to the first floor to meet the ambulance in an instance where every second counts. They shocked him so many times in the ER that he had burns on his back, but his heart started again, and he awakened with a beating heart aided by four new stints.

It was hard to imagine that this handsome, sixty-five-year young, gray-headed, blue-eyed, muscular man had experienced even one heart attack. He won his state's decathlon in high school forty-seven years ago. He then competed at a high level in track and field for the University of Arkansas, the most decorated NCAA program in the nation. To top it all off, he took a stress test at a local hospital a short time before, and they gave him a clean bill of heart health. It was even harder to imagine that this heart attack was the first of three!

He told us, all very sober and intently listening now, that there were no bright lights for him. Death was just like being unplugged. He just felt the life go out of him. He related that the hospital cardiac staff knew him well after the first attack and started calling him "Superman" because his name was Clark, and he had survived these normally-fatal heart attacks. They worked on him for forty-five minutes during his last heart attack, with him flatlining multiple times. A muscular male nurse came to work the next day, incredulous that Clark had survived the night, then walked over to his wife to apologize for breaking all his ribs. Subsequent x-rays showed his ribs to be unbroken and fine?! The attending physician told Clark later that he had screamed into his ear, "Come on, Clark, dammit, you can do this!" Clark had no recollection of it, but his heart started beating again and hasn't stopped since.

He awakened a bit dazed and confused in a hospital room with his wife staring at him. Also staring at him were John McDonnell and his wife. John was Clark's coach and the most successful coach in NCAA history. This was a moment between a legendary coach and one of his athletes —both with courage and heart. It takes one to know one.

Life not Death

But this is a story about life, not death like any worthwhile story is — even if it ends in death. And they all do. But the guy standing before us was exhorting men of all ages in front of him to "be men." It was starting to dawn upon us that he was a man among boys. But he was so humble it didn't seem like that nor matter much. He was a father, a husband, a coach, and a brother — a humble man, just encouraging men to be men. When men see real courage, something inside of us rises to meet it, and the journey to manhood begins again or is renewed with purpose. Hearing about sacrifice and witnessing true humility have a similar effect.

I think all the men there would agree it was a sacred moment — men relating to another man and in a tangible way to their creator, God.

In my continuing world of synchronicities with God coming near, I received a text from one of my best friends while writing this. We text each other our weights most days, trying to get to and stay at our goals and encourage each other to stay healthy and fit to enjoy and finish our races. He texted, "Nice rebound from last week. It's an endurance race."

I thought to myself, "That's Clark." He's broken many tapes in his day, but he's still running toward the essential tape with joy and purpose. And training between races — staying in the Word, in church, in community, in prayer, in serving, in leading — staying spiritually fit and healthy.

I told my texting friend I was writing about Clark and asked if he knew him well. He replied: "I've gotten to know him a bit in our Revelation Bible study and at a track and field meet where I talked to him and his grandson. First comes self-control, and [it] grows to perseverance — 2 Peter 1:6."

2 Peter 1:6 in context says: "Now for this very reason also, applying all diligence, in your faith supply moral excellence, and in your moral excellence, **knowledge, and in your knowledge, self-control, and in your self-control, perseverance, and in your perseverance, godliness**, and in your godliness, brotherly kindness, and in your brotherly kindness, love. For if these qualities are yours and are increasing, they render you neither useless nor unfruitful in the true knowledge of our Lord Jesus Christ [emphasis added]" (2 Peter 1:5-8).

Summation

"**Self-control, perseverance, and godliness**" is a good summation of Clark's talk and appeal to us men. I'll add a few of his quips, but it seems like the man standing before us was the message — distilled character with a "true knowledge of our Lord Jesus Christ." Clark is still running for an audience of One, Who finished His race so that we can run toward something that matters and helps us daily by His Spirit to do so.

Be that man. Get to know a man like that. Spend time with men like that.

This is the heart of the message of my first book, *A Friend of the King: David and His Mighty Men*. Clark is to me a picture of that man and that message. I sat amazed, humbled, and inspired to listen and looked about the room at the entranced faces of young men, eager to hear and walk in truth with the same courage and vision. I could only offer a silent, humble prayer of thanksgiving to God in my heart for hearing these truths and being with men who value them.

Clark's Quips

He started his talk by reading Psalm 119:9-12. He repeated: "I have hidden Your Word in my heart.... Lord, teach me your commandments." Then he went on to say we've not done this as men, and: "That is why I see our country blown up in so many ways. Dad's are not standing up, but rather interested in so many [other] things."

He said the Psalms had been life and salvation to him throughout his life and these times and mentioned quickly from memory Psalm 36, 42, and 51. He said: "We fall. Then we get back up."

He said we're made to be loved. Women are responders. They also help open up our hearts to life, beauty, relationship, and the glory of creation.

He recounted an important summer in 1972 when he spent the summer in Puerto Rico on an air force base where his LTC uncle was stationed. It was "a time when [Clark] started waking up spiritually." I will add we never know what generosity and hospitality might do for someone. Practice it. We do know from Scripture: "For the eyes of the Lord move to and fro throughout the earth that He may strongly support those whose heart is completely His" (2 Chronicles 16:9a).

He paused at one point and said, "The world is changing so fast." Then he said, "There are enemies within the church. There are woke churches!? If I'm stepping on your toes, good!"

He mentioned Psalm 1 and quoted a portion of it. Then he said, "When I came to Harvest Church, I heard Ben Wilson [the new pastor] say, 'My job is to teach men and women to obsess over the Word of God.'"

He mentioned that he recently read that the first class in The Master's Seminary in Sun Valley, California, teaches husbands how to love their wives. I would say that's insightful and so important for the road ahead, whether you're a theologian, pastor, or layperson. It's the road the Spirit calls us to in Ephesians: "Husbands, love your wives, just as Christ also loved the church and gave Himself up for her" (Ephesians 5:25).

Then he told a story about coming home late one night to a dark house with his two little boys in trail behind him. He had just stepped in the door when he received a sharp blow across his face! He crouched instinctively to a self-defense position, awaiting another blow to defend himself, and shouted to his little boys to alert them: "There's somebody in the house, boys!" After waiting a few moments, which seemed like hours, hearing only their loud breathing and nothing else, he ventured forward cautiously a few feet and turned on a light. It turns out he had stepped on a mop in the dark, which flew up and hit him in the face!

The moral of that story, he told the guys, is: "Out of the dark might come more than a mop! Get ready to protect your families."

In the end, he said the Scriptures tell us: "Be on the alert, **stand firm in the faith, act like men,** be strong [emphasis added]" (1 Corinthians 16:13). He said it in a way we all heard, understood, and wanted to do it — to be men like that.

If you meet him, he sometimes introduces himself: "Hi, I'm Clark Morman, with an 'a' — present-day saint." And he is. He needs little or no introduction. His big smile and infectious love will make itself known to you within minutes of an encounter.

I was with him and six other brothers an hour ago, where he's started leading the genesis of a men's weekly prayer group in the new church we joined only months ago. He's also a character coach for the Fellowship of Christian Athletes in local high schools, where he can love on the kids and encourage them in track, in their faith, and in life.

God has undoubtedly given Clark a new life and a new heart. And isn't that the story of us all? "For of His fullness we have all received, and grace upon grace" (John 1:16). Men, rise up and let's continually do something with our lives and hearts. The gift may be in its giving.

The End

Clark ended his talk by reading Psalm 1, and 2 Timothy 3:14-17. "How blessed is the man who does not walk in the counsel of the wicked, nor stand in the path of sinners, nor sit in the seat of scoffers! But **his delight is in the law of the Lord, and in His law he meditates day and night. He will be like a tree firmly planted by streams of water**, which yields its fruit in its season and its leaf does not wither; and in whatever he does, he prospers.

The wicked are not so, but they are like chaff which the wind drives away. Therefore the wicked will not stand in the judgment, nor sinners in the assembly of the righteous. For the Lord knows the way of the righteous, but the way of the wicked will perish [emphasis added]" (Psalm 1).

"You, however, **continue in the things you have learned and become convinced of**, knowing from whom you have learned them, and that from childhood **you have known the sacred writings which are able to give you the wisdom that leads to salvation through faith which is in Christ Jesus.** All **Scripture is inspired by God and profitable** for teaching, for reproof, for correction, for training in righteousness; **so that <u>the man of God</u>** may be adequate, equipped for every good work [emphasis added]" (2 Timothy 3:14-17).

"Moreover, **I will give you a new heart and put a new spirit within you**; and I will remove the heart of stone from your flesh and **give you a heart of flesh. I will put My Spirit within you** and cause you to walk in My statutes, and you will be careful to observe My ordinances [emphasis added]"

(Ezekiel 36:26-27).

"Then **I will make up to you for the years that the swarming locust has eaten,** the creeping locust, the stripping locust and the gnawing locust, My great army which I sent among you. **You will have plenty to eat and be satisfied and praise the name of the Lord your God, Who has dealt wondrously with you; then My people will never be put to shame.** Thus you will know that I am in the midst of Israel, **and that I am the Lord your God, and there is no other; and My people will never be put to shame** [emphasis added]"

(Joel 2:25-32).

PUZZLING CHAPTER 39

The Church

THREE YEARS AGO, MY WIFE and I moved an hour north of where we had lived for almost forty years. Our reasons were different, but we sensed the Spirit leading us to move. For me, it was to get out of a spiritual rut. Despite an active, faith-filled, vibrant past, our church of thirty-plus years had come to look very much like the culture. I longed for brothers and sisters, a community that wanted to go on with the Lord, called out upon the water "where feet may fail," as the song "Oceans" expresses so very well. Billboard ranked it as the No. 1 Christian song of the 2010's decade. Oceans was the No. 1 song in 2014 and 2016, No. 2 in 2015, and No. 10 in 2017. Was God calling you out on the water during those years and speaking to you about a new church? Or about the church in general in the USA?

"Don't Be Surprised"

As we found a new home, settled in, and wondered what this new chapter of our lives might look like, a good brother from our former church said something strange and out of character to me: "Don't be surprised if this chapter of your church life doesn't look like previous chapters." We both sensed it was a word from the Lord, but neither of us knew more than that.

We knew the value of community and attended church weekly to sense the Lord's leading on where He might plant us in a community. We mostly attended the two megachurches in our area because of their reputations. We had friends attending each. One was better known for missions. The other was well known for discipleship. Both were collegian churches. There was a fear of the Lord and solid Bible teaching in each place which we had found missing at our previous church as it experienced a slow fade during recent years. But neither of these large churches seemed right for us.

CR, The Journey, Nehemiah, & 2020

Soon the coronavirus would infect and affect the world and the church in predictable and mysterious ways. We'll get to that. But before and during that time, I found myself led to four different men's groups. Yes, they qualify as a Christian community but are specific to men and not churches.

Celebrate Recovery

Have you heard of Celebrate Recovery? I had heard about it but knew very little. I thought it was a ministry for people with addictions primarily. That would not be wrong, but it is much more.

One Sunday in one of the megachurches, a pastor introduced himself by saying something like: "Hi, I'm John, and I have a problem with alcohol, overeating, and pornography." The giant crowd seemingly answered with one voice, "Hi John."

I thought, "Did that just happen in a megachurch on a Sunday morning?" I knew that was how CR meetings begin, but in a massive church on a Sunday morning?! I was incredulous it happened, and at the next spiritual impression that came to me: "You should attend yourself."

A week later, I told my next-door neighbor about that spiritual impression. He quickly said, "I heard the same thing! Do you want to do it together?"

So we signed up and began a six-month journey with eight other men in freedom and discipleship. The worldwide and nationally known program is out of Saddleback Church in Southern California. They have their own Bible with additional notes, cross-references, and stories of recoveries.

The biggest takeaway for myself and my friend, both Christians since childhood, was that God by his Spirit is still rescuing people powerfully. He doesn't need our help to do it. In the weekly group meetings, what seemed perfectly odd to us was that the guys just shared what was transpiring between them and the Lord as they read their assignments and did their homework. There was no "cross talk" or counseling each other. Everyone was working out their own recovery with the Lord.

I saw one guy share a bit of his story initially, with his head down and voice so muted we could hardly hear. I thought to myself, "This guy doesn't have a snowball's chance in hell of making it through or finishing this program." But finish he did to my surprise. And he's doing very well two years later, walking in freedom, leading his family, and running his business. I had an enjoyable catch-up breakfast with him last week. We've become good friends.

As my friend and I continue to discuss takeaways from CR, we are both grateful we went through the course and saw the power of God work in needy, hopeless, powerless lives. That reality changed us. We each continue to disciple and mentor one or two guys we met there.

We now see CR as maybe the best expression of the church in America. The people coming have been humbled by life and know they have needs. They are the poor in spirit Jesus mentioned in His most famous sermon: "Blessed are the poor in spirit, for theirs is the kingdom of heaven" (Matthew 5:3).

The deception of self-effort and the works of religion have evaporated for them. They appear humbly but boldly now like the prostitute in the Pharisee's house recorded in Luke seven. We all hear Jesus say: **"When they were unable to repay, he graciously forgave them both. So which of them will love him more?"** And: "For this reason I say to you, **her sins, which are many, have been forgiven, for she loved much; but he who is forgiven little, loves little** [emphasis added]" (Luke 7:42,47).

We formerly regarded people in this program with their "hurts, habits, and hang-ups" as most at risk and unlikely to succeed. Now we see them as more spiritually advanced than most, and the same as "us" because we are all in the same, needy human boat. They know their weakness to battle their flesh and dark spirits. And they've seen up close the ravages caused by sin. They cried out to God for help. Now they know their Redeemer and that He is strong. They live on a new path, in a new day, with the promise and hope of a vastly different outcome.

The Journey

"The Journey" is a nine-month discipleship experience that originated in NWA, Northwest Arkansas, and enjoys a worldwide embrace.

My CR friend and I were invited to participate in a group with ten men as COVID-19 began in 2020, on the heels of our Celebrate Recovery experience. The visionary author and originator of *The Journey* discipleship model is Rocky Fleming. You can investigate it further at www.influencers.org.

The whole experience centers around a single Bible verse: "I am the vine, you are the branches; **he who abides** in Me and I in him, he bears much fruit, for apart from Me you can do nothing [emphasis added]" (John 15:5).

There are some books to read, a workbook with Bible verses for meditation, and many discussions, getting to know the group members. It's everyday discipleship and Christian community but focused and intentional on living a life with God, building on the proper Biblical foundation, using the disciplines (abiding) of the faith, and experiencing anew the Spirit of God Who Jesus sent to us.

Another outcome is new friendships or strengthened friendships. Typically, you'll be in a group of people from different denominations or spiritual DNAs within the body of Christ (churches). That is refreshing and mind-expanding, as one sees how God is working in other parts of His vineyard.

But **the personal "abiding" habit is the focus, beauty, and joy** of *The Journey*.

Nehemiah and 2020

My next-door neighbor, spiritual adventurer, septuagenarian, and beautiful friend is the other part of the "we" I reference above. By coincidence (for those who have too small a picture of God—and we all do!), we became next-door neighbors upon moving to NWA three years ago. Since then, we've become close friends and amazed as we've watched and experienced the Holy Spirit move in and around us in ever-increasing measure. We've experienced His power separately in our realms. And we've seen it in the four groups the Spirit led us to be part of during the past three years and the COVID-19 years, 2020 to the present.

After CR and during *The Journey*, two men in their 40s who worked for Ron's former company came to him with a request. It went like this: "We are halfway through our lives, and we are so burned out! We want the last half of our lives to count more than the first half. Will you mentor us?" Ron thought and prayed about it, then told them yes. Because of our spiritual adventures in CR and *The Journey*, Ron asked me to join the group. It was a short commute, a twenty-second walk across our lawns or sidewalk, so I agreed. A year later, another young man from the same company joined us at the Spirit's leading, making us five.

The very first study or Bible book we looked at was Nehemiah. The Spirit led Ron to begin there, using a video series by Chip Ingram called "Holy Ambition" to focus the group and facilitate discussion about where we are and where we want to go.

Nehemiah had a cushy but vital job as a wine taster for the king of Persia, the most sovereign ruler in the world of his day. It was an easy job, if a bit risky, but it also gave him personal contact and access to the king. He, like a bodyguard, was considered almost like one of the family.

Amid all this success and luxury, Nehemiah was still very concerned about the things and purposes of God. He had **a holy ambition**. When he learned there was an entourage of travelers in town from Israel, he inquired about Jerusalem. He learned that: "The people who survive the captivity are in great distress and reproach, and the wall of Jerusalem is broken down and it's gates burned with fire" (Nehemiah 1:3).

Does that description sound like our culture and churches today? Are our **walls broken down, gates burned with fire, and our people in great distress**? We finished that study, then looked at eschatology (the study of end-time events), prayer, and a host of relevant issues discussed in the Bible. But we still call our group the Nehemiah group because our original orientation and focus are still the same. We care that the walls are broken down, and the gates are burned with fire. We see God's people in distress everywhere, including our families at times. **We choose to have a holy ambition to do something about it, if God will help us.** The Scripture describes our hope and goal the best:

> **"Those from among you will rebuild the ancient ruins;**
> **you will raise up the age-old foundations; and you will be**

called the repairer of the breach, the restorer of the streets in which to dwell [emphasis added]" (Isaiah 58:12).

2020

Just before COVID-19 struck the USA in the spring of 2020, I felt the Spirit lead me to begin a bi-monthly men's friendship group in our home. The format, a book club of sorts interspersing books of the Bible, came to me, as did the frequency of the meetings and who to invite. There were five of us initially, and one came later. We call ourselves the 2020 group because we began in 2020, and our aim is 20/20 spiritual vision. We want to help each other see and hear what God is doing and saying in our times.

We aim to better know God, each other, and enjoy the journey toward both. We share what's going on in our lives, in our families, and with our friends. And we pray for each other.

The vision for this book began a few years ago. But it came into sharp focus during COVID-19, starting in 2020. And it was written mainly in these four communities while sharing the life God was giving us and showing us.

What About Church?

What about the church, the topic of this essential piece of the puzzle? We started our 2020 group by reading two books. First, we read *A Knowledge of the Holy* by A.W. Tozer to take a fresh look at God. Then we read *Beautiful Outlaw* by John Eldridge to take a new look at Jesus, Who is God in the flesh, Emmanuel, as He claimed, and the prophets and Scripture attest.

Discussing the second book and Eldridge's writings in general, we kept bringing up the modern church and its deficiencies. One of our number, Bill, spoke up and said, "It sounds like you guys are bride bashing." I answered that the rest of us had never heard that expression before, but we get it, and we certainly want no part of that.

The Bible tells us Jesus loves the church, His bride. He gave His life for her: "Just as Christ also loved the church and gave himself up for her" (Ephesians 5:25b). All in our group have a healthy fear of the Lord. We respect His ways and love the relationships He provides for us and all who believe.

We do not want to speak disparagingly about Christ's bride, the church, or attack her. He would certainly take offense at that, and rightfully so.

Besides, even in her weakened, anemic, and dysfunctional state, the church is still where disciples are made, and people learn about Christ, salvation, and the Person and purposes of God. It's where they experience love in its purest form, God's love, and have that modeled and imparted to them. The church gives the individual members making up the community of faith, the bride, the chance to experience and practice this fulfilling love.

Bride Bashing or Reformation

Most of us experienced different expressions of the church in our past and had firsthand knowledge of others. So our exasperation was not toward the church of Scripture, nor the church in general. It was toward abuses and neglect, wrong attitudes and actions we saw and experienced. These bad attitudes and actions are too widespread. They need to be addressed, corrected, and cautiously criticized, with the attitude to help and heal.

Stated another way: "The church in America, a part of the global bride of Christ, is living far below how she could be and should be. Her garments are soiled, and she doesn't properly love and respect her Lord. She's lost her way and much of her beauty due to self effort and self absorption. She doesn't even know it. She doesn't function in the

Spirit with the power or intimacy available to her."

We need not talk badly about her nor curse the darkness but light a candle. We need to be aware of what's happening, point it out when led, but mainly try to reform her and help restore her to her high position before her King. If you are a Christian, surely you know you are the church. Be the best part of His bride you can be, abiding with Him. Search out a functioning (not perfect) expression of the community of Christ, a local church, and be a part.

In the last book of the Bible, we see Jesus, the Husband of the bride, standing in the middle of lampstands, addressing seven expressions of His early church only sixty-two years after He laid His life down for her. She's already going astray. He is lovingly, truthfully laying out the reality of the situation in ways they and we can understand. She can act if she wishes and wills to be faithful and true — a fitting bride, washed by the Word and empowered by the Spirit to know the King and make Him known. She can return to the One her heart loves (Revelation 1-3).

Who's Responsible?

If the bride, the church, is to be beautiful, spotless, and wrinkle-free, who's responsible? The bride or her Husband? That is an interesting question, isn't it? Maybe it deserves a Hebrew *Selah* — stop and think about that.

It occurs to me now that Christ takes some if not the bulk of the responsibility for His bride's cleanliness and beauty and holiness.

Paul says a lot in Ephesians about the church and the family and how they relate. About the church and Christ, we read: "But as **the church is subject to Christ**, so also the wives ought to be to their husbands **in everything** [emphasis added]" (Ephesians 5:24).

Later we read: "Husbands, love your wives, just **as Christ also loved the church and gave Himself up for her**, so **that He might sanctify** her, having cleansed her by the washing of water with the word, that He might present to Himself the church in all her glory, having no spot or wrinkle or any such thing; but that she would be holy and blameless [emphasis added]" (Ephesians 5:25-27).

Sidebar-The Family

Isn't it strikingly peculiar and wonderful how God uses things in the natural to teach us about the spiritual and eternal? He uses the family, something familiar to every human, to teach us about the relationship of Christ and His bride. His bride is the church, the community of faith, the redeemed — those chosen and who choose to live with God forever from the time they believe, as a part of His eternal family. They are friends and suitable companions for His Son the King.

I just thought about the gender ratio in the world and looked it up. I thought it was about even, and sure enough, the 2021 estimates are that males in the world represent 50.42% of the world population. In 2020 it was about 102 men for every 100 women. It's about one to one, or one man for every woman and vice versa. Pretty convenient for family formation, procreation, and experiencing life on the earth in families, huh? It's God's plan evidently for us to get the most out of life on this gorgeous planet — beauty, peace, security, joy, laughter, destiny, dignity, understanding, wisdom, with relationships to share all the above. And it's preparing us for eternity. The natural comes first, and then the spiritual. We learn all of this from the Bible, in church, listening to preaching and teaching every Sunday, then discussing it in community, and practicing it in life.

Church Focus

What then should be the focus of the church? Last week, I met with our young pastor for breakfast and asked him the same question. His short answer without hesitation was "discipleship." He went on to say that a properly functioning church would also be concerned about social justice and caring for the poor, the sick, and the needy. Still, Christ's clear admonition to his disciples was: "**Go** therefore and **make disciples** of all the nations, baptizing them in the name of the Father and the Son and the Holy Spirit, **teaching them to observe all that I commanded you**; and lo, I am with you always, even to the end of the age [emphasis added]" (Matthew 28:19-20).

Even though pastor Ben Wilson is young, he is wise. Since his youth, he's been a Christian, walked in the ways of God, reveres the Word, and teaches it verse by verse, unapologetically. After college, he attended Talbot Seminary in California, obtained a Ph.D. from Cambridge in England, then taught at the Moody Bible Institute in Chicago. So he's well educated and well-traveled.

With all that, he and his wife, with four small children, felt called to pastor a local church in a college town. That is where he feels he can be of the most value to the King and His kingdom — serving a local church. He sees it as primary and essential to God's plan. We are glad he does! I think God is too.

The church has the Great Commandment and the Great Commission to help her focus. The Great Commission is recorded above by Jesus (Matthew 28:19-20). The Greatest Commandment is in Matthew's Gospel too: "Jesus replied: '**Love the Lord your God with all your heart and with all your soul and with all your mind.** This is the first and greatest commandment. And the second is like it: **Love your neighbor as yourself. All the Law and the Prophets hang on these two commandments** [emphasis added]'" (Matthew 22:37-40). Very simple. Very important. Don't lose your focus in these hazy, confusing times. And He will be with you by His Spirit to the end of the age. Enjoy your journey to relationship and destiny!

Our Church

I told you a bit about our three-year journey in a new place. But I didn't tell you about our new church. We were searching for a church community, but it took us a while to find one. Meanwhile, the Spirit led me to be in community with Christian brothers in four different men's groups. Also, for a short time before COVID-19 broke out, we were in a home group associated with one of the megachurches. Still, we hadn't found a church community or a local church that felt like home, or where we heard His voice for us. The Scriptures say: "**My sheep hear My voice**, and I know them, **and they follow Me** [emphasis added]" (John 10:27).

The Bible is clear that Christians should be a part of a body of believers. Jesus' disciples and apostles established the early church in every city. The Bible is full of instructions and guidance for those churches. Much is said about the gifts the Spirit gives to members of the churches to build up the whole church. And there's much said about leadership: elders, deacons, and pastors. This guidance is God's plan for His body, His bride, for her well-being and maturation.

The Lord's plan and command are that Christians meet together regularly and not forsake this practice. We read: "Let us hold unswervingly to the hope we profess, for he who promised is faithful. And **let us consider how we may spur one another on toward love and good deeds, not giving up meeting together, as some are in the habit of doing, but encouraging one another—and all the more as you see the Day approaching** [emphasis added]" (Hebrews 10:23-25 NIV).

This is in the Word and not an option, as some suggest, if one is a Christian or disciple of Christ. Jesus reminds us about obedience to Him, saying: "**Why do you call Me, 'Lord, Lord,' and do not do what I say?** [emphasis added]" (Luke 6:46). You can't have it both ways. My wife and I attend church and have seen the extreme value of attendance all of our lives, but the teaching and commands of Scripture determines things for us. As the Scripture says, "**Let God be found true, though every man be found a liar**, as it is written, 'That You may be justified in Your words, and prevail when You are judged [emphasis added]'" (Romans 3:4). We were looking for a church to join, but the bizarre events of 2020, and the Spirit led us on a delayed path.

Three years ago, upon moving to our new city, I noticed a church in a strip mall called Harvest Bible Chapel. I don't often notice such churches, but it seemed like the Spirit pointed it out to me, and I felt some curiosity about it. That same week, we met a close personal friend in a megachurch meeting who asked if we had found a church. She suggested we try this Harvest Church. "If it is so good, why don't you go there?" I responded. She told me her family was pretty connected to the church where we were standing. Then nothing much happened for three years except for the men's groups and COVID-19.

One Sunday, I felt a strong urge to attend this church. I did so, and to my surprise, I heard the young pastor, who was new to the church himself preach about the church in Ephesus. He said that the culture didn't change the church in Ephesus. The church in Ephesus changed the culture. There were many other synchronicities and confirmations in the coming weeks that this was where the Spirit was planting us. We followed their church membership procedure, and a few weeks later, along with twenty-seven other people, officially joined one Sunday morning. It's been a joy ever since. It's a multigenerational college church that fears God and teaches His word. Unsurprisingly, many of its members, full of love, welcomed us with open arms and hearts. The church's mantra is: "You Are Loved." We're now on a kingdom journey and adventure with them, a local church family.

The Church in America 2022 Going Forward

You should find a church like I've described, or where the Spirit leads you, and be a part. Be invested with sacrifice and service. You'll find it rewarding by reaping what you sow, but mainly you're obeying and honoring your King. Trust Him with the results. He's perfect, and His plans for you are better than yours. And yes, there is a cost, sacrifice, and opposition to following Jesus. He promised it would be so. He also promised that He'd be with you, and you'd come to know Him better and receive His reward in the end.

You need the benefit of the other gifts that the Spirit gives the church. Especially spiritual vision and hearing in the days ahead will help you prosper and fare well. It's also about the relationships you'll forge, the battles you'll fight together, and the joy of knowing the King better through it all — a Friend that sticks closer than a brother.

Derek Prince said: "The purposes of God are born in fellowship [the church]."

In the first paragraph of *The Tale of Two Cities,* Dickens writes: "**It was the best of times, it was the worst of times,** it was the age of wisdom, it was the age of foolishness, it was the epoch of belief, it was the epoch of incredulity, it was the season of Light, it was the season of Darkness, it was the spring of hope, it was the winter of despair, we had everything before us....[emphasis added]" Yesterday, I heard an eighty-three-year-old, black pastor and sage quote that first part, then say: "**I think the church can make her choice**" (Bishop Joseph L. Garlington, Sr.).

I do too! That's what COVID-19 is all about. It is a grace attack from God to show the culture how blind and disoriented it is. And how in need of truth and direction it is. God also sent it to purify His church. It stripped away a lot of blinding activity and raised the following questions: "What do you really value?" "Who do you really trust?" "Are you content or refreshed when your idols are shown to be what they are and stripped away?" "Do you long for your idols back?" There are more such questions, but you get the drift.

The Bible tells us judgment begins with the church: "For **it is time for judgment to begin with the household of God**; and if it begins with us first, what will be the outcome for those who do not obey the gospel of God? [emphasis added]" (1 Peter 4:17). The Bible also tells us that the church has the power to stop God's hand of judgment if they act: "If I shut up the heavens so that there is no rain, or if I command the locust to devour the land, or **if I send pestilence among My people, and My people who are called by My name humble themselves and pray and seek My face and turn from their wicked ways, then I will hear from heaven, will forgive their sin and will heal their land** [emphasis added]" (2 Chronicles 7:13-14). We see where judgment begins in these two verses — in the community of faith! And we see that God's people, the church, have the power to stop pestilence and bring healing if they humble themselves, seek God's face, and pray.

On the positive side of the pestilence, people were reintroduced to people. People valued getting together and the joy of a simple meal prepared in the kitchen of a home. They appreciated the outdoors, sunshine, and the park. They enjoyed visiting with neighbors they barely knew before, even if from six feet away. The whole puzzling thing reintroduced us to life stripped of some idols. It re-oriented us to important priorities and illuminated what was stealing our lives while we rushed along our way.

It showed church people we may all be in the same storm, but we're not all in the same boat. There were many differences in how church members reacted and churches responded to all the unknown health concerns, the governmental measures, and who they trusted or didn't trust.

Bob Mumford said: "Lord if you're doing anything on the earth, I want to be a part of it." That's a good reflection of the importance of the church and a proper attitude in following her Lord. At a recent Christian leadership conference, one of the keynote speakers, Joseph L. Garlington of Pittsburg, said: **"The church is the greatest institution on the earth today."**

It's true because God's people house God's Spirit. And because they, by faith, have responded to His love and chosen to value Him above all else. They have accepted His offer to know Him in a relationship of love and trust. This relationship is lovely to Him. He has expressed loving thoughts about such a community of faith: "In a desert land he [God] found him [Israel, by extension people of faith, the church], in a barren and howling waste. He shielded him and cared for him; he [God] guarded him as the apple of his eye" (Deuteronomy 32:10 ESV). And the Psalmist replies: "Keep me as the apple of your eye; hide me in the shadow of your wings" (Psalm 17:8). God describes us as the apple of His eye.

David, "a man after God's own heart" (1 Samuel 13:14, Acts 13:22) and one who "accomplished the purposes of God in his generation" (Acts 13:36), beautifully describes this relationship poetically and realistically in Psalm 139. A couple of excerpts are: "Where can I go from Your Spirit? Or where can I flee from Your presence? If I ascend to heaven, You are there; if I make my bed in Sheol, behold, You are there. If I take the wings of the dawn, if I dwell in the remotest part of the sea, even there Your hand will lead me, and Your right hand will lay hold of me" (Psalm 139: 7-10). He further says: "How precious also are Your thoughts to me, O God! How vast is the sum of them! If I should count them, they would outnumber the sand. When I awake, I am still with You'" (Psalm 139: 17-18).

"Deep calls to deep" (Psalm 42:7a). As far as the deep feelings the King of Heaven has for the church, His family, His bride, the Bible records: "The Lord Jesus in the night in which He was betrayed took bread; and when He had given thanks, He **broke it and said, 'This is My body, which is for you**; do this in remembrance of Me [emphasis added]'"

(1 Corinthians 11:23b-24).

PUZZLING CHAPTER 40

Living Stones

LET'S CONSIDER LIVING STONES IN connection with the church. A Scripture comes to mind: "**And coming to Him as to a living stone which has been rejected by men, but is choice and precious in the sight of God, you also, as living stones,** are being built up as **a spiritual house** for a holy priesthood, to offer up spiritual sacrifices acceptable to God through Jesus Christ [emphasis added]" (1 Peter 2:4-5).

My point in this puzzle piece is that living stones, individual Christians, make up the church. And that we are to be lively and active as God is building us up by His Presence within us. Jesus was the original stone men rejected, by and large, but was most precious to God. As living stones cut in His likeness, we are precious to God and constitute the church. The church is God's idea to cultivate friends and a bride acceptable for His Son, the King.

Livings Stones Are Loving Stones

Before beginning this discussion, please allow me a few quotes on love to get us thinking and our minds running on a proper track. Someone has wisely said, "It doesn't matter how fast you're going, if you're on the wrong track."

"Love means to love that which is unlovable, or it is no virtue at all"
(G. K. Chesterton).

"Loving can cost a lot, but not loving always costs more, and those who fear to love often find that want of love is an emptiness that robs the joy from life"
(Merle Shain).

"I believe that love is the greatest thing in the world; that it alone can overcome hate; that right can and will triumph over might"
(John D. Rockefeller, Jr.).

"The porcupine, whom one must handle gloved, may be respected, but never loved"
(Arthur Guiterman).

Reflect on those quotes, and you're ready to reflect on living stones and loving stones. I just returned from a Charles Simpson Conference in Gatlinburg, TN. The theme was "First Love." Charles is an octogenarian who has discipled me by tapes and CDs for forty years now. More than any other expositor I know, he seemingly leans on the Lord's chest and speaks to the church what he hears. The man and the words from God continue to make a significant impact on my life. So with rapt attention and anticipation, I awaited the theme and messages from the conference this year. They did not disappoint but were right on target. I believe the Lord, by His Spirit, is telling the church, all the individuals that constitute the church, to return to our first love. That's God's message of the hour to His people.

This is hardly a new message. But there is not a more important one.

If the vine is not connected to the branch, there is no life flowing, and there is no fruit. Soon there will be dryness, barrenness, and death. We were created for more.

Biblical Refresher on Love

God loved us first. This is pointed out many times in Scripture but perhaps most succinctly here: "We love, because He first loved us" (1 John 4:19).

We have a descriptor of God's divine love in 1 Corinthians 13, which is natural to Him. John, the disciple who leaned on Jesus' breast, tells us plainly how organic and vital this attribute of God is: "**God is love, and the one who abides in love abides in God, and God abides in him** [emphasis added]" (1 John 4:16b).

The Apostle Paul, who early in his life was not known for his love, tells us just how vital and transformational God's love is: "**That you, being rooted and grounded in love, may be able to comprehend with all the saints what is the breadth and length and height and depth, and to know the love of Christ which surpasses knowledge**, that you may be filled up to all the fullness of God [emphasis added]" (Ephesians 3:17b-19).

The cross of Calvary is the ultimate, silent, pervasive statement of God's love and His magnificent character of grace and humility, considering His unimaginable power and might. He is an unrivaled Being, known more for His love than anything else. We can count on Him to be the same and always do His part in the love relationship.

What about us?

Needed — A Touch From God

Charles Simpson's keynote address centered around: "We need a second touch." Taking an incident from Elijah's life (1 Kings 18:17-39) in apostate and idol-ridden Israel, he noted: "You can restore the altars, but you can't send the fire."

He then turned to the story about the blind man from Bethsaida, Peter's hometown: "And they **brought a blind man to Jesus and implored Him to touch him**. Taking the blind man by the hand, He brought him out of the village; and after spitting on his eyes and laying His hands on him, He asked him, **'Do you see anything?' And he looked up and said, 'I see men, for I see them like trees, walking around.'** Then **again He laid His hands on his eyes**; and he looked intently and was restored, and **began to see everything clearly**. And He sent him to his home, saying, 'Do not even enter the village [emphasis added]'" (Mark 8:22-26).

Bethsaida was in Galilee of the gentiles, not a religious place. Friends begged Jesus to touch this blind man. Begging is a good posture and attitude. Jesus took him by the hand and led him out of town. Sometimes you have to get away to receive a touch from Jesus.

Jesus touched him a second time. We need our vision, and Jesus knew this was important. **Jesus restored the man's vision with his second touch** and told him not to enter the village but to go home. Just let people see that you see, don't blab it to everyone. Live with vision, and people will notice.

Those who need to know, those close to you, will soon learn or come to see you've had a second touch from Jesus. They'll see you walking differently with sight, vision, and new direction. We all need another touch. The roads are dusty, and we need the Lord to wash our feet.

Charles Simpson said: "We must not be too casual with the things of God. It's too important, we must take it seriously." He went on to say: "Baptists don't believe in backsliding. But we do practice it."

God touched Isaiah's lips. His touch is cleansing. He touched Jeremiah and put prophecy in his mouth. The woman with the issue of blood touched Jesus and was healed. He wants to touch us to warm our hearts. He even touched lepers.

The Bible is full of stories about second touches. Peter's life is a good case in point. One day he proclaimed: "You are the Christ, the Son of the living God" (Matthew 16:16b). Shortly after that, Peter argued with Him: "Peter took Him aside and began to rebuke Him, saying, 'God forbid it, Lord! This shall never happen to You.'" (Matthew 16:22). Fifty days after the resurrection, Peter was the leading preacher at the birthing of the church. We would have kicked him out of our churches for denying Christ. But Christ continued to touch him.

Charles went on to say: "We will shake the places around us or we will be shaken. We are touched for others, and not just for ourselves. It's a wonderful time to be a believer but we have to get higher than we are — maybe higher than ever before. The revival coming will be greater than ever before."

Peter touched people, Paul touched people, and we can touch people. I think an excellent summation of Charles' remarks to us might be: "Fresh fire is needed, build new altars, and seek a second touch."

The lively stones need to recall: "[The] Lord of heaven and earth does not dwell in temples made with hands" (Acts 17:24b). And He's not far from you as Paul told the intelligentsia of Athens atop Mars Hill: **"That they would seek God,** if perhaps they might grope for Him and find Him, though **He is not far from each one of us** [emphasis added]" (Acts 17:27).

We must return to our first love, the Corner Stone. Or He will be a rock of offense, a stumbling stone! We must get this right and do so quickly. Jesus changed Simon's name to Peter, which means "stone or rock," and Peter writes to us: "For this is contained in Scripture:

'Behold, I lay in Zion a choice stone, a precious corner stone, and **he who believes in Him will not be disappointed.**' **This precious value, then, is for you who believe;** but **for those who disbelieve, 'The stone which the builders rejected, this became the very corner stone,' and, 'A stone of stumbling and a rock of offense;' for they stumble because they are disobedient to the word,** and to this doom they were also appointed [emphasis added]" (1 Peter 2:6-8).

Jesus also refers to this Psalm's prophecy (Psalm 118:22) about the Corner Stone, which is to be our first love: "Jesus said to them, 'Did you never read in the Scriptures, **the stone which the builders rejected, this became the chief corner stone; this came about from the Lord, and it is marvelous in our eyes**? Therefore I say to you, **the kingdom of God will be taken away from you and given to a people, producing the fruit of it.** And **he who falls on this stone will be broken to pieces; but on whomever it falls, it will scatter him like dust** [emphasis added]'" (Matthew 21:42-44).

More Thoughts for Lively Stones

It's the best of times and the worst of times for the church. Choose to see the best — the many opportunities available, then run to them. Fear and anxiety are terrible ways to use your imagination.

As shared in another piece of the puzzle: "We Christians may be in the same storm, but evidently we're not all in the same boat." If Jesus is in your boat, He will calm the storm. But then He's going to work on you. It's time to wake up! Wake up to the reality of Who is in the boat with you.

Bishop Garlington told the story of a beautiful, exotic bush in their garden that would not bloom. His gardener tried tilling, fertilizers, everything he could think of for a few years, but no blooms appeared. Then he remembered an old remedy someone once told him. He dug the plant up, shook it vigorously until most of the dirt was off the roots, then stuck it back into the ground. The following year it bloomed. Some of us need a violent shaking! And replanting.

Bishop Garlington told the story of being kicked out of his denomination early in his life in the same context. After that, he said: "I discovered the body of Christ." The issue is, "Do you want what He has for you?"

Bishop Garlington went on to say: "I needed to understand Jacob, Peter, and David [his favorites] were great guys who had a journey with God." "They were like the verse that described my early life: '[He] will go in and out and find pasture'" (John 10:9b). "**God doesn't judge you for who you are, but who you refuse to become.**"

The Ark or The Presence

In 1 Samuel 4-7, we read about a time in Israel's history when they were in a battle with the Philistines and brought the Ark of the Covenant into the war, hoping to turn the tide of the warfare. It caused quite a stir in both armies, but Israel lost, and the Philistines captured the Ark at the end of the day. Israel had the form but not the power of their former relationship with God.

We learn a couple of essential things from the story. The Presence of God relationally is more important than the shell of religion or form of what once was. And we learn the Ark can take care of itself.

The New Testament is full of similar imagery, but it's in the form of new wine and new [renewed] wineskins. New wine is symbolic of the Spirit of God, with its positive chemical reactions causing expansion of gases and eventually joy for the imbibing. And old wineskins are representative of the form of religion that once contained new wine, the life of God, but now are dry.

Old wineskins are too valuable to destroy, so they can be renewed. They are soaked in water (the Word), then rubbed with oil (the Spirit), and any hard spots pounded between rocks until the old vessel is soft, pliable, and ready for new wine (spiritual life) once more.

Marc Dupont says: "It's time to elevate our heart above our head." I think you can see the beauty and wisdom of that statement immediately. We've elevated our minds, thoughts, and intellectualism too much for too long. This has hurt us spiritually, and our whole being. We shouldn't put our minds to sleep, but we should give our hearts their proper function in the crucial matters of life and living.

Our speaker shared a true story of labor and delivery in peril. The doctor told the expectant mother: "Your baby is in trouble. You have to put your head below your heart now!" "How do I do that?" the mother replied. "Get on your knees and put your head on the floor," the physician explained before soon performing a C-section, and a healthy baby was born. Its umbilical cord had wrapped around its neck. Keeping your head below your heart can be life-saving and life-enriching for yourself and others.

One of the keynote speakers at the conference urged us to quit talking so much about "He is returning any minute," even if it seems imminent to you and many. Instead, take up your sword, as Caleb did, saying: "'**Now then, give me this hill country about which the LORD spoke on that day**, for you heard on that day that Anakim were there, with great fortified cities; **perhaps the LORD will be with me**, and **I will drive them out as the LORD has spoken.**' So Joshua blessed him and gave Hebron to Caleb the son of Jephunneh for an inheritance. Therefore, **Hebron became the inheritance of Caleb** the son of Jephunneh the Kenizzite **until this day, because he followed the LORD God of Israel fully** [emphasis added]" (Joshua 14:12-14). The speaker went on to say: "I want to burn out, not rust out."

Bishop Garlington made that point, then spoke of "**staying power.**" He suggested in the spiritual battles of life, we "stay low, stay humble, and stay out of the way!" One of his friends recently told him about life **in Christ: "If you don't quit, you win."**

Jesus' Disguises and His Ways

The Bishop went on to say, "Jesus doesn't always take the same form." He cited the road-to-Emmaus disciples walking with Jesus, unaware on the afternoon of His resurrection (Luke 24:13-25). They began to tell Jesus about Jesus.

Then Jesus began to say to them, "**How foolish and slow of heart to believe are you**." Wouldn't you love to have an audio file of that conversation? It ended with: "They began to relate their experiences on the road and how **He was recognized by them in the breaking of the bread** [emphasis added]" (Luke 24:35).

We see so much in this beautiful story. We see that disciples who walked with Jesus physically and knew Him needed a second touch. We see He is gracious, loves them, and will provide that touch. When He breaks the bread of revelation for us, we see and know Him. Get to know that relationship, and live there. It's life, love, inspiration, and joy.

Immediately after they told their story to the other disciples in a locked room, Jesus appeared to them, touching them again and allowing them to touch Him. It happened like this: "**While they were telling these things, He Himself stood in their midst** and said to them, 'Peace be to you.' But they were startled and frightened and thought that they were seeing a spirit. And He said to them, 'Why are you troubled, and why do doubts arise in your hearts? See My hands and My feet, that **it is I Myself; touch Me and see,** for a spirit does not have flesh and bones as you see that I have.' And when He had said this, **He showed them His hands and His feet**. While they still could not believe it because of their joy and amazement, He said to them, 'Have you anything here to eat?' They gave Him a piece of a broiled fish; and He took it and ate it before them [emphasis added]" (Luke 24: 36-43).

I think we can see that these ongoing touches are normal and essential for living stones, as is the breaking of bread with Him and communion.

Three Actions Empowering Living Stones

Jesus had **a supernatural birth**. You can read where it was prophesied seven hundred years before it happened in passages like Isaiah 9 or Micah 5, and how it happened in passages like Luke 2. Jesus would tell Nicodemus and all of us that a supernatural birth is necessary for us too in John 3.

Jesus said that **baptism in water** was necessary for us too. It's a symbol of our faith, and our commitment to walk in obedience to the Lord's commands. It demonstrates to us and the world our sins are forgiven, washed away, now as distant as the east is from the west. When Jesus came to John to be baptized, John rightfully recognized Jesus was sinless and need not be baptized, but Jesus requested John do it anyway to "fulfill all righteousness." The scene is recorded here: "Then **Jesus arrived from Galilee at the Jordan coming to John, to be baptized** by him. But **John tried to prevent Him, saying, 'I have need to be baptized by You**, and do You come to me?' But **Jesus answering said to him, 'Permit it at this time; for in this way it is fitting for us to fulfill all righteousness.**' Then he permitted Him [emphasis added]" (Matthew 3:13-15).

Thirdly, Jesus was **baptized in the Spirit**: "After being baptized, Jesus came up immediately from the water; and behold, the heavens were opened, and he saw the Spirit of God descending as a dove and lighting on Him, and behold, a voice out of the heavens said, 'This is My beloved Son, in whom I am well-pleased'" (Matthew 3:16-17). Like most things dealing with the Spirit of God, they are easily witnessed, easily experienced, but not easily explained or analyzed. Obviously, from the above passage, we see the Baptism of the Holy Spirit sealed Jesus' sonship. "This is my beloved Son, in whom I am well-pleased." And it seemed to be a setting apart, or consecration, of Jesus for His being the promised Messiah: "He is before all things, and in Him all things hold together. **He is also head of the body, the church; and He**

is the beginning, the firstborn from the dead, so that He Himself will come to have first place in everything. For it was the Father's good pleasure for all the fullness to dwell in Him [emphasis added]" (Colossians 1:17-19).

Oddly, a Wikipedia article may say it best: "Jesus is considered the first person to receive the baptism with the Holy Spirit. The Holy Spirit descended on Jesus during his baptism and anointed him with power. Afterward, Jesus began his ministry and displayed his power by casting out demons, healing the sick, and teaching with authority." It's clear from Jesus' practice and teaching that He intended his disciples would experience the same Baptism of the Holy Spirit. John prophesied it when he said: "He [Jesus] will baptize you with the Holy Spirit and fire" (Matthew 3:11b).

Living stones need the same three experiences our Lord planned and modeled for us. We need a supernatural birth, a water baptism, and a baptism in the Holy Spirit.

Jesus told his disciples to wait until they were endued with power from on high: "And behold, I am sending forth the promise of My Father upon you; but you are to stay in the city until you are clothed with power from on high" (Luke 24:49). They waited for the power, and then came the day of Pentecost: "And suddenly there came from heaven a noise like a violent rushing wind, and it filled the whole house where they were sitting" (Acts 2:2). Lively stones must let the sound of heaven fill their houses and quit trying to do God's work without God's power: "We have this treasure in earthen vessels, so that the surpassing greatness of the power will be of God and not from ourselves" (2 Corinthians 4:7).

This Funny Language

Eighty-three-year-old Bishop Garlington devoted almost an entire session of the recently cited conference to praying in the Spirit or praying in tongues. He said, "I want to talk to you about this funny language." I found this interesting because most attendees had come through the charismatic renewal of the 1960s and 1970s and probably had experienced the gift. So why preach to the choir? But I think that was precisely his point and the leading of the Spirit in the situation.

Like Paul reminding Timothy: "Therefore **I remind you to stir up the gift of God which is in you through the laying on of my hands.** For God has not given us a spirit of fear, but **of power and of love and of a sound mind** [emphasis added]" (2 Timothy 1:6-7).

The Language of Wonder

The Bishop used verses to remind us of what Paul taught and practiced: "For **anyone who speaks in a tongue does not speak to people but to God**. Indeed, no one understands them; **they utter mysteries by the Spirit** [emphasis added]" (1 Corinthians 14:2). He called tongues the language of wonder.

He went on to say, "Apparently, God sometimes wants us to pray but doesn't want us to understand." When he spoke, it occurred to me that it may be like the Holy Spirit living inside of us talking to the Father and Son. The Bishop said: "I'm bigger on the inside than I am on the outside. I'm a God container." This sounds funny but it is Scriptural — the clear teaching of Jesus and the Bible. (See: Col 1:27, Eph 3:20, 2 Cor 4:7, John 15:5, Isa 66:1-2, Zech 4:6)

He pointed out what some of the Apostles said about praying in the Spirit or praying in tongues. Paul said: "**I thank God that I speak in tongues more than all of you** [emphasis added]" (1 Corinthians 14:18). He goes on in that chapter to clearly say he favors the gifts that build up the church and hints this is why the Spirit gives the gifts. But he in no way detracts from the value to the individual, the living stone, of this intimate communication gift for praying and talking to God.

He quoted the letter of Jude, the half brother of Jesus: "But you, beloved, **building yourselves up on your most holy faith, praying in the Holy Spirit, keep yourselves in the love of God**, waiting anxiously for the mercy of our Lord Jesus Christ to eternal life [emphasis added]" (Jude 20-21).

There appears to be a little latitude or mystery about the question: "Is praying in the Spirit necessarily the same as praying in tongues?" I think this is a valid distinction without a clear resolution. It seems when you read everything Paul says about the subject in context, they are the same thing to him. But not enough is said to be sure this is the only meaning.

This morning, I was in a men's group studying intercession and prayer. The subject of praying in the Spirit came up. I'm the only guy in the group of five that has a prayer language, but we're all gut-level honest with each other and God-seekers, so I asked: "If you don't have the gift of tongues, what does praying in the Spirit look like to you?" One of the members said it's like "a lot of silence, slowly praying and listening, contemplating and waiting for new thoughts or ideas to come on the subject at hand, and then praying those." That's plausible.

While we're on this subject, and at this juncture, I'm in two men's groups with eleven guys total, and only three of us have the gift of tongues or a prayer language. Yet all of the guys are Spirit-filled and hear from God regularly, acting on these impressions or praying them faithfully. Some have questioned: "Am I filled with the Holy Spirit, or had the Baptism of the Spirit if I don't speak in tongues?" Then they will quote something they think is in the Bible: "Baptized in the Holy Spirit with the evidence of speaking in tongues."

My answer at this point in my life, reading the Word, living in a church community, exposed to a cross-section of Christianity in our country and abroad, with a better than average knowledge of church history, is this: The gifts of the Spirit are precisely that. He gives or gifts them as He wills, for the building up of His body, the church, of which we are a part. I've experienced the gift of tongues personally as a prayer language and find it to be as described in Scripture and widely experienced in the church. If it's something you desire, you can ask Him for it in prayer. It's Scriptural to do so. Is praying in tongues evidence of being Baptized or filled with the Holy Spirit? I don't find that anywhere in the Bible. It's in a few church doctrinal statements, where some logic and deduction are applied to some occurrences of being baptized in the Holy Spirit and then speaking in tongues. This may or may not be warranted, and is a matter of opinion.

The Scriptures say that whoever prays in the Spirit edifies himself. Is there anything wrong with that? There is something right about that! No one has a problem with someone who runs stairs or rides a bike to keep their physical body in the best condition. "One who speaks in a tongue edifies himself" (1Corinthians 14:4a). The Apostle also says: "What is the outcome then? I will pray with the spirit and I will pray with the mind also" (1Corinthians 14:15a).

The Bishop also said, "Tongues is a language of worship." "I will sing with the spirit and I will sing with the mind also" (1Corinthians 14:15b).

He said, "Tongues is a language of warfare." "For if the bugle produces an indistinct sound, who will prepare himself for battle?" (1Corinthians 14:8). He also gave a recent example where some witches were picketing the Supreme Court over the abortion issue. A group of high school students came upon the situation and began to pray in the Spirit aloud. Within fifteen minutes, the witches left.

Lastly, he said: "Tongues is a language of weakness." "In the same way the Spirit also helps our weakness; for we do not know how to pray as we should, but the Spirit Himself intercedes for us with groanings too deep for words; and He who searches the hearts knows what the mind of the Spirit is, because He intercedes for the saints according to the will of God" (Romans 8:26-27).

Summary

A summary of the tongues issue for me and anyone who has a prayer language would be: "Use it!" Don't let the fact that others do not or that there is some controversy about it slow you down. Do you want to sink to the lowest common denominator or set the bar as low as you can? These times of intense spiritual opposition and warfare call for our best conditioning and most potent weapons. "For the weapons of our warfare are not of the flesh, but divinely powerful for the destruction of fortresses" (2 Corinthians 10:4).

Maybe more importantly, if God gave you a gift to use for yourself and the church, and you let it fall into disuse, is that wise or honoring the Gift Giver? God celebrates and appreciates desire and passion. "Pursue love, yet desire earnestly spiritual gifts" (1Corinthians 14:1a). Honor Him by using the gifts He gives you often and much.

A summary of being living stones might be to fix our eyes on the Chief Corner Stone. "**Fixing our eyes on Jesus, the author and perfecter of faith**, who for the joy set before Him endured the cross, despising the shame, and has sat down at the right hand of the throne of God [emphasis added]" (Hebrews 12:2). **Remember love**, and **seek constant touches and intimacy with God. Abide** in the shadow of the Almighty. **Experience the power of the Spirit, then function in that power and the gifts** of the Spirit to **build up the body into the living, lively stones He desires us to become** —the house and family of God. Amen.

PUZZLING CHAPTER 41

Martyrs

"REMEMBER THE PRISONERS, AS THOUGH in prison with them, and those who are ill-treated, since you yourselves also are in the body" (Hebrews 13:3).

What a beautiful verse and admonition to the church, set between two relational verses, one that encourages hospitality (grace) and the other that honors an undefiled marriage bed (loyalty). All three point to a unified church, walking in loving concern for its own and all others.

"Martyr" as a noun is: "a person who voluntarily suffers death as the penalty of witnessing to and refusing to renounce a religion" or "a person who sacrifices something of great value and especially life itself for the sake of principle" (Merriam-Webster). As a verb, martyr is: "to put to death for adhering to a belief, faith, or profession" or "to inflict agonizing pain on : torture" (Merriam-Webster).

Who knew? Merriam-Webster has a kid's definition of words. Since I want this writ to be straight-forward and childlike, something our Lord recommends, I'll include their simple definition: noun -"a person who suffers greatly or dies for a religion or cause," verb - "to put to death for refusing to give up a belief."

The etymology of words, their origins, and their original meanings are always enlightening and fascinating. The word "**martyr**" comes originally from the ancient Greek legal term for "**witness**," for someone who gives testimony or evidence in a court of law. Indeed, someone willing to give his or her life for the truth they profess is the strongest possible witness.

Why is this a piece of the puzzle in our day? It points out that our American culture and American Christians are asleep to martyrdom's prevalence on the earth. We are asleep or apathetic or both. These are other words for deceived and deluded. Are we so concerned about ourselves that we don't care about others suffering for the faith? That's not the way Jesus showed us, and it's an indicator of deception and delusion.

Have you ever asked yourself, "Why does martyrdom happen?" Have you looked at the bulk of the instances in history? Why does it seem the vast majority of martyrs are Christians and Jews? Isn't that curious? Surely there must be some unseen reason or cause for that mostly one-sided aggression? Is there some spiritual reality here valuable to know for our good and the good of humankind? God has an enemy, and he hates the family of faith.

Incredulous

I spoke with two young siblings recently in their late 30s or early 40s, raised in a Christian home, about some Christian martyrdom going on in Asia and the Middle East. They looked at me incredulous as if to say: "Is that still going on? I can't believe it's true." Their reaction was incredulous to me, but telling about the church in the USA today. Yet the scope of martyrdom in the world is even more incredible.

Forbes, in a January 13, 2021, article reported: "On average, every day, 13 Christians are killed for their faith, 12 churches or Christians buildings are attacked, 12 Christians are unjustly arrested, detained or imprisoned, and 5 Christians are abducted for faith-related reasons. In the 21st century, it is still not possible to practice religion or belief safely."

Open Doors reports in 2021: "Over 360 million Christians [were] living in places where they experience high levels of persecution and discrimination. 5,898 Christians [were] killed for their faith. 5,110 churches and other Christian buildings [were] attacked. 4,765 believers [were] detained without trial, arrested, sentenced or imprisoned" (opendoorsusa.org).

Encouragingly, Open Doors also reports another side to this truth: "These numbers are heart-breaking. And yet, they do not tell the whole story. James 1:2-4 says, 'Consider it pure joy, my brothers and sisters, whenever you face trials of many kinds because you know that the testing of your faith produces perseverance.' That joy is what we see when we hear and work with Christians all over the world who suffer because they serve Jesus. God cares for His people, and He will never leave or forsake them."

What to Do?

The Bible shows martyrdom to have happened throughout history. It still happens. What should we do about it? Pray to the God of Heaven for martyrs and their families. Pray those persecuted be protected, helped, and comforted by Him. He instructs us to remember them:

> **"Remember the prisoners, as though in prison with them, and those who are ill-treated,** since you yourselves also are in the body [emphasis added]" (Hebrews 13:3). They are a part of us.

Wouldn't you want people to pray for you and your family if you faced persecution, prison, or decapitation by the sea? One of Jesus' most famous commands was: "**Do to others whatever you would like them to do to you**. This is the essence of all that is taught in the law and the prophets [emphasis added]" (Matthew 7:12 NLT).

The sons of Issachar understood their times and what they should be doing (1 Chronicles 12:32). Giving an ear to this ongoing and increasing injustice of persecution on the earth will help you understand our times and what you should be doing.

Let me recommend the book *Bonhoeffer: Pastor, Martyr, Prophet, Spy* by Eric Metaxas. It will give you a deep, personal, insightful look at a well-known twentieth-century martyr, Dietrich Bonhoeffer, and the actual phenomenon of martyrdom. A New York Times bestselling biography, the book takes both threads of Bonhoeffer's life — pastor and spy — and shows how a humble man of courage and faith navigated his evil time and place. Does this sound possibly relevant?

For an inside look at the underground church in China read *The Heavenly Man* by Brother Yun. For an inside look at martyrdom in Africa and the Middle East read *The Insanity of God* by Nik Ripken. I heard this author speak and visited with him personally, shortly after reading the book. He and his wife are the real deal.

Let me also suggest that you get involved with a ministry that supports Christians worldwide who are persecuted only for their faith. One such ministry is VOM. "The Voice of the Martyrs (VOM) is a nonprofit, interdenominational missions organization that serves persecuted Christians around the world. Founded in 1967 by Richard and Sabina Wurmbrand, VOM is dedicated to inspiring believers to deepen their commitment to Christ and fulfill His Great Commission — no matter the cost" (persecution.com). Open Doors (opendoorsusa.org) is another. Supporting such a ministry will help you stay aware, pray, and give something to those suffering for their faith.

I encourage you to light a candle, and not curse the darkness. Please don't get into Christian humanism, thinking you caused this situation or must fix it yourself. Just be humbly aware. Pray and trust God to answer those prayers with real help in time of need. He tells us what to do in His Word. "**Remember the persecuted**" with your prayers and giving. Do something. Do what you would want others to do for you in these matters of real-life and genuine faith.

"When the Lamb broke the fifth seal, I saw underneath the altar the souls of **those who had been slain because of the word of God, and because of the testimony which they had maintained;** and they cried out with a loud voice, saying, "**How long, O Lord, holy and true, will You refrain from judging and avenging our blood on those who dwell on the earth**?" And there was given to each of them a white robe; and **they were told that they should rest for a little while longer** [emphasis added]"

(Revelation 6:9-11a).

"Of the sons of Issachar, **men who understood the times**, with knowledge of what Israel should do [emphasis added]"

(1 Chronicles 12:32a).

PUZZLING CHAPTER 42

Slavery

SLAVERY IS A SIMPLE PIECE of the puzzle. Yet it seems complex, dark, burdensome, and blinding to our secular humanist culture and the woke church in our day. It is a piece of the puzzle for the benefit of those who might wonder about all the fuss.

Look at history, and you'll see God has been working to help humankind fix the problem of slavery over time. I would recommend *Amazing Grace: William Wilberforce and the Heroic Campaign to End Slavery* by Eric Metaxas to see how a group of committed Christians stood against slavery and had it outlawed in the mighty British empire where it was entrenched. Wilberforce's life was a passionate twenty-year fight to abolish the British slave trade and efforts to abolish slavery in the British colonies, a victory achieved just three days before his death in 1833.

Before Wilberforce, few thought slavery was wrong. After Wilberforce, most societies came to see it as a great moral wrong. He was a hero to Abraham Lincoln and an inspiration to the anti-slavery movement in America.

Along with reading *Amazing Grace*, or maybe before you read it, I recommend reading *Steal Away Home: Charles Spurgeon and Thomas Johnson, Unlikely Friends on the Passage to Freedom* by Matt Carter and Aaron Ivey. You will see some profound truth about slavery in the USA, reconciliation, and the ways of God. You'll get a double bang for your buck because you'll see how God was working in America to eradicate the institution of slavery, plus you'll get to know the prince of preachers, Charles Haddon Spurgeon, intimately and personally. Additionally, you will learn about his unlikely best friend, Thomas Johnson, a freed black man and former American slave. I promise you'll never forget this book or their lives and times. The book was written and researched from both men's journals. The book touches heaven, and it touches the heart.

Slavery — Facts of History

Slavery has been an institution in the world's cultures since antiquity, and it was so until less than two centuries ago. In ancient Rome, estimates are that one-third of the population were slaves. Some sold themselves into slavery so they could eat, have shelter, and learn a trade. Many were captives of war and sold in the marketplace. Most could work to buy their freedom, and a typical length of slavery was seven years. Many chose to remain slaves (then called bondslaves) if they had kind masters who met their needs or they had no better choices. There was no welfare system in Rome. Slaves and ordinary citizens worked for food and shelter day to day. Some probably thought slavery was an injustice, while others considered it a blessing because someone met their needs. All probably considered it a fact of life and the way things were.

Roman slavery usually wasn't slavery for life, and it wasn't based on race, as in Britain or the colonies. Nor did the bulk of slaves come voluntarily from around the world or through conquered peoples, as in Rome. Britain and the colonies' supply of slaves came from African tribes capturing and selling their enemy tribe members to slave traders. So in a sense, they did come from conquered peoples. These are differences, but do we know what it was like in either case? In the fulness of time, some Christians like Wilberforce and friends, the Clapham Sect, made the horrors of the slave trade widely known when communication and government structures made such communication and dialogue possible.

The Bible on Slavery — Rome and Beyond

It's important to know what the Bible says about slavery because that would be what God thinks about it. For some salient insights and to get to the heart of the matter quickly, let's see what Paul wrote to the Church in Ephesus, one of the ten largest cities in the largest, most powerful empire the world has known.

"Slaves, obey your earthly masters with respect and fear, and with sincerity of heart, just as you would obey Christ. Obey them not only to win their favor when their eye is on you, but as slaves of Christ, doing the will of God from your heart. **Serve wholeheartedly, as if you were serving the Lord, not people, because you know that the Lord will reward each one for whatever good they do, whether they are slave or free. And masters, treat your slaves in the same way. Do not threaten them, since you know that he who is both their Master and yours is in heaven, and there is no favoritism with him** [emphasis added]" (Ephesians 6:5-9 NIV).

Some today would have moral objections immediately and cry foul. What, the Bible doesn't decry slavery! No, it doesn't. Instead of addressing the ethical challenges of the future, which He would in time, God addressed the practical difficulties that worked then and have ever since, whether or not people were involved in the institution of slavery.

To stay on the straight and narrow path of truth and not box shadows or joust windmills, we must not avoid any part of Scripture. Let

Scripture speak to every issue and heart because it does. Tozer said: "It takes the whole Bible to make a whole Christian."

Some of Paul's audience were slaves, and some were owners. What Paul said about slaves and to slaves was unprecedented in Rome and all of history. It gave slaves dignity and unknown equality with all people. Paul also encouraged them to seek their freedom if they could. Paul reminds masters of slaves to treat them kindly, with respect, and as fellow servants of Christ, before God Who will judge everyone by these standards.

See how counter-cultural from the mores of men God's ways are and Christians should be. Jesus and his followers could never be a subculture of Rome, Britain, Germany, or America — we were always and forever to be a counterculture. We are to show the way, the truth, the light. We are to preach Jesus and him crucified, then, in the power of His living Spirit, change the culture about us to reflect the kingdom of God. We know from Scripture what the kingdom of God looks like: "**For the kingdom of God is not eating and drinking, but righteousness and peace and joy in the Holy Spirit** [emphasis added]" (Romans 14:17). There are times when the Spirit of God comes strongly to a people in an area, and the counter culture of Christendom affects so many willing and hungry souls that it becomes the culture and is pervasive for a time. Then, for a while, large numbers of people experience righteousness, peace, and joy as they emulate Christ.

The Worst Slavery

The worst slavery is sin. It ends in addiction, codependency, sex trafficking, unhealthy relationships, alienation from God, and death — a slow miserable death.

All the while, a life alive to Christ enjoys a continual feast, no matter our earthly circumstances. Because there is a God who cares, sees, knows, and will act in justice and mercy at all times and every time.

God's judgments are high and out of our sight much of the time on earth, hidden if you will, for reasons known to Himself. Yet He is always in the process of seeing that people reap what they sow while awaiting final adjudication and justice at His great white throne.

Many, many Scriptures support this reality. All of Psalm 10 would be a good meditation. That God's judgments on the earth are many times hidden from us is recorded here: "**The wicked, in the haughtiness of his countenance, does not seek Him. All his thoughts are, 'There is no God.'** His ways prosper at all times; **Your judgments are on high, out of his sight;** as for all his adversaries, he snorts at them. [emphasis added]" (Psalm 10:4-5). Psalm 37 and Psalm 73 are excellent meditations on this truth and how it works, and their numbers are easy to remember. Solomon tells us: "**For God will bring every act to judgment, everything which is hidden, whether it is good or evil** [emphasis added]" (Ecclesiastes 12:14).

A Blame Game

In the meantime, the best secular humanists can do is come up with a blame game. At the moment, they go by the name of BLM, touting CRT in our country. A small group of people influenced by the darkness are trying to divide the country based on race and gain unmerited power and influence for themselves. It occurs to me now that they are, in essence, shaking their angry fists at God, trying to undo all the racial healing and freedom from slavery He has brought forth in the past few centuries.

People who have never been enslaved demand that people who never owned slaves give them money. Doesn't this sound odd to you? And a wee bit unjust — it's neither social justice nor justice. It's a blatant deception, except for those who can see it.

Voddie Baucham says that: "Like all critical theories, Critical Race Theory (CRT) is about assigning fault and casting blame." In truth,

CRT tries to blame America's ills, real or perceived, on a part of our past already dealt with by our Civil War, then further by the civil rights movement of the 1960s, and ongoing by the hand of God. It is He Who rights every wrong now and in the future. He's always present and always seeing the hearts, intentions, and actions of every human being in real-time. And they are recorded for dealing with in our time on the earth and the future. If you think this is hard for our Creator, consider the 150-200 billion galaxies we know about, springing suddenly into existence 14 billion years ago. Or think about the 37 trillion cells in your human body, each a little factory with coded instructions for your creation and well-being.

Black Lives Matter (BLM), which is the same thing and an outgrowth of CRT, is how the darkness is trying to cover up or obscure the real reason for America's ills, real or imagined. The actual cause and one secular humanists loathe to hear is this: "Men have forgotten God; that's why all this has happened" (Aleksandr Solzhenitsyn, 1983 Templeton Address).

I'm not trying to be divisive in calling out the confusion and delusion in the cultural and church landscape. I pray and trust God will take care of this, and He will, just like He did slavery in the first place. I would encourage you to pray that God helps our churches and country turn back to more just, truthful, healthy, helpful, and spiritual ways in the future. My concern and motive for writing about this are your well-being and peace. In this obscured and debris-strewn battlefield with all its smoke and confusion, I want you to see clearly so you can escape to safety and help those around you. Don't put on the BLM goggles! They are very dark, blinding really, and will only hinder your escape to safety from the battlefield.

Try to understand what's going on so you can speak to it. You can pray if you can't talk about it or don't think you have a voice. In any instance, choose to light a candle. Don't waste time or your life cursing the darkness.

In the daily language of the airlines: "Put your oxygen mask on first. Then you can help those seated around you." The flight attendants tell you this before every flight because if the airplane loses cabin pressure at high altitudes, you only have between 60 - 90 seconds to don your oxygen mask. After that, the lack of oxygen to your brain renders you disoriented and unable to think, confused about where you are and what's happening, until you quickly become unconscious. Without oxygen, a short time later, you will die from the lack of sight-giving, brain-enabling, life-sustaining oxygen. Our country and church are in a spiritual decompression right now. Some parts of it are worse off than others, but we're all suffering and in immediate peril unless we get those oxygen masks firmly on our faces and breathe in the life-giving and preserving Word and Spirit of God.

You can read Voddie Baucham's book *Fault Lines* for the truth about the BLM/CRT issue, and be armed with reality to share with those in the market for the truth. Or you can point folks to it once you know what it says. And you can tell folks what the Bible says about slavery in Ephesians 6:5-9. God cares more about your heart and how you act, as master or slave, than He does about the institution of slavery. He's involved in every life, and He will right every wrong. It's His nature and within His power. He's given His Word. And He's given us freedom, more than we can handle without His help, and the freedom to accept or reject that help.

The most important book I read in 2021 was *Fault Lines* by Voddie Baucham. The best book I read in 2021 was *Steal Away Home* by Carter and Ivey.

The End

The end of forced slavery has already been purchased and secured. The date by our present way of reckoning time was April 3, 33 AD. The place was a hill, just outside the Jerusalem city gates, in the Kingdom of

Israel, part of the Roman Empire. The exorbitantly high price was paid by the King of the Jews, Who also happens to be the King of Heaven. His Name be praised, forever. Amen.

✜

"Say, therefore, to the sons of Israel, 'I am the Lord, and I will bring you out from under the burdens of the Egyptians, and I will deliver you from their bondage. I will also redeem you with an outstretched arm and with great judgments'"

(Exodus 6:6).

"For I will go through the land of Egypt on that night, and will strike down all the firstborn in the land of Egypt, both man and beast; and against all the gods of Egypt I will execute judgments—I am the Lord"

(Exodus 12:12).

"After these things I heard something like a loud voice of a great multitude in heaven, saying, 'Hallelujah! Salvation and glory and power belong to our God; because His judgments are true and righteous; for He has judged the great harlot who was corrupting the earth with her immorality, and He has avenged the blood of His bond-servants on her.' And a second time they said, 'Hallelujah! Her smoke rises up forever and ever'"

(Revelation 19:1-3).

"And he said, 'Lord, I believe. And he worshiped Him. And Jesus said, 'For judgment I came into this world, so that those who do not see may see, and that those who see may become blind'" (John 9:38-39).
"Therefore do not go on passing judgment before the time, but wait until the Lord comes who will both bring to light the things hidden

in the darkness and disclose the motives of men's hearts; and then each man's praise will come to him from God"

(1 Corinthians 4:5).

"For it is time for judgment to begin with the household of God; and if it begins with us first, what will be the outcome for those who do not obey the gospel of God?"

(1 Peter 4:17).

"Promising them freedom while they themselves are slaves of corruption; for by what a man is overcome, by this he is enslaved"

(2 Peter 2:19).

"But false prophets also arose among the people, just as there will also be false teachers among you, who will secretly introduce destructive heresies, even denying the Master who bought them, bringing swift destruction upon themselves....The Lord knows how to rescue the godly from temptation, and to keep the unrighteous under punishment for the day of judgment"

(2 Peter 2:1,9).

"There is no wisdom and no understanding and no counsel against the Lord"

(Proverbs 21:30).

PUZZLING CHAPTER 43

Delusion from the Lord

IF THAT SOUNDS FUNNY TO you, it should. And then again, like many puzzles or puzzle pieces, it shouldn't. Delusion is the only logical explanation for most of what we see happening in the church and culture right now — things remarkably and unbelievably different than a mere generation ago. Have you ever heard a sermon or teaching that the Lord might send a delusion? It's in the Bible. It's in the Bible more than once. We must read the Bible for ourselves and ask our pastors, teachers, and friends questions. We must also spend time meditating on Scripture — asking the Lord for illumination.

I recently heard a speaker quote something I had never heard before but loved: "It takes the whole Bible to make a whole Christian." I looked up the source of that quote, and it is A.W. Tozer, who I have read somewhat extensively. I had to smile inside and be glad because I love Tozer. And it's refreshing to discover the childlike wonder of what you don't know. Another of my all-time favorite quotes is: "I'm still learning" (Michelangelo).

The entire quote by Tozer is even more insightful than the shortened, more often quoted version: "The Word of God well understood and religiously obeyed is the shortest route to spiritual perfection. And we must not select a few favorite passages to the exclusion of others. Nothing less than a whole Bible can make a whole Christian" (A.W. Tozer). This is the clear teaching of the Bible, and the Bible is the foundation of our faith. It's the Word of God to his people and to all people who dwell on His earth. "**All Scripture is inspired by God and profitable for teaching, for reproof, for correction, for training in righteousness**; so that the man of God may be adequate, equipped for every good work [emphasis added]" (2 Timothy 3:16-17).

That makes me ponder another Michelangelo quote: "The greater danger for most of us lies not in setting our aim too high and falling short; but in setting our aim too low, and achieving our mark." Could that apply to our search for what we can learn about God and His ways? I think so. We should read the whole Bible as if it were the secret to the treasure of His kingdom and His very Personage, because it is.

Delusion

Delusion sounds very ominous, and it is. It's not something that sounds like it should come from the Lord, so this should grab our attention immediately. Moses by the Spirit 3500 years ago gave us this insight about God: "**God is not a man, that He should lie**, nor a son of man, that He should repent [emphasis added]" (Numbers 23:19a). We have also pointed out in other pieces of this puzzle how the Lord loves and values truth: "**Make them holy by your truth; teach them your word, which is truth** [emphasis added]" (John 17:17 NLT). He even uses it as a synonym for His Son and thus Himself: "**I am** the way, and **the truth**, and the life; no one comes to the Father but through Me [emphasis added]" (John 14:6b). And lastly, we see God loves the truth in people, His creation, and family: "Behold, **You desire truth in**

the innermost being, and in the hidden part You will make me know wisdom [emphasis added]" (Psalm 51:6).

So I'm not sure how you will reconcile this piece of the puzzle. But I trust with God's help, you will be able to do so. Whether you do or not, whether I do or not, we must accept it because it's recorded by the Spirit in the Bible. My mind turns to another famous quote about Aslan the lion, a fictional character representing Jesus: "**Course he isn't safe. But he's good.** He's the King, I tell you [emphasis added]" (C.S. Lewis, *The Lion, the Witch, and the Wardrobe*).

"Yes, But He's in Prison"

In an adjacent piece of this puzzle, you saw or will see something about "lies and deception" in the spiritual realm from the lives of two prophets, an old prophet and a young prophet (1 Kings 13). A second bizarre look or glimpse into the spiritual realm of "lies and deception" comes from the lives of two kings in ancient Judah and Israel (1 Kings 22). It seems like spirits of "lies and deception" are most intense and numerous around power, money, and religion.

Wicked King Ahab and his evil queen Jezebel once ruled in Israel, the ten northern tribes of God's chosen people. At the same time, Jehoshaphat, a godly and good king, ruled in Judah (c. 873–c. 849 bc), the two southern tribes of God's chosen people, usually collectively called Israel — a bit confusing, I know. But Abraham, Isaac, and Jacob (Aka Israel), were fathers of them all.

The people of the two kingdoms were brothers but divided after Solomon and were sometimes at war with each other. Sounds too familiar, doesn't it?

For some reason, probably involving power, money, and mutual self-protection from outside enemies, King Jehoshaphat reached out to King Ahab saying in essence: "Let's be friends." The good king's speech to the evil king went like this: "Jehoshaphat said to the king of Israel,

'I am as you are, my people as your people, my horses as your horses'" (1 Kings 22:4b). But he should have known that wasn't true and understood better than to desire this relationship, even if they were united by common ancestry and God's purposes in the past.

What in common does light have with the dark, or good with evil? The Scripture says: "**Do not be bound together with unbelievers**; for what partnership have righteousness and lawlessness, or **what fellowship has light with darkness?** Or what harmony has Christ with Belial, or **what has a believer in common with an unbeliever?** [emphasis added]" (2 Corinthians 6:14-15). I realize this is in the New Testament, but the Old Testament repeats the same theme and truth in many stories and multiple verses. One such verse would be: "**He who walks with wise men will be wise, but the companion of fools will suffer harm** [emphasis added]" (Proverbs 13:20). Another would be: "**The righteous is a guide to his neighbor, but the way of the wicked leads them astray** [emphasis added]" (Proverbs 12:26). The best reference might be David, the second king of Israel: "How **blessed is the man who does not walk in the counsel of the wicked, nor stand in the path of sinners**, nor sit in the seat of scoffers! But **his delight is in the law of the Lord, and in His law he meditates day and night** [emphasis added]" (Psalm 1:1-2).

Jehoshaphat should have known better than to make a pact with the devil or be unequally yoked with an evil king. But a common enemy had presented itself as a threat to both, and warfare loomed as an option or eventuality. Even with his spiritual vision a little blurred, Jehoshaphat knew to seek the Lord's thinking or advice on such a critical matter as war, from a prophet — one who hears from God.

With the stage set, here's what happens next: "Jehoshaphat said to the king of Israel, '**Please inquire first for the word of the Lord.**' Then the king of Israel gathered the prophets together, about four hundred men, and said to them, 'Shall I go against Ramoth-gilead to battle or shall I refrain?' And they said, 'Go up, for the Lord will give it into the hand of the king.' But Jehoshaphat said, '**Is there not yet a prophet of the Lord here that we may inquire of him?**' The king of Israel said to Jehoshaphat, 'There is yet one man by whom we may inquire of the Lord, but I hate him, because he does not prophesy good concerning me, but evil. **He is Micaiah** son of Imlah [emphasis added]'" (1 Kings 22:5-8a).

The plot thickens. The prophet of God does not tell evil people what they want to hear, and they are miffed. Sound familiar? We have two ancient kings sitting on their thrones in their royal robes, listening to counsel about whether to go to battle against a common enemy together. The evil king's prophets say to go to war, and the Lord will deliver your enemies into your hand. Jehoshaphat, the good king, saw and listened to all this but didn't resonate with them and asked whether there was a genuine prophet of the Lord they could consult. Ahab replied there is one, but "I hate him." He never prophesies anything good about me, and he's in prison. Jehoshaphat said, "Send for him."

As we read the story, Ahab's servants retrieve Micaiah, from prison, clean him up to be presentable before the kings, and ask him to prophesy what the other prophets have said. "But Micaiah said, 'As the Lord lives, what the Lord says to me, that I shall speak'" (1 Kings 22:14). He appears before the kings, and Ahab asks for his counsel. Remarkably, amazingly, and humorously (if you know the end of the story), the prophet says: "Go up and succeed, and the Lord will give it into the hand of the king" (1 Kings 22:15b).

Evidently, God has a sense of humor, as does His prophet. The way Micaiah said what he said must have been with sarcasm or otherwise witty and unbelievable because Ahab immediately said: "**How many times must I adjure you to speak to me nothing but the truth in the name of the Lord?**' So he said, '**I saw all Israel scattered on the mountains, like sheep which have no shepherd.**' And the Lord said, 'These have no master. **Let each of them return to his house in peace** [emphasis added]'" (1 Kings 22:16-17). We learn from what happened that this was the Lord's Word and precisely what would transpire. But we get additional insight into how it came about in the spiritual realm, which is fascinating and telling for us in our day — deception from the Lord.

"Then the king of Israel said to Jehoshaphat, 'Did I not tell you that he would not prophesy good concerning me, but evil?'" (1 Kings 22:18). But the prophet's only reply was to say what he saw in the spiritual realm about the situation at hand: "Micaiah said, '**Therefore, hear the word of the Lord. I saw the Lord sitting on His throne, and all the host of heaven standing by Him on His right and on His left. The Lord said, 'Who will entice Ahab to go up and fall at Ramoth-gilead?' And one said this while another said that. Then a spirit came forward and stood before the Lord and said, 'I will entice him.' The Lord said to him, 'How?' And he said, 'I will go out and be a deceiving spirit in the mouth of all his prophets.' Then He said, 'You are to entice him and also prevail. Go and do so.'** Now therefore, behold, **the Lord has put a deceiving spirit in the mouth of all these your prophets; and the Lord has proclaimed disaster against you** [emphasis added]'" (1 Kings 22:19-23).

2 Thessalonians 2

I hope you'll read the rest of the story in eleven verses (1 Kings 22:29-40). It's so intriguing. I'm sure you will. I can hardly stand not to tell it here, but I don't want to take away from our main point, "deception from the Lord." Indeed that is a significant theme and piece of *Puzzling 2020*. It speaks to how we got here and where we're going as a church and culture. I could say it's the essential part of the puzzle. But upon reflection, the essential part would be, "How then should we live?" Look for those crucial pieces throughout the puzzling process.

Yet it is critically important to understand how we got here and what we're up against. Supposing God sent this delusion changes everything. It points to a different strategy and how to live in these times. The story and spiritual insight above help you understand what Paul tells us in 2 Thessalonians 2. "**Let no one in any way deceive you, for it [Christ's return / the day of the Lord] will not come unless the apostasy comes first** [emphasis added]" (2 Thessalonians 2:3a). And: "**For this reason God will send upon them a deluding influence so that they will believe what is false** [emphasis added]" (2 Thessalonians 2:11).

What to do?

So if this delusion is from the Lord, **can we stand against it?** I think the obvious answer would be "no." We're not gods. Trying to be so is what got us into this mess and quandary — secular humanism, Christian humanism, and our spiritual blindness. But an obvious, immediate truth to put into practice is the old saying: "If you're trying to get out of a rut, first, stop digging." Or a new quote I ran across today: "If you don't know where you are going, any road will get you there" (Lewis Carroll). This seems related to the adage: "Slow down. If you're on the wrong track, it doesn't matter how fast you're going."

So if this delusion is from the Lord, **should we stand against it?** I think the answer would be "yes," but only seeking His wisdom, power, and leading on when and where to do so. This delusion accomplishes His greater purpose: to show the world and the church what we are without Him. We can't and shouldn't think we can stop that, nor would we want to do so. It would be like interfering with a surgeon in the middle of a delicate and life-saving operation. It's better to cooperate in any way he suggests or is helpful or simply stay out of the way.

We need only maintain the perspective that we should: "**Stand by the ways and see and ask for the ancient paths, where the good way is, and walk in it**; and you will **find rest for your souls** [emphasis added]" (Jeremiah 6:16). Speak the truth in love, and be led by the Spirit. Use the Word of God, but always recall it is the sword of the Spirit, not your sword. Use it when and as directed: **"the sword of the Spirit**, which is the word of God [emphasis added]" (Ephesians 6:17b). This calls for spiritual sensitivity, which is gained by practice and abiding with Christ (John 15:5). Keep in mind that the battle is not yours. It's His, as another prophet of God reminded the king and people of Israel who were in a predicament: **"Listen, all Judah and the inhabitants of Jerusalem and King Jehoshaphat: thus says the Lord to you, 'Do not fear or be dismayed because of this great multitude, for the battle is not yours but God's** [emphasis added]" (2 Chronicles 20:15). Remember where the power and might for the battles of our lives and times come from: "This is the word of the Lord to Zerubbabel saying, **'Not by might nor by power, but by My Spirit,' says the Lord of hosts**. 'What are you, O great mountain? Before Zerubbabel you will become a plain; and **he will bring forth the top stone with shouts of "Grace, grace to it!** [emphasis added]'" (Zechariah 4:6-7). We must understand where the power is and that there is untold power in His Grace. Paul ends most of his letters with a blessing and prayer: **"the grace of God be with you all."**

Perspective of Delusion

Just being armed with this correct perspective of delusion in our present darkness should comfort many parents who wonder, "Where did I go wrong with my kids?" Much of **their wandering and waywardness is due to this delusion.** It's aided by the media, the media used by the dark side, permitted by the Lord (or sent by Him!). The pervasive influence of lies and the cultural draw of peer pressure and secular humanism taught in our schools and universities for decades have our young people in a chaos of conscience, class, and cliques — very wayward and confused. More dangerous or threatening is that they are opposed to the ways and Person of God. This never ends well, except for His mercy and grace. Much prayer is the order of the day.

Of course, we weren't perfect parents. There are none. We should humbly own our mistakes and ask forgiveness, making amends where needed or appropriate. We need to operate in love, grace, and truth toward our children and youth. They want and need our blessing, and we shouldn't withhold it, but tell them the truth about what you believe and why. Don't be too concerned about the seemingly polarized relationships brought about mainly by social media and skin deep or screen deep relationships. Tell them the truth in love, if you love them. Love covers a multitude of sins. Trust God with the results. Let them see and sense your faith. And pray to God for vision and healing in every relationship you have. Missing life here and in eternity is at stake.

What do you make of a story like the one in 1 Kings 22? Have you ever heard a sermon or teaching on this event? It's in the Bible. The Spirit saw purpose in relating it. It's a trustworthy and accurate account of things that happen in the heavenlies, and it's supported elsewhere by the Scriptures (Ephesians 6:12, Daniel 10:13).

The first thing that comes to mind is don't be smug in your understanding of the spiritual realm. Don't be afraid of it either. Trust God, choose your alliances wisely based on their character and the leading of the Holy Spirit. Trust God, not your theology or church doctrine, and live life in the Spirit. That's what Scripture teaches. Don't be afraid of anything or anyone but fear God. He's trustworthy and true.

Could God send a deceiving spirit? The Bible says He's going to, as attested by Paul in 2 Thessalonians 2. The same Bible gives us an account of a time He did just that in 1 Kings 22. This is a good reminder that He is God and we are not. Let's try to trust Him, and live the life He's provided and empowered by His grace and His Spirit.

To sulk or blame God or anybody for misleading you instead of taking responsibility for yourself and reading the Bible He provided you is like walking out into a clear area or sitting down under a tree during a lightning storm. Good luck.

Live local. Live in the Spirit. Acts17:23-31 tells us that is God's plan and design for us. Live courageously and enjoy your journey.

Summary — Living with Delusion

At the end of his second letter to the church in Thessalonica, Paul sums up his advice and instruction concerning the attempted deception there. I think it speaks volumes of counsel and guidance for us today. Paul the Apostle says: "But **we should always give thanks to God for** you, **brethren beloved by the Lord**, because God has chosen you from the beginning for salvation **through sanctification by the Spirit and faith in the truth.** It was **for this He called you** through our gospel, **that you may gain the glory of our Lord Jesus Christ**. So then, brethren, **stand firm and hold to the traditions which you were taught, whether by word of mouth or by letter from us.** Now **may our Lord Jesus Christ Himself and God our Father, who has loved us and given us eternal comfort and good hope by grace, comfort and strengthen your hearts in every good work and word** [emphasis added]" (2 Thessalonians 2:13-17).

"There's a wideness in God's mercy,
Like the wideness of the sea;
There's a kindness in His Justice,
Which is more than liberty.
But we make His love too narrow
By false limits of our own,
And we magnify His strictness
With a zeal He will not own.

> There is welcome for the sinner,
> And more graces for the good;
> There is mercy with the Saviour;
> There is healing in His blood.
> For the love of God is broader
> Than the measure of Man's mind;
> And the heart of the Eternal
> Is most wonderfully kind.
> If our lives were but more simple,
> We should take Him at His word;
> And our lives would be all sunshine
> In the sweetness of our Lord"
>
> (John G. Lake).

"At this also my heart trembles, and leaps from its place. Listen closely to the thunder of His voice, and the rumbling that goes out from His mouth. Under the whole heaven He lets it loose, and His lightning to the ends of the earth. God thunders with His voice wondrously, doing great things which we cannot comprehend"

(Job 37:1-3, 5).

"The coming of the lawless one will be in accordance with how Satan works. He will use all sorts of **displays of power through signs and wonders that serve the lie,** and all the ways that wickedness deceives those who are perishing. **They perish because they refused to love the truth and so be saved. For this reason God sends them a powerful delusion** so that they will believe the lie and so that all will be condemned who have not believed the truth but have delighted in wickedness [emphasis added]"

(2 Thessalonians 2:9-12 NIV).

PUZZLING CHAPTER 44

Peter and Faith

I AWAKENED EARLY ONE MORNING thinking about Peter and his great walk of faith. He certainly wasn't perfect in it, but as far as I know, he was one of only two water-walkers in human history. He was willing to get out of the boat when no one else was. It was his idea. He was a little bit hot and cold in his walk of faith as he learned to walk more by faith than by sight. The progression came as he became more and more enamored with and trusting of his Lord. It's a bit that way for all of us, is it not?

Paul had a lot of faith too. He exercised it and wrote about it extensively. Most of our insights about faith — what it is, how foundational it is, and how vital — come from Paul's analysis and pen. He was more cerebral about it than Peter but just as powerful and practical.

Peter admired how Paul could write about faith and analyze it along with other spiritual truths. He told us all: "And regard the patience of our Lord as salvation; just as also **our beloved brother Paul, according to the wisdom given him, wrote to you, as also in all his letters, speaking in them of these things, in which are some things hard to** understand, which **the untaught and unstable distort, as they do also the rest of the Scriptures, to their own destruction** [emphasis added]" (2 Peter 3:15-16).

Paul was a lawyer and very well educated in the Greco-Roman school of logic, rhetoric, knowledge, and organized thought. It's a miracle of no small proportion that Paul was also a mystic and understood faith and grace were the real keys to the kingdom. He subjugated his great mind to these instead of exalting his mind and becoming famous or prideful.

We read a caution that "knowledge puffs up" in Scripture: "**Knowledge makes arrogant, but love edifies**. If anyone supposes that he knows anything, he has not yet known as he ought to know; but **if anyone loves God, he is known by Him** [emphasis added]" (1 Corinthians 8:1b-3). And we also read that Paul's intellectual prowess was known by kings as well as by Peter: "**While Paul was saying this in his defense, Festus said in a loud voice, "Paul, you are out of your mind! Your great learning is driving you mad** [emphasis added]" (Acts 26:24).

But "his great learning" didn't drive him mad! Paul's faith completed him — it didn't compete within him. Once faith opened his eyes and mind, he saw so much farther that it excited his brain and intellect. He valued both knowing facts and that the spiritual was surpassingly valuable, more awesome, more powerful, and the prescribed path to knowing God and the things of God.

He could effectively write about it, having experienced both learning and faith, more than perhaps anyone in history, by his prowess or giftedness and the Lord's direction and grace. He wrote compellingly about the struggle between the mind and the heart, the intellect and faith. This has been important to us during the two millennia since he wrote about both to help us see the bridge of trust and encourage us to cross it to the beautiful land of the Spirit and our creator God.

One example from Scripture of how he could see both realms and write about them so beautifully is in his letter to the church in Rome: **"Because that which is known about God is evident within them; for God made it evident to them. For since the creation of the world His invisible attributes, His eternal power and divine nature, have been clearly seen, being understood through what has been made**, so that they are without excuse. For even though they knew God, they did not honor Him as God or give thanks [emphasis added]" (Romans 1:19-21a). Paul is one of many intellectuals, academics, and geniuses who experienced knowledge and reason, faith and grace. Newton, Pascal, Galileo, Kepler, Copernicus, and Augustine are others. The list is long, yet relatively few have the intellectual prowess of these listed.

Nevertheless, anyone can experience through the gift of faith with whatever reasoning powers they have, access to the fantastic, beautiful, enlightening realm of the Spirit. This brings us back to Peter.

Peter seems to see into the spiritual realm as far or farther than even Paul. Their names are synonymous with the early founders of the church and history makers. They changed the course of history perhaps more than anyone else we know or read about, except the object of their affection and worship, Jesus Christ, the Son of God.

If you have a sense of history, you should be able to see how Christianity changed the Roman empire, then swept into Europe, across the Atlantic into the Americas, across the Pacific to Asia, and now back to its starting place, the Middle East. The Twelve Apostles are primarily responsible for this invasion of the kingdom of God, enabled by faith, the Bible, and empowered by the Spirit as planned by God before time. The Book of Acts gives us snippets of their stories, how they operated, and how they did this.

In our Bibles, it's titled *The Acts of the Apostles*. Some have suggested it could more appropriately be called *The Acts of the Holy Spirit*. By God's grace, it's both. And the two preeminent apostles were Peter and Paul.

It's fun and enlightening to look at them individually as apostles through the lens of faith and grace and their natural gifting and human abilities. It's also interesting to note that they seldom, if ever, did. After they experienced God's grace and accessed it by faith, that's all they talked about, wrote about, and walked out.

They conclude almost all of their writings, which comprise much of the New Testament, with similar phrases and not just for show or to be uniform in appearance. Those phrases include prayers and blessings they knew God would answer for the recipient individuals and churches. Those prayers and blessings were for grace, peace, love, and power in the Holy Spirit — but always grace, the unmerited favor and power of God, which includes the others.

Paul's prayer for grace bookends Ephesians at the beginning and ending: "**Grace to you and peace from God** our Father and the Lord Jesus Christ" (Ephesians 1:2), and: "**Peace be to the brethren, and love with faith, from God** the Father and the Lord Jesus Christ. **Grace be with all those who love our Lord Jesus Christ** with incorruptible love [emphasis added]" (Ephesians 6:23-24). At the end of other letters, we see this too: "I, Paul, write this greeting with my own hand. Remember my imprisonment. **Grace be with you** [emphasis added]" (Colossians 4:18). Peter stressed grace too in his letters: "but **grow in the grace and knowledge of our Lord and Savior Jesus Christ**. To Him be the glory, both now and to the day of eternity. Amen [emphasis added]" (2 Peter 3:18).

Faith and grace, grace and faith, these are the undisputed keys to the kingdom. "By grace, you are saved through faith," or as some European reformers couched it: "By grace alone, through faith alone, in Christ alone." This became the mantra of the reformation, a rediscovery of the apostles' teaching and lifestyle with their Creator, Redeemer, Father, and Friend through His only begotten Son, Jesus Christ. Since then, it's been shared with many sons and daughters. I hope you are one, or will become one!

This writing has taken a different direction from focusing on Peter as intended initially. But in the end, enough is said.

Of late, my favorite books of the New Testament to read over and over are the two letters of Peter. They have a mysterious, compelling draw, not just for their brevity, conciseness, profound and distilled truth. You sense the power, peace, and spiritual seeing ability in his life when you read it, along with his beautiful, comfortable, confident relationship with his Savior and Friend.

How did he get it? I think he would smile and say, "Grace and Faith." Faith opens the realm of the Spirit to you, and then you can write what you see and hear, by God's grace.

Epilogue

Mystery? Yes, there is and always will be some mystery involved. It's mysterious — anything we can't fully process or explain with our minds is what we call mystery. But it's not that complicated. Mystery doesn't mean complex, just unknown.

Faith and its exercise are as simple as a trusting child jumping from some height into a trustworthy parent's arms. Grace, the faithful catching, is God's part.

Hopefully, discussing it in this way using non-religious, non-theological terms and keeping it as simple as it is has caused you to think about the grace and faith proposition again or anew. You'll need to function in it in the days ahead. But then again, you always did.

"For **by grace you have been saved through faith**. And this is not your own doing; it is **the gift of God**, not a result of works, so that **no one may boast** [emphasis added]'"

(Ephesians 2:8-9 ESV).

"Now when Jesus came into the district of Caesarea Philippi, He was asking His disciples, 'Who do people say that the Son of Man is?' And they said, 'Some say John the Baptist; and others, Elijah; but still others, Jeremiah, or one of the prophets.' He said to them, 'But who do you say that I am?' **Simon Peter answered, 'You are the Christ, the Son of the living God** [emphasis added]'"

(Matthew 16:13-16).

"Then **Peter said**, 'Silver or gold I do not have, but what I do have I give you. **In the name of Jesus Christ of Nazareth, walk** [emphasis added]'"

(Acts 3:6 NIV).

"**Peter, an apostle of Jesus Christ**,…**May grace and peace be yours in the fullest measure** [emphasis added]'"

(1 Peter 1:1-2).

PUZZLING CHAPTER 45

The Fool

"THE FOOL HAS SAID IN his heart, 'There is no God'" (Psalm 14:1a).

This is a chapter I didn't expect to write. But I feel the Spirit leading me to discuss it as a piece of the puzzle, especially considering what the Bible says about fools.

I think it's safe to say none of us wants to be a fool. None of us wants to be fooled or deceived. None of us wants to act like a fool. So let's pause and see if we can get the Creator's thoughts on the matter. Evidently, it's on His mind and pervasive in human history from antiquity until today.

Why is this important?

Do you think you can fool God? About anything? Do you think you can pick and choose from His Word, the Word He says He divinely inspired? Do you think by selective obedience to some of His Word, you can fool Him into thinking you're a Christian or a follower of His

Son the Christ? If you feel that or live like that, you have only succeeded in fooling yourself.

"The essence of idolatry is the entertainment of thoughts about God that are unworthy of Him" (A.W. Tozer).

The Bible tells us and also demonstrates in story after true-life story that God, who created everything and sustains everything that He made, knows everything, including the number of hairs on your head and the thoughts and intentions of your heart.

So if you think you're fooling Him, you are only fooling or deceiving yourself. In essence, you have become a fool and are playing the fool.

We're using the Biblical definition of a fool here: "The fool has said in his heart, there is no God." So if you have your image of God and not how He paints Himself in the Bible, aren't you saying: "There is no God [like that]." If so, you may be a fool and have been fooled, according to the Bible.

I'm not calling you a fool! God has some powerful words for anyone who calls someone a fool: "But I say to you that **everyone who is angry with his brother** shall be guilty before the court; and **whoever says to his brother, 'You good-for-nothing,'** shall be guilty before the supreme court; and **whoever says, 'You fool,' shall be guilty enough to go into the fiery hell** [emphasis added]" (Matthew 5:22).

Doing any of the things listed in the verse above puts you, a human, in a place of judgment, self-exaltation, and pride before the Almighty. He will stomach nothing of the sort. Don't be foolish is the strong warning from Jesus Himself. All three of these behaviors and attitudes are stepping stones toward calling others "a fool" and thus becoming a fool, in danger of perishing, which is the end of fools.

This discussion is for self-examination and rumination of what the Bible and God say about being a fool. It's for our illumination and benefit in living life with a truthful and healthy paradigm.

There seems to be a connection between being a fool and being deceived — especially concerning one's notion or belief about God and one's relationship to God.

Throughout history, the fool is considered a human who acts out of a distorted view of reality.

A Dictionary Look At The Fool

A Dictionary exercise using Merriam-Webster supports the tricked or deceived connection with being a fool or acting a fool. The noun "fool" means: "a silly or stupid person; a person who lacks judgment or sense." Or: "a person who has been tricked or deceived into appearing or acting silly or stupid."

As a verb, "fool" means: "to trick, deceive, or impose on." Common verb phrases include "fool around," which means: "to putter aimlessly; waste time," "to philander or flirt," and "to be sexually promiscuous, especially to engage in adultery." To "fool away" means: "to spend foolishly, as time or money; squander." To "fool with" means: "to handle or play with idly or carelessly," as in "to be hurt while fooling with a loaded gun."

I think we know these definitions and word usages from our language, culture, and history. We think of "fools or fooled" as undesirable and that certainly couldn't include us, but do we consider the significance of applying the concept to our relationship with our Maker? What does He think? And what does He see?

A Bible Looks At The Fool

Three ancient Hebrew words are translated as "fool" in our English Bibles. "Nabal" used by David in Psalm 14:1, is used eighteen times in the KJV. The BDB Lexicon, arguably the best Hebrew-English dictionary in the world, written by German scholars in the 1800s, defines "nabal" as: "foolish, senseless, fool." Strong's Definitions define "nabal" as a "stupid, wicked (especially impious), vile person."

A second word translated "fool" in our KJV English Bibles seventy times is "kesiyl." BDB defines it as: "fool, stupid fellow, dullard, simpleton, arrogant one." Strong defines it as: "properly fat, (figuratively) stupid or silly, fool (-ish)."

A third word translated "fool" twenty-six times in our KJV English Bibles is "eviyl," and BDB defines it as: "(1) one who despises wisdom, (2) one who mocks when guilty, (3) one who is quarrelsome, (4) one who is licentious." Strong defines it as: "silly, fool (-ish) (man)." It comes "from an unused root meaning to be perverse."

Wow! Those ancient meanings of the word "fool" speak deeply into how one defines a fool, becomes a fool, and the end of the fool.

It's a matter of what one says or believes in his heart. It's a matter of the heart. It's a matter of will. Truth and deception come to you during your lifetime. What you believe or accept as truth will determine your reality and outcome.

Is God True or Mankind?

The Bible is clear concerning the ultimate source of truth: "What then? If some did not believe, their unbelief will not nullify the faithfulness of God, will it? May it never be! Rather, **let God be found true, though every man be found a liar** [emphasis added]" (Romans 3:3-4a].

Or is God a liar and humanity true? That determination is left to you by a magnanimous God who grants you free will. It is up to you to decide for yourself and act accordingly.

Oh, it won't alter the truth that God is who He says He is and rules over all. But you are given the freedom to believe differently and act that way if you choose.

If this is your desire, may it go well with you. But this is clearly not the best path and the path God has proffered you by His love, light, and grace. Two courses are described in His Word for acceptance or rejection, along with the consequences of each.

Proverbs

The foolish and wise are contrasted in Proverbs, an ancient book of wisdom written mainly by Solomon about 1000 BC. These sage collections of timeless wisdom are written to young men or men in general but apply to both sexes in every way.

The Proverbs encourage wise behavior and warn of the pitfalls of foolish behavior with examples. They indicate a person will be tempted to be deceived, usually in the area of sex and money, and that life and success, or death and failure, will result from each individual's decisions.

The Proverbs tell us God has given us this honor to enjoy life and decide how we want to live it. He has also painted an accurate and timeless picture of the outcome of both paths to help truth-seeking humans along their way to the best result.

Oddly, he paints wisdom as a Person or companion on life's journey — a Guide to the best life can offer and indicates the relationship with this Guide is more important than life's outcome. Guidance must be believed, then discovered true or false along the way. Wisdom is proven by her actions, or as the Bible says: "Yet **wisdom is vindicated by her deeds** [emphasis added]" (Matthew 11: 16-19).

A Man Named "Fool"

This is an odd one! We have an account in the Bible of a man actually named "Fool." To top it off, he was wealthy and had a beautiful, wise wife. The story involves David, the noblest king of Israel, about 1000 BC. You can read the whole whimsical, jarring story in I Samuel 25.

What were his parents thinking? They named their son Nabal, one of three Hebrew words for "fool." I've read that in this culture and day, parents would watch the actions of their small children to note some character trait or bent, then name them accordingly. I still can't imagine naming or calling your young boy "Fool."

That's not the point of the discussion, however. It's to see what can we learn or what might benefit us from a man named "Fool"? As the story develops to one of its most suspenseful junctures, we know what Fool's wife and the household thinks the name means. It's instructive and insightful for us today. His wife tells us as she addresses David the King: "Please **do not let my lord pay attention to this worthless man,** Nabal, for as his name is, so is he. **Nabal is his name, and folly is with him** [emphasis added]" (1 Samuel 25:25).

Then there is another definition of a fool to ponder. It's one to remember if you don't want to be a fool or play the fool. Nabal's servants told his beautiful, sensitive, and wise wife Abigail a further definition of a "fool," saying: "**He's such a worthless man nobody can speak to him** [tell him anything] [emphasis added]" (1 Samuel 25:17b).

This foolishness almost cost Nabal his life and that of every male servant he had. It eventually did cost him his life, wife, and fortune. He should've listened to his servants. Fools aren't prone to listen to anyone else. That's the point. They are so sure of themselves and convinced of their position, importance, and judgment on most matters.

I loved my father-in-law like my father. Both were great men and leaders, examples to young men and their communities. And even though my father-in-law honored me, I honored him, and we loved each other, he would often say something marginally offensive. He enjoyed saying: "You can tell a fighter pilot, but you can't tell them much."

I know he was proud of me. He expressed it in many ways and kept some models of fighter jets I had flown in the lobby of his automotive repair shop. It was his way of saying, man-to-man, father-to-son: "Stay humble and be willing to listen to others."

A beautiful, poetic verse in one of David's Psalms says the humble shall hear. "My soul will make its boast in the Lord; **the humble will**

hear it and rejoice [emphasis added]" (Psalm 34:2). Humility is an aid to hearing in the spirit and knowing God. You might say it's a prerequisite.

Hubris, or pride is deafening, blinding, and deceiving — incredibly offensive in the presence of the Holy, which would be everywhere and always. The most important thing you can do in your life is to choose humility, be humble, hear and obey God.

Eighteen Inches or Michael's Story

Eighteen inches, one cubit, the distance between most peoples's elbow and longest fingertip, was a common unit of measurement in antiquity. It is also the approximate distance between the head and the heart. Once I had a young college-age man who grew up in our church approach me and ask to discuss faith and religion. He told me he had become an atheist and wanted to talk to someone about it, but not his closest friends because they were Christians, and he didn't want to hurt their faith. He remarked, "I don't think I can hurt your faith."

I told him I would be glad to talk to him anytime he wished, and we met several times over a beverage or lunch, to share a book, or to watch a movie of interest to us. Once there was a young guy from Idaho who many considered a prophet, visiting our town and talking to me about joint village work in Belize. Following a spiritual impression, I seized the opportunity to have him meet and speak with my young friend Michael in case he might have a prophetic word to help Michael on his journey.

I arranged a meeting at a local coffee shop Michael and I frequented. Michael didn't show. When I called to see if he was coming, he told me he needed to cancel. I was disappointed but asked my young prophetic friend if he might have a word for Michael anyway. He replied, "I think I do. Your friend has said there is no God in his head, but he hasn't said it in his heart."

I later shared this with Michael, then looked at him for an answer or reaction. He simply said: "That's true."

It seems like this situation is valid for believing and non-believing people alike. The lies or truths must make the journey eighteen inches from your head to your heart before it ultimately matters and has its effect. This is the most critical eighteen inches in history, certainly personal history. It's the crucial distance thoughts traverse for a person determining truth or lies, which are the matters and essence of life and death.

Scripture Meditations on Fools and Foolishness

A fool does not delight in understanding, but only in revealing his own mind"

(Proverbs 18:2).

"The fear of the Lord is the beginning of knowledge; fools despise wisdom and instruction"

(Proverbs 1:7).

"A fool always loses his temper, but a wise man holds it back"

(Proverbs 29:11).

"Do not be eager in your heart to be angry, for anger resides in the bosom of fools"

(Ecclesiastes 7:9).

"When a wise man has a controversy with a foolish man, the foolish man either rages or laughs, and there is no rest"

(Proverbs 29:9).

"A fool's mouth is his ruin, and his lips are the snare of his soul"

(Proverbs 18:7).

"The lips of the wise spread knowledge, but the hearts of fools are not so"

(Proverbs 15:7).

"Leave the presence of a fool, or you will not discern words of knowledge. The wisdom of the sensible is to understand his way, but the foolishness of fools is deceit. Fools mock at sin, but among the upright there is good will"

(Proverbs 14:7-9).

"Everyone who hears these words of Mine and does not act on them, will be like a foolish man who built his house on the sand"

(Matthew 7:26).

"Do not answer a fool according to his folly, or you will also be like him. Answer a fool as his folly deserves, that he not be wise in his own eyes"

(Proverbs 26:4-5).

"Like the legs which are useless to the lame, so is a proverb in the mouth of fools"

(Proverbs 26:7).

"Like an archer who wounds everyone, so is he who hires a fool or who hires those who pass by"

(Proverbs 26:10).

"Do you see a man wise in his own eyes? There is more hope for a fool than for him"

(Proverbs 26:12).

"He who conceals hatred has lying lips, and he who spreads slander is a fool"

(Proverbs 10:18).

"He who troubles his own house will inherit wind, and the foolish will be servant to the wise hearted"

(Proverbs 11:29).

"The wise fear the Lord and shun evil, but a fool is hotheaded and yet feels secure"

(Proverbs 14:16 NIV).

"A truly wise person uses few words; a person with understanding is even-tempered. Even fools are thought wise when they keep silent; with their mouths shut, they seem intelligent"

(Proverbs 17:27-28 NLT).

Is Atheism Dead?

An octogenarian friend of mine recently recommended to me the book *Is Atheism Dead?* by Eric Metaxas. My wise, older friend is a brilliant lawyer, an adventurer, well-read, and a naturalist. He related he had read the book through ten times! I didn't care for the title much at first, but an intellectual friend who read the book when I did thought it was brilliant. It's in direct reference to the April 8, 1966 cover of *Time* magazine, "*Is God Dead?*"

I knew about Metaxas from his best known work, *Bonhoeffer: Pastor, Martyr, Prophet, Spy*, which is a must read. He did a beautiful job on this latest book too, as one might expect of a Yale graduate, whose speciality is biographies with investigative attention to detail. Basically he took all the arguments of the leading atheist scientists in 1966 and shows us what science has learned since then in the first section of the book. In the second section he looks at what archeology has shown us since then, validating the ancient Biblical record with not a single find refuting it. Then in the third and final section he deals with the young atheists of the time on their philosophy — where it leads and their willful distain for truth if it points away from their positions.

He did such a masterful job showing how science, archeology, and philosophy have done nothing but point us toward God since 1966, that after reading his book I would agree, atheism is dead. It's dead factually, logically, and scientifically with what we know today and has been discovered since the time of the 1966 article. But it's not dead as long as deception is alive — as long as there are people who don't want to know the truth or facts, but had rather believe in their hearts there is no God.

Summary

"**But to what shall I compare this generation?** It is like children sitting in the market places, who call out to the other children, and say, 'We played the flute for you, and you did not dance; we sang a dirge, and you did not mourn.' For John came neither eating nor drinking, and they say, 'He has a demon!' The Son of Man came eating and drinking, and they say, 'Behold, a gluttonous man and a drunkard, a friend of tax collectors and sinners!' Yet **wisdom is vindicated by her deeds** [emphasis added]"

(Matthew 11: 16-19).

"**And if you call on him as Father who judges impartially according to each one's deeds, conduct yourselves with fear throughout the time of your exile, knowing that you were ransomed from the futile ways** inherited from your forefathers, not with perishable things such as silver or gold [emphasis added]"

(1 Peter 1:17-18 ESV).

"The way of a fool is right in his own eyes, but **a wise man is he who listens to counsel** [emphasis added]"

(Proverbs 12:15).

"**Do not be wise in your own eyes; fear the Lord and turn away from evil** [emphasis added]"

(Proverbs 3:7).

"**The eyes of the Lord are toward the righteous** and His ears are open to their cry. **The face of the Lord is against evildoers**, to cut off the memory of them from the earth [emphasis added]"

(Psalm 34:15-16).

"**The fool has said in his heart, 'There is no God.'** They are corrupt, they have committed abominable deeds; there is no one who does good. The Lord has looked down from heaven upon the sons of men to see if there are any who understand, who seek after God. They have all turned aside, together they have become corrupt; there is no one who does good, not even one [emphasis added]"

(Psalm 14:1-3).

PUZZLING CHAPTER 46

Stay in Your Lane - Men

Motivation for the Journey

Allow me first to say a few words about the woman's lane. I do this for two reasons. First, so you may know what the woman's lane looks like in God's economy. The lines have blurred in our day and culture, even in our churches, so the sexes collide. They are not making peaceful, orderly progress in their journeys, but instead suffering crashes, hurt, injury, and setbacks. Secondly, you'll be encouraged to do your part, trusting God and His Spirit to lead and help your wife do her part because at least you are in your lane. Be sure about the lanes and your target. You may recall what Zig Ziglar said: "If you aim at nothing, you will hit it every time."

These brief descriptions of the woman's lane come primarily from Tony Evans and a video titled "Kingdom Woman." You may want to access that for more insight. Also, a piece of the puzzle on the woman's lane comes in the next chapter.

Dr. Evans says when considering the woman's alignment (lane), we first have to ask if the man is in alignment (his lane). Because he is the husband (a gardening term) and is responsible to some significant degree for how his garden (wife) looks and grows. That you reap what you sow is a time-honored axiom, and it's especially true about our wives. It's not the whole story. Of course, they are free-will creatures before God like we are. But I've noticed in life, and predict you have too, that wives seem to accentuate husbands' strengths and weaknesses. So be careful what you sow. You may be more responsible for what you loathe in your wife than you're aware. Take care of your garden in healthy ways, and you'll have good produce all your days. Of course, you'll need God's help, but it's available.

Our lanes have nothing to do with the equality of persons. We are joint heirs and equal partners in life, equal in value but not equal in function. Very quickly, we come in the Scriptures to the hated word (in our day) submit: "**Wives, submit yourselves** to your own husbands as you do to the Lord. For **the husband is the head of the wife** as Christ is the head of the church, his body, of which he is the Savior [emphasis added]" (Ephesians 5:22-23 NIV). And we read: "But I want you to understand that Christ is the head of every man, and the man is the head of a woman, and God is the head of Christ" (1 Corinthians 11:3).

God values authority and order very much. Do it His way, and you'll experience peace and His promises. Do it your way, and you'll endure pain with steep precipices and divides.

In every age where feminism is strong, and men are abdicating their positions, situations that are connected, these words "submit yourself" or "subject yourself" seem like roadblocks or big stones blocking freedom and happiness for women. God says they are instead touchstones to happiness, joy, peace, and more freedom. Who do you believe?

The Bible goes even further in talking to wives about their lane: "In the same way, you **wives, be submissive to your own husbands so that even if any of them are disobedient to the word,** they may be won without a word by the behavior of their wives [emphasis added]"

(1 Peter 3:1). Men, this is not for you to know so you can hold a gun to your wife's head. But so you know these are God's words and wisdom for peace and life — the way things should be to invoke His pleasure and promises — a target for harmonious living and joyful lives. But you must focus on your lane, something you can control by your vision and will.

Dr. Evans describes the woman's lane as: "without a word — don't nag." Your adornment must not only be external. He says: "Look in the mirror of God's word and see if you're pretty on the inside." And he reminds us about a gentle and quiet spirit: "Your adornment must not be merely external—braiding the hair, and wearing gold jewelry, or putting on dresses; but let it be the hidden person of the heart, with the imperishable quality of a gentle and quiet spirit, which is precious in the sight of God" (1 Peter 3:3-4).

He encourages wives to be a help-mate, not a hurt-mate. And to be like Sarah, "calling Abraham lord" (1 Peter 3:6). He reminds us all when you rebel against legitimate authority, we rebel against God.

Husband's Understand

God's instructions to stay in our lanes are sprinkled throughout the Word. They are important. One of the best summaries, with practical details and God's heart in the matter, is 1 Peter 3. Looking at just one verse, we see: "You **husbands** in the same way, **live with your wives in an understanding way**, as with someone weaker, since she is a woman; and **show her honor as a fellow heir of the grace of life**, so that **your prayers will not be hindered** [emphasis added]" (1 Peter 3:7).

Please read the whole chapter several times, men; if you want all the nuances and insights. The Spirit will show you wisdom and God's heart on this matter of your lane. Nothing can bring you more joy in your earth life than getting this right, or more pain if you don't.

A verse worth mentioning and meditating upon concerning understanding our roles as husbands is: "**Who are you to judge the servant of another?** To his [or her] own master he [or she] stands or falls; and he [or she] will stand, for the Lord is able to make him [or her] stand [emphasis added]" (Romans 14:4). Once when I was judging my wife for some leadership issues in the family with our children I didn't think appropriate, the Lord through a Sunday School class teacher showed me this verse the very same morning. Then the thought came from another realm: "**She's your helpmeet, but she's My servant. Don't judge her.**"

Live with her understanding she's a woman. Seek to understand grace for yourself so you can honor her as a fellow heir with the grace she craves, and God extends. Understanding your wife and extending grace is tied to effectiveness in prayer, perhaps the most potent force in the universe because it moves the most powerful Being in the universe by His invitation and design. Indeed, as I was writing these three chapters on the man's lane, the woman's lane, and prayer, I felt the Spirit impress me, "These are the three most important topics in the book, practically speaking."

Like Gravity

Some basic tendencies of men and women are woven into men and women from creation by God's design and His decree. We see it in Genesis, the account of the creation and actions of the earliest humankind.

The women's lane is a creation issue, not a political or cultural issue. And so is man's. God's wisdom squares against that of secular humanism. She tends to want to control her husband or a man but will not be happy and fulfilled unless she overcomes that desire and voluntarily chooses to give up control to her husband or male authority in her life, trusting what God says and looking to His support as she does. It's the way of humility and trust that works itself out as submission and respect or honoring men and the role God gave them.

In the first book of the Bible, as a result of rebellion and disobedience toward God, we see God's action in the life of the first woman and women's DNA ever since: "To the woman He said, 'I will greatly multiply your pain in childbirth, in pain you will bring forth children; yet **your desire will be for your husband, and he will rule over you** [emphasis added]'" (Genesis 3:16). You can remember how basic and pervasive this is by remembering John 3:16, the often quoted and most familiar verse in the Bible summarizing salvation and restored relationship with God.

The Hebrew word for "desire" used here is only used two times in the Bible in a similar context, and it means "to control." The other time is before Cain killed his brother Abel and was sulking because God accepted Abel's sacrifice over his own: "And the Lord had regard for Abel and for his offering; but for Cain and for his offering He had no regard. So Cain became very angry and his countenance fell. Then the Lord said to Cain, 'Why are you angry? And why has your countenance fallen? If you do well, will not your countenance be lifted up? And if you do not do well, **sin is crouching at the door; and its desire is for you, but you must master it** [emphasis added]'" (Genesis 4:4b-7). So we see the Lord God telling Cain that sin desires to control him, but he must rule over it. And in the same manner, the woman is told going forward, she has an innate desire to rule over her husband, but she must rule over that desire, submit to him, obey him, and thus honor him.

How about gravity and man? Simply said in the vernacular, men have in them from the Garden of Eden the desire to put their feet up and rest or vegetate. As our sentence, we must get out of the easy chair, work, and lead, even though it will be more challenging than before. This is a judicial sentence and an invitation to grace, as submission and honor are for the woman.

We read in Genesis about the original man and men ever since:

"Then to Adam He said, '**Because you have listened to the voice of your wife**, and have eaten from the tree about which I commanded you,' saying, "You shall not eat from it;" cursed is the ground because of you; **in toil you will eat of it all the days of your life**. Both thorns and thistles it shall grow for you; and you will eat the plants of the field; **by the sweat of your face you will eat bread, till you return to the ground**, because from it you were taken; for **you are dust, and to dust you shall return** [emphasis added]'" (Genesis 3:17-19).

Man forfeited eternal life by disobedience, and also must struggle against his nature to work and lead, to find fulfillment and joy, as he relates to God and people.

You know about gravity and what will happen if you jump off a building or a cliff. If you've lived very long on the earth, you know the tendencies laid out above and in the Bible are true about men and women too.

Take Responsibility

What does leading your family or leading in life look like today? How are we to rule over creation and our wives and children? There is plenty of talk, print, and speculation about this. It's a conversation topic in churches, taverns, and byways of the culture. It's obvious it goes against our nature and the mores of today's culture for men to lead, but to ignore it is the source of much pain and similar to ignoring gravity. Leading requires intentionality, conviction, and continual movement in the proper direction. Leading also requires fine-tuning and frequent adjustments due to missteps, failures, and complacency.

Ouch, did I say complacency? Someone said: "Apathy is the world's biggest problem — but who cares?" That's funny, and not so much. It's something I struggle with, and I think every man does. God hates it. It's not like Him; He cares deeply and acts consistently, constantly, and sacrificially on behalf of others. So that's our charge and calling as men, from our Maker and Lord. I recently ran across an anonymous quote: "A man's failure to lead is him actually leading in failure."

We need help! And we'll find we have it as we are obedient and practice ruling and leadership. You find grace (unmerited assistance and power) when you need it. And you usually don't find grace (unmerited help and strength) until you need it. That's a quality and the beauty of grace. It's poured out on a life that's being lived.

I've canoed thousands of miles in my lifetime. Some beginners along the way called me Legend. But I believe there are only two kinds of canoeists: those who have crashed (turned over) and those who will. Of course, tips, advice, and classes can be helpful, but I also say: "You learn how to canoe with a paddle in your hands." Translated, this means you learn to lead by leading every time it's called for, which is often and much. Men who wish to honor and trust God and His ways, who want the best for their families, friends, churches, and country will lead — even and especially in a day and time when it's seemingly not valued, desired, or honored.

I will not be exhaustive or discuss ways men can lead in our day. I'm just going to encourage you to lead. I will point you to one trait of a leader, one I'm impressed to share right now. Maybe it's a beginning for all others? Indeed, it's an excellent place to start! Take personal responsibility for your own mistakes and your position of influence, and lead as a man. If you believe it's God's plan for men, then take that responsibility and act on it all of your days.

To make this point, I'm going to share an incident in the life of David. He was a poet, shepherd, warrior, and king — some say he is the world's most universally admired man. He had some significant successes, and he made some big mistakes. Maybe those go together? At any rate, God blessed his life amazingly, and he taught us a lot about a life lived with God in a world at war.

David Numbers Israel

When my children were small, I used to tell them Bible stories or read them Bible stories every night before bedtime, sometimes together, but mostly separately, and let them choose if they wished what they would hear. For one long period, my little daughter, who was five or six, asked me repeatedly to tell her three stories.

The story of Esther, an orphan girl who became queen of the vast Persian empire when it ruled the whole earth, makes sense for a little girl. I love it too (Esther)! She also liked to hear the miracle from Elisha's life, where he caused a valuable, borrowed, lost, iron axehead to float so that it could be retrieved and returned to its owner (2 Kings 6:1-6). "Tell me the story about the axehead," she would say. That might seem strange, but I happily complied with her request to satisfy her curiosity and to know as much about this mighty prophet as we could learn. But I could never figure out her motive for her third request.

As we snuggled on her bed, or she lay happily on her pillow, content that her dad was with her and reading to her, willing to serve her and answer her questions as best he could, she would ask: "Daddy, tell me about when David numbered Israel." This is a fantastic story — but dark. I often smiled inside and wondered why my little girl liked this story or what she was trying to puzzle out within this event.

This story teaches us a lot, especially about authority, manhood, and God. Watching David take responsibility for a wrong decision and the situation it caused is perhaps the biggest lesson we men can learn, and also how he took the responsibility to lead out of it. Let's look.

"Then Satan stood up against Israel and moved David to number Israel. So David said to Joab and to the princes of the people, 'Go, number Israel from Beersheba even to Dan, and bring me word that I may know their number.' Joab said, 'May the Lord add to His people a hundred times as many as they are! But, my lord the king, are they not all my lord's servants? Why does my lord seek this thing? Why should he be a cause of guilt to Israel?' Nevertheless, the king's word prevailed against Joab. Therefore, Joab departed and went throughout all Israel, and came to Jerusalem. Joab gave the number of the census of all the people to David. And all Israel were 1,100,000 men who drew the sword; and Judah was 470,000 men who drew the sword. But he did not number Levi and Benjamin among them, for the king's command was abhorrent to Joab" (1 Chronicles 21: 1-6).

Why Number Israel?

Why number Israel? Or why not? Both are good questions. Joab, the commander-in-chief of David's army, asked the first question. We can ferret out why it wasn't wise to take a census of Israel from Scripture, but that is not the main point of this story for us. Perhaps it is something along the lines of: "If riches increase, do not set your heart upon them" (Psalm 62:10c). Or: "No king is saved by the size of his army; no warrior escapes by his great strength" (Psalm 33:16 NIV). Or: "The strutting rooster, the male goat also, and a king when his army is with him. If you have been foolish in exalting yourself...." (Proverbs 30:31-322a).

At any rate, when a story starts with Satan standing up against Israel and moving David to number Israel, you know it's not a good thing. And we immediately read: **"God was displeased with this thing, so He struck Israel. David said to God, 'I have sinned greatly, in that I have done this thing**. But now, please take away the iniquity of Your servant, for I have done very foolishly [emphasis added]'" (1 Chronicles 21: 7-8).

The Scripture doesn't say precisely how God struck Israel or how David knew it was happening and it was his fault. But we can see clearly that David took responsibility and asked God for forgiveness.

God's Ways

The memorable events from here to the end of the chapter tell us a lot about God, the possible results of free will used errantly by earthly authorities, and the relationship God was still forging with David, a man after God's own heart.

We read earlier in David's life that Saul, the first king of Israel and David's predecessor, was fearful, trusted his own ways instead of God's, and willingly disobeyed God at a critical juncture. To make it worse, he made excuses and didn't take responsibility for his actions and disobedience. God told him by the prophet Samuel who called him out: "But now your kingdom shall not endure. **The Lord has sought out for Himself a man [David] after His own heart**, and the Lord has appointed him as ruler over His people, **because you have not kept what the Lord commanded you** [emphasis added]" (1 Samuel 13:14).

Similarly, the Lord sent a different prophet to David in this instance: "The Lord spoke to Gad, David's seer, saying, 'Go and speak to David, saying, "**Thus says the Lord, I offer you three things; choose for yourself** one of them, which I will do to you."' So Gad came to David and said to him, 'Thus says the Lord, "**Take for yourself either three years of famine,** or **three months to be swept away before your foes, while the sword of your enemies overtakes you,** or else **three days of the sword of the Lord, even pestilence in the land,** and the angel of the Lord destroying throughout all the territory of Israel." Now, therefore, consider what answer I shall return to Him who sent me.' David said to Gad, 'I am in great distress; **please let me fall into the hand of the Lord, for His mercies are very great. But do not let me fall into the hand of man** [emphasis added]'" (1 Chronicles 21:9-13).

Wow, what would you have chosen? We read of David's decision: "So **the Lord sent a pestilence** on Israel; **70,000 men of Israel fell. And God sent an angel to Jerusalem to destroy it**; but as he was about to destroy it, **the Lord saw and was sorry over the calamity, and said to the destroying angel, 'It is enough**; now relax your hand.' And the angel of the Lord was standing by the threshing floor of Ornan the Jebusite. Then **David lifted up his eyes and saw the angel of the Lord** standing between earth and heaven, with his drawn sword in his hand stretched out over Jerusalem. **Then David and the elders, covered with sackcloth, fell on their faces. David said to God**, 'Is it not I who commanded to count the people? Indeed, **I am the one who has sinned and done very wickedly,** but these sheep, what have they done? O Lord my God, please **let Your hand be against me and my father's household, but not against Your people that they should be plagued** [emphasis added]'" (1 Chronicles 21:14-17).

There is much to notice and learn here. Seventy thousand is about the entire population of the city where I live. I'm not sure what part of the population of Israel that was at the time. According to the CDC as of August 12, 2022, "COVID-19 has caused more than 1,030,000 deaths in the United States since the start of the pandemic," which is about .3% of the population. I looked up the Hebrew word for men in David's instance: it is "males." Only men were killed in this instance. Interesting.

It entered the Lord's mind to destroy Jerusalem. Still, He was "sorry over the calamity," had compassion, and showed mercy even before David and the elders, covered in sackcloth fell on their faces, and prayed. The timing and the number of "men" killed are significant, and the humble posture of David and the elders is telling. Taking responsibility, asking for forgiveness, and being concerned for the welfare of the people, are characteristic of David and pleasing to God. The plague stopped. But there was more action to this bizarre event.

The Lord shows His redemptive but very accountable, relational side: "**Then the angel of the Lord commanded Gad to say to David, that David should go up and build an altar to the Lord on the threshing floor of Ornan the Jebusite**. So David went up at the word of Gad, which he spoke in the name of the Lord. Now Ornan turned back and saw the angel, and his four sons who were with him hid themselves. And Ornan was threshing wheat. As David came to Ornan, **Ornan looked and saw David, and went out from the threshing floor and prostrated himself before David with his face to the ground.** Then David said to Ornan, 'Give me the site of this threshing floor, that I may build on it an altar to the Lord; for the full price you shall give it to me, that the plague may be restrained from the people.' Ornan said to David, 'Take it for yourself; and let my lord the king do what is good in his sight. See, I will give the oxen for burnt offerings and the threshing sledges for wood and the wheat for the grain offering; I will give it all.' But King David said to Ornan, '**No, but I will surely buy it for the full price; for I will not take what is yours for the Lord, or offer a burnt offering which costs me nothing.**' So **David gave Ornan 600 shekels of gold by weight for the site.** Then **David built an altar to the Lord there and offered burnt offerings and peace offerings**. And **he called to the Lord and He answered him with fire from heaven on the altar of burnt offering**. The Lord commanded the angel, and **he put his sword back in its sheath** [emphasis added]" (1 Chronicles 21:18-27).

If you're a man, your head is abuzz at all this. There are so many intense things happening with such meaning and ramifications. Ornan touches me — especially his response to the king. He is so honoring and sacrificial. His work ethic with his sons shows a united family of some means. Yet he's immediately willing to give David the king his land, and his animals used to make his living, as well as his tools, all of it, at the king's request.

David's famous response to Ornan's generous gesture is telling and instructive for men today and of every age. Yet I don't think we get it. Lord, help us see that we don't deserve the sacrifice, even if we are king. It is You Who deserve sacrifice and offerings. My prayer is for You to show us what and how to make sacrifices and offerings that are pleasing to You and meaningful. We can see it must cost us something, or we don't value You, as David did. As a good friend once told me, "Show me your checkbook, and I'll tell you your priorities and what's important to you." For those curious, at today's spot gold prices (240 oz @1757), David paid Ornan $421,680 for the place of sacrifice the angel of the Lord picked.

Obedience Rewarded—Sacrifice Accepted

As many times as I've read and meditated on this chapter in David's life and told the story to my daughter, I don't think I noticed until this reading that the Lord answered him with fire from heaven on the altar. That's awe inspiring, and was to David and the elders! The Lord commanding the angel to put his sword back in its sheath is a decisive end to the saga for all concerned.

Yet there's an interesting afterword to the story: "At that time, when David saw that the Lord had answered him on the threshing floor of Ornan the Jebusite, he offered sacrifice there. For the tabernacle of the Lord, which Moses had made in the wilderness, and the altar of burnt offering were in the high place at Gibeon at that time. But David could not go before it to inquire of God, for he was terrified by the sword of the angel of the Lord" (1 Chronicles 21:28-30).

If you know Bible history, you may know David eventually brought the tabernacle to this spot. There Solomon built the temple in Jerusalem. It was on this very same mountaintop where Abraham offered up Isaac a thousand years before David's time. In three events spanning centuries, one can see the finger of God tracing His precise and beautiful plan of relationship by sacrifice. It's as easy to puzzle out as it is awe-inspiring if one wants to know the truth and will look at the facts.

I recently read Spurgeon's insightful and beautiful take on this event in David's life: "No chisel of mason, or hammer of carpenter can build a holy place. Without either of these a spot may be none other than the house of God, and the gate of heaven. God chose a threshing-floor for his audience with David, just as aforetime he had chosen to reveal himself in a bush to Moses. His presence had been glorious on the sandy floor of the wilderness, in the midst of the curtains of goats' hair; and now it was gracious among the sheaves and the oxen. How can he that filleth all things care about a house which is made with hands? You know how curtly Stephen dismisses even Solomon's Temple with a word— 'but Solomon built him a house. Howbeit, the Most High dwelleth not in temples made with hands.' What was that golden fane to the Infinite Majesty? Is not his own Creation sublimer far? No arch can compare with the azure of heaven, no lamps can rival the sun and moon, no masonry can equal that city whose twelve foundations are of precious stones. Thus saith the Lord by the prophet: 'Heaven is my throne, and the earth is my footstool: where is the house that ye build unto me? and where is the place of my rest? For all those things hath mine hand made.' Wherefore, then, should he not choose the hill whereon Oman had made a hardened floor whereon to thresh his corn? At any rate that was the Lord's meeting-place with David, his audience chamber with the suppliant king; as if to show that he careth not for tabernacles or temples, but by his own presence makes that place glorious wherein he reveals himself" (Charles Haddon Spurgeon, 1894).

Fear of God Restored — A Good Beginning

Before I retired from the airlines, I wrote my first book entitled *A Friend of the King, David and His Mighty Men*. The names of the chapters sum up its message: Be a Leader, Be a Man, Be a Friend, and Understand Your Times and What You Should Be Doing.

Life ends well when you take responsibility for what God entrusted to you and are obedient. It ends well even if you fail, if you are quick to repent and ask forgiveness in prayer, accepting God's judgment. It ends well when you obey God rather than man. It starts if you fear God more than man. Fear God and keep His commandments. Fear God and live. Fear God and lead. That's God's simple and profound message to men.

Do you need a slap in the face to remember it? I pray God will do something like that, some act of grace, to keep it fresh on men's minds and spirits in our day and the days ahead. So much depends on it!

I often ask younger men how they walk this out in real life and in real-time. What graces are they experiencing? They should share it as it encourages all men — sacrifice and courage, truth and honor. Godspeed on your journey in leading, and may you farewell.

As you grow older, it doesn't get easier as one might think. At times it seems even more faith is required. It does get easier if you learn to live by faith. But you might recall that some of Abraham's most challenging tests of faith came late in his life. But what should we expect if we read in Scripture: "Behold, as for the proud one, his soul is not right within him; but **the righteous will live by his faith**" (Habakkuk 2:4). And: "And **without faith it is impossible to please Him [God]**, for he who comes to God must believe that He is and that He is a rewarder of those who seek Him [emphasis added]" (Hebrews 11:6).

More faith will likely be required the longer we live. It's part of the adventure and relationship with God. But we do have some promises from our Heavenly Father: "Even to your old age I will be the same, and even to your graying years I will bear you! I have done it, and I will carry you; and I will bear you and I will deliver you" (Isaiah 46:4). And one of my personal favorites: "Yet those who wait for the Lord will gain new strength; they will mount up with wings like eagles, they will run and not get tired, they will walk and not become weary" (Isaiah 40:31).

But You Don't Know My Wife

I hope this puzzle piece has encouraged and inspired men to lead who aren't doing so. I hope it's caused all of us to reexamine our roles or lanes and how we've been doing. As Socrates said: "The unexamined life isn't worth living." Or in Bible speak perhaps: "'Come now, and let us reason together,' says the Lord" (Isaiah 1:18a).

Some of you no doubt will say that you don't know my wife. Like the woman coming to the unrighteous judge, your wife has worn you down. Have you given up? You might even quote the parable of Jesus: "by continually coming she will wear [has worn] me out" (Luke 18:5b). First of all, the quote is not in this context, but most men can identify with it. The context is that we should be persistent in prayer. Shouldn't we men be as relentless in leading? Especially if that's God's command and what He promises will make things better.

I recently ran across a humorous, profound quote by Mary Kay Ash: "Every silver lining has a cloud." You can expect opposition. God's plan is to make us strong and those around us stronger and healthier. It's an opportunity to lead.

Another quote that has some application in this context comes from Napoleon Bonaparte: "Never interrupt your enemy when he [or she] is making a mistake." While this makes perfect and profound sense in warfare against a real enemy, your spouse is not your enemy. Remember what God said: "… a man shall leave his father and his mother, and be joined to his wife; and **they shall become one** flesh [emphasis added]" (Genesis 2:24). The two become one. If one of you takes a step backward, you both do. So don't be complacent or passive about this — interrupt her if she's making a mistake. Be kind, of course, and ask for the grace to be so, but say what you feel is the truth and do what you need to do to lead. Be humble too, and willing to change if the shoe is on the other foot. That's part and parcel of being a good leader. Humility is requisite.

John Maxwell says: "A leader is someone who knows the way, shows the way, and goes the way."

Remember what is said about God: "**If we are faithless, He remains faithful**, for He cannot deny Himself [emphasis added]" (2 Timothy 2:13). Want to be like Christ in this matter of marriage and stay in your lane no matter what your spouse does? Be faithful to your part and lead. Trust the Lord will change her heart as needed. Pray. But be faithful anyway! There will be fewer crashes if at least one of you stays in your lane.

The Power of God

Are you still not convinced that it's the man's job to lead? Or are you so beat up by the enemy that you don't think you can recover and become the leader God calls you to be to your wife and family? We might call that deception.

I will risk quoting a Scripture out of context, something I try never to do. But it makes the point clearly, and it fits. One time a group of religious leaders approached Jesus and tried to convince Him of their flawed beliefs that there was no resurrection. After hearing them out, he answered: "**You are mistaken, not understanding the Scriptures nor the power of God** [emphasis added]" (Matthew 22:29). You can lead, and you should, or you don't understand the Scriptures or the power of God to help you.

Take responsibility! It is necessary. It makes you a good candidate for grace. It's an excellent start, especially if you've made a big mistake. It involves humility, confession, and the realization you are a leader appointed by God. Risk and lead. It's the only way you win. And who knows, it may be the only way you lose, if you don't lead. Note the parable of the three stewards (Matthew 25:14-29). If you bury what the Lord gives you and believe a lie about Him, then act that out; you lose — everything. If you risk investing what He's given you, you win — everything, and enter into the joy of your Lord. LEAD! Risk! Love!

"Why do you call Me, 'Lord, Lord,' and do not do what I say?"
(Luke 6:46).

PUZZLING CHAPTER 47

Stay in Your Lane - Women

MY WIFE HAS OFTEN TOLD me she's happy she's a female.

Women are seemingly the human race's heart, not the head. Why would they want to be both? Isn't God wise? Or is He not doing an excellent job at being God? It seems some would say so by their attitudes and actions.

Do some women feel they are entitled to something more? Do they have a lack of trust in God and His ways? Let's call it what it is. And let's resolve to understand our lane and stay in it. God's lane for us is a beautiful place. Being out of your lane isn't flattering, and your shortcomings will be exposed, hopefully, sooner rather than later, so you may receive His grace for correcting the rest of your journey and for the rest of your days.

I have a good friend who was the CEO of a large hospital. He once told me, "Entitlement is the biggest problem in our nation today."

Why would you think that the Almighty owes you anything? Or that anyone else does? Is it your pride? Or your self-asserted importance? Self-exaltation?

Who gave you life? This beautiful planet for a home? Air to breathe? Water to drink? Destiny? Purpose? Love? I'll give you a hint. There are three letters in His most commonly ascribed name.

Worth

Worth is a complex issue to discuss, yet it's simple in light of the Bible and the Creator. We are made in His image. He made creation for our habitation. This says we are very valuable to him. We are His image bearers, witnesses to angels, and to those who do not yet know Him. Yet our value to Him goes deeper still.

If being made in His image with this beautiful planet to enjoy wasn't enough, God gave us free will to make a mark, good or bad, on His creation and to use or abuse the same. Then if that wasn't enough, we are twice bought, created by Him, then redeemed from sin and death by His cross. So what are we worth to Him? It would seem a price too great to pay!

Tell me again, what does God owe you? Only a rebellious, spoiled child would think God owed them something or anything. Feeling entitled in light of the gift of life and creation is the height of hubris, the very pinnacle of pride.

That's why God won't stomach it. That's why He will welcome grace and reject forever self-effort and works or those who claim and act as though they are entitled to something more than the marvelous gifts He has given and ascribed to them. "For **by grace** you have been saved through faith; and that not of yourselves, it is the gift of God; **not as a result of works, so that no one may boast** [emphasis added]" (Ephesians 2:8-9). This element is a theme painted into many pieces of the puzzle, and you may yet see it again.

Forgive

One might wonder what forgiveness has to do with worth? The Spirit is impressing me they are connected along the lines of trust, especially trusting the worth God ascribes to you and His protection of you in a sometimes painful world.

Allow me to try to explain the truth about forgiveness with examples. By the way, this particular suggestion of staying in our lanes applies to both sexes, men and women. I suppose I'm led to share it in the female chapter because women seem to have more sensitive souls, feel hurt more deeply, and struggle more with forgiveness than most men. But don't lose track of the fact forgiveness applies equally to all humankind.

To fail to forgive is to be out of your lane. You are putting yourself in God's lane. "Who can forgive sins but God alone?" (Mark 2:7b). "There is only one Lawgiver and Judge, the One who is able to save and to destroy; but who are you who judge your neighbor?" (James 4:12). "Never pay back evil for evil to anyone. Respect what is right in the sight of all men. If possible, so far as it depends on you, be at peace with all men. Never take your own revenge, beloved, but leave room for the wrath of God, for it is written, 'Vengeance is Mine, I will repay,' says the Lord" (Romans 12:17-19).

God forgives you as you ask, only after forgiving others. "Forgive us for our sins, just as we have forgiven those who sinned against us" (Matthew 6:12 NCV). Forgiveness is like breathing in and out, a rhythm of life and living for a follower of Christ. Forgiveness is releasing the demand of justice, of being paid back, into God's hands.

Forgiveness is not forgetting or excusing the wrong, but the opposite. It's relinquishing the demand of justice to someone more qualified. Evil will be repaid. What would make it right in your mind? God wants justice more deeply than you do. Justice is God's job. Our job is to partake of forgiveness and to extend it.

This is a most crucial concept and issue with God! It is mentioned in Jesus' Sermon on the Mount and the Lord's Prayer. "**Whenever you stand praying, forgive**, if you have anything against anyone, **so that your Father who is in heaven will also forgive you your transgressions** [emphasis added]" (Mark 11:25). "And **forgive us our debts, as we also have forgiven** our debtors [emphasis added]" (Matthew 6:12).

There should be no limit to forgiveness. Why? Because God commands it (Matthew 18: 21-22). It's what He does and makes available to all. The cross triumphs over the devil, evil, and demons. Forgiveness was Christ's weapon of choice (Ephesians 4:26-27). It should be ours.

Our way to fight sin against us is not to fight but forgive, leaving vengeance and justice to God. Satan loves it when we flee from forgiveness and run to judgment. That makes us less effective stewards of grace and keeps us in chains.

Hurt people hurt people. Forgiven people forgive people. By the Spirit, forgiveness overflows. If you can't forgive, you probably are painting a picture of how you see God's forgiveness of you.

Do you believe God would lie, or can be fooled? Do you think you can ask for forgiveness and not forgive? How are your actions speaking about this in your life at the moment?

Forgiveness doesn't mean reconciliation. But forgiveness is a call on your life today. A name probably came to your head when I mentioned forgiveness if there is still a root of bitterness in you. In non-forgiveness, you are allowing something done to you to define you. Decide to forgive them. Ask God to forgive you as you have forgiven them. Drink from the cup of forgiveness. Today is the day. Don't let the sun go down: "Be angry, and yet do not sin; do not let the sun go down on your anger" (Ephesians 4:26).

Experience forgiveness, extend forgiveness, and live. You will discover the ability to love more deeply and experience the depths of God's mercy. It's healing and cleansing and will help keep you in your lane, where you're safe and can move unimpeded. Enjoy the journey to freedom.

Forgiveness is the mark of one who walks with God. I pray for your freedom and a lifestyle of forgiveness. This is part of the gospel that saves you and keeps saving you. "For I am confident of this very thing, that He who began a good work in you will perfect it until the day of Christ Jesus" (Philippians 1:6). Ask for His mercies every morning in prayer, and expect to see them. "Through the Lord's mercies we are not consumed, because His compassions fail not. They are new every morning; great is Your faithfulness" (Lamentations 3:22-23).

The Woman's Lane Described In the Bible

The woman's lane is simple and straightforward, as God's commands are. They also fly in the face of secular humanism and the feminism accepted in our culture and day, which God's ways often do.

The women's lane is a creation issue, not a political or cultural issue. God's wisdom squares against that of secular humanism. What is the best belief system and course of action for women, men, and families? You can read and decide for yourself. He's given us that privilege. Ponder for yourself God's ways as revealed in Scripture versus the mores of the culture and feminism, then decide which sounds right. Who will you believe, God or the religion of secular humanism? What you are acting out is what you believe. You can change your thinking if you want to trust God and then ask Him for help in prayer to follow through. Expect to see Him in action on your behalf if this is your decision.

God's designed lane for women to best enjoy their lives can be described by two words and concepts: submission and respect.

Submission and Respect

These two words sum up what God has said to women about His plan for women and what will make them happy and cause them to experience the most joy in life and eternity. It also gives their husbands the greatest pleasure and their families tremendous peace. Let's have a look.

I don't intend to do a complete Bible study on the subject. There are plenty of such studies if you want to verify what I'm sharing. I want to give you enough detail from the Bible so that you know this is really what the Bible teaches and God's heart on the matter. Hopefully, you'll be intrigued or inspired to search the Scriptures on your own. I strongly suggest that getting these truths into your head and letting them move eighteen inches to your heart is key to your joy and happiness as a woman. Living them causes you to become even more beautiful than you already are.

Foundation

"In the beginning God created the heavens and the earth" (Genesis 1:1). I know what you're thinking: "If he is starting there, this is going to be a very long chapter or very BIG puzzle piece!" Not at all. I just want you to see this truth was in the beginning and is for all time. God creates man and woman in the same chapter, just like they are and have always been. I want us to be mindful that our sexuality is a creation issue, not a political, philosophical, or cultural issue. "God created man in His own image, in the image of God He created him; male and female He created them. God blessed them; and God said to them, 'Be fruitful and multiply….' God saw all that He had made, and behold, it was very good. And there was evening and there was morning, the sixth day" (Genesis 1:27-28a,31).

It's noteworthy that perhaps the most instructive insights into the nature of two sexes are given in Genesis, at the very beginning, by the wisdom and hand of the Creator. I was about to launch into an abbreviated explanation of the seminal verses in Genesis, trying to convey the woman's lane, when I received a blog from one of my best friends and long-time mentor, Charles Angel. Not only is it a beautiful synchronicity and validation that what I'm writing is right on track, but it also allows me to dive into the subject matter after just stating the truth. You can read Charles' beautiful hermeneutic as an addendum to this puzzle piece if you want to dig deeper or meditate on these truths in Scripture. The name of his blog site is *"Been Pondering."* His concise and well-researched summary is an excellent example of the age-old, time-honored truth: "The Bible is the best commentary on the Bible."

Simply said, as a ramification of Eve's deception and willful disobedience in the Garden of Eden, her "desire" became to rule over her husband. God said: "And you will desire to control your husband, but he will rule over you" (Genesis 3:16b NLT). The second part of that verse and God's decision is the husband's lane, and we discuss that in an adjoining puzzle piece.

In essence, God said: "Yes, Satan deceived you, but you willed to disobey, so I'm making it such that you, and all women after you, must will to obey and submit to your husbands to be happy." And for the man's willful complicity in the disobedience, God said to Adam in essence: "Your work will be harder and you'll desire to sit in an easy chair with your feet up, but will only be happy if you will rule, work, lead." Again that's part of the man's lane discussed in another piece of the puzzle, but it's so connected I note it here.

There are two touchstones on one beautiful path to happiness and wholeness for women. They also make for a happy husband and a healthy family if known and practiced. They are named submission and honor or respect.

Would you like to see what that looked like four thousand years ago and still looks like today?

Sarah (Aka Sarai)

Women are exquisite creatures in the eyes of men, and I think of all humankind. Their shapely, soft bodies and seemingly softer souls give them a beauty, aura, and unique place all their own. Beauty is somewhat challenging to define. But when you see or experience it, you know it and are arrested by it in your spirit and soul. Think of a vast mountain range or seascape, the sunrise or sunset playing on the clouds at the advent or benediction of the day, a Peter Paul Rubens canvas, the marble "David" by Michelangelo in Florence, or Venus de Milo beautifully displayed in the Louvre in Paris. Gazing in the presence of such beauty takes human beings to another place within themselves. It is a place that transcends the ordinary places of our lives and the spaces of our beings. It makes us hungry for more beauty to be sought, discovered, and experienced. It speaks to our spirit about the vastness of creation, and the beauty that's knowable, yet other, to be known.

Such is the beauty of a woman, just being herself, and living in the lane or place God created for her takes her to another level of mystery and beauty.

In another piece of our puzzle, I mentioned Esther, Ruth, and Abigail in the same context as Sarah. They share in common the knowledge, beauty, and joys of staying in their lane while trusting God and the men in their lives.

Let's look at some events in Sarah's life that speak loudly and confidently to this truth and trust. About 2000 BC, Abram took his beautiful wife Sarai from their comfortable home in one of the most progressive cities in the ancient world near Babylon, called Ur of the Chaldeans, on a journey to a place God would show them. They knew not where.

We know the area today as Israel, named after Abraham and Sarah's grandson. It's one-fifth the size of Arkansas, yet it is in the world headlines almost daily for some reason or other. It also happened to be on the ancient Via Maris, or Way of the Sea, the trade route and road connecting the two ancient empires of Egypt and Babylon.

The couple and their entourage were destined to meet in this remote land with trials, trouble, beauty, and success. If you read Genesis and the story of Abraham's life, you certainly will come away with the idea he was a man's man and a leader. He was a man of courage and faith. In the Bible, he's given the title "Father of the Faith" (Galatians 3:29, Romans 4:11-13, Hebrews 11:8-10, Isaiah 51:1-2). But it wasn't so every day and at every juncture. And that's where we see the qualities that made Sarah even more beautiful than she naturally was. Those qualities are submission and honor, the path or lane God prescribes for women. If they trust Him and His word enough to risk obedience, although against their nature, He will show Himself to be their protector and benefactor — indeed, He shows them a beautiful side of Himself.

It happened this way: "Now there was a famine in the land; so Abram went down to Egypt to sojourn there, for the famine was severe in the land. It came about when he came near to Egypt, that he said to Sarai his wife, 'See now, I know that you are a beautiful woman; and when the Egyptians see you, they will say, "This is his wife;" and they will kill me, but they will let you live. Please say that you are my sister so that it may go well with me because of you, and that I may live on account of you.' It came about when Abram came into Egypt, the Egyptians saw that the woman was very beautiful. Pharaoh's officials saw her and praised her to Pharaoh; and the woman was taken into Pharaoh's house. Therefore he treated Abram well for her sake; and gave him sheep and oxen and donkeys and male and female servants and female donkeys and camels" (Genesis 12:10-16).

Well, I know what you ladies think of that! And even you men are probably thinking, "What was he thinking!?" But none of us live in their times, nor do we apprehend the power of Egypt and Pharaoh. And I would submit that all our lives, we are still learning how powerful God is, compared to the world, and if we can risk trusting Him. Keep that in mind, but let's look at this through Sarai's eyes. Wouldn't she think: "My husband who said he loved me and would protect me with his life is putting me in harm's way to save his own skin." She was probably tempted to try and save herself, revealing she was a married woman. But she did the almost unthinkable and submitted to her husband's request, honoring him with her trust and obedience. She did so when it seemed he didn't deserve it, trusting God to help her and honor her obedience.

What happened? "But the Lord struck Pharaoh and his house with great plagues because of Sarai, Abram's wife. Then Pharaoh called Abram and said, 'What is this you have done to me? Why did you not tell me that she was your wife? Why did you say, "She is my sister," so that I took her for my wife? Now then, here is your wife, take her and go.' Pharaoh commanded his men concerning him; and they escorted him away, with his wife and all that belonged to him" (Genesis 12:17-20).

So the Lord God shows the first couple of Israel, and the future house of faith, that He can protect those who walk according to His ways. We see what is plainly written a thousand years later in the Bible: "The king's heart is like channels of water in the hand of the Lord; He turns it wherever He wishes" (Proverbs 21:1).

Most importantly, Sarai sees and feels the closeness of the Lord as He protects her in the house of a powerful emperor. God honors her for obedience to her husband, honoring His ways, and trusting Him. Trust is a powerful, intimate force and a thing of profound beauty. Submission shows humility and trust. Perhaps there is nothing closer to God's heart.

I think I've made the point for submission and honor. Rather, Sarai did. There's more to the story because this happens one more time!? I will not tell the whole story but let you read it for yourself (Genesis 20). "Unbelievable," you might say. But humans are slow learners and suitable candidates for grace, which may be the point. Honesty, humility, grace, and trust are all attributes of God we can experience with His modeling and help. They make for inner beauty and outward wholeness. We also learn a few other things worth mentioning in this second round of trust, submission, and honor in Sarai's life with Abraham and God.

The story's ending, where another powerful king is smitten by Sarah's beauty and wants her for himself, goes like this: "Then Abimelech called Abraham and said to him, 'What have you done to us? And how have I sinned against you, that you have brought on me and on my kingdom a great sin? You have done to me things that ought not to be done.' And Abimelech said to Abraham, 'What have you encountered, that you have done this thing?' Abraham said, 'Because I thought, surely there is no fear of God in this place, and they will kill me because of my wife. Besides, she actually is my sister, the daughter of my father, but not the daughter of my mother, and she became my wife; and it came about, when God caused me to wander from my father's house, that I said to her, 'This is the kindness which you will show to me: everywhere we go, say of me, "He is my brother." Abimelech then took sheep and oxen and male and female servants, and gave them to Abraham, and restored his wife Sarah to him. Abimelech said, 'Behold, my land is before you; settle wherever you please.' To Sarah he said, 'Behold, I have given your brother a thousand pieces of silver; behold, it is your vindication before all who are with you, and before all men you are cleared.' Abraham prayed to God, and God healed Abimelech and his wife and his maids, so that they bore children. For the Lord had closed fast all the wombs of the household of Abimelech because of Sarah, Abraham's wife" (Genesis 20:9-18).

In this riveting story from antiquity, yet seemingly from today, there is plenty of room for imagination and the Spirit to speak to you about things that were at play here. We see that Abraham and Sarah were indeed siblings by the same father, but not the same mother. I'll leave that one alone and write it off to antiquity and their culture. But we see that half-truths, told to deceive, are not in line with God or His ways. God makes that clear to Abraham as this serious situation gets sorted out. Half-truths to deceive point to a lack of trust in God's goodwill and power to save, protect, and provide.

Most intriguing to me and pointing to Sarah's beauty, trust, and obedience is how God protects and honors her. He uses her obedience and deep trust to set up this learning experience making both Abraham and a powerful, foreign king more God-fearing. God goes to bat for Sarah! Everyone knows it after the fact. But she knows it personally and intimately — her own "very great reward" (Genesis 15:1).

Abimelech's servants were called together early in the morning and told about the dream — that Sarah was Abraham's wife and that they would all have been killed by God had he touched her! After the truth was known and everyone's motives exposed by the Almighty, the king said to Abraham that he could settle anywhere he wanted in the land — in effect, he had the king's permission, protection, and blessing going before him. To Sarah, he says: "I've given your 'brother' a thousand pieces of silver" so that all may know your name is honored and cleared of any wrong. Last we see that God's judgment of Abimelech and his people had already broken out as "closed wombs" because Abimelech wrongly took Sarah into his house. Abraham, "a prophet," as God told Abimelech in the dream, prayed to God for the plague to be lifted from Abimelech's household, and God honored Abraham's prayer.

All these lessons sprang from the submission and honor, obedience and trust of a beautiful woman, and the responding action of a loving God, Who honors such attitudes and actions. Sarah was the beneficiary, but so are we all.

We might sum up God's comments on Sarah's part like this: "Just as **Sarah obeyed Abraham, calling him lord,** and **you have become her children if you do what is right without being frightened by any fear** [emphasis added]" (1 Peter 3:6). Maybe God's pleasure with Sarah is also captured in this thought: "**In the same way, you wives, be submissive to your own husbands** so that even if any of them are disobedient to the word, they may be won without a word by the behavior of their wives, as they observe your **chaste and respectful behavior. Your adornment must** not be merely external—braiding the hair, and wearing gold jewelry, or putting on dresses; but let it **be the hidden**

person of the heart, with the imperishable quality of a gentle and quiet spirit, which is precious in the sight of God [emphasis added]" (1 Peter 3:1-4).

If you read the Bible stories of any famous women, even the infamous, through these glasses (submission and respect), you'll see true beauty and the effects of true beauty on the world around them. You'll see the beauty and blessings that accompany staying in the lane God created and planned for you.

It's worth mentioning that many of these beautiful women of the Bible didn't have a great start. Ruth was from Moab, a nation under a curse, and she was a young widow. Esther was an orphan and likely a captive of war. Abigail was living in a lousy marriage situation. Sarah moved away from her family to settle in a foreign land, probably never to see them again. Mary Magdalene had seven demons before meeting Jesus. So you know, it's not about race, sex, advantage or disadvantage. It's about knowing your lane and a committed decision to stay and live there. It's about submission and honor, trust and obedience. It's about the inner beauty that comes from such a heart. And it's about a powerful, loving God who honors, protects, and values such a "gentle and quiet spirit," which is pleasing to Him and others. Godspeed as you journey.

"Why do you call Me, 'Lord, Lord,' and do not do what I say?"
(Luke 6:46).

PUZZLING CHAPTER 48

Prayer Privilege

Opulence

After sleeping peacefully one evening, pleasantly tired, I awakened at 3:16 AM thinking about prayer, knowing it would be a piece of the puzzle and chapter in this book. The word "opulence" came to me. My mind turned to when the Queen of Sheba visited Solomon during his reign in Israel about 1000 BC: "Now when the queen of Sheba heard about the fame of Solomon concerning the name of the Lord, she came to test him with difficult questions. So she came to Jerusalem with a very large retinue, with camels carrying spices and very much gold and precious stones. When she came to Solomon, she spoke with him about all that was in her heart. Solomon answered all her questions; nothing was hidden from the king which he did not explain to her. When the queen of Sheba perceived all the wisdom of Solomon, the house that he had built, the food of his table, the seating of his servants, the attendance of his waiters and their attire, his cupbearers, and his stairway by which he went up to the house of the Lord, there was no more spirit in her. Then she said to the king, 'It was a true report which I heard in my own land about your words and your wisdom. Nevertheless I did not believe the reports, until I came and my eyes had seen it. And behold, the half was not told me'" (1 Kings 10:1-7a). Opulence, indeed.

She went on to say with the history and experience of a royal: "'You exceed in wisdom and prosperity the report which I heard. How blessed are your men, how blessed are these your servants who stand before you continually and hear your wisdom. Blessed be the Lord your God who delighted in you to set you on the throne of Israel; because the Lord loved Israel forever, therefore He made you king, to do justice and righteousness.' She gave the king a hundred and twenty talents of gold, and a very great amount of spices and precious stones. Never again did such abundance of spices come in as that which the queen of Sheba gave King Solomon" (1 Kings 10:7b-10). Solomon's court was thus acknowledged and applauded by this beautiful royal.

For the king's part, we see: "King Solomon gave to the queen of Sheba all her desire which she requested, besides what he gave her according to his royal bounty. Then she turned and went to her own land together with her servants" (1 Kings 10:13).

If you read to the end of the chapter, you'll find that Solomon was more wealthy than any earthly king at the time in wisdom and money, according to the promise the Lord gave him as a young man. We read: "So God said to him, 'Since you have asked for this [wisdom] and not for long life or wealth for yourself, nor have asked for the death of your enemies but for discernment in administering justice, I will do what you have asked. I will give you a wise and discerning heart, so that there will never have been anyone like you, nor will there ever be. Moreover, I will give you what you have not asked for—both wealth and honor—so that in your lifetime you will have no equal among kings'" (1 Kings 3:11-13 NIV).

If you read to the end of the chapter and do the math on Solomon's wealth, as some have done in today's values, you'll discover he was the wealthiest man who ever lived, eclipsing today's billionaires. So was this earthly king's court. We read further: "So King Solomon became greater than all the kings of the earth in riches and in wisdom. All the earth was seeking the presence of Solomon, to hear his wisdom which God had put in his heart" (1 Kings 10:23-24).

Consider the opulence of the greatest of earthly kings. Compare it with the King of the Universe and the Kingdom of Heaven. We hear Jesus ending the famous Lord's Prayer: "For Yours is the kingdom and the power and the glory forever. Amen" (Matthew 6:13b). To Whom do you pray?

Pray Tell

"Pray tell" is a phrase my grandparents used more often than we do today. Merriam Webster defines it as an idiom: "used for emphasis to demand an answer when asking someone for a reason, explanation, etc."

What can one say about prayer, pray tell, as profound and as significant as it is, in a simple book or as a piece of a simple puzzle?

Prayer was and is very important to the Father, the Son, and the Holy Spirit — the Triune God.

In the Old Testament, we read: "For My house will be called a house of prayer for all the peoples" (Isaiah 56:7c). Then, in His day, Jesus quoted the prophets Isaiah (above) and Jeremiah (7:11), saying: "It is written: 'My house will be called a house of prayer; but you are making it a den of robbers'" (Matthew 21:13). "In the same way the Spirit also helps our weakness; for we do not know how to pray as we should, but the Spirit Himself intercedes for us with groanings too deep for words"(Romans 8:26).

Perhaps the most extraordinary building ever built by the wisest, wealthiest man who lived was for God's glory and habitation — and the purpose of prayer. God then dwelled with His people in a place open for all people to come. One could experience the presence of God and petition One so great and good you could ask Him anything.

Jesus, on earth as the very Son of the very God, was passionate about many things – the will and rule of His Father; love for other people; family; many sons and daughters; justice and right living; and the glory of His Father. But the thing we see Jesus get violent about is prayer, the intimate relationship and communion with our Father, being hindered (Matthew 21:12-13, Mark 11:15-18).

The dedication of the temple by Solomon about 1000 BC accentuates the purpose and promise of the temple. The Scriptures record Solomon's words: "God of Israel, let your word that you promised your servant David my father come true. But **will God really dwell on earth?** The heavens, even the highest heaven, cannot contain you. How much less this temple I have built! **Yet give attention to your servant's prayer and his plea for mercy, Lord my God. Hear the cry and the prayer** that your servant is praying in your presence this day. **May your eyes be open toward this temple night and day, this place of which you said, 'My Name shall be there,' so that you will hear the prayer** your servant prays toward this place. **Hear the supplication of your servant and of your people Israel when they pray toward this place. Hear from heaven, your dwelling place, and when you hear, forgive** [emphasis added]" (1 Kings 8:26b-30).

God's response to the dedication accentuates the purpose and promise of the temple — to be a house of prayer for all people. The Scripture records God's actions and blessing immediately before Solomon's dedication prayer: "Then the priests brought the ark of the covenant of the Lord to its place, into the inner sanctuary of the house, to the most holy place, under the wings of the cherubim. **It happened that when the priests came from the holy place, the cloud filled the house of the Lord, so that the priests could not stand to minister because of the cloud, for the glory of the Lord filled the house of the Lord** [emphasis added]" (1 Kings 8:6,10-11).

Temple Dedication Prayer Is Telling

Solomon's temple dedication prayer is telling and touching. It has many ramifications for prayer and for us today. Please read the whole chapter if you're interested. A summary tells us: "If there is famine in the land, **if there is pestilence, if there is blight or mildew, locust or grasshopper, if their enemy besieges them in the land of their cities, whatever plague, whatever sickness there is, whatever prayer or supplication is made by any man or by all Your people Israel, each knowing the affliction of his own heart, and spreading his hands toward this house; then hear in heaven Your dwelling place, and forgive and act and render to each according to all his ways, whose heart You know, for You alone know the hearts of all the sons of men, that they may fear You all the days that they live in the land which You have given to our fathers** [emphasis added]" (1 Kings 8:37-40).

Solomon's prayer that God will always hear prayers offered toward His dwelling place continues: "When they sin against You (for there is no man who does not sin) and You are angry with them and deliver them to an enemy, so that they take them away captive to the land of the enemy, far off or near; if they take thought in the land where they have been taken captive, and repent and make supplication to You in the land of those who have taken them captive, saying, '**We have sinned and have committed iniquity, we have acted wickedly'; if they return to You with all their heart and with all their soul in the land of their enemies who have taken them captive, and pray to You toward their land which You have given to their fathers**, the city which You have chosen, and the house which I have built for Your name; **then hear their prayer and their supplication in heaven Your dwelling place, and maintain their cause, and forgive Your people who have sinned against You and all their transgressions which they have transgressed against You**, and make them objects of compassion before those who have taken them captive [emphasis added]" (1 Kings

8:46-50). It sounds like Solomon is a seer into the future, humanity, and the mercy and grace of the God of Israel, the Creator and King of the Universe.

Devalued

When the people no longer valued the house of prayer, God destroyed it, and it was taken away in 586 BC, along with most of the nation. This happened about 500 years after it was built. The people and the furnishings of the Temple were transplanted in Babylon.

For seventy years, they languished in Babylon! Did they realize what they had lost? Did they miss it? Did they miss Him — their Creator, Father, God? And the nearness of His presence?

Around 500 BC, with the leadership and the supernatural power of the Holy, Israel rebuilt the temple against all odds in a climate of warfare, threats, and spiritual opposition. They rebuilt the wall around Jerusalem in a miraculous 52 days, complete with a moat and gates. Then the temple was completed – the house of prayer was valued and restored. Intimacy, communion, and prayer were possible again and practiced anew with God at the center of His house.

This wasn't the structure that had fallen into abuse and disuse, except to become an idol in service of humanity and religion with the façade of communion with God. This second temple functioned again, as initially purposed, but not with the former outward beauty, which partly led the people to worship the form and not value the Presence, the power, and the prayer to the Almighty.

This house of prayer continued for about 500 years until the same forces of idolatry and (false) religion culminated in it being destroyed again. Herod, an evil king but one of the world's greatest architects, made splendid, eye-popping improvements to placate the people and make it appear the Lord was again in His house of prayer.

The Son of Man, also the Son of God, overturned the tables of money changers and false religionists, driving them from this house of prayer. Jesus loudly proclaimed that they had made it rather a den of thieves — stealing away from the people the precious communion and prayer desired by the people and the Holy One.

This happened just before His temple (body) was destroyed on April 3, 33 AD. A few days before that, His disciples were in Jerusalem with Jesus admiring the marvel of Herod's refurbished Second Temple. When they pointed out its grand appearance, Jesus told them plainly that soon not one of those beautiful, huge stones would be left on top of another.

And so it was in 70 AD, the Roman general Titus, who would become emperor, utterly destroyed the city and the magnificent temple lavishly refurbished in grand style just a few decades earlier.

That house of prayer for all people was no more and is no more.

You can visit the temple mount in Jerusalem, as I have a few times. You can lay your hands on the giant stones of the Western Wall and pray. That's what people do 24/7. They pray in the open air before a small section of the ancient, colossal foundation stones laid by Solomon 3000 years ago. People write their prayer requests on tiny pieces of paper and fold and insert them in the tiny crevices between the massive stones. Periodically they are all removed, and the process starts anew or continues beneath where the magnificent, ancient House of prayer stood.

You can look to your right and see a pile of ancient temple stones lying where they landed 2000 years ago when the Roman army destroyed the temple and took down every stone to get the gold. Gold was so plentiful to Solomon that he used it in the mortar between the great stones causing the temple to glisten in the morning desert sun and making it one of the wonders of the ancient world. His masons worshipfully cut and placed these stones without the sound of a hammer or chisel at the site. The 2000-year-old stone pile is now a silent witness to the Presence of God in the lives of His people, faithfulness to His Word, purposes, and plans.

But the Stone cut without human hands, falling from heaven in the time of Rome, as prophesied by Daniel (Daniel 2:34-45), has become the chief cornerstone, a Living stone, the first of many sons and daughters. These living stones are the temple of God (1Peter 2:5), a house of prayer — a kingdom expanding that will never end.

Again we see that God does not dwell in a temple made with human hands (Acts 7:48-49, Acts 17:24)! For a time, he permitted it in an intimate, humble setting for Him. But no more. God's dwelling is as intimate, spiritual, and invisible as spirits are. But for our understanding, God showed us first what He was going to do in the natural realm through prototype and prophecy, before sending His Spirit to our individual and corporate temples, our bodies.

There are hints in Scripture that Solomon's Temple is patterned after God's opulent, without-precedent, unfathomable throne room in heaven. At its center was the Ark of the Covenant, a tiny box of wood overlaid with the purest gold, containing three symbols of His presence. In the original there was the law written in stone given to Moses (a moral code for righteous living), Aaron's rod that budded (symbolizing the miracle of life after death), and manna (angel food, nourishing over a million people in the desert for forty years, supplied daily). But that's not all.

These were artifacts of the Exodus — God leading his people out of a demon-worshiping culture where they were redeemed by His mighty hand and outstretched arm. To Israel, they were a memory of the past and a hope for the future. They represented assurance of God's faithfulness and His promise to always be with his people — a prayer away.

A natural substance overlaid with a symbol of the divine (gopher wood overlaid with gold) adorned the top of the ark, fashioned as a mercy seat. Here two golden cherubim stretched their wings toward the center, where the very Presence of the Creator dwelled.

The Ark with the mercy seat was the focal point of the tent of meeting, sprinkled with blood and oil as prescribed by God and carried out by His priests. It was hidden from the people but accessible to the high priest in the Most Holy Place once a year. Just outside, also hidden from the people but accessible to the priests, was the Holy Place, containing three (again) constantly-attended items representing communion with God. There was a lampstand with oil lamps shining their light on the space; directly across from the lampstand was a table of fresh bread, presented to the Lord weekly, then eaten by the priests when replaced. In front of the Ark of the Presence, the Ark of the Covenant, separated by only a thick blue, purple, and crimson linen curtain with cherubim worked in it, was the Altar of Incense. Here the prayers of the priests for the people were offered to the Holy One, dwelling behind the veil only inches away.

The Tabernacle, the tent of meeting, the tent of prayer was in the center of the camp. Anyone could come to the outer court and be near the Presence after making a blood sacrifice through priests who also entered with a blood sacrifice and washed with water.

God was near, tangible, powerful, but lovingly approachable by his choosing, initiative, and decree. Anyone, anywhere in the camp for these forty wilderness years, could see the evidence above the tent of meeting. Each and every person could see and would see a cloud that led them by day and a cloud of fire that illuminated the camp and guided them by night. God's continual, humble, loving presence was with His people in an intimate setting far away from the world's noisy, pagan, idle-ridden kingdoms — primarily Egypt and Babylon.

He was getting His promised people out of slavery, and He was getting slavery out of them. He gently, lovingly, and powerfully led them to a promised land and a deeper relationship. It was land promised to Abraham, Sarah, and their descendants, some 500 years earlier, now 4000 years ago.

It was a House of Prayer and a Tent of Meeting, proffered and provided by the Creator Himself.

This Tent of Meeting, treasured and carried by the faithful, God honored with His presence from the time of Moses around 1500 BC until the time of David around 1000 BC. The judges ruling Israel gave way to the time of the monarchy, and David brought the Ark of the Presence to the place where God would allow Solomon, his son, to build The Temple, a house of prayer, lasting for 1000 years, although destroyed once and built back on the same foundation after a seventy year interlude in Babylon. Solomon did this using the same layout as the humble, extraordinary Tent of Meeting.

One thousand years earlier, Abraham had looked for a city whose architect and builder was God (Hebrews 11:10). He found one.

He found all three — a City, the Architect, and the Builder at the remote mountain top of Moriah, where he obediently, in faith, offered Isaac, his only son, up to God as a sacrifice. He could only see by faith, but he did see by faith and action, the continual presence of God with his family and friends. His house was a home of communion with God, by sacrifice for prayer.

We don't know what Abraham saw by faith that God might do in the future. But he believed, and his confidence has become sight to his descendants and the whole world.

We've heard of the Ark of the Covenant—God's presence with His people. We know about the tent of meeting—a place of sacrifice, making communion possible, and prayer. The Bible and history tell us about the temple in Jerusalem—a house of prayer for all people and the city of the great King (Psalm 48:2, Matthew 5:35).

From there, we've gone to God dwelling within His people by His Spirit to the ends of the earth, until the end of the age, then forever, amen. We are houses of communion and prayer — God's continual, indwelling presence with His people, His image bears, proffering this life of prayer and communion to all people, everywhere.

"The Spirit and the bride say, 'Come!' And let the one who hears say, 'Come!' Let the one who is thirsty come; and let the one who wishes take the free gift of the water of life" (Revelation 22:17 NIV).

The prophet says: "Come, all you who are thirsty, come to the waters; and you who have no money, come, buy and eat! Come, buy wine and milk without money and without cost" (Isaiah 55:1). The Prophet says, "If you knew the gift of God and who it is that asks you for a drink, you would have asked him and he would have given you living water" (John 4:10).

Pray, people, pray night and day, give Him no rest. He needs none. You only need to apprehend the omnipotent One you address and honor His Grace with your humble petition and act of worship. Experience Him. Experience His presence and power. Experience prayer — real prayer, simple, child-like, no-pretense prayer.

Prayer changes things—every prayer matters. If you have enough faith to pray, you can move mountains by addressing the mountain mover. Pray!

This piece of the puzzle introduces prayer. The actual prayer piece of the puzzle will be much shorter. Prayer, like canoeing, is best learned with a paddle in your hands — practice.

The essential elements are yourself, God, and talk. Please keep it simple. Keep it child-like. Keep in mind prayer is primarily about Him. Seek to know Him better each day. As with living, the joy is in the journey. In the end, prayer doesn't change God. Prayer changes us. But there is much joy and many surprises in the process. It's called supernatural for a reason.

So let this serve as an introduction to prayer — an introduction and a benediction. "For thine is the kingdom, and the power, and the glory, for ever. Amen" (Matthew 6:13b KJV).

PUZZLING CHAPTER 49

Prayer Helps

SINCE THIS LITTLE PUZZLE ISN'T exhaustive in any sense, I feel OK to proffer a few helps in our quest to understand and practice prayer, which may be the most important, influential, and productive spiritual discipline available to us by God's design and decree. It's relationship 101 — talking things out, telling someone Who cares how you feel and your thoughts, listening with interest, and respecting His thoughts.

The most important thing to remember is that you are conversing with the most powerful and loving Being in the universe — One you would like to know better and have that opportunity each time you meet. Prayer is a two-way conversation, so listening is essential to the meeting and an equation to keep in mind.

Where do we meet? And at what time? Those are necessary and telling things to know if you're meeting someone. Thankfully you can meet God anywhere you wish and at any time. The One you address is always available, attentive, and not restricted by place, space, or time.

A Special Privilege

I am starting to see prayer as the special privilege it is. Is how we see it practiced in our churches the way it is? Is it what we see practiced through recorded history? I don't know. I often hear the phrase: "I guess all we can do is pray." Really? That's all we can do? Do you know Who you're addressing in prayer? I'm coming to hate that phrase, and partially because it hits too close to home.

In light of God's unfathomable power, sovereignty, and otherness from His creation — maybe so. Maybe our requests, pleas, and thoughts are to Him like a two-year-old pleading with their parents for something, no matter how spiritually mature or immature we might be.

He is other than His creation. But then, He chose to become a part of His creation. He lowered Himself to pick us up, become one of us, and relate to us on our level. He chose to be more intimately involved in our pains and joys, to walk with and talk with us.

So in that reality, prayer takes on new meaning indeed. It's up to each individual to discover and determine, at least in part, how closely and intimately you will walk with your Maker, Brother, and Friend.

Indeed there is a great gulf fixed between us and Him, with Whom we have to do. But He has arranged a bridge called the Cross to make a pathway to Him. And then, in great humility, He made it possible for Him to dwell with us and intimately within us — spirit to Spirit. Amen.

If this sounds foreign or weird to you, I humbly suggest that you haven't read your Bible closely enough. Or that you sit under teachers teaching in churches that don't read or believe their Bibles. Jesus based His church, His family, and the community of faith known as the Kingdom of God on this reality. This is how the Kingdom of Heaven invades this earth's kingdoms and is prevailing and growing into the eternal family of God until this very day. In one sentence, it is this: "To them God has chosen to make known among the Gentiles the glorious riches of **this mystery**, which is **Christ in you, the hope of glory** [emphasis added]" (Colossians 1:27 NIV). (I proffer these verses for your further meditation and consideration of this reality: Isaiah 66:1-2, Acts 17:24-28, 30, Ephesians 3:20, Galatians 2:20, John 3:1-8, John 15:5.)

In all fairness, one must note that God's Spirit within us is a mystery, as pointed out in the verse above. But it's also necessary to realize that: "In him [God] we live, and move, and have our being" (Acts 17:28 KJV). How did you come to be? I predict a man and woman came together, two cells united one from each, and they began to divide exponentially into different body parts, knowing their various functions. Then you were born a living soul and began to mature. Now you live and move and are a being. You know that much, but I predict not much more than that or how it possibly could happen. Life in the Spirit and life lived with God are like that. This verse comes to mind: "For those who are led by the Spirit of God are the children of God. The Spirit you received does not make you slaves, so that you live in fear again; rather, the Spirit you received brought about your adoption to sonship. And by him we cry, 'Abba, Father.' The Spirit himself testifies with our spirit that we are God's children" (Romans 8:14-16 NIV).

What About Prayer?

So what does that have to do with prayer? If your kids ask you for something compared to someone else's asking you for something, do the requests carry the same weight?

I do realize we're talking about God here. And in a sense, He is the Father of us all. We also read this about Him: "But love your enemies, and do good, and lend, expecting nothing in return; and your reward will be great, and you will be sons of the Most High; for **He Himself is kind to ungrateful and evil men.** Be merciful, just as your Father is merciful [emphasis added]" (Luke 6:35-36).

But that your own children have a special place with you and in your heart is something easily understood in the natural and should be evident in the spiritual. So we can move on from here. Interestingly, God has so orchestrated creation that He teaches us, like children, spiritual truths by first showing us how things work in the natural: "However, the spiritual is not first, but the natural; then the spiritual" (1 Corinthians 15:46).

Is prayer mysterious? Yes, it is. But it seems intrinsic to every human being. Many people report praying daily, and some admit not knowing to whom they pray. It may be a creation issue, a bit like breathing. So it's a mystery we live with, but so common we don't think of it as a mystery.

I love Acts chapter seventeen. The older I get and the more I read it, the more I love it. Here we see Paul, a very well-educated Jewish lawyer, speaking to the intelligentsia of the day in Athens about truth, philosophy, and God. He notices they are polytheistic by their many idols to many gods at the base of Mars Hill, among them an idol to "The Unknown God."

A mystery — so Paul speaks to this mystery in their audience. A few believed and were born by the Spirit into the family of God. They enjoyed immediate and continual access to their Father. We read: "But some men joined him and believed, among whom also were Dionysius the Areopagite and a woman named Damaris and others with them" (Acts 17:34). It will be fascinating to one day speak to Damaris and learn of the things she asked of God. Also, what became of the people she lifted to God in prayer?

We also read in Scripture that God disciplines His children: "Because the Lord disciplines the one he loves, and he chastens everyone he accepts as his son. Endure hardship as discipline; God is treating you as his children. For what children are not disciplined by their father? If you are not disciplined—and everyone undergoes discipline—then you are not legitimate, not true sons and daughters at all. Moreover, we have all had human fathers who disciplined us and we respected them for it. How much more should we submit to the Father of spirits and live! They disciplined us for a little while as they thought best; but God disciplines us for our good, in order that we may share in his holiness. No discipline seems pleasant at the time, but painful. Later on, however, it produces a harvest of righteousness and peace for those who have been trained by it" (Hebrews 12:6-11 NIV).

So welcome to the table, where you have continual access to the Father of Lights. You are an honored, disciplined, discipled, valued, and loved child. It's good to be part of the family and free to ask Father anything you like! If you hold back, you don't yet know how big and good He is. But you will learn, by His grace.

Prayer Helps

This chapter is named prayer helps because **prayer helps** with about anything and everything in life. Also, I include **some helps to prayer** that you might find motivational or inspirational.

My wife and I recently spent a weekend at the lake with friends. Early morning, we were getting around — reading, thinking, journaling. After some small talk on the deck, I told the guys I was writing and thinking about prayer. Then our ladies informed us it was time for breakfast. After breakfast, I asked the whole group a question. "All of you have been Christians for many years. What are the most important things you have learned, or God has taught you, about prayer?"

Patty spoke up first, "He hears my prayers. It's not that I hope He hears. He desires to answer my prayers." Then David added, "I'm learning to pray the Scriptures. Many of them are tied to His promises. It helps me to pray what I know He desires. I find myself praying back to Him His good pleasure."

After a thoughtful pause, Debbie said, "Be exactly honest with God, and don't cover up. He'll bring you to repentance, and then you can freely ask what you will. Trust Him at all times. Pour out your heart to Him. If you have trash in your heart, let Him speak to it and cleanse you." She referenced a Psalm: "Trust in him at all times, you people; pour out your hearts to him" (Psalm 62:8 NIV).

Connie then added her significant thought on prayer, "Have faith and pray in faith. Fear doesn't move mountains." Bill spoke next, "Listen! So much of prayer is listening. Wisdom shouts in the streets, but one must be quiet and listen." He also added, "Come [in prayer] with expectation! But also come with humility."

Stan spoke to the question last and said, "I've been learning recently to pray, 'Let the Lord do what seems best to Him.'" He said it came to him from a prayer of Joab before a critical battle: "Be strong, and let us show ourselves courageous for the sake of our people and for the cities of our God; and **may the Lord do what is good in His sight** [emphasis added]" (2 Samuel 10:12).

One of the girls spoke up in disagreement, saying, "No, but we should ask the Lord boldly what we want." Both have a point, but the Lord will probably do what seems best to Him anyway in response to our request. And praying as Joab did, and Stan is learning to do, may show spiritual maturity and a heightened awareness of Who God is. The New Testament tells us: "His judgments are true and righteous" (Revelation 19:2a), and the Old Testament says the same: "The fear of the LORD is clean, enduring forever; the judgments of the LORD are true; they are righteous altogether" (Psalm 19:9). If we know Him, it's easy to believe that His plans for us are better than our plans for us.

Home Group on Prayer

A few weeks earlier, we were in our church small group, and I asked the same question after we had gone around the room and prayed for needs that were on our hearts and touched our lives.

Energetically, Hilary, John, Clark, Kim, Rochelle, Bruce, Rick, Ron, and others voiced their most poignant thoughts on prayer: "Distraction is a tool of Satan against me. I'm too busy not to pray!" "Prayer changes us." "Seventy-three of the one hundred fifty Psalms are about prayer or contain prayers. For example, 'Hear my cry O God, You have been my Rock.'" "Daniel was the prime minister of a world empire, yet he paused to pray three times a day." "Do you see prayer as talking to your eternal, heavenly Father?" "When you pray coincidences happen. When you don't, they don't." "I use the acronym ACTS as a format for my prayer; adoration, confession, thanksgiving, and supplication."

Clark, who miraculously survived multiple heart attacks, said, "I am an answer to prayer — that I am still here." He added, "I realized that God wants me to pray. He doesn't need me to pray. But I have a privilege of seeing prayers come true."

Rochelle added that she was a single mom for twelve years and, "Prayer taught me I'm never alone." She also shared an acronym that helped her practice prayer as it should be practiced: "PUSH — pray until something happens." In other words, perseverance, or persevere in prayer. Clark added to that thought: "George Muller prayed for his best friend to come to faith for fifty-seven years. The day they buried Muller, his friend bowed beside his grave and gave his heart to Christ."

John quoted Adrian Rogers, who said: "There is no promise God cannot keep; no prayer He cannot answer." Hilary added, "A spirit cannot survive in a hurried soul" (Dallas Willard). She mentioned how much *The Ruthless Elimination of Hurry: How to Stay Emotionally Healthy and Spiritually Alive in the Chaos of the Modern World* by John Mark Comer had touched her life and prayer life. The title intrigues me, and I must read it. Here are the two most highlighted quotes from Kindle readers. "*Corrie ten Boom once said that if the devil can't make you sin, he'll make you busy. There's truth in that. Both sin and busyness have the exact same effect—they cut off your connection to God, to other people, and even to your own soul.*" And: "*If you want to experience the life of Jesus, you have to adopt the lifestyle of Jesus.*"

I added three recent things that motivate me to pray. The first is a confession. I often say that I believe prayer is the most important spiritual discipline. Someone said, "If you preach you move men, but if you pray you move God. Who would you rather move?" In the same breath, I usually say prayer is my weakest spiritual discipline, which I believe it is. It's as if I wear that as an excuse or a badge of some kind, admitting failure or deficiency in prayer with a hope to do better. I recently felt the Spirit impress me to stop saying that and instead pray! I've started to do so.

I'm coming into some new revelational awareness of grace, one I've just scratched the surface of and will continue to expand for the rest of my life. In part, it is a belief I often voice: "I believe God's plans for me are better than my plans for me." That thought is beginning to inform and influence my prayer life. I can pray fearlessly and with reckless abandon, so to speak, because I see experientially and in faith that God will do with my prayer as He sees fit, and that is precisely what I'd want Him to do because of His wisdom, goodness, and power. Said another way, He hears my voice, knows it's important to me, sees my heart of care and compassion for others or my pain, and knows how to best address the matter and bring a good result. His plans for us are better than our plans for us! Pray.

Last I shared my favorite Bible verse on prayer with our group of friends: "…**there was silence in heaven for about half an hour**. And I saw the seven angels who stand before God, and seven trumpets were given to them. **Another angel came and stood at the altar, holding a golden censer; and much incense was given to him, so that he might add it to the prayers of all the saints** on the golden altar which was before the throne. And the smoke of the incense, with **the prayers of the saints, went up before God out of the angel's hand.** Then **the angel took the censer and filled it with the fire of the altar, and threw it to the earth; and there followed peals of thunder and sounds and flashes of lightning and an earthquake** [emphasis added]" (Revelation

8:1-5). One has to marvel at and love the imagery of prayer and the importance and power of prayer portrayed in this glimpse from The Apocalypse. Pray.

PUZZLING CHAPTER 50

The Threshing Floor

"DAVID WAS FOR MANY YEARS searching for a site for the great temple which he purposed to build for Jehovah his God. It had been ordained that the sacrifices offered to the one God should be offered by all Israel upon one altar; but as yet the ark of the Lord was within curtains, near to David's palace, and the altar of burnt offering was situated at Gibeon. Where should the one altar be erected? Where should the ark find its permanent dwelling-place?" This is how Charles Haddon Spurgeon began his sermon on I Chronicles 21:28, November 9, 1884, from the Metropolitan Tabernacle Pulpit in London.

This is a more important question with a more important answer than any of us realize.

God's heart was in a dance with that of a courageous, shepherd king. The result was in effect one that would make all the earth and creation sing. A romance of cosmic yet intimate scale was unfolding on a threshing floor atop a mountain named Moriah, just outside what was then the City of David, and capital of Israel 1000 BC. Both locations would soon be encompassed by the city of Jerusalem, meaning in the Hebrew language "the foundation or city of peace." This was foundational for peace with God, and the peace of mankind.

Jerusalem is also known appropriately as the city of the Great King: "Beautiful in elevation, the joy of the whole earth, is Mount Zion in the far north, the city of the great King" (Psalm 48:2). "But I say to you, make no oath at all, either by heaven, for it is the throne of God, or by the earth, for it is the footstool of His feet, or by Jerusalem, for it is the city of the great King" (Matthew 5:34-35). The city and this mountain would become the center of the earth to God, and to those who love and worship Him.

This is one of the most important pieces to a cosmic puzzle involving God, angels, and humankind. Surely you can see it, if you read the Bible or if you read history. You'll see if you watch the nightly news, which I don't recommend unless you can separate the events from the slanted meaning given them by a mostly-deceived, secular-humanist media. It's more enlightening to read the Bible and history than to watch only the sensationalism and violence the media seeks to market, painting a very distorted picture of reality. It's better to dwell in the secret place of the Most High, and pray from the shelter of the Almighty. But I digress.

Jerusalem, Jerusalem!

Jerusalem is a microcosm of Israel's history and mankind's history on the earth. Who is God there? And Who will be worshiped there? In the city of the Great King? Jesus said as he looked over the city: "Jerusalem, Jerusalem, who kills the prophets and stones those who are sent to her! How often I wanted to gather your children together, the way a hen gathers her chicks under her wings, and you were unwilling" (Matthew 23:37).

If you believe God's Word is holy and inspired (2 Timothy 3:16), and God keeps his word to a thousand generations (Deuteronomy 7:9), you might be interested in some of the things He says in the Bible about Jerusalem.

"But to his son I will give one tribe, that My servant David may have a lamp always before Me in Jerusalem, the city where I have chosen for Myself to put My name"
(1 Kings 11:36).

"Remember the word which You commanded Your servant Moses, saying, 'If you are unfaithful I will scatter you among the peoples; but if you return to Me and keep My commandments and do them, though those of you who have been scattered were in the most remote part of the heavens, I will gather them from there and will bring them to the place where I have chosen to cause My name to dwell'"
(Nehemiah 1:8-9).

"Now David built houses for himself in the city of David; and he prepared a place for the ark of God and pitched a tent for it. Then David said, 'No one is to carry the ark of God but the Levites; for the Lord chose them to carry the ark of God and to minister to Him forever.' And David assembled all Israel at Jerusalem to bring up the ark of the Lord to its place which he had prepared for it"
(1 Chronicles 15:1-3).

"Then Solomon began to build the house of the Lord in Jerusalem on Mount Moriah, where the Lord had appeared to his father David, at the place that David had prepared on the threshing floor of Ornan the Jebusite"
(2 Chronicles 3:1).

"Now in the first year of Cyrus king of Persia, in order to fulfill the word of the Lord by the mouth of Jeremiah, the Lord stirred up the spirit of Cyrus king of Persia, so that he sent a proclamation throughout all his kingdom, and also put it in writing, saying: 'Thus says Cyrus king of Persia,' "The Lord, the God of heaven, has given me all the kingdoms of the earth and He has appointed me to build Him a house in Jerusalem, which is in Judah. Whoever there is among you of all His people, may his God be with him! Let him go up to Jerusalem which is in Judah and rebuild the house of the Lord, the God of Israel; He is the God who is in Jerusalem"

(Ezra 1:1-3).

"'Then they shall bring all your brethren from all the nations as a grain offering to the Lord, on horses, in chariots, in litters, on mules and on camels, to My holy mountain Jerusalem,' says the Lord, 'just as the sons of Israel bring their grain offering in a clean vessel to the house of the Lord'"

(Isaiah 66:20).

"Blessed be the Lord from Zion, Who dwells in Jerusalem. Praise the Lord!"

(Psalm 135:21).

"At that time they will call Jerusalem 'The Throne of the Lord,' and all the nations will be gathered to it, to Jerusalem, for the name of the Lord; nor will they walk anymore after the stubbornness of their evil heart"

(Jeremiah 3:17).

"Speak kindly to Jerusalem; and call out to her, that her warfare has ended, that her iniquity has been removed, that she has received of the Lord's hand double for all her sins"

(Isaiah 40:2).

"On your walls, O Jerusalem, I have appointed watchmen; all day and all night they will never keep silent. You who remind the Lord, take no rest for yourselves; and give Him no rest until He establishes and makes Jerusalem a praise in the earth"

(Isaiah 62:6-7).

"Rejoice greatly, O daughter of Zion! Shout in triumph, O daughter of Jerusalem! Behold, your king is coming to you; He is just and endowed with salvation, humble, and mounted on a donkey, even on a colt, the foal of a donkey. I will cut off the chariot from Ephraim and the horse from Jerusalem; and the bow of war will be cut off. And He will speak peace to the nations; and His dominion will be from sea to sea, and from the River to the ends of the earth"

(Zechariah 9:9-10).

"If I forget you, O Jerusalem, may my right hand forget her skill. May my tongue cling to the roof of my mouth if I do not remember you, if I do not exalt Jerusalem above my chief joy"

(Psalm 137:5-9).

"Why are the nations in an uproar and the peoples devising a vain thing? The kings of the earth take their stand and the rulers take counsel together against the Lord and against His Anointed, saying, 'Let us tear their fetters apart and cast away their cords from us!' He who sits in the heavens laughs, the Lord scoffs at them. Then He will speak to them in His anger and terrify them in His fury, saying, 'But as for Me, I have installed My King upon Zion, My holy mountain'"

(Psalm 2:1-6).

PUZZLING CHAPTER 51

Wonder or Wander

WONDER: NOUN "A FEELING OF surprise mingled with admiration, caused by something beautiful, unexpected, unfamiliar, or inexplicable"

(Oxford Languages Dictionary).

Wonder: verb 1. "desire or be curious to know something," 2. "feel doubt"

(Oxford Languages Dictionary).

Wander: verb "walk or move in a leisurely, casual, or aimless way"
(Oxford Languages Dictionary).

Wander: noun "an act or instance of wandering"
(Oxford Languages Dictionary).

These two English words are sometimes confused. I awakened early one morning to journal and quickly found myself musing and meditating on how they apply to our relationship with the Almighty. They certainly do.

Thoughts about these two words awakened me along with some lyrics of a beautiful song by MercyMe, "Even If."

Wonder

You can wonder about paradoxes and hidden things or unclear things about God. He invites you to do so. This invitation is something along the lines of: "Be angry, and yet do not sin" (Ephesians 4:26a). Or you could say doubt, but don't depart. You can question things but do not wander from faith in God, as demonstrated by holding fast to his ways and commands. Obedience is faith, genuine faith, in the absence of complete understanding. This morning, a brother in a Bible study said: "Obedience is love, or shows real love."

I think of Job amid personal pain after all ten of his children died in a violent storm that destroyed the house where they were feasting (Job 1:13-22). His faith proclamation is one of the loudest in history and the Bible: "Though He slay me, yet will I trust Him" (Job 13:15a).

Job's faith proclamation, backed up by his worship of God and obedience to God's ways, speaks as boldly and loudly as anything in history of the kind of faith that pleases a very worthy God — One worthy of that trust, One all-powerful, faithful, and good.

Job's words rank right up there with phrases uttered by God himself during His time on earth: "Father, forgive them; for they do not know what they are doing" (Luke 23:34a). Also: "Father, if You are willing, remove this cup from Me; yet not My will, but Yours be done" (Luke 22:42). And: "It is finished!" (John 19:30b).

It's OK to wonder and ponder. Job did. Jesus did. It's not OK to give up on God and wander — to use your wonder as an excuse to wander from God and his ways and go your own way. Or to try to re-create God in your image of Him.

That's pride, hubris, disobedience, and dishonoring to the Holy One. He has not left that option open to us or anyone. Not even his Son. Well, on second thought, He has left that option available.

Some advocate that this kind of wondering is necessary to genuine faith, coming to faith, and testing faith. They say wondering refines, proves, and strengthens faith and its validity. A well-known and respected Quaker theologian said: "We need to be agnostics first and then there is some chance at arriving at a sensible system of belief" (D. Elton Trueblood).

Honest questioning from a heart that trusts God is "wondering" permitted. It's even an invitation for God to show you truth and reveal perhaps some of His hidden ways or answer your questions. But don't let your wondering giveaway to wandering. You'll be showing your faith isn't faith as defined by God. It may still be in the process like Peter's was from the beginning to late in his life. But in the end, you will show whether you built your house on His or your ways, faith in God or faith in man (secular humanism), on the rock or on sand (Matthew 7:24-27). Wonder, but do not wander.

Wonder — An Antidote to Wander

Wonder, as first defined above, is an antidote to wandering away.

If one is filled with awe at creation and the paragon of God's attributes shown in what He has made — that is a healthy wonder. A heart filled with that wonder will not be tempted to wander often or much.

A heart is filled with wonder when it meditates on God's beautiful, holy, and other attributes described in the Scriptures and demonstrated toward individuals and nations. A heart fills with wonder at the thought of One so powerful, just, loving, generous, creative, and kind.

This wonder causes a heart not to want to wander but stay near — to continually dwell or tabernacle with God. David said it this way: "One thing I have asked from the Lord, that I shall seek: that I may dwell in the house of the Lord all the days of my life, to behold the beauty of the Lord and to meditate in His temple" (Psalm 27:4).

A hymn writer from yesteryear has pinned it this way as a song and prayer:

> "O to grace how great a debtor / Daily I'm constrained to be! / Let Thy goodness, like a fetter, / Bind my wandering heart to Thee. / Prone to wander, Lord, I feel it, / Prone to leave the God I love; / Here's my heart, O take and seal it, / Seal it for Thy courts above"
>
> ("Come Thou Fount of Every Blessing," Robert Robinson, 1758).

The 3000-year-old Psalms and Proverbs are an invitation to dwell with God or the implied and proffered freedom to dwell elsewhere if you choose. The ramifications of each one's decisions are laid out.

Dwell is the keyword: "Thus says the Lord, 'Heaven is My throne and the earth is My footstool. Where then is a house you could build for Me? And where is a place that I may rest [dwell]? For My hand made all these things, thus all these things came into being,' declares the Lord. 'But to this one I will look, to him who is humble and contrite of spirit, and who trembles at My word'" (Isaiah 66:1-2). Abide is the crucial word: "I am the vine, you are the branches; he who abides in Me and I in him, he bears much fruit, for apart from Me you can do nothing" (John 15:5). It's a lifestyle you choose, do, and practice — a rhythm. To dwell and abide is a choice, then an action.

You can choose a lifestyle with solitude, silence, reading the Word, prayer, meditation, reading good books, exercise in creation, and sharing with others, or you can dwell in front of a TV and do a plethora of self-absorbed or people-pleasing activities. You choose to live in wonder or to wander.

Poet, prophet, and king of Israel, David said it best in Psalm 23.

Please read it and let the peaceful succinct phrases wash over your soul and re-center you to a place of wonder. Psalm 1 will do the same thing. They bring you to the King or keep you mindful of Him as described in Psalm 24, where you know Him and can say with David: "You will make known to me the path of life; in Your presence is fullness of joy; in Your right hand there are pleasures forever" (Psalm 16:11).

Be continually filled with wonder; you won't wander or even want to wander. I know that's a lot of "w"s.

Wander as a Bridge to Wonder

There are strong warnings to avoid a life of wander(ing) by living in appropriate and continual wonder. But it must be said that wander(ing) often leads to wonder — the wonder of grace, which is the wonder of God.

Possibly the most famous hymn in the world was written by a 19th-century British slave trader who was rescued from the depths of despair. The lyrics are known the world over and start like this: "Amazing grace how sweet the sound that saved a wretch like me. I once was lost, but now I'm found, was blind but now I see" (John Newton, 1725-1807).

And there was a woman of the night whose wandering turned to wonder at knowing and being forgiven by Jesus. She was so emboldened that she dared enter a Pharisee's home to express her appreciation and worship Jesus. He aptly explained the reality of the situation to both of them and us: "You [Simon the Pharisee] did not give me a kiss, but this woman, from the time I entered, has not stopped kissing my feet. You did not put oil on my head, but she has poured perfume on my feet. Therefore, I tell you, her many sins have been forgiven—as her great love has shown. But whoever has been forgiven little loves little" (Luke 7:45-47 NIV). Jesus also told her: "Your sins are forgiven. Your faith has saved you; go in peace" (Luke 7:48b,50b).

In this case and millions like it, a life of wandering led to a life of wonder. Grace was shown to be what it is — a magnanimous and freely given gift. Grace is a gift undeserved, life-giving, eternal, and accessible. These words are feeble to describe something so powerful, noble, and grand. I realize this more and more as I experience grace more and more. Grace may be as much a descriptor of Who God Is as what He does. John tells us about Jesus: "And **the Word became flesh, and dwelt among us**, and we saw His glory, glory as of the only begotten from the Father, **full of grace and truth** [emphasis added]" (John 1:14). Then to emphasize the point John writes: "For **of His fullness we have all received,** and **grace upon grace** [emphasis added]" (John 1:16).

Maybe the monarchs of the last millennium apprehended a bit of this reality when they addressed each other and were addressed: "Your Grace." Most of them knew they ruled by God's permission and decree. They experienced and exalted the attribute of grace. It is a wonder, enabling one to experience wonder, seldom more to wander.

Even If

The contemporary music group MercyMe released a song entitled "Even If" in 2017 that was nominated for the Dove Award Song of the Year. It is timeless in its truth and message and addresses in a way only a song can do the concept of how we're prone to wander but must choose wonder. To summarize this piece of the puzzle, I'll share some lyrics and encourage you to watch it performed on YouTube or listen on your favorite music app.

In a magazine interview, the lead singer of MercyMe, Bart Millard, said that the band's hit song "Even If" is about his son's lifelong battle with diabetes.

The song's lyrics read: "They say it only takes a little faith/ To move a mountain/ Well good thing/ A little faith is all I have, right now/ But

God, when You choose/ To leave mountains unmovable/ Oh give me the strength to be able to sing/ It is well with my soul. ... I know You're able and I know You can/ Save through the fire with Your mighty hand/ But even if You don't/ My hope is You alone." (The Christian Post, christianpost.com).

"He who made the Pleiades and Orion
And changes deep darkness into morning,
Who also darkens day into night,
Who calls for the waters of the sea
And pours them out on the surface of the earth,
The Lord is His name"

(Amos 5:11).

PUZZLING CHAPTER 52

Prayer at Shiloh

Authority and Prayer

Yesterday our pastor began a series of sermons on First and Second Samuel. His theme and focus is "redeeming spiritual authority." This is important to God, and He redeemed it during a bleak time of moral decay and chaos in ancient Israel. That certainly seems germane to our day, doesn't it?

Joshua led the children of Israel into the promised land about 1500 BC, where they continued under the theocratic leadership of judges lasting almost 500 years. During this period, there were cycles of moral decay and then revival to a healthy relationship with God. At the very end of the period, we see extreme moral decay, homosexuality defended, chaos, social upheaval, open conflict, and cultural breakdown, not unlike the USA today. The very last verse in the book of judges gives us insight and the reason for what happened: "In those days **there was no king in Israel; everyone did what was right in his own eyes** [emphasis added]" (Judges 21:25). That last phrase could be the watchword of secular humanism.

God was about to do something insightful and helpful for His chosen people Israel. This would also signal a chapter change in how God works among the peoples of the earth — the evolution of government, if you will, demonstrating to man, man's inability to rule himself successfully and the grace of God helping humankind on their journey despite that reality. The system of judges was about to give way to the rule of kings in Israel.

We would probably like to immediately have a good and noble king ride into the situation with his army of like-minded warriors and set the condition right so the people could live in freedom and peace without fear. But we read about God's ways: "'For My thoughts are not your thoughts, nor are your ways My ways,' declares the Lord. 'For as the heavens are higher than the earth, so are My ways higher than your ways and My thoughts than your thoughts'" (Isaiah 55:8-9).

Shiloh

So as you might suspect, God didn't do it this way, at least not initially. It started with a prayer of a barren woman offered up in great distress from Shiloh.

Shiloh is a name as mysterious as it is beautiful. Its ancient meanings are: "He Whose It Is," and "Tranquility Town." It is also a messianic name for Jesus the coming King: "The sceptre shall not depart from Judah, nor a lawgiver from between his feet, until Shiloh come; and unto him shall the gathering of the people be" (Genesis 49:10 KJV).

Another translation has it: "The scepter shall not depart from Judah, nor the ruler's staff from between his feet, until Shiloh comes [or Until he comes to Shiloh; or Until he comes to whom it belongs], and to him shall be the obedience of the peoples" (Genesis 49:10 NASB).

Shiloh's etymology is insightful. Its meaning comes from two smaller words: "to extract or be at prosperous rest" and "if only, would it be that, may it be."

The town of Shiloh is most famous for being the first seat of government in Israel under Joshua after the conquest of Canaan. At Shiloh, the tent of meeting was set up (Joshua 18:1), the land was divided (Joshua 18:10), and judges were established up to the time of Eli and Samuel (1 Samuel 1:9). The Tabernacle was there for over 300 years, about the same amount of time our country has existed.

It was here that Hannah (a Hebrew name meaning: favor, grace, or God has favored me) with her husband Elkanah (a Hebrew name meaning: God has purchased, God has possessed, God has created) came up to worship and sacrifice each year. The Bible tells us: "Now this man would go up from his city **yearly to worship and to sacrifice to the Lord of hosts in Shiloh** [emphasis added]" (1 Samuel 1:3a). We can also see that Hannah believed it to be, and found it to be, a special place of prayer.

To learn her touching story, one must read the first two chapters of First Samuel. But I want to cut to our main point, her prayer. After eating a meal with her husband at his request: "Then Hannah rose after eating and drinking in Shiloh. Now Eli the priest was sitting on the seat by the doorpost of the temple of the Lord. She, greatly distressed, prayed to the Lord and wept bitterly. She made a vow and said, 'O Lord of hosts, if You will indeed look on the affliction of Your maidservant and remember me, and not forget Your maidservant, but will give Your maidservant a son, then I will give him to the Lord all the days of his life, and a razor shall never come on his head'" (1 Samuel 1:9-11).

Her prayer and oath are as bizarre as what happens next: "Now it came about, as she continued praying before the Lord, that Eli was watching her mouth. As for Hannah, she was speaking in her heart, only her lips were moving, but her voice was not heard. So Eli thought she was drunk" (1 Samuel 1:12-13). The aging and not-so-spiritually-sensitive judge and high priest hadn't grasped what was going on with Hannah, but we hear it from her own gentle, humble mouth and heart: "No, my lord, I am a woman oppressed in spirit; I have drunk neither wine nor strong drink, but I have poured out my soul before the Lord. Do not consider your maidservant as a worthless woman, for I have spoken until now out of my great concern and provocation" (1 Samuel 1:15-16). So we learn that God hears hearts, even if prayers are silent or inward, especially of passionate and desperate people, even if pastors, priests, or overseers do not.

We also see God is in the business of grace and answering such prayer. The story continues: "Then Eli answered and said, 'Go in peace; and may the God of Israel grant your petition that you have asked of Him'" (1 Samuel 1:17). Hannah's cheerful reply was: "... 'Let your maidservant find favor in your sight.' So the woman went her way and ate, and her face was no longer sad" (1 Samuel 1:18). Something significant happened to Hannah in the middle of those two prayers — her prayer and Eli's! She heard something in the Spirit and believed it would happen. She knew only by faith, but she believed God heard her prayer, and the answer was imminent.

We read elsewhere in the Bible: "This is the confidence which we have before Him, that, if we ask anything according to His will, He hears us. And if we know that He hears us in whatever we ask, we know that we have the requests which we have asked from Him" (1 John 5:14-15). Hagar and her only son Ishmael were alone in the desert, about to die from thirst, when she prayed. God answered her prayer, and she gave God the name: "You are a God who sees" (Genesis 16:13b).

We read that God followed through on His part and gave Hannah a son. Samuel (a Hebrew name meaning "God hears") was born about nine months later. Hannah carried through on her promise and gave him back to serve Eli and the Lord in the tabernacle at Shiloh after she weaned him, probably at five or six years of age.

Samuel grew up to effectively become a prophet, priest, and king in Israel before there was a king. He was the last judge. He showed himself faithful to God, constantly hearing and obeying the word of the Lord.

He was not swayed by power and always cared about and carried out his Father's business. In that, Samuel was a type of Jesus, the coming messiah and King. Samuel was one of the greatest leaders in Israel's history, and he would figure prominently in the transition from the judges to the kings in Israel. He acknowledged and anointed the first two kings of Israel at God's leading. It all began with Hannah's prayer and God's answer at Shiloh.

Hannah's Prayer of Thanksgiving

Hannah's second recorded prayer is even more remarkable than her first one. It's a prayer of thanksgiving to her Lord, Who showed Himself to her in the most intimate and revelational ways imaginable. It flows to her heart from the Lord's heart — beautiful truths about His person and ways, like a love poem between them. The Spirit shared it with us via our Bibles.

"Then Hannah prayed and said,
'My heart exults in the Lord;
My horn is exalted in the Lord,
**My mouth speaks boldly against my enemies,
Because I rejoice in Your salvation.
There is no one holy like the Lord,
Indeed, there is no one besides You,
Nor is there any rock like our God.
Boast no more so very proudly,
Do not let arrogance come out of your mouth;
For the Lord is a God of knowledge,
And with Him actions are weighed.
The bows of the mighty are shattered,
But the feeble gird on strength.**
Those who were full hire themselves out for bread,

But those who were hungry cease to hunger.
Even the barren gives birth to seven,
But she who has many children languishes.
The Lord kills and makes alive;
He brings down to Sheol and raises up.
The Lord makes poor and rich;
He brings low, He also exalts.
He raises the poor from the dust,
He lifts the needy from the ash heap
To make them sit with nobles,
And inherit a seat of honor;
For the pillars of the earth are the Lord's,
And He set the world on them.
He keeps the feet of His godly ones,
But the wicked ones are silenced in darkness;
For not by might shall a man prevail.
Those who contend with the Lord will be shattered;
Against them He will thunder in the heavens,
The Lord will judge the ends of the earth;
And He will give strength to His king,
And will exalt the horn of His anointed.'

"Then Elkanah went to his home at Ramah. But the boy ministered to the Lord before Eli the priest [emphasis added]"

(1 Samuel 2:1-11).

More on this Story of Grace and Prayer

God often does more than we ask or think because that's Who He Is — gracious beyond our imaginations. Paul says of God and His Spirit when writing to the church in Ephesus: "Now to Him who is able to do far more abundantly beyond all that we ask or think, according to the power that works within us" (Ephesians 3:20).

That measure of grace shows itself after the prayer of Hannah as we read: "Now Samuel was ministering before the Lord, as a boy wearing a linen ephod. And his mother would make him a little robe and bring it to him from year to year when she would come up with her husband to offer the yearly sacrifice. Then Eli would bless Elkanah and his wife and say, **'May the Lord give you children from this woman in place of the one she dedicated to the Lord.'** And they went to their own home. **The Lord visited Hannah; and she conceived and gave birth to three sons and two daughters.** And **the boy Samuel grew before the Lord** [emphasis added]" (1 Samuel 2:18-21). Whoever said, "You can't have your cake and eat it too," may not have experienced prayer or grace.

Another Secret to Prayer

It's not that obvious, but our pastor pointed out in his sermon that perhaps even more than Hannah desired to have a son, she wanted to encounter God. She wanted to know He took note of her situation, her hurting heart, and her prayer — that He cared.

This seems probable when one considers how quickly and willingly she gave her son up to the Lord's service as promised. Note also how quickly her sadness was turned to gladness when she knew God heard her prayer. Then, lest there be doubt, her convincing prayer of thanksgiving shows her intimacy with the Lord and knowledge of Him. She is overjoyed at being noticed by the Lord more than even the blessing of bearing a son.

Our pastor quoted one of his closest mentors: "If all that you want in life is God, you'll have everything you want in life." It seems this is true in Hannah's life. May it be true in yours and mine, is my prayer.

Hanani, a prophet speaking to a future king in Judah, tells us about God: "For the eyes of the Lord move to and fro throughout the earth that He may strongly support those whose heart is completely His"

(2 Chronicles 16:9a). It was true in Hannah's life and may that truth inform and influence our prayer lives as well. Our pastor said that God uses humble people whose deepest desire is simply to know God. Said another way: "All God needs is people who only need God."

An Odd Turn of Events

I wrote these puzzle pieces on prayer before Sunday's sermon illuminated Hannah's important, telling examples of prayer. That's synchronicity easy to see and worthy of pause and reflection. Then this afternoon, as I met with my editor friend to discuss the completion of this book, he said to me: "You do realize the original name of our city was Shiloh?"

I replied: "I did not, but I am overjoyed to learn such!" It just underscores the personal aspect of prayer, and God's activity with His people. A quick web search confirmed what my friend told me. *Goodspeed's History of Arkansas* states that: "The settlement of Springdale (Shiloh) began around 1838 and it was 'due to religious purposes' with the immediate reason being 'the noble spring near a tree across the road.'" Research also revealed that the original site of Shiloh in Israel was unknown since the time of Jerome (420 AD), but was rediscovered in 1838 with important digs and discoveries continuing to our day (christiananswers.net).

Find your Shiloh and go there often, to "worship and sacrifice," which are elements of true prayer. Godspeed on this rewarding journey for yourself and others. *Selah.*

Shiloh שילה
The focus is properly on the
One who is to come, the
One to whom it belongs, the
One we meet in prayer, the
Amen אמן of God,

> One who tabernacles (lives, dwells, meets) with us, the
> One who Himself dwells in unapproachable light,
> Gopherwood overlaid with purest gold,
> Immanuel, God with us.

"Until Shiloh comes...." Indeed, He has come. He dwells with His people. He hears hearts. He answers prayer. He's coming again soon in a very different way. The same Bible tells us: "Behold, He is coming with the clouds, and every eye will see Him, even those who pierced Him... So it is to be. Amen" (Revelation 1:7). And: "For this reason also, God highly exalted Him, and bestowed on Him the name which is above every name, so that at the name of Jesus every knee will bow, of those who are in heaven and on earth and under the earth, and that every tongue will confess that Jesus Christ is Lord, to the glory of God the Father" (Philippians 2:9-11). Come, Shiloh, come. Amen.

Hannah's prayer teaches us: "There is none holy like the LORD." Shiloh is a place of prayer, "The place that belongs to Him."

"But you, when you pray, go into your inner room, close your door and pray to your Father who is in secret, and your Father who sees what is done in secret will reward you"

(Matthew 6:6).

"For the eyes of the Lord are toward the righteous, and His ears attend to their prayer"

(1 Peter 3:12).

"We know that God does not hear sinners; but if anyone is God-fearing and does His will, He hears him"

(John 9:31).

"Then you will call upon Me and come and pray to Me, and I will listen to you. You will seek Me and find Me when you search for Me with all your heart"

(Jeremiah 29:12-13).

"Until now you have asked for nothing in My name; ask and you will receive, so that your joy may be made full"

(John 16:24).

PUZZLING CHAPTER 53

Disciple Prayer

Prayer — the Final Frontier

Prayer is the most important of the spiritual disciplines I would suggest. Spiritual disciplines such as Bible study, meditation, service, staying in community, and prayer are ways we connect to God and stay connected to God in our day-to-day life. Why do I say prayer is the most important? It has the potential to move the most powerful being in the universe. And we have His invitation to do so.

This immediately gets to the heart of the matter, which is a matter of the heart. What do you believe about God? Then what do you know about and think about prayer? Do you accept the God to whom you pray is the most powerful being in the universe? Do you believe He is good, as the Bible says and His track record shows? Do you think, as one of His children, He has invited you to talk to Him at any time about anything on your heart? Your answers will affect how you pray. And how you pray will demonstrate your answers to these questions.

Is the end of prayer to move God? Or is it to know God and ourselves better — to refine our relationship? Maybe to define our relationship? Maybe all the above?

Talking or sharing hearts is the basis of all relationships. That's how we get to know one another and see what we have in common. It is also to discover what we might agree about or disagree. Talking is where we settle our disagreements and work through them. It's how we determine if there is a kind, unselfish, insightful heart in a person we want to know better, walk alongside, and call a friend.

If you have had a significant romance, do you remember how many hours you spent talking on the phone or anywhere you could meet? Enough said.

Talking is important. It's natural. It's a means to an end. And it's an end unto itself, akin to the saying: "The joy is in the journey, not in reaching your destination." So it is with prayer. These are elements and considerations in prayer. Prayer can and should be as natural as romance or friendship.

So What's the Issue

So what's the issue with prayer? Isn't it understood and practiced effectively by Christians everywhere?

In a recent sermon, our pastor quoted some statistics from a survey among Christians about prayer. Most Christians surveyed rated their prayer life a "3" on a scale from "1" to "10." Only 2% of Christians rated their prayer life as a "9" or "10." No matter where you feel you are personally on the scale, this points out what many of us suspected, that the prayer life of the church in America is seriously anemic. This is a real problem for our church, our culture, and our country — and for us personally, more to the point.

Let's not try to fix America or the American church for the moment. Let's learn how to pray. And then, let's pray.

Have you been taught how to pray? A somewhat-mature person

with a bit of experience and instruction will catch a lot more fish than a kid with a string and hook, so let's learn together. This jigsaw puzzle isn't exhaustive and undoubtedly is inadequate to cover a far-reaching and influential subject such as prayer. But we can look at what Jesus said about prayer. We can look at what is said about the Holy Spirit and prayer. And we can look at the simple but powerful connection between Communion and prayer. That will get us a long way down the road toward effective praying and knowing the God to Whom we pray — the most valuable outcome.

Jesus on Prayer

David, king of Israel, said about prayer: "O Lord, I call upon You; hasten to me! Give ear to my voice when I call to You! May my prayer be counted as incense before You; the lifting up of my hands as the evening offering" (Psalm 141:1-2). That's beautiful and sets the tone for understanding prayer and what it means to God and humankind. We're told in Scripture that David was a man after God's own heart. So we can trust that what he says about prayer reflects God's heart.

One thousand years later, the King of Kings walked the same roads and climbed the same hills. After watching His prayer habits and seeing the power in His life, His followers asked: "Will you teach us to pray?"

Luke records Jesus' response like this: "When you pray, say:

'Father, hallowed be Your name.
Your kingdom come.
Give us each day our daily bread.
And forgive us our sins,
For we ourselves also forgive everyone who is indebted to us.
And lead us not into temptation'"

(Luke 11:2-4).

That's only thirty-seven words by my count — very profound and simple. It brings to mind some words of Solomon: "Do not be hasty in word or impulsive in thought to bring up a matter in the presence of God. For God is in heaven and you are on the earth; therefore let your words be few" (Ecclesiastes 5:2). And yet we're invited to pour out our hearts to Him in prayer: "Trust in Him at all times, O people; pour out your heart before Him; God is a refuge for us" (Psalm 62:8). It must be a matter of humility and the heart, but everyone respects **the force of few words**. Back to Jesus' model prayer, Matthew records it like this:

"Our Father in heaven,
Hallowed be Your name.
Your kingdom come.
Your will be done
On earth as it is in heaven.
Give us this day our daily bread.
And forgive us our debts,
As we forgive our debtors.
And do not lead us into temptation,
But deliver us from the evil one.
For Yours is the kingdom and the power and the glory forever. Amen"
(Matthew 6:9-13 NKJV).

That's sixty-six words, profound and simple. What can we quickly glean from this prayer? I know people have spent lifetimes studying and meditating on it. One cannot put too much importance on capturing a conversation of God talking to God. And this one Jesus crafted for us.

Abba — Father

When looking at the original language in this prayer, I noticed Jesus used the word Abba for Father. That had gotten entirely by me and undid me a bit. I have a very high view of God, albeit not as high as it should be, so I had a little trouble with Jesus using the word "daddy" or "papa" in prayer. It's such an important, profound prayer prayed so often — probably more than any uttered in the past 2000 years. Except maybe: "Lord, help me!"

But there it was, Jesus encouraged His disciples and all disciples to address the Almighty, His Father, as "our Dad." I know this can be problematic for some because they had poor examples of fathers or dads. But not everyone did, and in this way, God chooses to identify with us on a human, personal, imperfect level — a family level. I had a really good dad. He wasn't perfect. No dads are, save One. But probably 99% of dads have some of the dad quality in their hearts that is turned toward the welfare of their kids, wanting them to live in a safe environment, enjoy their growing-up years, and keep a lasting relationship.

Dads, you know you can be both tender and accessible, resolute and strong. This is perhaps a microcosm of how the Lord is with us, as His only begotten Son teaches us in the disciple's prayer, commonly known as The Lord's Prayer. Jesus prayed it as a model for his disciples.

Focus of Prayer

Let's see where Jesus focused in this model prayer.

Focus: What? Your kingdom — to come, Father's will to be done.

Focus: Where? On earth, our circumstances, our times, our family and friends, strangers who cross our path, or the Spirit brings to our attention.

Focus: Close? Daily bread, food for each day, day to day, looking to Him with trust and confidence: physical bread (food) and spiritual bread (revelation).

Focus: Important Issue? Forgive, in every instance possible, because it's powerful and healing and freeing for you. And our forgiveness from God, although already purchased and provided, is tied to our forgiveness of others. Jesus tells us elsewhere: "And his lord, moved with anger, handed him over to the torturers until he should repay all that was owed him. My heavenly Father will also do the same to you, if each of you does not forgive his brother from your heart" (Matthew 18:34-35).

Focus: Following? Lead us not into temptation. This simple, profound line would indicate the opposite could be true. We don't need a complete understanding of this or God's mind or ways, but we do need to pray this as modeled. It's in the most quoted prayer in the universe for a reason.

Focus: Warfare? Deliver us from evil. We have an enemy bent on our destruction and missing eternity with a good God because he did. Pray this! And Abba will deliver you! Do your part not to empower the enemy or make your situation worse by disobedience to God and His Word. Satan probably tells his fellow fallen angels, commonly known as demons, to honor the advice Napoleon Bonaparte gave his commanders: "Never interrupt your enemy when he is making a mistake."

Focus: Eternal? Thine is the kingdom — the now and the not yet! The power — He wins, we win. The glory — goodness. Forever — eternal, no time, no death. Amen — it is so, may it be so, we believe. Jesus is called the Amen of God (Revelation 3:14), so we know it is so.

Pray like this often and much. Pray *The Lord's Prayer* often and much. Pray it with an honest and sincere heart, knowing and expecting to be heard.

The Spirit and Prayer

The Holy Spirit is, well, a Spirit. There is not much one can say about Him that the Bible has not told us. There are continual and continuing instances of His activity on the earth, especially in the lives of God's family of faith. Like the wind, we can see the leaves of His activity move and evidence of upheaval where it's blown strong. Those with keen spiritual sensitivity may see it as it's happening, immediately afterward, or even when it's coming. But He's mysterious and hidden, no doubt one of His favorite traits about Himself — understated is an understatement. That said, He's deeply personal, even internal, and dwelling within the believer — as close as your breath or your DNA.

Read John chapter three, Jesus' conversation with Nicodemus, the teacher of Israel, about the Holy Spirit. Then ask God in prayer to give you more insight if you want it. As understanding comes, put on Holy Spirit glasses or lens and read Acts and the rest of the New Testament. Then you can read the Old Testament with the same lens, and it will surprise you as God grants you insight. You'll be shocked and pleased at how much you can know of Him and how little.

Let's get to a few understated instances where the Scripture mentions the Holy Spirit in the context of prayer. Then we'll move on, realizing He hides Himself and is understated, seemingly for a reason.

I imagine Him sometimes like lightning. We don't understand lightning or electricity to a large degree. But lightning comes out of thunderstorms, one of the most potent forces in nature. They move in and around people, villages, and cities and usually don't do much damage. They say lightning doesn't usually discharge from a cloud downward but from the ground upward — earth calling forth something from the sky. They say if we could harness the energy in a single lightning bolt, it would power a major city for a year. "Every second on earth, 100 lightning bolts strike the planet. That's about 8 million strikes per day, and 3 billion a year, on average" (axis.com). The NOAA says: "There are between 100 million and 1 billion volts in a lightning flash" (weather.gov). Lightning can heat surrounding air to over 50,000°F. That's five times hotter than the surface of the sun. It's known this phenomenon puts needed ozone back into our atmosphere, but there is still much mystery surrounding lightning, as with the Spirit, and much awe. If you are near a lightning storm, you know what I mean — a beautiful, awful mystery which adds much value to our lives.

Then in my imagining, I step back and recall the Holy Spirit isn't like lightning. He's much more powerful. He made lightning, the planet, our solar system with its perfectly distanced sun, moon, and some 200 billion known galaxies we call the universe. This is the One Who hovers around and within us as He wills.

What does the Bible tell us of His connection with prayer? Paul by the Spirit tells us: "In the same way, **the Spirit helps us in our weakness.** We do not know what we ought to pray for, but **the Spirit himself intercedes for us** through wordless groans. And **he who searches our hearts knows the mind of the Spirit, because the Spirit intercedes for God's people in accordance with the will of God** [emphasis added]" (Romans 8:26-27 NIV). This has double weight and insight because the Spirit inspired Paul to write it, and Paul probably experienced the Holy Spirit more than any other human we know about, save our Lord.

It's hard to connect the dots in the spiritual realm unless you go there often and much — maybe dwell there, with Him. Some of the following verses aren't explicitly connected to prayer, but I think you can see how they are connected. John, perhaps Jesus's closest friend and the most spiritually sensitive and mystical of His disciples, recorded by the Spirit: "If you love Me, keep My commandments. And **I will pray the Father, and He will give you another Helper, that He may abide with you forever—the Spirit of truth**, whom the world cannot receive, because it neither sees Him nor knows Him; but **you know Him, for He dwells with you and will be in you**. I will not leave you orphans; **I will come to you** [emphasis added]" (John 14:15–18 NKJV).

John further shares Jesus' teaching on the Holy Spirit: "Nevertheless I tell you the truth. It is to your advantage that I go away; for if I do not go away, the Helper will not come to you; but if I depart, **I will send Him to you. ... I still have many things to say to you**, but you cannot bear them now. However, when He, the Spirit of truth, has come, **He will guide you into all truth**; for He will not speak on His own authority, but **whatever He hears He will speak; and He will tell you things to come.** He will glorify Me, for **He will take of what is Mine and declare it to you** [emphasis added]" (John 16:7,12-14).

Luke, a gentile doctor and servant to Paul records these words of Jesus in his gospel account: "For **the Holy Spirit will teach you in that very hour what you ought to say** [emphasis added]" (Luke 12:12). While this verse isn't given in the context of prayer, it's undoubtedly consistent. It fits with the verses above, pointing to the intimacy of the Spirit in the believer's life in speaking and hearing — prayer.

Paul again speaks about the Spirit and prayer: "For if I pray in a tongue, my spirit prays, but my mind is unfruitful. What is the outcome then? **I will pray with the spirit and I will pray with the mind also** [emphasis added]" (1 Corinthians 14:14-15a).

The prophet speaks about the Spirit and prayer: "I will pour out on the house of David and on the inhabitants of Jerusalem, the Spirit of grace and of supplication" (Zechariah 12:10a).

Our Lord taught us to pray, "Our Father — Abba." "Because you are sons, God has sent forth the Spirit of His Son into our hearts, crying, 'Abba! Father!'" (Galatians 4:6).

Communion and Prayer

The connection between communion and prayer isn't at first obvious. But the leader in one of the men's groups I attend, after intending to start teaching us about prayer this past January, felt the Spirit lead him to look first at Communion. By Communion, I mean the Eucharist, the Lord's Supper. Along with water baptism, Communion is one of two ordinances our Lord instructed his followers to practice. Jesus said: "Do this in remembrance of me" (Mark 14:22-25, Luke 22:18-20, 1 Corinthians 11:23-25).

We do this to remember and proclaim to ourselves and others what Christ did: "For as often as you eat this bread and drink the cup, you proclaim the Lord's death until He comes" (1 Corinthians 11:26).

"How beautiful is the Rider on the white horse, how beautiful is the Lamb that was slain, how beautiful is the Rider on the white horse, worthy is Your Name." These are lyrics playing in my hearing as I type this paragraph. They are part of the song "Beautiful Rider" by Jake Hamilton. And it makes my point precisely.

When a believer takes communion, there is a real awareness of the One we worship and the magnitude of His sacrifice. It's a time of still hearts and solemn attention. The Father is also there, by His Spirit, to honor His Son, so you can ask Him what you want — prayer. By His sacrifice, we have this access. By the magnitude of His love and sacrifice, things seem to take their proper importance, and we often have nothing to say. We sit in silent awe, undone by the awareness of Who He Is and what He has done.

In our modern world, it's one of the times we come close to experiencing what the Psalmist heard from the Spirit and encouraged us to do: "Be still, and know that I am God; I will be exalted among the nations, I will be exalted in the earth" (Psalm 46:10).

The Heart of Prayer

The heart of prayer is the heart. Prayer changes things — you and the things around you.

Pray with heart. Pray with compassion. If you start, the Spirit will help you. But you have it within you. Pray the Lord's Prayer with your heart and your spirit's eye toward heaven for what you might see or hear when you do. Write it out. Pray it in phrases, and wait. Pray it in sentences and wait. Pray it all at once, slowly, with awareness of each thought. Listen for the impressions and presence of the Holy One to Whom you pray. He is near.

A popular, recent song about prayer perfectly expresses this idea of praying with your heart and passion. I recommend you get alone and watch it on YouTube or listen on your favorite music app. The song is "In Jesus Name (The God of Possible)" by Katy Nichole.

In this kind of heart-felt prayer, you sometimes feel your heart beating together with the Holy. This is a special place of awareness and change — of perceived audience with the King of the Universe, Who is also known as Jesus of Nazareth. The One Who wept at Lazarus' grave, seeing the pain and loss of those around Him. The Lord watched Hannah's lips move with no sound coming forth as she poured out her heart and pain to Him at Shiloh and then gave His answer through the simple prayer of Eli, the High Priest: "Go in peace; and may the God of Israel grant your petition that you have asked of Him" (1 Samuel 1:17).

Practice Prayer

Prayer helps us to be disciplined, and discipline helps us to pray. Daniel is an excellent example of this. Prayer helps us to fight the busyness of mind and spirit with solitude and silence. With prayer, it helps to be simple, to be sincere, to pray in secret, to pray in groups, to pray to God, an audience of One. Amen.

Before saying amen and leaving this all-important subject, I want to recommend a little book on prayer. The title is *Before Amen* by Max Lucado, the author of almost 100 books with 130 million copies in print. We read it during COVID-19 for insight and instruction on prayer in the "2020 Reading Club and Friendship Group" that meets in our home twice each month. We all thought it was short, simple, and excellent — helpful and encouraging, in understanding and practicing prayer. Since then, in retrospect, I would add it is deeply profound. Read it and be propelled into prayer's beauty, practice, and power. Leonardo da Vinci's quote comes to mind: "Simplicity is the ultimate sophistication." That is how I regard this little book on prayer.

"Now He was telling them a parable to show that at all times they ought to pray and not to lose heart"

(Luke 18:1).

PUZZLING CHAPTER 54

God's Prayer

The Lord's Prayer

Jesus prayed a prayer known as the High Priestly Prayer. It's recorded in John 17 and it seems like the real Lord's Prayer, one He prayed to His Father on His own initiative.

"God talking to God," is a fantastic thought to accompany any prayer we see Jesus pray. I heard it first expressed in the jungle of Belize on a short mission trip with friends. We were on a high porch overlooking the Belize River in the early morning, praying over the day's plans and activities. Our host finished our prayer time with passionate prayer, committing our requests to God for His consideration, favor, help, power, and answers. Then he acknowledged, although we passionately wanted God to move and help the local people as we had prayed, we needed to remember how Jesus prayed: "… not as I will, but as You will" (Matthew 26:39b).

Our host was referencing Jesus' prayer in a different garden near Jerusalem just before his arrest. We read: "And He went a little beyond them, and fell on His face and prayed, saying, 'My Father, if it is possible, let this cup pass from Me; yet not as I will, but as You will'" (Matthew 26:39). As we see in this prayer and the disciple's prayer, "Thy will be done" was a theme of Jesus' life.

The passion, self-sacrifice, humility, and obedience mirrored in that prayer and Jesus' subsequent actions pierce deep into one's heart, touching us at our core. So does the thought of Incarnate God praying from earth to God Almighty, His Father, in heaven. Our host finished his prayer that morning: "… as Jesus prayed, God talking to God, not our will but Your will be done." The Spirit wrote those thoughts deep in my heart.

Our Lord's Prayer

Jesus prayed the high priestly prayer during His last month on earth as God in the flesh, with all the mysterious limitations incarnation imposed upon Him. He spoke to his disciples very plainly about what would happen to Him. He shared thoughts about the Kingdom of God He wanted to drive home before leaving. His candor and clarity are compelling, as you can read in John 16. After talking to them, thinking of what their lives without Him would look like, He slipped away for private prayer for them. Parts of His prayer read like this:

"After saying all these things, Jesus looked up to heaven and said, **Father, the hour has come. Glorify your Son** so he can give glory back to you. For **you have given him authority over everyone. He gives eternal life to each one you have given him.** And **this is the way to have eternal life—to know you, the only true God, and Jesus Christ**, the one you sent to earth. I brought glory to you here on earth by completing the work you gave me to do. Now, Father, bring me into the glory we shared before the world began"

(John 17:1-5 NLT).

"**I have revealed you to the ones you gave me from this world.** They were always yours. You gave them to me, and they have kept your word. Now they know that everything I have is a gift from you, for **I have passed on to them the message you gave me. They accepted it and know that I came from you, and they believe you sent me** [emphasis added]"

(John 17:6-8 NLT).

"**I'm not asking you to take them out of the world, but to keep them safe from the evil one.** They do not belong to this world any more than I do. **Make them holy by your truth; teach them your word, which is truth. Just as you sent me into the world, I am sending them into the world. And I give myself as a holy sacrifice for them so they can be made holy by your truth** [emphasis added]"

(John 17:15-19 NLT).

"**I am praying** not only for these disciples but also **for all who will ever believe in me through their message. I pray that they will all be one, just as you and I are one—as you are in me, Father, and I am in you. And may they be in us so that the world will believe you sent me** [emphasis added]"

(John 17: 20-21 NLT).

"**Father, I want these whom you have given me to be with me where I am. Then they can see all the glory you gave me because you loved me even before the world began!** O righteous Father, the world doesn't know you, but I do; and these disciples know you sent me. **I have revealed you to them, and I will continue to do so.** Then your love for me will be in them, and **I will be in them** [emphasis added]"

(John 17:24-26 NLT).

John 17 is the entirety of the prayer. It's worth many readings and meditations. Please read it as much for what you can learn about God as about prayer. Both are incredibly insightful.

Some Meditations

I just read through the entire prayer and was overwhelmed with the Grace and magnanimity of Jesus. The Godhead's intentions and goodwill toward humankind are fully displayed for those who will hear and see.

What a prayer! This seems to be the highest bar in prayer, God talking to God about us, His plan, His commitment, and His purpose to bless us with His presence within us, dwelling with us, that we may always be where He is, eternally — knowing each other and being fully known. Jesus prays that we know it, and that we live like it by His Spirit, enjoying the gift and showing others how that looks. Amen.

Last Prayer

The last words of anyone are usually significant and insightful. They often summarize a person's life and what they value most. As such, they are brief and weighty — a summary of what the person holds dear in their purpose and personal journey. I think you can say the same about a person's last prayer.

This prayer seems like Jesus' last prayer with His Father before leaving earth. I think He knew it was. He would say a few more short prayers recorded for us. There were prayers at Passover with his disciples, which would become the Lord's Supper for more generations of disciples. There was His prayer in the garden referenced above. And there were sentence prayers during His last hours. Remember, this is God talking to God, so all are monumental and of supreme importance to humankind. Until the very end, He was praying — for you and me.

Do you think His Father heard His prayer? And granted His plea? Of course, He did and would!

Please ponder with me a few of Jesus' final prayers: "Father, forgive them; for they know not what they do" (Luke 23:34b). "It is finished" (John 19:30b). "Father, into your hands I commit my spirit" (Luke 23:46b).

"Who is it that overcomes the world? Only the one who believes that Jesus is the Son of God"

(1 John 5:5 NIV).

PUZZLING CHAPTER 55

Passionate Prayer and Grace

How Not to Pray

At the very end of Jesus' famous and fabulous Sermon on the Mount (Matthew 5-7), we read: "When Jesus had finished saying these things, the crowds were amazed at his teaching, because he taught as one who had authority, and not as their teachers of the law" (Matthew 7:28-29).

He delivered this insightful, challenging discourse on the north end of the Sea of Galilee. He looked up the mountain at the large crowd sitting in a natural amphitheater. They looked down at Him and the blue, sparkling Galilee with desert mountains on either side and beyond — a beautiful and breathtaking setting. Because of the location, there was every kind of person in the audience: the people who knew the Scriptures best, those taught by them weekly in the synagogues, pagans, gentiles, Roman soldiers of the occupying army, and merchants from Egypt and Babylon who traveled the ancient trading route, the Via Maris or Way of the Sea, which passed nearby. It was a fascinating group. It's almost as if someone planned this historic event's place, time, and setting to get the word out.

Jesus' theme in simplest terms seemed to be: "Let's get real, people." He knew the "teachers of the law" taught the people many things from the Scriptures as if they had written them, and they taught many things as Scripture that the Scriptures didn't say or support. He told them plainly that a life lived with God wasn't for show and didn't depend on them as much as they thought and were taught. He reminded them that God sees all your ways precisely as they are, even the intent of your heart. He cares more about your motives and simple actions than the enormous show that religion had come to be.

What Did Jesus Say About Prayer

In this famous sermon, Jesus addressed prayer as essential and got right to the point. In keeping with the theme of His message, He told them and us first how not to pray (Matthew 6:5-6). Avoid praying to be seen by people. It's not a performance. The gap between how you pray before others and how you pray before God alone is the essence of hypocrisy. If you pray just to be seen by others, you have your reward.

Jesus then shared the positive and proper way to pray. Shut the door of some private place. Pray in secret in front of God. That act alone shows your sincerity — that you indeed are praying to God and expect that He sees, hears, and cares.

He didn't say not to pray in public. There is a time to pray in community, to share your faith, and unite your faith with others — seeking the Lord's presence and action together. In another Scripture, we're told: "For where two or three have gathered together in My name, I am there in their midst" (Matthew 18:20). And: "Again I say to you, that if two of you agree on earth about anything that they may ask, it shall be done for them by My Father who is in heaven" (Matthew 18:19).

Your prayer in public or with others should be the same as your prayer in your closet. That's the essence of Jesus' message. Be genuine and avoid hypocrisy. God sees. And God is the One Who rewards.

Don't Try to Manipulate

Don't try to manipulate God. Prayer is not a magic formula. Putting faith in how you craft your prayer is meaningless, and Jesus discourages it: "… when you are praying, do not use meaningless repetition as the Gentiles do, for they suppose that they will be heard for their many words. So do not be like them; for your Father knows what you need before you ask Him" (Matthew 6:7-8). He knows, and He sees. Imagine that.

With a heart aware that God knows all, Jesus gives us what we know as the Lord's Prayer (Matthew 6:9-13). Praying the Lord's Prayer starting with this awareness and in this spirit will guide you to a beautiful place in prayer. It's like a portal that opens the heavens to the purposes and person of God, where He is ready to meet you.

Passion and Grace

I think it's safe to say that God is passionate. He loves passion and passionate people. I'm sure he loves fervent prayer. In fact, He just comes right out and says it in His Word: "The effective, fervent prayer of a righteous man avails much" (James 5:16c NKJV).

When I think of passionate people, Jacob comes immediately to mind. His passion led him eventually to Bethel. Bethel, in Hebrew, means "the house of God." Jacob's passion led him to a desperate place. He went to be alone with God in the desert and pray. With a stone for a pillow, Jacob's passionate God met him in that lonely place and blessed him. It was a strong blessing we enjoy today, along with millions in the family of God.

"'Was not Esau Jacob's brother? declares the Lord. 'Yet I have loved Jacob; but I have hated Esau'" (Malachi 1:2b-3a). That is a strong, shocking insight the prophet gives us by the Spirit into God's heart. What do you make of it? Years ago, one of my best friend's beautiful, sensitive wife said, "I couldn't love or trust a God like that." After experiencing much of God's love, grace, and goodness in the following years, she abandoned that position entirely. But it still cries out for some explanation; if we can know it.

Consider Jacob, who passionately pursued the favor and blessing of God. He went to great lengths and took risks, made mistakes, deceived, and was deceived, yet ended up with God's blessing. God even changed his name to Israel, meaning "a prince with God."

Consider Esau, his older brother and only sibling, who was the legal heir to the blessing. Yet it meant so little to him he bartered it for a bowl of soup — a transaction God honored. How did God feel about someone who valued His blessing so lightly? Malachi told us.

How passionate are you about God's blessing? How passionately do you pray for yourself, your family, and others?

God valued Jacob's passion and his desire. Passion and desire are similar. It would be best if you value some things and passionately want them. God respects that in people. Pray like that — from the heart — and see what happens.

Do you remember Hannah's prayer for Samuel? The priest thought she was drunk. She was drunk with desire and care and longing to love. She poured out her heart to God in prayer, and you know the rest of the story.

David was passionate and had a heart like God's. Read the Psalms he wrote, and you'll get it. You'll see plenty of prayers to emulate. Some will become your favorites to read and pray. As you pray, remember that it was three thousand years ago, and you will worship our timeless and timely God, Who is the same yesterday, today, and forever. He also dwells with His people and leads them like a flock.

Grace and Prayer

That leads us to the grace aspect of prayer. Do you recall how we are saved? By grace — the Bible clearly tells us that no man can boast and get caught up in pride, which is the original sin and perhaps the most deadly. "For by grace you have been saved through faith; and that not of yourselves, it is the gift of God; not as a result of works, so that no one may boast" (Ephesians 2:8-9).

My favorite prayer of all times is Mary's prayer at Cana in Galilee. The prayer sparked Jesus' earthly ministry of signs and wonders. This miracle and this prayer show us God's heart, power, compassion, commitment, loyalty, spiritual sensitivity, and love from the beginning — His grace.

Mary's prayer was looking into Jesus' eyes and saying: "They have no wine." Let's look at the context and what happened:

> "On the third day there was a wedding in Cana of Galilee, and the mother of Jesus was there; and both Jesus and His disciples were invited to the wedding. When **the wine ran out**, the mother of Jesus said to Him, '**They have no wine.**' And Jesus said to her, 'Woman, what does that have to do with us? My hour has not yet come.' His mother said to the servants, '**Whatever He says to you, do it.**' Now there were six stone waterpots set there for the Jewish custom of purification, containing twenty or thirty gallons each. Jesus said to them, 'Fill the waterpots with water.' So they filled them up to the brim. And He said to them, 'Draw some out now and take it to the headwaiter.' So they took it to him. When the headwaiter tasted the water which had become wine, and did not know where it came from (but the servants who had drawn the water knew), the headwaiter called the bridegroom, and said to him, '**Every man serves the good**

wine first, and when the people have drunk freely, then he serves the poorer wine; **but you have kept the good wine until now**.' This beginning of His signs Jesus did in Cana of Galilee, and manifested His glory, and His disciples believed in Him [emphasis added]"

(John 2:1-11).

There is so much to see and tell here! I am mystified that John is the only disciple to record this miracle and to tell us it was Jesus' first. I have visited this spot in Galilee and seen the humble church standing on a foundation laid by emperor Constantine's mother in the fourth century. It has a rather backcountry, back-water, obscure, forgotten feel. But it was of supreme importance to a young couple on their wedding day and very important to Mary, the compassionate mother of Jesus.

It sounds sacrilegious, but it seems to me that Mary, in this case, was more spiritually sensitive than Jesus. Or at least she heard first in her spirit what the Spirit wanted to do. When Jesus heard His mom say they had run out of wine, He knew she was asking Him to do something about it. And He told her that He hadn't heard it was time for Him to do anything extraordinary. But she heard it and, acting in faith that He would hear it too and do something special, turned to the servants and told them to do whatever Jesus said. Then she walked away. Beautiful!

This is a beautiful picture of praying with expectancy, acting, then resting on the fact God will act if He wants. Mary trusted He would be gracious, grant a heart-felt request, have compassion for a young couple starting out without many resources, care about their feelings and reputation, and desire Himself the happy celebration of a wedding. She evidently had some spiritual premonition God would act.

We know from Jesus Himself how He operated on earth. John, who knew Him best, recorded it when Jesus said: "I can do nothing on my own. I judge as God tells me. Therefore, my judgment is just, because I carry out the will of the one who sent me, not my own will" (John 5:30 NLT). Jesus did only what He heard the Father tell him to do. The inference is He heard by the Holy Spirit. Jesus said elsewhere: "I don't speak on my own authority. The Father who sent me has commanded me what to say and how to say it" (John 12:49).

What are some things we can quickly and easily learn from Mary's prayer?

1. Know well the Person you're addressing.
2. Be listening for the Spirit yourself.
3. Be engaged with people, present in their lives, and aware of their needs.
4. Leave the results with God after you pray.
5. This shows honor and trust in His heart to know and do what's best for everyone in the situation.
6. Expect wine.
7. You will probably be surprised by the quality and quantity of God's goodness — grace.
8. God loves weddings.
9. Get ready for a spectacular wedding — one for the ages, the wedding supper of the Lamb.

The Half-hearted and Weddings

Do you recall Jesus' parables about inviting guests to a great feast and then getting some lame excuses (Luke 14:16-24)? They ignored a most gracious dinner given by a significant, influential person. The consequences were most unfortunate for them but caused those who would come, who would value the invitation to come, to enjoy the honor and beauty, and to partake freely, without cost of a fabulous event with ongoing relationship implications.

Do you recall the five foolish virgins (Matthew 25:1-13)? "Same song, second verse," as the old saying goes. You can't be casual or play games with someone as important as God. He's gracious beyond your comprehension, but as Bonhoeffer taught us, His grace is costly to Him, and He will not take kindly or lightly to those who think lightly or unkindly about Him and refuse or rebuff His invitation to Grace.

There were five wise virgins, too, if you recall. To which group do you belong? Are you sure? Do you keep oil in your lamp and the wick trimmed with others? Are you listening for the shout at the bridegroom's coming — and the King of Glory (Psalm 24)?

We're back to passion and prayer. And we're back to grace. Expect Grace when you pray to Him Who is gracious and good. Enjoy the feast, every wedding, and with eyes wide open, anticipate the unimaginable wedding to come, the wedding feast of the Lamb!

PUZZLING CHAPTER 56

Cell Phones

Well Said

Last summer, one of my best friends from Air Force days visited me. He was an F-16 instructor pilot in a squadron that helped our fighter squadron transition from the F-4 Phantom to the F-16 Falcon. Now we both are retired from flying fighters and the airlines. He was in the area with friends for an annual canoeing adventure on the Buffalo River. He came a couple of days early at my invitation so I could introduce him to the Ozark backcountry by bush plane and then fly us to the cabin to spend the night renewing and celebrating our friendship.

Dave is a funny, serious guy. I know that sounds conflicted, but it's not, and it's true. His tactical callsign (the name fighter pilots call each other on the radio) illustrates the funny side. As a lieutenant stationed in Alaska, he attacked another airplane in the middle of dropping bombs on the range. This is *verboten* for safety reasons because the fighter dropping bombs is already task-saturated with hitting the target, not hitting the ground, and looking for threats, flying in the neighborhood of 500 MPH. But it sometimes happens, akin to lion cubs playing with each other, honing their hunting skills. Unfortunately, on this day, the fighter he attacked was the squadron commander, earning him a little time away from flying and doing less desirable duties. His peers awarded him the callsign "Mugger" immediately.

On the serious side, Mugger is a thinker, philosopher, truth seeker, and Christ follower. He cares deeply about people, friends, the church, the culture, Israel, and the kingdom of God.

We were talking about this book, and the topic of cell phones came up — how much they affected the world's population, especially the youth or the next generation. We were talking about deception, but our discussion was broad. I asked Mugger to recap some of the thoughts we shared, mostly his. Here they are:

"Social media is a way to inform and influence the entire world instantly. The control of SM (social media) controls the message people receive, a good way to get a consensus on social and moral issues since most people do not filter what they receive. It has instant credibility, especially with young people and the unthinking. It used to be 'as seen on TV,' now it's 'as seen on Twitter.' Controlling people's thoughts makes a one-world government easier to sell.

"Cell phones now connect the world because the infrastructure is much easier than landlines. Only a couple of decades ago, a significant percentage of the world population was isolated in its location and culture. Now kids in third-world countries can explore an entire world their parents never even knew existed. That can be good, except when the content is controlled. It's a great way to indoctrinate the next generation. Maybe there was safety in isolation.

"Kids now live through their phones rather than reality. Their reality is what's on the phone. They sit together in groups working on their phones rather than interacting with the person next to them. Apparently, the virtual reality in their phone is better than the reality of the present moment. They develop a false sense of what real life is. They are exposed to humanistic junk, porn, and leftist ideology, all at an early age, rather than having a chance to grow up as kids playing sandlot ball, etc. Despite parental controls, they can get exposed to all kinds of stuff well above their maturity level that they can't process properly.

"Cell phones and SM are the perfect tools to generate one-world group think."

I would piggyback on Mugger's thoughts and say: "How can you control news, media, banking, education, and become the social police? How can you divide people, which is an excellent path toward seizing power?"

One friend who uses all the social media platforms in his volunteer work with forest fire alerting and tracking told me about the upsides and downsides of SM. Then he said, "Twitter is the cesspool of SM."

I can't speak to that because I'm hardly on social media. I have a blog to make my books known and share insights I get from reading and journaling. I have a Facebook page to make the blog known, but I access it very infrequently. In the past, I've used it enough to see it can suck you in and be time and thought-consuming. Exercise caution, restraint, and even abstinence if necessary. Remember some of the hard words of Jesus in the Sermon on the Mount: "If your right hand makes you stumble, cut it off and throw it from you; for it is better for you to lose one of the parts of your body, than for your whole body to go into hell" (Matthew 5:30).

Cell Phones and Faith

In my middle ages, I visited my grandmother with a voice recorder and asked her to tell me about her life. I wanted to hear her experiences in her voice and from her heart. It was a precious, slow, mesmerizing time chocked with beautiful life stories in a simpler but less comfortable time. I asked her if she remembered the first car she saw. She perked up and said, "Sure! Me and Martha Middleton were in a field picking up rocks. We heard it, so we put our shoes on and ran down the hill. And there it come, no team [of horses] pulling it or nothing!" The wonder of it was still in her eyes and voice.

That was beautiful and shocking to me when I heard it. I realized that my grandmother and her generation, only two generations ago, had more in common with Abraham, and those of the intervening four thousand years, than with the generation of their children and grandchildren, my generation. She had seen the invention of the electric light bulb, the automobile, and the airplane in her lifetime. At the same time, she lived a good part of her life with horses, mules, and wagons — growing their food, sharing with neighbors, and walking or riding horses from place to place.

Since then, there have been thousands of life-changing technologies I could mention to illustrate my point and invoke amazement, from medicine and DNA to splitting the atom and nuclear energy. But the cell phone you have in your pocket or very close at hand may be the most unique, personal, and far-reaching.

With more computing power than NASA had to put a man on the moon fifty-three short years ago, you can access information, people, and more technologies worldwide in seconds, 24/7/365, than is almost imaginable. "You can also use it to call people" as one friend often reminds me.

I needn't say more. You know the empowerment you feel by using all the apps for daily navigating your world of communication, banking, driving about, shopping, research, and you name it. So be invigorated, pleased, and grateful. But also beware. Your servant, the cell phone, can also become a master and rob you of your life in insidious ways. Like the tail wagging the dog — you know what I mean. Gamers know what I mean, or maybe they don't, which illustrates the problem. If you don't get outside and breathe air, interact with people, and get alone with your thoughts, you're missing out on real life and trading that for a virtual counterfeit, robbing you of meaning and joy.

My son sent me a funny, telling meme a few months ago. There was a cartoon image of a guy texting and printed below it was a text invitation that read: "Hey, what are you doing tonight? I've invited a few of our friends to come over and stare at our phones."

There is a best-selling book entitled *The Purpose Driven Life*. I would call the situation above the virtual-driven life or the idol-driven life. Beware of idols and what the Scripture tells us: "Their idols are silver and gold, the work of man's hands. They have mouths, but they cannot speak; they have eyes, but they cannot see; they have ears, but they cannot hear; they have noses, but they cannot smell ... they have hands, but they cannot feel; those who make them will become like them, everyone who trusts in them" (Psalm 115:4-8).

The blistering technological progress has resulted in what some have coined "future shock." We are shocked by it more than we know, and at the same time, seemingly anesthetized, addled, or dazed by it, going about our business in what we suppose is the new normal, but with too much information to process pouring into our minds and consciences.

Our cell phones have almost become our drug of choice. The device is what we use to anesthetize ourselves from the overload of information we get from the device. Do you see the quandary? Or the threat?

But cell phones are here, for good or bad. We must deal with them, use them as servants, avoid their mastery of us, and be aware of their ability to distract and deceive, most insidiously.

As I sit here and ponder it, the most significant thing they rob us of is solitude and silence. I've realized by the Spirit's leadership in the last two years how valuable and beautiful those are. I never want to go back to margin-less living or let anyone or anything rob me of those two beautiful spiritual disciplines. Solitude and silence were practiced for millennia but are scarcely known in our day. They not only accentuate a well-lived life but are also a lens for seeing and experiencing life — real life and living, not the virtual counterfeit.

Reality is better — don't waste your life. Reality versus virtual is the difference between worshiping and knowing our living Creator God or carrying worthless idols around on our backs. Choose wisely and live. Choosing is the part you do for yourself and by yourself. That's why it's so important — it's personal.

With what's in the pipeline (the web — interesting word and thought) available instantly from the device, you are bombarded by others. Ideology and deception, as described by Mugger above, are everywhere. Social, and not-so-social, media where people can rant, spew anger, hurt, and their ideology in a not-so-civilized manner from the secret lair of their dwelling — things they would never have the courage to say face to face or in public — right to you in your home.

Everything contrary to the love of the Father can be facilitated and magnified mightily by your cell phone: "For all that is in the world, the lust of the flesh and the lust of the eyes and the boastful pride of life, is not from the Father, but is from the world" (1 John 2:16). Pride that comes from knowledge and porn, deceiving and deceptive, are lurking and readily available for those who will drink from that well. Please don't do it! There are supposed to be gatekeepers on the web, and whole industries have grown around the gatekeeping issue for a reason, so you know you must keep your own gate. Remember what David said and do the same: "I will set no worthless thing before my eyes; I hate the work of those who fall away; it shall not fasten its grip on me" (Psalm 101:3).

The Good

We certainly shouldn't fail to mention the good things that come with cell phones and the technologies they make possible, to serve us and the greater good. GPS and navigation apps save untold amounts of gas and time each day, helping us navigate efficiently to where we are going. There are similar aviation apps that I use in flying. It makes simpler and safer the once-challenging art of aviation navigation. Language translation apps help us communicate with friends abroad or in other cultures. Banking apps, shopping apps, church and community apps — the list is endless and grows daily.

Let that empower you but not overwhelm you. Apps on your phone may be like clothing — less is more. May God lead us to simpler lifestyles, where we have a few things that serve us well but not so much that we end up serving our possessions. Simplicity is a spiritual discipline worth looking into and embracing for the peace and rest it brings. It's also an aid to spiritual sight and seeing and an antidote to deception. Please give it a look, then make simplicity your goal and practice. If you're not familiar with the discipline of simplicity, I wholeheartedly recommend *The Celebration of Discipline* by Richard Foster for an explanation, inspiration, and application.

Back to the apps for a moment; my favorites are the Bible apps. YouVersion, with over 500,000,000 installs, is my favorite for reading and searching the Bible. You can use it online or install several versions of the Bible for free and have access to them anytime, even if you have no web connection. KAIROS is my favorite app for looking up the original meanings of Hebrew or Greek words. It's tied to the KJV and Strong's Concordance, powerfully easy to use and robust. The Blue Letter Bible is a good one. There are many! Get familiar with and use one. They make it super easy to copy and paste Scripture verses, then text or email them (to family and friends.)

As far as searching goes, I find that Google is as good as Logos or the best purchased Bible software for laptops or computers. If you have a word, sentence, or phase memorized or hidden in your heart, just Google it as best you remember it. Soon you'll be looking at the very word of God, written and preserved over millennia, and can study it or copy and paste it into documents, letters, emails, or texts to your friends, as the Spirit leads.

Or better yet, meditate on it in silence and solitude as you look at similar passages, the original languages, and contemplate while writing in your journal what you are discovering—Godspeed on your beautiful journey to better knowing God and the meaning of life.

"He said, 'Go your way, Daniel, for these words are concealed and sealed up until the end time. **Many will be purged, purified and refined, but the wicked will act wickedly; and none of the wicked will understand, but those who have insight will understand** [emphasis added]'"

(Daniel 12:9-10).

"But as for you, Daniel, conceal these words and seal up the book until **the end of time; many will go back and forth, and knowledge will increase** [emphasis added]"

(Daniel 12:4).

"Then that lawless one will be revealed whom the Lord will slay with the breath of His mouth and bring to an end by the appearance of His coming; that is, the one whose coming is in accord with the activity of Satan, with all power and signs and false wonders, and **with all the deception of wickedness for those who perish**, because they did not receive the love of the truth so as to be saved. For this reason **God will send upon them a deluding influence so that they will believe what is false, in order that they all may be judged who did not believe the truth, but took pleasure in wickedness** [emphasis added]"

(2 Thessalonians 2:8-12).

"**He who stops his ears from hearing about bloodshed and shuts his eyes from looking upon evil; he will dwell on the heights**, his refuge will be the impregnable rock; **his bread will be given him, his water will be sure** [emphasis added]"

(Isaiah 33:15b-16).

"Study to shew thyself approved unto God, a workman that needeth not to be ashamed, rightly dividing the word of truth"

(2 Timothy 2:15 KJV).

"**Finally, brethren, whatever is true**, whatever is **honorable**, whatever is **right**, whatever is **pure**, whatever is **lovely**, whatever is of good repute, if there is any excellence and if anything worthy of praise, **dwell on these things** [emphasis added]"

(Philippians 4:8).

PUZZLING CHAPTER 57

Church and Religion

SOMETHING VERY PLAIN AND DIRECT needs to be said about church and religion. A church or any religion built on the works and good deeds of humans (the strength of man) is sick and dysfunctional. This should be obvious to anyone with spiritual sight (Ephesians 2:8-9, 2 Corinthians 4:7, John 15:5).

That's precisely the situation God sent his only Son to speak into and correct between the BC and AD years. That was the situation of moral decay and religious deception in Israel at the end of the judges' time. God anointed a king named David to lead His people into a renewed relationship with Him and be an example for the kings of the earth to follow going forward. That was the situation of moral decay and religious deception two thousand five hundred years later when God moved in the life of a young Augustinian friar from Saxony, Germany, named Martin Luther. He was a catalyst to recall truth and set things on the right trajectory again, to lead God's people in a renewed relationship with Him. You can look for other examples yourself. It seems this happens about every five hundred years in history.

This is not new. We should learn from it. But there are probably some good reasons we don't apprehend it. Those reasons involve our original bent, the fact we have an enemy, and also God's good pleasure in preparing a bride of trust and beauty, a suitable companion for His Son, the King. Also, the fact that God has no grandchildren, only children. But that discussion is beyond the scope of this humble writ and puzzle.

False Religion

What do we do with false religion? How do we see it? How do we define it? What would God have us do if we live in such a time? These are critical questions, and your answers and actions are life-enriching or shattering for you and yours.

It's somewhat easy to see hypocrisy — the gap between how the people in a deceived church act and what they proclaim to be the truth. Their lives are powerless and lukewarm toward their faith, and they look very similar to the culture around them. Many believers stop attending such a church and strike out on their own to find their way spiritually. Many see this as an excuse to stop attending church and never return, deciding this was a false hope and system. Some hop from church to church in search of the real thing — faith, hope, love in relationships and community. But it's harder and harder to find, and the journey can get long while looking. It's a time of spiritual war, dislocation, and moving about looking for safety and shelter.

But God

Paul, in a beautiful letter to the church in Ephesus, writes: "**But God, being rich in mercy**, because of **His great love** with which He loved us, **even when we were dead** in our transgressions, made us alive together with Christ (**by grace** you have been saved) [emphasis added]" (Ephesians 2:4-5).

Please read the whole chapter for fuller understanding and revelation, but if God could save you from the world, sin, yourself, and destruction to begin with, He can certainly lead you onward and home. Follow the Lamb.

But Church

You don't want to go to church because the church is weak and dysfunctional. You must go to church because you are weak and dysfunctional. So it's like finding a hospital or doctor when you are sick — find the best one you can. That's what you would do in the natural. Ask friends and do research because your situation is deteriorating and demands it. You can't heal yourself or even know what's wrong with you. Remember the sage adage: "A doctor who treats himself or herself, has a fool for a patient." It's as accurate in the spiritual realm as in the medical sphere. The biggest problem with deception is that if you are deceived, you don't know it. But if you're walking among loving, spiritually-sensitive people, they will notice and help you walk in truth, becoming healthy and free to enjoy life as a gift.

Two Edged Sword

Seeing deception is the key to understanding and surviving this tightrope situation. You need to be in a community of faith to survive and thrive. But if you're in a deceived or dysfunctional community, you will get sicker and sicker spiritually. You end up being a part of the problem instead of the solution. And you negatively influence others to stay where you are with everyone stuck in the mud of dead religion and deception.

If you see and believe this is going on in the church, if you sense that Satan is deceiving churches and leaders, or that God is purifying

His church, or all the above, then you feel freer to act. You'll feel compelled to act. Your loyalty isn't the question any longer. It's a matter of obedience and survival.

These are tough decisions, I know from experience. You often feel like you're betraying your spiritual family if you leave. But it's the Lamb we must follow. You must trust Him to know what's best for you, your family, and His church. It's a time of warfare, turmoil, smoke, and debris — a time of tearing and healing. Follow the Lamb. Thankfully His Spirit abides within you and can show you the way. Take courage and follow.

In these times of intense spiritual warfare, it is a matter of spiritual life and death. Find a community of faith that preaches the Word and practices what it says. Stay in the community. Read the Word daily, alone and with your spouse. Pray daily, alone and with your spouse. If you do, you'll probably live through the warfare and thrive. If you don't, there's a good chance you'll end up wounded or spiritually dead, along with family members. Given the deception element of this warfare, you'll probably never know what hit you.

Jesus' brother Jude in his short, powerful book, reminds us of the Apostle's words about the end-time church: "'In the last time there will be mockers, following after their own ungodly lusts.' These are the ones who cause divisions, worldly-minded, devoid of the Spirit. But you, beloved, building yourselves up on your most holy faith, praying in the Holy Spirit, keep yourselves in the love of God, waiting anxiously for the mercy of our Lord Jesus Christ to eternal life. And have mercy on some, who are doubting; save others, snatching them out of the fire; and on some have mercy with fear, hating even the garment polluted by the flesh" (Jude 18b-23).

Wake up! Find a good church or community of faith and throw your life's joys and cares in with theirs, humbly experiencing God together. We did. After experiencing the first two years of COVID-19 in a spiritual wilderness, mainly without a church, the Spirit led us to a beautiful community. It's like a fresh oasis of joy, relationship, and purpose. I pray that you find one too.

Then Jude's beautiful benediction will take on new meaning for you and yours: "Now to Him who is able to keep you from stumbling, and to make you stand in the presence of His glory blameless with great joy, to the only God our Savior, through Jesus Christ our Lord, be glory, majesty, dominion and authority, before all time and now and forever. Amen" (Jude 24-25).

"These are the ones who follow the Lamb wherever He goes. These have been purchased from among men as first fruits to God and to the Lamb"

(Revelation 14:4).

"…not giving up meeting together, as some are in the habit of doing, but encouraging one another—and all the more as you see the Day approaching"

(Hebrews 10:25 NIV).

"Why do you call Me, 'Lord, Lord,' and do not do what I say?"

(Luke 6:46).

"Beloved, while I was making every effort to write you about our common salvation, I felt the necessity to write to you appealing that you contend earnestly for the faith which was once for all handed down to the saints. For certain persons have crept in unnoticed, those who were long beforehand marked out for this condemnation, ungodly persons who turn the grace of our God into licentiousness and deny our only Master and Lord, Jesus Christ"

(Jude 3-4).

"Now I desire to remind you, though you know all things once for all, that the Lord, after saving a people out of the land of Egypt, subsequently destroyed those who did not believe"

(Jude 5).

"These are the men who are hidden reefs in your love feasts when they feast with you without fear, caring for themselves; clouds without water, carried along by winds; autumn trees without fruit, doubly dead, uprooted; wild waves of the sea, casting up their own shame like foam; wandering stars, for whom the black darkness has been reserved forever"

(Jude 12-13).

"But you, beloved, building yourselves up on your most holy faith, praying in the Holy Spirit, keep yourselves in the love of God, waiting anxiously for the mercy of our Lord Jesus Christ to eternal life"

(Jude 20-21).

"Ascribe to the Lord, you heavenly beings, ascribe to the Lord glory and strength. Ascribe to the Lord the glory due his name; worship the Lord in the splendor of his holiness"

(Psalm 29:1-2 NIV).

"The Lord sat as King at the flood; yes, the Lord sits as King forever. The Lord will give strength to His people; the Lord will bless His people with peace"

(Psalm 29:10-11).

"The fear of man brings a snare, but he who trusts in the Lord will be exalted"

(Proverbs 29:25).

"To the angel of the church in Sardis write: He who has the seven Spirits of God and the seven stars, says this: 'I know your deeds, that **you have a name that you are alive, but you are dead. Wake up**, and strengthen the things that remain, which were about to die; for I have not found your deeds completed in the sight of My God. So remember what you have received and heard; and keep it, and repent. Therefore **if you do not wake up, I will come like a thief, and you will not know at what hour I will come to you. But you have a few people in Sardis who have not soiled their garments; and they will walk with Me in white, for they are worthy. He who overcomes will thus be clothed in white garments; and I will not erase his name from the book of life**, and I will confess his name before My Father and before His angels. **He who has an ear, let him hear** what the Spirit says to the churches [emphasis added]'"

(Revelation 3:1-6).

"For I am confident of this very thing, that He who began a good work in you will perfect it until the day of Christ Jesus"

(Philippians 1:6).

PUZZLING CHAPTER 58

The Holy Bible

God's Word

Nothing needs to be said about the Bible, as it speaks for itself. But it seems something needs to be said about the Bible in a book like this. I'll try.

It jumps into my mind now that John starts his Gospel: "In the beginning was the Word, and the Word was with God, and the Word was God. He was in the beginning with God. All things were made through Him, and without Him nothing was made that was made. In Him was life, and the life was the light of men. And the light shines in the darkness, and the darkness did not comprehend it" (John 1:1-5 NKJV).

John's discourse about the Word is a bit mystical but not hard to puzzle out, as he continues down to verse fourteen, where he tells us plainly that Jesus Christ is the Word of God, just as the Bible is the Word of God. "And the Word became flesh and dwelt among us, and we beheld His glory, the glory as of the only begotten of the Father, full of grace and truth" (John 1:14 NKJV).

The Greek word used for Word is "logos," a masculine noun that Thayer's Lexicon defines as "a word, uttered by a living voice, embodies a conception or idea," and "what someone has said, a word, the sayings of God, decree, mandate or order, of the moral precepts given by God." It's fascinating that the Bible, God's written Word, is called and put on the same level as Jesus, God's living Word. They are the same in essence, importance, and value for us. Amen.

Two things jump out at me before we continue: (1) The darkness did not comprehend it — the living or written Word. (2) The Word is full of grace and truth. Grace and truth keep popping up in the Bible as I write this book.

The Bible

Josh McDowell, a leading apologist in our times, identifies seven reasons the Bible is unique. The seven reasons that make the Bible unique are its "continuity, circulation, translation, survival, teaching, and influence on literature and civilization." The uniqueness of the Bible does not prove that the Bible is divinely inspired, but rather its superiority over any other writing.

McDowell goes on to say: "The Bible was written over a period of fifteen centuries, by over forty authors in different places and times, in different languages and styles and yet has one central unified theme that of the relationship between mankind and the only Living God expressed in His offer of salvation through the Lord Jesus Christ." It is incredible to contemplate the chances of that happening with so many authors, scribes, translators, etc. involved over so long a time — not to mention some enemies.

My Thoughts

You are probably aware *The Holy Bible* is the best-selling and most published book in history. There is not even a close second. Not only that, but the second most published book in history is *The Imitation of Christ*, written by a German monk, Thomas à Kempis, around 1470 AD, seeing 745 editions before 1650 AD and published in more languages than any other book in the world, other than the Bible. It is a devotional book so chocked full of the Scripture; you are reading the Scripture as you go. The third best-selling book of all time and the second best seller in the English language after the Bible is *The Pilgrim's Progress from This World, to That Which Is to Come*, a 1678 Christian allegory written by John Bunyan. It has been translated into more than 200 languages and has never been out of print since he wrote it from an English prison.

My point is this. If you or anyone you know is making a flimsy excuse for not reading the Bible or doubting its merit, that may say more about you or them than it does the Bible. It points to deception. A humble person, looking for truth, in light of the above evidence, would read it expecting to find merit due to the great cloud of witnesses.

It also claims to be the Word of God: "And so **we have the prophetic word** confirmed, which **you do well to heed as a light** that shines in a dark place, **until the day dawns and the morning star rises in your hearts;** knowing this first, that **no prophecy of Scripture is of any private interpretation, for prophecy never came by the will of man, but holy men of God spoke as they were moved by the Holy Spirit** [emphasis added]" (2 Peter 1:19-21 NKJV). And: "**All Scripture is inspired by God** and profitable for teaching, for reproof, for correction, for training in righteousness [emphasis added]" (2 Timothy 3:16).

Note the incredible Scripture preservation stories against all odds and enemies. The Dead Sea Scrolls are one such two-thousand-year-old witness surviving to our day after the Romans sought to expunge every written thing Jewish around the revolt they finally put down in 73 AD, with the fall of Masada. Consider the people who died willingly to preserve, print, and spread the Scriptures, like William Tyndale, who was burned at the stake on October 6, 1536 at the age of 42. And people like Gutenberg, who lived to invent the printing press "to give the Scriptures wings."

Lastly, I love the history the Bible brings to life and its record for all the world to see. I was a mathematics major in college, but I liked history more. Then I saw history as a haphazard system of events, dates, personalities, or leaders. It wasn't easy to tie it together in a unified whole. That was until I started to look at history through the lens of the Bible. Then the exciting stories of every event or culture I researched or studied began to make sense. That has continued to this day. It's valuable for the history it records and just as helpful as a lens to view history in every era and epoch.

I recently heard an interview with a well-known Egyptologist, David Rohl, who said: "Herodotus is supposed to be the world's first historian, but I believe it was Moses."

A Few Other Thoughts

A theologian named Sper adds: "... the Bible is unique in four other ways.

1. Its view of God. The God of the Bible is Sovereign and a God of love, mercy, and goodness.
2. Its view of man. The Bible provides a realistic portrayal of man, in which he is neither more nor less than he is.
3. Its view of salvation. The Bible alone offers salvation as a gift.
4. Its view of history. The facts of history and geography confirm the truth of the Bible."

Another theologian adds: "No book has ever been the subject of more continued attacks upon it than the Bible. Despite the assaults mounted upon it for millennia, it has emerged unscathed" (Richard M Riss).

F. Bettex of Stuttgart, Germany, wrote: "Unchanged and unchangeable, this Bible stands for centuries, unconcerned about the praise and the reproach of men. With sublime freedom, it strides through the history of mankind, dismisses entire nations with a glance, with a word, in order to tarry a long time with the deeds of a shepherd. It rises like an angel to heights that make peoples, passing hither and thither, appear like swarms of grasshoppers, yea, all nations like a drop in a bucket."

That quote brings to mind a particular Scripture and the fact that all Scripture seems to point to a King, the Messiah: "Why are the nations in an uproar and the peoples devising a vain thing? The kings of the earth take their stand and the rulers take counsel together against the Lord and against His Anointed, saying, 'Let us tear their fetters apart and cast away their cords from us!' He who sits in the heavens laughs, the Lord scoffs at them. Then He will speak to them in His anger and terrify them in His fury, saying, 'But as for Me, I have installed My King upon Zion, My holy mountain'" (Psalm 2:1-6).

Let's end with some thoughts on the uniqueness of the Bible by John Ankerberg:

20 REASONS FOR THE UNIQUENESS OF THE BIBLE

The Bible is the only book in the world that offers objective evidence to be the Word of God. Only the Bible gives real proof of its divine inspiration.

The Bible is the only religious Scripture in the world that is inerrant.

The Bible is the only ancient book with documented scientific and medical prevision. No other ancient book is ever carefully analyzed along scientific lines, but many modern books have been written on the theme of the Bible and modern science.

The Bible is the only religious writing that offers eternal salvation as a free gift entirely by God's grace and mercy.

The Bible is the only major ancient religious writing whose complete textual preservation is established as virtually autographic.

The Bible contains the greatest moral standards of any book.

Only the Bible begins with the creation of the universe by divine fiat. It contains a continuous, if often brief and interspersed, historical record of mankind from the first man, Adam, to the end of history.

Only the Bible contains detailed prophecies about the coming Savior of the world, prophecies that have proven accurate in history.

Only the Bible has a totally realistic view of human nature, the power to convict people of their sins, and the ability to change human nature.

Only the Bible has unique theological content, including its theology proper (the trinity; God's attributes); soteriology (depravity, imputation, grace, propitiation atonement, reconciliation, regeneration, union with Christ, justification, adoption, sanctification, eternal security, election, etc.); Christology (the incarnation, hypostatic union); pneumatology (the Person and work of the Holy Spirit); eschatology (detailed predictions of the end of history); ecclesiology (the nature of the church as Christ's bride and in a spiritually organic union with Him); etc. [Forgive the theological speak!]

Only the Bible offers a realistic and permanent solution to the problem of human sin and evil.

Only the Bible has its accuracy confirmed in history by archeology, science, etc.

The internal and historical characteristics of the Bible are unique in its unity and internal consistency despite its production over 1500 years by 40-plus authors in three languages on three continents, discussing scores of controversial subjects yet having agreement on all issues.

The Bible is the most translated, purchased, memorized, and persecuted book in history. For example, it has been translated into some 1700 languages.

Only the Bible is fully one-quarter prophetic, containing a total of some 400 complete pages of predictions.

Only the Bible has withstood 2000 years of intense scrutiny by critics and not only survived the attacks but prospered and had its credibility strengthened by such criticism. (Voltaire predicted that the Bible would be extinct within 100 years, but within 50 years, Voltaire was extinct, and his house was a warehouse for the Bibles of the Geneva Bible Society.)

Only the Bible has molded the history of Western civilization more than any other book. The Bible has had more influence on the world than any other book.

Only the Bible has a Person-specific (Christ-centered) nature for each of its 66 books, detailing the Person's life in prophecy, type, antitype, etc., 400 to 1500 years before that Person was born.

Only the Bible proclaims a resurrection of its central figure that can be proven in history.

Only the Bible provides historical proof that the one true God loves mankind. (The John Ankerberg Show, 2014, jashow.org).

"Let God be found true, though every man be found a liar"
(Romans 3:4a).

"Heaven and earth will pass away, but My words will not pass away"
(Matthew 24:35).

"So will My word be which goes forth from My mouth; it will not return to Me empty, without accomplishing what I desire, and without succeeding in the matter for which I sent it"
(Isaiah 55:11).

"Forever, O Lord, Your word is settled in heaven. Your faithfulness continues throughout all generations; You established the earth, and it stands. They stand this day according to Your ordinances"

(Psalm 119:89-91b).

"I shall delight in Your statutes; I shall not forget Your word"

(Psalm 119:16).

"I am God, and there is no one like Me, declaring the end from the beginning, and from ancient times things which have not been done, saying, 'My purpose will be established, and I will accomplish all My good pleasure'"

(Isaiah 46:9-10).

PUZZLING CHAPTER 59

Predestined

Fuzzy for a Reason

Few things seem to stir up theologians or modern churchmen as much as predestination. For the life of me, I don't see why. Oh, I have looked into it. It's hard to read your Bible without running across verses that support both sides of the controversy. The rhetoric or debating side of me has often thought about making a case for both sides independently from the Scripture because there are Scriptures that seem to support both sides.

This seeming paradox, some think, must be solved! To me, it's a conundrum for sure, but not necessarily a paradox. I believe God hasn't given us enough information to know for certainty how we are saved or the truth of the matter about free will or predestination. And that, He has done for His reasons.

I think those on either side of the argument, and that's what it always becomes, think God is more than able to communicate anything He wants. Most believe that we could probably understand it if He spoke it clearly or answered some of our questions about a few verses. I think He made it fuzzy for a reason, so we'd keep seeking Him, asking Him, and trying to figure it out until He answers us or we find peace about it. I've included other complex or fuzzy issues in the Bible as puzzle pieces that I believe are there for the same reason — hell and eternal punishment, divorce and remarriage, to name two. I address them to point out that we shouldn't believe everything we've been taught but search and read the Scriptures ourselves. Get to know your Maker this way, and let Him reveal your heart's desire and what you can understand. It's a healthy, active way to stay away from deception under the wing of the Almighty.

Where is Your Faith

A lot can be known if one keeps looking, seeking, asking, and questioning. I think that's the point of God keeping it a bit fuzzy. Also, these quandaries say a lot about us and our relationship with our Father.

Aren't we supposed to hold some things as a mystery? Or are you putting your faith in your faith, your understanding of Scripture, and thus yourself? Doesn't Scripture clearly say: "For who has known the mind of the Lord, or who became His counselor? Or who has first given to Him that it might be paid back to him again? For from Him and through Him and to Him are all things. To Him be the glory forever" (Romans 11:34-36).

I would also ask those who are dogmatic on either side: "Is this an issue that really must be known, or determines if a person comes to faith or not?" It seems to me that it is not. Then why be so dogmatic about it?

I have known many friends who have come to faith in Christ, are indwelled by His Spirit, and produce fruits as the Scripture promises, without even knowing this debate exists. What do you make of that?

I would suspect if anyone has a morbid desire to prove one side or the other from the Scripture, they may be doing so to exalt themselves and their understanding of the Word, more than making it about a search for truth. Is your faith in God or yourself and your sure knowledge of Scripture? Is this topic that important, and can we know the whole truth? People should ask themselves those questions if they continue far into this fray.

Sure, study the issue to your heart's content. The Scripture encourages us to do so: "Be diligent to present yourself approved to God as a workman who does not need to be ashamed, accurately handling the word of truth" (2 Timothy 2:15). But humbly realize your knowledge of the Word and truth probably has its limits. And the Scripture further instructs us: "But refuse foolish and ignorant speculations, knowing that they produce quarrels. The Lord's bond-servant must not be quarrelsome, but be kind to all, able to teach, patient when wronged" (2 Timothy 2:23-24). "But avoid foolish controversies and genealogies and strife and disputes about the Law, for they are unprofitable and worthless" (Titus 3:9).

So What Is the Debate

Predestination is the biblical doctrine that God in His sovereignty chooses specific individuals to be saved. There are several verses in the Bible that seem to say that. As many verses say, we have choices to make and thus free will. Corollaries of these positions produce phrases like: "Once saved always saved," or "the eternal security of the believer," which are related but not the core issues.

Wikipedia has it: "The history of the Calvinist–Arminian debate begins in early 17th century in the Netherlands with a Christian theological dispute between the followers of John Calvin and Jacobus Arminius, and continues today among some Protestants, particularly evangelicals. The debate centers around soteriology, or the study of salvation." The article says that Augustine was debating some of these issues in the 5th century, which supports my theory that it's fuzzy for a reason, and I'll get to that possible reason.

A handy website that is usually very helpful has this to say in the end about the debate and does a good job stating the issue: "If God is choosing who is saved, doesn't that undermine our free will to choose and believe in Christ? The Bible says that we have the choice—all who believe in Jesus Christ will be saved (John 3:16; Romans 10:9-10). The Bible never describes God rejecting anyone who believes in Him or turning away anyone who is seeking Him (Deuteronomy 4:29). Somehow, in the mystery of God, predestination works hand-in-hand with a person being drawn by God (John 6:44) and believing unto salvation (Romans 1:16). God predestines who will be saved, and we must choose Christ to be saved. Both facts are equally true. Romans 11:33 proclaims, "Oh, the depth of the riches of the wisdom and knowledge of God! How unsearchable his judgments, and his paths beyond tracing out!" (gotquestions.org).

That doesn't answer all the questions, but it's about as close as folks who debate this ever get. And it makes one's head spin.

What Do You Think?

Well, I think the truth is the truth, and God is God, so it doesn't much matter what I believe, nor is it all that important to know how salvation works or how one comes to faith in Christ. It's mysterious like conception, but you know when a baby starts to grow and when it comes out into the world.

I will tell you that Arminianism, Aka freewill, makes the most sense to me. Considering all the verses, it seems more logical and gives me peace. I have plenty of friends who are Calvinist and think that is the clear teaching of Scripture. But to me, too many choices seem to be involved for that to be true or the whole truth.

"Whoever will call on the name of the Lord will be saved" (Romans

10:13). "Choose for yourselves today whom you will serve...but as for me and my house, we will serve the Lord" (Joshua 24:15). "And opening his mouth, Peter said: 'I most certainly understand now that God is not one to show partiality; but in every nation, the man who fears Him and does what is right is welcome to Him'" (Acts 10:34-35). "Then they will call on me, but I will not answer; they will seek me diligently but they will not find me, because they hated knowledge and did not choose the fear of the LORD" (Proverbs 1:28-29). These verses indicate that God has given man a choice about his relationship with God.

A Bride for His Son, the King

Ultimately, I think all the commotion and fuzziness are intended and designed to find a suitable bride for God's Son, the King. We're told in Scripture the church is His Bride. God doesn't want a robot bride anymore than any man would. He wants a bride who will trust Him and choose Him, with her own free will, with no compulsion to do so, or it's meaningless. There are many stories like this in the Bible.

The earliest and the one that quickly comes to mind is Abraham sending his servant to find his son Issac a suitable wife among her mother's people. Once I asked my good friend and long-time mentor, Charles Angel, to speak about this issue. He has the gift of wisdom, has walked with the Lord a long time, and is an astute student of the Bible. He replied with a sixteen-page letter laying out his findings from the Word of God. It was awe-inspiring and confirmed, for me, what I already believed. Here are a couple of paragraphs from what he shared with me:

"When a young man chooses the woman that he wants to wed, he asks her if she will marry him. Then she has a choice to make. The white robe of righteousness that is required of those who are in the Bride of Christ is a gift. We must, however, make ourselves ready and clothe ourselves in it (Matt. 22:1-14, Rev. 19:7-8). He has offered it to us; we must choose to receive it or not. Abraham is a type of God the Father, and Isaac is symbolic of Christ. Abraham sent his steward to find a bride for his son (Gen. 24). The steward fulfilled the role for Isaac that the Holy Spirit fills for Christ. Rebekah was chosen to be the wife, yet she was given a choice as to whether she would follow the servant back to marry Isaac (Verses 44, 57-58). Likewise, the Holy Spirit invites us to be united with Christ, but we choose whether we will do so.

"The Lord desires to save every person, but He has left us the choice of whether to receive His gift. 'This is good and acceptable in the sight of God our Savior, who desires all men to be saved and to come to the knowledge of the truth. For there is one God, and one mediator also between God and men, the man Christ Jesus, who gave Himself as a ransom for all, the testimony given at the proper time' (1 Tim. 2:3-6). 'The Lord is not slow about His promise, as some count slowness, but is patient toward you, not wishing for any to perish but for all to come to repentance' (2 Pet. 3:9). Yes, God wishes for all to repent and live. He prepared the lake of eternal fire for the devil and the fallen angels, not for man (Matt. 25:41). Man goes there only when he spurns the forgiveness that God offers." Thank you, Charles.

So How Do You Answer

How do you answer when people ask you about this if they do? I'd humbly say that you don't know for sure because you probably don't. But you can tell them what you think and why, of course.

One of my best fighter pilot friends, Brian Fields, who was also a theologian of sorts, and very knowledgeable about the Bible, was asked once what he believed about the eternal security of the believer. He replied: "I believe in once saved, always saved — probably." I also heard him tell another person in the squadron another time: "If it's important to you, you ought to look into it."

Knowing Brian as I did, he probably did believe in "once saved, always saved," or rather "If saved, always saved." But he didn't put stock in a sinner's prayer without conviction and a "quality decision," as he called it — a choice. But after a quality decision, he put a lot of faith in God's faithfulness to keep us all our lives and present us to His Father for eternity. "For I am confident of this very thing, that He who began a good work in you will perfect it until the day of Christ Jesus" (Philippians 1:6).

But he and I also noted some troubling verses that we discussed often, indicating free will or choice might come into play even after one is saved. Jesus, when He was walking the earth, said things like: "Therefore everyone who confesses Me before men, I will also confess him before My Father who is in heaven. But whoever denies Me before men, I will also deny him before My Father who is in heaven" (Matthew 10:32-33). And: "If you abide in Me, and My words abide in you, ask whatever you wish, and it will be done for you" (John 15:7). "If" seems like a conditional word, that requires a choice. Abiding is like being married and requires choice too. Can a name be erased, due to some choice? Jesus said to the church in Sardis: "He who overcomes will thus be clothed in white garments; and I will not erase his name from the book of life" (Revelation 3:5a).

So there you have it. It sounds like the best verse to describe the situation may be: "So then, my beloved, just as you have always obeyed, not as in my presence only, but now much more in my absence, **work out your salvation with fear and trembling** [emphasis added]" (Philippians 2:12).

You know — if you've chosen a mate and are in a good marriage, and you've chosen to make it work and are committed to it in thought and action daily — you then enjoy the relationship and don't think about it much. You know you're committed to each other and are enjoying the journey. These questions of security hardly even enter your mind. Continue to enjoy the security and your relationship.

Also, enjoy the mystery. We are the finite pursuing the infinite. We are the imperfect pursuing the perfect. Yet we read: "**He has made everything beautiful in its time.** He has also **set eternity in the human heart;** yet **no one can fathom what God has done from beginning to end** [emphasis added]" (Ecclesiastes 3:11NIV). He put something in our hearts to draw us to Himself, or we find no rest. Then we can decide how we'll respond. It sounds like the Song of Solomon, doesn't it? It's time to put away the debate, stop the talk, and enjoy the romance. "I am my beloved's and my beloved is mine" (Song of Solomon 6:3).

PUZZLING CHAPTER 60

Coffee Shop Problem Solving

Our Nation

Sitting in a local coffee shop today with fellow pilgrims, we fancy ourselves as truth seekers pondering God our Father and His activity on the earth throughout history and in our present day. We enjoy talking about the truths He has shown us and what insights He might yet reveal.

We talked about this present darkness, insight into our times, and warfare in the spiritual realm that affects us all. If you know it's real and have some weapons or armor to employ, you are in the game. If you don't know it's real, the opposite is true; you are way behind.

It appears we are living in a reprise of the first century. The book of Acts and the Gospels are very relevant today. We live in a pagan, truth-starved, hostile culture.

Maybe this USA chapter of 400 years is the latest installment of governments the Lord has allowed to rule on the earth. We started well with His help and an infusion of truth, light, and divine intervention.

Michael Medved is one good author who writes books about God's favor (called exceptionalism in academic circles) in America's early history. His book, *God's Hand on America: Divine Providence in the Modern Era,* is a great read.

One can't read the Bible with its amazing miracles of God helping His people and read the history of the United States with its amazing miracles of God assisting this nation and not see the coincidences or synchronicities. But even when God gives a country light and help, as people become prosperous and left to themselves, they turn to idols. Then soon, the Lord must act to keep people from destroying themselves and each other.

It's like a 6000-year lesson or experiment on how men and nations fare with free will, government, and empire.

"We the people" was unique in its beginning, but it won't be in its end unless God acts to rescue and deliver us. We are not unique in that we've gone the way of other peoples and governments before us of late. We are rejecting the rule of God and choosing to go our own way.

Much has been written about our beginning by truth-loving and truth-speaking people who lived then. But we are in a time when people in positions of influence want to rewrite history and bend the truth to their image or what they think instead of bending themselves to the truth — the time-tested truth of the Bible and actual history. Truth and freedom go together. Deception and slavery go together.

We'll soon know what the end of this matter will be. Slavery to fear, government, and sin? Or the freedom to live in truth, light, and love. God knows how far he will allow us to go for our well-being and His purposes.

In a sense, all humans are his children, and he acts for our benefit as a whole while ensuring individual and corporate justice. The flood is one account of how far God will let things go before acting redemptively on a big scale.

The Nations

But the flood also shows how He cares for his own amid a storm or a significant correction. I once had an Air Force commander who said: "When the bombs start falling, they destroy believers and nonbelievers alike."

This is true, of course, yet not altogether true. The God of the cell, the earthquake, and the supernova is the creator of physics and not bound by these laws, as we see numerous times in Scripture.

Indeed, in times of great upheaval, we see His prophets say things like: "**Then those who feared the Lord spoke to one another, and the Lord gave attention and heard it, and a book of remembrance was written before Him for those who fear the Lord and who esteem His name.** 'They will be Mine,' says the Lord of hosts, 'on the day that I prepare My own possession, and **I will spare them as a man spares his own son who serves him.**' So you will again distinguish between the righteous and the wicked, between one who serves God and one who does not serve Him [emphasis added]" (Malachi 3:16-18).

God can and does care for his own. He does so to a different standard because they trust Him. They trust even when it might not go their way, believing that His ways are high, out of our sight, and better than ours. History shows the blood of the martyrs is the seed of the church, so some sacrifice and suffering come with the territory and warfare. He's coming back soon, and His reward with Him. Then it will be clearly seen and known.

Israel as a Model

The Holocaust in Europe during my parents' lifetime bears witness to many perishing (6 million Jewish victims and 5 million non-Jewish), some as martyrs like Bonhoeffer, hours before allied forces liberated his concentration camp. But many were supernaturally and miraculously delivered. I've visited Anne Frank's home in Amsterdam, where many Jews were hidden, then smuggled to life-preserving freedom. You've probably seen the movie *Schindler's List*, based on a true story of saving Jewish lives. In Jerusalem, on the Mount of Remembrance by the *Yad Vashem* memorial, the peaceful "Garden of the Righteous" serves to honor those non-Jews who, during the Holocaust, risked their lives to save Jews from extermination by the Nazis.

Before 586 BC, prophets like Isaiah, Jeremiah, Micah, and Habakkuk told the idolatrous peoples of Judah that God was about to judge their nation for its adultery and injustices. God's final judgment resulted in the destruction of their Temple, the looting of its treasures, and most of the people who survived the brutal Babylonian onslaught being carried away into captivity. Jeremiah even told them they would go into captivity for seventy years, one year for every year they had not let the land rest as commanded by the Lord.

But the prophets also spoke to those in Judah (perhaps like the church of today), those who feared the Lord and demonstrated their love by obeying Him, saying the Lord noticed them and would protect them with His eye on them. Things started to deteriorate again after Judah came back from Babylon, and the Persian empire ruled the earth. That's when Malachi, a contemporary of Ezra and Nehemiah, prophesied. In the last book of the Old Testament, he writes: "'For behold, **the day is coming, burning like a furnace**; and all the arrogant and every evildoer will be chaff; and the day that is coming will set them ablaze,' says the Lord of hosts, 'so that it will leave them neither root nor branch. **But for you who fear My name, the sun of righteousness will rise with healing in its wings; and you will go forth and skip about like calves from the stall**. You will tread down the wicked, for they will be ashes under the soles of your feet on the day which I am preparing,' says the Lord of hosts [emphasis added]" (Malachi 4:1-3).

Other prophets say the same things in different but similar times, demonstrating this is the mind and will of the Lord in all these times of correction and judgment. That gives us courage, peace, and the motivation to act and experience the Lord's grace, power, and favor in such times. It's also an invitation to be still and enjoy His presence and safety while He acts: "In repentance and rest you will be saved, in quietness and trust is your strength" (Isaiah 30:15b). "The remnant of Israel will do no wrong and tell no lies, nor will a deceitful tongue be found in their mouths; for they will feed and lie down with no one to make them tremble" (Zephaniah 3:13).

Other prophets speak to God's plans and purposes in these times of correction: "'For I,' declares the Lord, 'will be a wall of fire around her, and I will be the glory in her midst'" (Zechariah 2:5). "By smooth words he will turn to godlessness those who act wickedly toward the covenant, but the people who know their God will display strength and take action" (Daniel 11:32). "The Lord sat as King at the flood; yes, the Lord sits as King forever. The Lord will give strength to His people; the Lord will bless His people with peace" (Psalm 29:11-12).

I find it fascinating that the Holocaust Museum in Jerusalem is called "*Yad Vashem*," which means "The Hand of God." The Scripture over the entrance reads, "Can these bones live?" (Ezekiel 37). That's a good question for governments and nations. It's a good question for churches and people. God is working His plan for the ages. Rest in Him, and in that posture, actively be a part by His leading by His Spirit (Zechariah 4:6).

"For by grace you have been saved through faith; and that not of yourselves, it is the gift of God; not as a result of works, so that no one may boast"

(Ephesians 2:8-9).

"'But let him who boasts boast of this, that he understands and knows Me, that I am the Lord who exercises lovingkindness, justice and righteousness on earth; for I delight in these things,' declares the Lord"

(Jeremiah 9:24).

"Why are the nations in an uproar and the peoples devising a vain thing? The kings of the earth take their stand and the rulers take counsel together against the Lord and against His Anointed"

(Psalm 2:1-2).

"Now therefore, O kings, show discernment; take warning, O judges of the earth. Worship the Lord with reverence and rejoice with trembling. Do homage to the Son, that He not become angry, and you perish in the way, for His wrath may soon be kindled. How blessed are all who take refuge in Him!"

(Psalm 2:10-12).

"Behold, the nations are like a drop from a bucket, and are regarded as a speck of dust on the scales; behold, He lifts up the islands like fine dust…All the nations are as nothing before Him, they are regarded by Him as less than nothing and meaningless"

(Isaiah 40:15,17).

"The grass withers, the flower fades, when the breath of the Lord blows upon it; surely the people are grass. The grass withers, the flower fades, but the word of our God stands forever. Get yourself up on a high mountain, O Zion, bearer of good news, lift up your voice mightily, O Jerusalem, bearer of good news; lift it up, do not fear. Say to the cities of Judah, 'Here is your God!' Behold, the Lord God will come with might, with His arm ruling for Him. Behold, His reward is with Him and His recompense before Him. Like a shepherd He will tend

His flock, in His arm He will gather the lambs and carry them in His bosom; He will gently lead the nursing ewes"

(Isaiah 40:7-11).

"'Remember the former things long past, for I am God, and there is no other; I am God, and there is no one like Me, declaring the end from the beginning, and from ancient times things which have not been done,' saying, 'My purpose will be established, and I will accomplish all My good pleasure'"

(Isaiah 46:9-10).

PUZZLING CHAPTER 61

Value Life

FROM MY JOURNAL JUNE 5, 2022: "We had a great day yesterday with Rick and Melinda taking us to Williamsburg and Yorktown for a splendid day of viewing American history, including a two-hour sunset sail from Yorktown aboard the majestic schooner *Alliance*. That caused me to awaken this morning thinking about a sailing poem Tozer introduced to me in one of his books and how it applies to the spiritual life."

"Tis The Set Of The Sail"

"But to every mind there openeth,
A way, and way, and away,
A high soul climbs the highway,
And the low soul gropes the low,
And in between on the misty flats,
The rest drift to and fro.
But to every man there openeth,
A high way and a low,

And every mind decideth,
The way his soul shall go.
One ship sails East,
And another West,
By the self-same winds that blow,
'Tis the set of the sails
And not the gales,
That tells the way we go.
Like the winds of the sea
Are the waves of time,
As we journey along through life,
'Tis the set of the soul,
That determines the goal,
And not the calm or the strife [emphasis added]"

(Ella Wheeler Wilcox).

It is a beautiful poem and telling. I sit on the patio, meditating on the verse in the early morning stillness of Newport News, drinking coffee. Melinda soon joins me, and we share some recent spiritual experiences.

She tells me of a girlfriend having many self-worth issues, so she felt the Spirit impress her to send this girlfriend the Lauren Daigle song "You Say." The girlfriend later reported that the following three times she got into her car, that song was playing on the radio. Synchronicity? Shame was a significant issue with this young woman, and we discussed that one must let God deal with shame, or it will control your life. We were impressed the wind of the Spirit is blowing among God's people for help and healing these days, more so than we've seen in previous days, as we share story after story. Or maybe we're just becoming spiritually sensitive enough to sense it.

It was soon time to go to church. Rick and Melinda were excited to show us their home church. We had attended the same church as young adults many years earlier but hadn't seen each other much in the intervening years.

Rick told us as we drove south it was a relatively large church, with a primarily military family makeup, due to its proximity to the Norfolk Naval Base. On the way, Rick and Melinda said many good things about their pastor, a middle-aged African American man they both loved. But as soon as we sat down and relaxed, listening to the worship team warm up, Rick noticed that their beloved spiritual leader was out of town, and we were to have a guest speaker.

Nigel — Legin

"Nigel 'Legin' Anderson is a spoken word artist, gospel hip hop artist, podcaster and preacher/speaker who uses transparency to connect and art to communicate with his listeners. Inspired by his father's battle with addiction, Legin speaks about fatherlessness to forgiveness, as well as racial reconciliation and urban apologetics among other topics, and the hope of the gospel in his music" (legin.tv). That introduction is from his website. But before I knew any of that, I heard a young, intelligent black man speak powerfully from his heart. He rapped some too, and he was real.

We sang several worship songs, including: "Your Love Never Fails" and "Break Every Chain." Then Nigel began talking about his life, faith, God's kingdom, and abortion. I wasn't expecting any of what I heard. It surprised and humbled me in a good way. The Spirit of God was so strong with this young man. It was the best talk about abortion I've ever heard — a message so timely and relevant to our day, with a different slant than is usually heard.

He told us his name was Nigel, but he chose Legin (Nigel spelled backward) as a stage name because God had turned his life around. He titled his message "Life, Value, Mercy."

Life

He asked, "What's the definition of life? What's the definition of me?" Then Nigel quoted the verse: "For You formed my inward parts; you wove me in my mother's womb. I will give thanks to You, for I am fearfully and wonderfully made; wonderful are Your works, and my soul knows it very well" (Psalm 139:13-14).

He continued, "I am awesome, not because I'm awesome, but because He made me. Your value is unchangeable in God's eyes." And if that's not enough, Jesus said: "I'm going to exchange my infinite life for your temporary one."

Value

Nigel said that our value comes from being made in the image of God. We are his image bearers: "God created man in His own image, in the image of God He created him; male and female He created them" (Genesis 1:27). He then asked the question: "What determines the value of something? It's who owns it. And how much someone is willing to pay for it."

To continue making his point, he said: "For we are His workmanship, created in Christ Jesus for good works, which God prepared beforehand so that we would walk in them" (Ephesians 2:10). He added: "There is an Artist involved. And He's interested in my goodness."

He said: "From now on we regard no one from a worldly view like we used to regard Christ from a worldly view — just a good man or a historical figure." Everyone in His image has value: "So we have stopped evaluating others from a human point of view. At one time we thought of Christ merely from a human point of view. How differently we know him now!" (2 Corinthians 5:16 NLT).

"We don't get to assign value to life — God does" (Nigel Anderson).

Mercy

Nigel went on to talk about the father in abortion situations. He was right in saying that almost no one thinks about the father. He said, "I used to not care about the dad who suffers in an abortion situation too, probably because I was abandoned and had issues because of it. But I'm a hypocrite if I don't. Because I'm forgiven."

Then came a powerful statement: "Each of you is one bad decision from becoming everything you hate." He said one could argue that David broke all ten commandments in one bad decision and wrongful act. We need to understand mercy: "But God, being rich in mercy, because of His great love with which He loved us, even when we were dead in our transgressions, made us alive together with Christ (by grace you have been saved)" (Ephesians 2:4-5). And: "For I was hungry, and you gave Me something to eat; I was thirsty, and you gave Me something to drink; I was a stranger, and you invited Me in; naked, and you clothed Me; I was sick, and you visited Me; I was in prison, and you came to Me" (Matthew 25:35-36).

Nigel said he was ashamed of the list he kept of people who don't deserve mercy. But we should all ask ourselves if we do the same. Mercy is when you don't get what you deserve.

He said, "I want the church to be known for radical mercy!" He finished with: "And what does the Lord require of you? To act justly and **to love mercy** and to walk humbly with your God [emphasis added]"(Micah 6:8b NIV).

Pointing to Jesus as our model and guide, he mentioned: "Father, forgive them; for they do not know what they are doing" (Luke 23:34). He humbly finished the discussion of mercy, saying: "Jesus forgave the guy about to stab Him. I'm not there. I want to be. Maybe someday."

Defend the Fatherless

Nigel said: "I don't know anyone weaker or more fatherless than the baby on the way to the abortion clinic." Then he cited this verse: "Vindicate the weak and fatherless; do justice to the afflicted and destitute. Rescue the weak and needy; deliver them out of the hand of the wicked" (Psalm 82:3-4).

He ended his talk with: "Find a way to fight for the value of every life."

Secular Humanism and Abortion

As I sit at the cabin months later and ponder Nigel's message, it occurs to me that abortion is secular humanism on steroids. It is also feminism on steroids. Have we come so far down this road from God and his Bible that we think we are little gods that can decide who lives and dies? That we can commit a murder, the willful destruction of human life, for our convenience, on a whim, or for what we think is the betterment of society? God help us must be our prayer. And God have mercy on us. We are becoming, or have become, the victims of our seared consciences and are very much deceived and deluded.

Abortion is probably the largest body of evidence in the argument that our church and culture are deceived and deluded. When one looks at the historical, ethical, biological, and Biblical evidence pointing to its ghastly horror, and the ramifications of child sacrifice in ancient cultures, it's wrong and an insult to the Creator. He always addresses this evil. The fact we don't see that speaks loudly to our delusion and spiritual blindness.

I mentioned ethics. Who gets to decide what is right or wrong? God or man? There you have the quandary and definition of secular humanism. "God, through the Bible says this, but I think...[differently]."

By his grace, may we come to see the magnitude of the honor God bestows on humankind called free will. By his grace, may we come to know the extent of our genocide, turn from it and ask for mercy. And by his grace, may we come to see and experience the magnitude of his mercy. There is forgiveness with God that we may fear Him (Psalm 130:4).

But fear Him we must. As I have pointed out in previous books and this puzzle, child sacrifice was present in ancient Israel, and Judah (Isaiah 57:5-9, Jeremiah 32:35, 2 Kings 21:6, Leviticus 20:2–5), just before their destruction or significant corrections. I don't expect it will be different here unless we turn and turn quickly to honor life, value it, and thus honor Him and His ways. He Who is the judge of nations, also the galactic judge, does not change.

I feel I can hear Him saying to the church, culture, and nation: "**These things you have done and I kept silence; you thought that I was just like you;** I will reprove you and state the case in order before your eyes [emphasis added]" (Psalm 50:21). And: "**Whom have you so dreaded and feared that you have not been true to me,** and have neither remembered me nor taken this to heart? **Is it not because I have long been silent that you do not fear me?** I will expose your righteousness and your works, and they will not benefit you. When you cry out for help, let your collection of idols save you! [emphasis added]" (Isaiah 57:11-13a NIV).

Usually, people who want to go their own way or have a better idea on abortion, proffer the question: "When does life begin? Is it at conception or birth?" They decide it's at birth, so they can terminate what happens before that without calling it murder or homicide. That's a pretty flimsy distinction considering we can't even define life or have any idea how to create it. When cells start to divide at conception, they come out as a fully formed human if left alone. You did. It seems like a moot point and a miracle so extraordinary no one would argue about it, but instead worship the Creator in awe. But we've elevated ourselves to gods that can make such determinations on a whim to fit our situation and desires with no care about the miracle or our Maker. This is the highest hubris and insolence I can imagine — blinding and damning. May the Lord have mercy on us and help us regain our spiritual sight and moral equilibrium, according to His ways and Word, which is a good prayer to be accompanied by whatever acts of repentance are in order.

I'm comforted that He takes note of our repentance and hears our prayers. The prophet prayed: "In wrath remember mercy" (Habakkuk 3:2c). The Bible tells us that: "Mercy triumphs over judgment" (James 2:13b). Let this be our prayer, our hope, and motivation for actions to correct this situation wherever and however we can. Lord, hear our prayer.

PUZZLING CHAPTER 62

Your Fast

Tell Me About Your Fast

I didn't intend to say that you are fast or move quickly. But in your world, do you fast? Do you slow things down to the speed of power and effectiveness? That's what happens when we pray and when we fast. We get still, focused, humble, and outside our physical selves. I'll explain.

The lack of fasting indicates that the bar may be set very low in our Christian experience and understanding in the west. Fasting is a pathway to power in living and muscle in prayer.

In Jesus' famous sermon on the mount, we read: "But you, **when you pray**, go into your inner room, close your door and pray to your Father who is in secret, and **your Father** who sees what is done in secret **will reward you** [emphasis added]" (Matthew 6:6). Note that Jesus expects His disciples will pray. He takes it for granted.

In the same teaching, Jesus says: "But you, **when you fast**, anoint your head and wash your face so that your fasting will not be noticed by men, but by **your Father** who is in secret; and your Father who sees what is done in secret **will reward you** [emphasis added]" (Matthew 6:17-18). Note Jesus expects His disciples will fast. He puts fasting on precisely the same level as prayer.

I know you're probably saying: "Dear me!" But we should be saying: "Oh my! Thank you, God, for giving us this key." The knowledge that prayer and fasting are mighty before God is a gift. Understanding that fasting is parallel or equal to prayer is also a gift. We'll get to "why" in just a second.

Martin Luther arrived at the same conclusion. John Wesley would not ordain a gospel minister if he did not commit to fast every Wednesday and Friday until 4 PM. Why is a fast so important?

Fasting Isn't About Eating But Humility

Fasting is a God-appointed way to humble ourselves. Pride is the primary inhibitor to effectiveness in prayer.

Andrew Murray, a prolific writer and spiritual seer from yesteryear, makes this point very well in *The Humility of our Lord*, republished as simply *Humility*. And I borrow most of the thoughts and truths expressed on this subject from Derek Prince, a spiritual giant from the greatest generation, who wrote about, taught about, and practiced this command of Jesus our Lord. His flagship book on the subject is *Shaping History Through Prayer and Fasting*.

Pride is a vicious adversary to God's blessing. If pride could cause an angel to lose his place, we should be very aware of its threat to our place with God and our spiritual well-being. On the other hand, humility is the pathway to power and a place of good standing with God.

In the parable of the dinner guests (Luke 14:7-24), Jesus sums up this truth: "For everyone who exalts himself will be humbled, and he who humbles himself will be exalted" (Luke 14:11).

Derek Prince says: "God can humiliate you. But only you can humble yourself." John Bunyan, author of the famous *Pilgrims Progress*, tells us: "He that is down needs fear no fall, he that is low, no pride; he that is humble ever shall have God to be his guide."

James the Apostle and half brother of Jesus reminds us: "'God is opposed to the proud, but gives grace to the humble.' Submit therefore to God. Resist the devil and he will flee from you. Draw near to God and He will draw near to you. Humble yourselves in the presence of the Lord, and He will exalt you" (James 4:6-8,10). Derek Prince adds: "There is no access to God with pride."

So how do we humble ourselves? David tells us how he did: "I humbled my soul with fasting" (Psalm 35:13). Your soul is the arrogant part of you. Humbling your soul brings it into subjection. Your stomach is an excellent servant but a terrible master.

Yom Kippur — The Fast

Oddly enough, I'm writing on Rosh Hashanah, the Jewish New Year, the beginning of their Days of Awe. They will celebrate their holiest day, Yom Kippur, the Day of Atonement, in ten days. It was a day for centuries and millennia when the High Priest would enter the Holy of Holies with the blood of a sacrificed lamb, and the people's sins would be carried away. Everything, the future of Israel, depended on that sacrifice. The people's part was to humble their souls.

They were to do no work because it was a sabbath of rest. But God told them to afflict their souls — fast. "On exactly the tenth day of this seventh month is the day of atonement; it shall be a holy convocation for you, and **you shall humble your souls** and present an offering by fire to the Lord. You shall not do any work on this same day, for it is a day of atonement, to make atonement on your behalf before the Lord your God [emphasis added]" (Leviticus 23:27-28).

Fasting is defined simply as "abstaining from food for spiritual purposes."

For 3500 years, the Jewish people have known that "afflicting our souls" is fasting. In the New Testament, Yom Kippur is called "The Fast."

We find another example of national fasting and the people of God humbling themselves during the Persian empire: "Then **I proclaimed a fast** there at the river of Ahava, **that we might humble ourselves before our God** to seek from Him a safe journey for us, our little ones, and all our possessions [emphasis added]" (Ezra 8:21).

Ezra describes his motive for fasting: "For I was ashamed to request from the king troops and horsemen to protect us from the enemy on the way, because we had said to the king, 'The hand of our God is favorably disposed to all those who seek Him, but His power and His anger are against all those who forsake Him.' **So we fasted and sought our God concerning this matter, and He listened to our entreaty** [emphasis added]" (Ezra 8:22-23). Ezra was leading a large group of families, carrying with them some of the most valuable items ever known to man, on a perilous journey, through lands infested with brigands. He put his money where his mouth was, and fasted.

Faith is deeply personal and mystical. Faith is also tangible and real. Be real. Fast and pray to the real God, and expect He will hear and answer your prayer with real results, especially if you humble yourself—that's the issue.

Fasting Aids Even Evil People and Nations

It's fascinating and points out how vital and powerful humility is before our holy, mighty, righteous, and merciful God. Do you know about Ahab's fast? He was one of Israel's most evil kings!

Ahab's situation is summed up like this: "Ahab said to Elijah, 'Have you found me, O my enemy?' And he answered, 'I have found you, because you have sold yourself to do evil in the sight of the Lord. Behold, I will bring evil upon you, and will utterly sweep you away, and will cut off from Ahab every male, both bond and free in Israel; and I will make your house like the house of Jeroboam the son of Nebat, and like the house of Baasha the son of Ahijah, because of the provocation with which you have provoked Me to anger, and because you have made Israel sin'" (1 Kings 21:20-22).

Evil King Ahab's response was to humble himself by fasting: "It came about when Ahab heard these words, that he tore his clothes and put on sackcloth and fasted, and he lay in sackcloth and went about despondently. Then the word of the Lord came to Elijah the Tishbite, saying, 'Do you see how Ahab has humbled himself before Me? Because he has humbled himself before Me, I will not bring the evil in his days, but I will bring the evil upon his house in his son's days'" (1 Kings 21:27-29).

If fasting could do that for overtly evil Ahab, what could it do for you and me?

In the story of Jonah, an evil king fasted and prayed for his nation, along with his people and their animals. They also repented of their sins in this state. But the fantastic thing is the Lord noted their humility evidenced by their fast and had mercy on them. They were spared judgment for many years.

We read of their predicament: "Then the people of Nineveh believed in God; and they called a fast and put on sackcloth from the greatest to the least of them. When the word reached the king of Nineveh, he arose from his throne, laid aside his robe from him, covered himself with sackcloth and sat on the ashes. He issued a proclamation and it said, 'In Nineveh by the decree of the king and his nobles: Do not let man, beast, herd, or flock taste a thing. Do not let them eat or drink water. But both man and beast must be covered with sackcloth; and let men call on God earnestly that each may turn from his wicked way and from the violence which is in his hands. Who knows, God may turn and relent and withdraw His burning anger so that we will not perish'" (Jonah 3:5-9).

We read the outcome: "When God saw their deeds, that they turned from their wicked way, then God relented concerning the calamity which He had declared He would bring upon them. And He did not do it" (Jonah 3:10).

Interestingly, the two evil kings above, one religious and the other secular, repented and humbled themselves by fasting after just one word from a prophet of God. Would the people of God be so humble and God-fearing and tremble at His Word today?

People of Faith Fast

Esther, the Jewish Queen of Persia, fasted and asked her people to fast with her when her cousin uncovered an evil plot to destroy the Jews. The plan and scheme were firm by law and decree, so only God and the king could stop it.

"Then Esther told them to reply to Mordecai, 'Go, assemble all the Jews who are found in Susa, and fast for me; do not eat or drink for three days, night or day. I and my maidens also will fast in the same way. And thus I will go in to the king, which is not according to the law; and if I perish, I perish.' So Mordecai went away and did just as Esther had commanded him" (Esther 4:15-17).

This perilous situation required God to answer prayer and for keen spiritual sensitivity in dealing with the highest political powers of the land. Esther was beautiful, no doubt, but it was forbidden to come into the king's presence uninvited, by penalty of death, and the king hadn't called for her for thirty days. Fasting food and water for three days couldn't have helped her appearance, so she wasn't trusting in any of her womanly persuasive powers, but God's favor and answered prayer in response to a humbling fast.

The Bible is pretty straightforward. People of faith, from the lowest to the highest, fast. It's a way of life. It's the way of faith. Is it time to start?

I haven't even mentioned Paul. Of fasting, we read: "But in all things we commend ourselves as ministers of God: in much patience, in tribulations, in needs, in distresses, in stripes, in imprisonments, in tumults, in labors, in sleeplessness, in fastings" (2 Corinthians 6:4-5 NKJV). And again: "in weariness and toil, in sleeplessness often, in hunger and thirst, in fastings often, in cold and nakedness" (2 Corinthians 11:27).

Hunger and thirst are one thing — you have nothing to eat. Fasting is another — you have food but refuse to eat.

The New Testament saints and elders of the early church demonstrate with their actions their belief in the importance of fasting: "Now there were at Antioch, in the church that was there, prophets and teachers: Barnabas, and Simeon who was called Niger, and Lucius of Cyrene, and Manaen who had been brought up with Herod the tetrarch, and Saul. While **they were ministering to the Lord and fasting**, the Holy Spirit said, 'Set apart for Me Barnabas and Saul for the work to which I have called them.' Then, **when they had fasted** and prayed and laid their hands on them, they sent them away [emphasis added]" (Acts 13:1-3). This was the most decisive moment in church history, and fasting played a significant role. Derek Prince adds, "God didn't call on us to improve His methods, but to follow them. Has God changed?"

While watching a Derek Prince YouTube video on fasting, one of the guys in our 20/20 group said: "Prayer itself is humbling. Bringing fasting with it is moreso." He then added: "Medicine is now telling me it's good for me [to fast]. It's a gift from God."

If My People

Fasting benefits us in ways we need like nothing else does. It can also help our culture and nation. We've mentioned a famous verse about prayer and humility from the time of Solomon: "**If My people** who are called by My name **will humble themselves, and pray** and **seek My face**, and **turn from their wicked ways**, then **I will hear** from heaven, and **will forgive their sin and heal their land** [emphasis added]" (2 Chronicles 7:14 NKJV). These are the words of the LORD to His people.

If we take the four steps listed above, God will take the three steps He promised. We **must humble ourselves (fasting), pray, seek His face, and turn from our wicked ways**. He will then **hear, forgive, and heal our land**. Please, people, let's resolve to do this and follow through on our part. As we are coming to see, the consequences of not doing so are dire. But the promise of help after our heart change, demonstrated by our actions, are most significant and sorely needed. It's the beautiful privilege of the family of God. The promise is born from His mercy, grace, loving and forgiving heart. If my people **will humble themselves (fast)**?

"'Now, therefore,' says the Lord, 'Turn to Me with all your heart, with fasting, with weeping, and with mourning. So rend your heart, and not your garments; return to the Lord your God, for He is gracious and merciful, slow to anger, and of great kindness; and He relents from doing harm'"

(Joel 2:12-13).

"Blow a trumpet in Zion, consecrate a fast...."

(Joel 2:15).

PUZZLING CHAPTER 63

Strange New World

Powerful Delusion

"For this reason God will send them a powerful delusion so that they believe the lie" (2 Thessalonians 2:11NIV).

I don't watch the news. I haven't watched a newscast in over twenty years, probably thirty years. I hear things here and there in the marketplace and have friends tell me what's happening in the world if they think it's pertinent, would interest me, or comes up in conversation. Then if I want, I can go to the web and try to figure out the story or event from an unbiased source without an agenda or slant — these days a scarce commodity.

That's good enough for me. Solomon, reported to be the wisest man who ever lived, about 1000 BC, said: "I've been young and now I am old, and there is nothing new under the sun" (Ecclesiastes 1:9). Isaiah, in about 700 BC said by the Spirit: "He who keeps his ears from hearing about bloodshed and his eyes from looking upon evil will dwell securely with me" (Isaiah 33:15-16). And Jesus said in about 30 AD:

"...your eyes are the lamp to your heart" (Matthew 6:22-23). Solomon chimes in again, saying: "above all else watch over your heart" (Proverbs 4:23).

So I read the Bible, and study history, believing, like Churchill, that we see more clearly what lies ahead by looking back at the past.

And then, I try to lead a quiet, peaceful life and work with my hands. And think upon beautiful and positive things as the Apostle Paul instructs the church in Thessalonica and Philippi and the church of all ages to do.

«... make it your ambition to lead a quiet life and attend to your own business and work with your hands" (1Thessalonians 4:11). "Finally, brothers and sisters, whatever is true, whatever is noble, whatever is right, whatever is pure, whatever is lovely, whatever is admirable—if anything is excellent or praiseworthy—think about such things" (Philippians 4:8 NIV).

Like King David, one of my heroes in the faith, I try not to consider things too difficult for me (Psalm 131:1). I leave all the heavy lifting to the Lord of creation and the Lord of human history (Isaiah 30:15, Zechariah 4:6). He is going to be up all night anyway, so I can peacefully sleep (Psalm 121:4).

The Evening News — Life Is Bad

My father was a news addict, especially later in life, and I would say typical of the population in that regard, certainly his generation. I was a news addict in college and earlier in life. But it's like I used to tell my dad about the news: "They don't tell you that 7.999 billion people get up, go to work, school or play, every day, and come home, without anything bad happening to them." Instead, they scour the earth for images and reports of bloodshed and violence and paste that on the evening news — these days the 24/7 news. We all know that's what attracts people's attention. People will watch it and also watch the advertising during the newscast. And subsequently, buy the products, so more such newscasts are produced for profit. But is this a correct representation of life on the planet? Is it the truth about what's going on each day? Is it the big picture? As best as we can envision it? I would say no! I would say it's a lie. It's a system perpetuating lies about life and living on the planet.

The Bible — Life Is Good

Life is good on the planet, especially for those who abide with the Lord (John 15:5, Psalm 91:1-2). It's a gift! A gift to be seized and enjoyed every day we awaken. *Carpe Diem*, and enjoy the gift!

The prophets of old attest to this, even as they predicted future judgment and doom on those who rejected the goodness of God and the close relationship he graciously and mercifully proffered, and proffers still. We see the last of them, Malachi, writing: "But for you who fear My name, the sun of righteousness will rise with healing in its wings; and you will go forth and skip about like calves from the stall" (Malachi 4:2).

At the same time, there does seem to be some spiritual "second law of thermodynamics" at play. Things with humans tend to disorder and decay without His sustaining life and activity on our behalf.

We'll call it a mystery because that's how the apostles described it, and that's what it is. It's observable in people of every race and every generation for which we have a record, every epoch from Job to this day (1Timothy 3:16).

So we observe it works but know not how it works — like believers and the wind John describes in John 3:8. This seems to be only communicated in the Bible, and from person to person, also involving a direct revelation or encounter with the Holy Spirit of God. That's the most beautiful and mysterious part. It's like a secret, but as Tozer tells us: "It's an open secret."

The church, disciples of Christ, of all people should know this and practice His presence in public and secret. But there seems to be a severe delusion at work. Perhaps a deception predicted and revealed to the Apostles that would occur in the latter days (2 Thessalonians 2:11).

Darwinism — Evolution

Some have suggested Darwinism is that delusion. What's commonly called the "Theory of Evolution" is not supportable by modern science. Evolution is proven more and more each year to be not only improbable but impossible. Yet it is painted as truth in textbooks and museums around the world. In the same time frame as Darwin came Karl Marx in the political world and Sigmund Freud in the psychological world, and other men of the age, in the spirit of the French Enlightenment, who wished to experience, create, or imagine a world without God — "a powerful delusion."

The Media

As I ponder this today, I see the media as "a powerful delusion" or a significant part of it. Day after day, night after night, they pour forth their lies and half-truths that bring them monetary gain and keep people watching. The media serve their financial goals and political agendas as they act like little gods helping us see the world of their "truth."

Secular Humanism — A House of Cards

Do you watch television news? Then you know how it makes you feel. I admit it appeals to the humanistic side of all of us. We want to know. That's what Satan had in mind when he said to Adam and Eve: "For God knows that when you eat from it [the tree of knowledge] your eyes will be opened, and you will be like God, knowing good and evil" (Genesis 3:5 NIV).

If the subtle work of secular humanism has crept in on you until you are possibly a Christian-humanist, which should be an oxymoron, then you think you must know these things to fix them, like a god. Okay, I better stop. Hopefully, you comprehend what I'm saying. If your life is built on this type thinking, it is a house of cards.

Unfounded Fear — A Judgment

One interesting, observable side effect of this negative news and sensationalism is that people living in the world's freest, safest, most prosperous country live in some measure of fear and dread. They forfeit the benefits of blessings because they fear situations that aren't substantiated or real.

I think you can add this as one of the judgments of the Lord on our land, along with hurricanes, wildfires, super winds, pestilence, and plague. It's a judgment of fear. Fear is typically a tool of Satan. Mostly, it is irrational. The propensity for fear in humans serves both good and bad purposes. It seems wired into us at our core. So without spiritual protection, we are susceptible to its ravages and angst.

So I will ask you," Why do you watch the news?" I see it like taking a little poison pill daily. You can feed your faith or feed your fears. Maybe you like people telling you lies? Or perhaps you feel like you're so important, you have to know? Or that knowing makes you more important to others? We're given insight and warning about this: "But knowledge puffs up while love builds up [emphasis added]" (1 Corinthians 8:1b NIV).

I don't want to make too big an issue of this. It could be that you want to be an active part of your culture, a change agent, and you think this is an integral part of life and living. Or maybe you have the calling of a watchman or prophet in your life? You decide, but give some thought to unplugging! Those around you and your own heart will thank you.

As I once said to my best friend, a very spiritual believer, maybe the best fighter pilot I ever knew, and a watchman: "Brian, promise me you'll read the Bible at least twice as much as much as you watch CNN, FOX, Etc.!" He said he would, and I know he did. You can't tell a watchman not to watch! But you can decide for yourself, what the Spirit would have you do, and do it.

Secular Humanism — The Great Delusion

At any rate, we are not like God, as the tenants of secular humanism would have us believe. God made us in his image, but His ways are higher than our ways (Isaiah 55:9). He is significantly "other" than his creation.

Come to think about it; the media may not be the great delusion. It may simply be the voice of this grand deception or a pawn in its service. Secular humanism is likely the great delusion. Man thinks he is God or tries to be like God and go forward without Him. Delusional! That is "a powerful delusion."

How does that happen? How does it work? Is it a valid explanation for what has befallen our churches, youth, and culture? Is it a piece of the puzzle? Maybe the most crucial element? We'll look at that again before finishing this puzzle.

Sex and The Great Delusion

Our young, Cambridge educated pastor started a book club or reading group recently. It meets every other Thursday from 6:30 AM to 8:00 AM. The makeup of the fifteen of us who participate is multigenerational, primarily men, but two female college students — a diverse group from many different walks of life. The book Ben chose is quite interesting, *Strange New World: How Thinkers and Activists Redefined Identity and Sparked the Sexual Revolution*, by Carl R. Trueman.

"It's an unusual book," I thought, "and unusual that it would draw this group of young professionals — present and future leaders." But it's timely and ties into this puzzle piece of deception, delusion, and our times. So I was anxious to be a part, and learn with friends.

In his introductory remarks, Ben said: "How did we get here as a culture? Reading this book together will be more about understanding where we are and how we got here than a Biblical response." Then he said: "I care more about what's right than being the person who is right. Maybe this will help us to understand and be better able to talk about it with others in the church and culture."

In a short video, Carl R. Trueman (Ph.D., University of Aberdeen) introduced us to his book and some of the primary thoughts and topics: 1. The speed of change in our time has given us vertigo. 2. Everything has become political. 3. In selling things, merchants go out of their way to say they support pride month, abortion, etc. 4. We've lost the distinction between public and private life. 5. The issue of sex, was formerly private not public. [The words of an old Janice Joplin song popped into my mind: "Nothin' ain't worth nothin', but it's free."] 6. The changing notion of the human self to autonomous, free-floating. 7. The only constant thing in this world is you. Everything else is contrarian. 8. God defines all people as dependent on Him and others. Note God's laws of hospitality.

In summation, he said the primary debate or root cause of the divide is the fundamental concept of self. Are we made in God's image and redeemed? Or are we at the center, being our god, determining our fate, and making our rules?

Tim spoke up and said: "I have lived in many cultures, and they are more about the family and clan than what we see here." Mike said: "It seems like we're not tethered to anything anymore." And about the loss of distinction between private and public life of previous generations without social media, Mike said: "I miss that" — the sense of private life, with family, a few friends, and God apart from public life.

It seems like this could be a valuable tool for conversation. And it may help us grow in curiosity and humility.

Delusion and Queen Elizabeth II

Hearing this British theologian drew my heart and mind to England, her beloved Queen, and what I read Alistair Begg, another theologian, report about her life.

"It so happened that this past weekend [July 2022] I was in the UK during the celebration of the Platinum Jubilee of Queen Elizabeth II. I was speaking at a conference in the town of Kilmarnock, which is in Ayrshire. It was there, in 1956, that I stood with my mum and waved my Union Jack as the Queen passed through town. For the past sixty-six years I have enjoyed the privilege of being one of her subjects."

"The Queen has lived successfully in the public eye for seventy years, causing us to wonder at the source of her strength. The Christian Institute reported, 'In an article for Parliament News, Lord Michael Farmer credited the Queen's faithfulness to her position and constancy in public life to her devotion to God,' writing, 'The answer lies in her continuous confession of her trust and reliance on Jesus her savior, and God her father.' There is only one person she addresses as 'Your Majesty,' and that is Jesus, who is King of Kings and Lord of Lords. She is the queen who has a King! Her identity, like all who trust in Jesus, flows not from wealth or social status but from her union with Christ" (Alistair Begg, truthforlife.org, "Learning for Living," July 2022).

Begg says: "In her Christmas addresses, the Queen has not surrendered to the temptation to universalize her message but has declared her trust in God, drawing strength from the hope of the Christian Gospel." Thank God for her humble, honest, strong stand in the face of widespread delusion. Thank God for the Queen.

Wheat, Tares, and The End of the Age

When pondering a powerful delusion sent from the Lord, it's hard to wrap your mind around it. Yet it's the only explanation for what is happening in our churches and culture at the moment. Where are we in the storm and where did it begin? These are good questions to ponder, trying to gain some frame of reference for what we're experiencing, and maybe find a way out.

But if you're near the eye of the storm, you haven't that luxury, instead hour to hour, and day to day you help others cope while surviving yourself. If you are in a different location, and watching on radar, you have an idea of the size of the storm, its intensity, and direction of movement, so you can better proffer advice for survival to those in the storm or harm's way, and start to plan some clean up and life restoring missions. That's how I see prayer, the Word, and dwelling in the secret place of the Most High.

I don't know if this powerful deception from the Lord began at the Renaissance and Reformation, or with the Enlightenment, or with Darwin, Marx, Freud, Et al. It seems tares were sown with the wheat at some point in time. And now the gale force winds of that harvest are upon us.

Jesus told a story about that, to help us understand, act with wisdom, and be at peace during the powerful delusion from the Lord: "The slaves of the landowner came and said to him, 'Sir, did you not sow good seed in your field? How then does it have tares?' And he said to them, '**An enemy has done this!**' The slaves said to him, '**Do you want us, then, to go and gather them up?**' But he said, '**No; for while you are gathering up the tares, you may uproot the wheat** with them. **Allow both to grow together until the harvest; and in the time of the harvest I will say to the reapers, "First gather up the tares and bind them in bundles to burn them up; but gather the wheat into my barn** [emphasis added]"" (Matthew 13:27-30).

Jesus speaks to this again in the final chapter of Holy Scripture: "And he said to me, 'Do not seal up the words of the prophecy of this book, for the time is near. **Let the one who does wrong, still do wrong; and the one who is filthy, still be filthy; and let the one who is righteous, still practice righteousness; and the one who is holy, still keep himself holy. Behold, I am coming quickly, and My reward is with Me, to render to every man according to what he has done.** I am the Alpha and the Omega, the first and the last, the beginning and the end [emphasis added]'" (Revelation 22:10-13).

"The eye is the lamp of the body. If your eyes are healthy, your whole body will be full of light. But if your eyes are unhealthy, your whole body will be full of darkness. If then the light within you is darkness, how great is that darkness!"

(Matthew 6:22-24 NIV).

"Above all else, guard your heart, for everything you do flows from it"

(Proverbs 4:23).

"Their idols are silver and gold,
The work of human hands.
They have mouths, but they cannot speak;
They have eyes, but they cannot see;
They have ears, but they cannot hear;
They have noses, but they cannot smell;
They have hands, but they cannot feel;

They have feet, but they cannot walk;
They cannot make a sound with their throat.
Those who make them will become like them,
Everyone who trusts in them"

(Psalm 115:4-8 NASB).

"Now to the King eternal, immortal, and invisible, the only God, be honor and glory forever and ever. Amen"

(1 Timothy 1:17).

PUZZLING CHAPTER 64

Israel ישראל

May 14, 1948

A couple of years before my mom passed away, she gave me a book for Christmas entitled *What in the World is Going On?: 10 Prophetic Clues You Cannot Afford to Ignore* by David Jeremiah. When I opened the cover, the first words staring at me were "May 14, 1948." I knew immediately it would be good and I read it in very few sittings.

Israel has been a part of the puzzle from the beginning, in God's mind and in God's eyes. And she will be until the end. You can't read the Bible or history and fail to see that. Her presence in the world and history are too remarkable to overlook. I would like to plunge into all the evidence for that statement, but a book like this won't permit it.

Accept it by faith and evidence. Then keep your eyes and ears open to whatever the Lord will show you about the small nation, and what she teaches us and the world about the Lord.

All you need to know is that Israel is highly favored by God, and any wise, God-fearing person will bless them and support them anyway possible. Abraham, the father of the faith, is also the father of Israel. In the first book of the Bible, about four thousand years ago, we see God make Abraham a promise: "And I will bless those who bless you, and the one who curses you I will curse. And in you all the families of the earth will be blessed" (Genesis 12:3).

A brief, telling look at history is to look at all the nations who have blessed Israel, and all the nations who have cursed Israel. Note what happens to them.

A couple of God's attributes acted out in history tell the tale. First, God doesn't lie or change His mind: "God is not human, that he should lie, not a human being, that he should change his mind. Does he speak and then not act? Does he promise and not fulfill?" (Numbers 23:19 NIV). Secondly, even if people or nations don't keep their word to God, He keeps His Word. It's Who He is: "If we are faithless, He remains faithful, for He cannot deny Himself" (2 Timothy 2:13).

Allow me to wrap up this introduction by quoting three observations about Israel by well-known people. King Louis XIV of France asked Blaise Pascal, the great French philosopher and mathematician, to give him proof of the supernatural. Pascal answered: "Why, the Jews, your Majesty — the Jews."

Mark Twain, the great American writer, intellectual, agnostic and a self-acknowledged skeptic, wrote: "The Egyptian, the Babylonian, and the Persian rose, filled the planet with sound and splendor, then faded to dream-stuff and passed away. The Greek and Roman followed, made a vast noise and they are gone. Other peoples have sprung up, and held their torch high for a time, but it burned out and they sit in twilight now or have vanished. The Jew saw them all, beat them all, and is now what he always was, exhibiting no decadence, no infirmities of age, no weakening of his parts, no slowing of his energies, no dulling of his alert and aggressive mind. All things are mortal, but the Jew. All other forces pass, but he remains. What is the secret of his immortality?"

The obvious and most plausible answer is Israel's immortal God, and His promises to Abraham, Isaac, Jacob, and their descendants forever.

Leo Tolstoy, the famous Russian intellectual and author best known for his classic *War and Peace* had this to say: "The Jew is the emblem of eternity. He who neither slaughter nor torture of thousands of years could destroy, he who neither fire, nor sword, nor Inquisition was able to wipe off the face of the earth. He who was the first to produce the Oracles of God. He who has been for so long the Guardian of Prophecy and has transmitted it to the rest of the world. Such a nation cannot be destroyed. The Jew is as everlasting as Eternity itself."

The words of Solomon come immediately to mind: "A time for war and a time for peace… He has made everything appropriate in its time. He has also set eternity in their heart, yet so that man will not find out the work which God has done from the beginning even to the end" (Ecclesiastes 3:8b,11). This is an insightful and universal truth. But it seems to especially describe the history and purpose of the Jewish nation we call Israel.

Image Bearers

It's a well known and published fact that one out of five Nobel laureates is Jewish. One web source says this: "Remarkably, Jews and people of Jewish descent represent less than 0.20% of the world's population, but they represent 22.4% of all Nobel laureates (208 out of 930)." So I could go off on how unusual that is, but you already get it. Or I could point out that the state of Israel is one fifth the size of Arkansas, or about the size of New Jersey, yet it's in the national headlines most days. What could be the reason for matters concerning Israel to be so statistically skewed?

I would suggest they are a favored nation of the one true God. They serve His purposes and communicate them to the rest of the world, serving His greater purposes, which is to draw from the earth a people for Himself, and a suitable bride for His Son, the King. In the process, the peoples of the earth have opportunity to learn about God, and this coming King.

The people of Israel have spiritual and natural enemies bent on their destruction because of God's favor. But they enjoy God's favor whether they walk in His ways or not, because of His faithfulness to His word to Abraham, Isaac, and Jacob (Israel). Only at stake in all of this is how they fare as a result of their faithfulness to the covenant. If they keep their covenant, they fare well. If not, they experience God's chastisement and correction. Faithful is God, so they will always exist in some form, eternally.

When and why did God pick them, and for what purpose?

Moses wrote by the Spirit: "**The Lord did not set His love on you nor choose you because you were more in number than any of the peoples, for you were the fewest of all peoples, but because the Lord loved you and kept the oath which He swore to your forefathers**, the Lord brought you out by a mighty hand and redeemed you from the house of slavery, from the hand of Pharaoh king of Egypt. **Know therefore that the Lord your God, He is God, the faithful God, who keeps His covenant and His lovingkindness to a thousandth generation with those who love Him and keep His commandments; but repays those who hate Him** to their faces, to destroy them; He will not delay with him who hates Him, He will repay him to his face. Therefore, you shall keep the commandment and the statutes and the judgments which I am commanding you today, to do them [emphasis added]" (Deuteronomy 7:7-11). You can read all of chapter seven for additional and telling insights.

It started with Abraham about 2000 BC. We have some hints from the Bible why God chose him, and I'll give a few. But keep in mind the overarching truth about God taught in Scripture is this: God is no respecter of races or people, but He can show favor to whom He wills (Romans 2:11-16, Exodus 33:19).

One reason that God chose Abraham is insightful and instructive for every generation: "For I know him, that he will command his children and his household after him, and they shall keep the way of the Lord, to do justice and judgment; that the Lord may bring upon Abraham that which he hath spoken of him" (Genesis 18:19 KJV). That's beautiful and important.

We learn of other reasons: "And he believed in the Lord; and he counted it to him for righteousness" (Genesis 15:6 KJV). "Yet, with respect to the promise of God [to have children and multitudes of descendants although he was very old], he did not waver in unbelief but grew strong in faith, giving glory to God, and being fully assured that what God had promised, He was able also to perform. Therefore it was also credited to him as righteousness" (Romans 4:20-22 NASB). Abraham trusted and believed God, and that touched God. Evidently so much that God trusted Abraham.

Probably the ultimate action and act of faith that set Abraham apart in God's eyes, and those of the world once it was known, was his willingness to sacrifice his only son, the son of the promise, at God's command (Genesis 22:1-19). "By faith Abraham, when he was tested, offered up Isaac, and he who had received the promises was offering up his only begotten son; it was he to whom it was said, 'In Isaac your descendants shall be called.' He considered that God is able to raise people even from the dead, from which he also received him back as a type" (Hebrews 11:17-19). You can see why this trust and willingness to sacrifice a son would get God's attention, and be very close to His heart.

Perhaps God's greater purpose in establishing Abrahams's descendants, Israel, is stated here: "**Even so Abraham believed God, and it was reckoned to him as righteousness.** Therefore, **be sure that it is those who are of faith who are sons of Abraham**. The Scripture, **foreseeing that God would justify the Gentiles by faith,** preached the gospel beforehand to Abraham, saying, '**All the nations will be blessed** in you.' So then **those who are of faith are blessed with Abraham**, the believer [emphasis added]" (Galatians 3:6-9). It was always God's plan for salvation to come from the Jews, in the person of His Son, the King. But salvation would come also to the Gentiles, whosoever will, by faith, just as with Abraham.

And finally the New Testament description of Abraham's life resonates with the faithful of all times: "**By faith Abraham, when he was called, obeyed** by going out to a place which he was to receive for an inheritance; and he went out, not knowing where he was going. **By faith he lived as an alien in the land of promise, as in a foreign land**, dwelling in tents with Isaac and Jacob, fellow heirs of the same promise; for he was **looking for the city which has foundations, whose architect and builder is God** [emphasis added]" (Hebrews 11:8-10).

It's interesting to note that Abraham was a gentile by bloodline, and a Jew by faith. His descendants after him, as uncountable as the stars, were Jews by his bloodline and by faith. It was God's plan that they bear God's image to the rest of the world. Then finally they would bear the King. To them belong the promises, and to them belongs the land.

Puzzling Israel?

You've already started puzzling about Israel and what you can learn about them and about God through them. Let's continue in that vein. I'll record a smattering of related Scriptures below, and let you puzzle how and if they fit into your paradigm about Israel and God's cosmic story. We'll let the Word speak to the purposes and promises of Israel — rather the purposes and promises of God for Israel.

The Word of the Lord and Israel

"Who has heard such a thing? Who has seen such things? Can a land be born in one day? Can a nation be brought forth all at once? As soon as Zion travailed, she also brought forth her sons" (Isaiah 66:8).

May 14, 1948! After almost 2000 years without a home, Israel came back to the land, retaining her language, religion, and culture — unprecedented in human history.

"By the rivers of Babylon, there we sat down and wept, when we remembered Zion. Upon the willows in the midst of it we hung our harps. For there our captors demanded of us songs, and our tormentors mirth, saying, 'Sing us one of the songs of Zion.' How can we sing the Lord's song in a foreign land? If I forget you, O Jerusalem, may my right hand forget her skill. May my tongue cling to the roof of my mouth if I do not remember you, if I do not exalt Jerusalem above my chief joy" (Psalm 137:1-6).

"But You, O Lord, abide forever, and Your name to all generations. You will arise and have compassion on Zion; for it is time to be gracious to her, for the appointed time has come. Surely Your servants find pleasure in her stones and feel pity for her dust. So the nations will fear the name of the Lord and all the kings of the earth Your glory. For the Lord has built up Zion; He has appeared in His glory. He has regarded the prayer of the destitute and has not despised their prayer. This will be written for the generation to come, that a people yet to be created may praise the Lord. For He looked down from His holy height; from heaven the Lord gazed upon the earth, to hear the groaning of the prisoner, to set free those who were doomed to death, that men may tell of the name of the Lord in Zion and His praise in Jerusalem, when the peoples are gathered together, and the kingdoms, to serve the Lord" (Psalm 102:12-22).

"I also was acting with hostility against them, to bring them into the land of their enemies—or if their uncircumcised heart becomes humbled so that they then make amends for their iniquity, then I will remember My covenant with Jacob, and I will remember also My covenant with Isaac, and My covenant with Abraham as well, and I will remember the land" (Leviticus 26:40-42).

"But I say to you, make no oath at all, either by heaven, for it is the throne of God, or by the earth, for it is the footstool of His feet, or by Jerusalem, for it is the city of the great King" (Matthew 5:34-35).

"Remember Abraham, Isaac, and Israel, Your servants to whom You swore by Yourself, and said to them, 'I will multiply your descendants as the stars of the heavens, and all this land of which I have spoken I will give to your descendants, and they shall inherit it forever'" (Exodus 32:13).

"God also said to him, 'I am God Almighty; be fruitful and multiply; a nation and a company of nations shall come from you, and kings shall come forth from you. The land which I gave to Abraham and Isaac, I will give it to you, and I will give the land to your descendants after you'" (Genesis 35:11-12).

"If they return to You with all their heart and with all their soul in the land of their enemies who have taken them captive, and pray to You toward their land which You have given to their fathers, the city which You have chosen, and the house which I have built for Your name; then hear their prayer and their supplication in heaven Your dwelling place, and maintain their cause, and forgive Your people who have sinned against You and all their transgressions which they have transgressed against You, and make them objects of compassion before those who have taken them captive, that they may have compassion on them (for they are Your people and Your inheritance which You have brought forth from Egypt, from the midst of the iron furnace), that Your eyes may be open to the supplication of Your servant and to the supplication of Your people Israel, to listen to them whenever they call to You. For You have separated them from all the peoples of the earth as Your inheritance, as You spoke through Moses Your servant, when You brought our fathers forth from Egypt, O Lord God" (1 Kings 8:48-53).

"For I do not want you, brethren, to be uninformed of this mystery—so that you will not be wise in your own estimation—that a partial hardening has happened to Israel until the fullness of the Gentiles has come in; and so all Israel will be saved; just as it is written, 'The Deliverer will come from Zion, He will remove ungodliness from Jacob.' This is My covenant with them, when I take away their sins" (Romans 11:25-27).

"For I say to you, from now on you will not see Me until you say, 'Blessed is He who comes in the name of the Lord!'" (Matthew 23:39).

Exceptionalism Then and Now

Of course Israel is an exceptional nation among the nations of the earth. Anyone can see that due to her successes, her continuing place among the nations, and the miracle of her survival over four millennia. Anyone who can't see it is deceived, ignorant of history and the facts, or has some self-serving view that's counter to history and reality.

An eternal, powerful God, Who keeps His word to a thousand generations is the only explanation for her surviving and thriving. Israel is God's national image bearer or *imago dei* among the nations of the earth. Remember, God told Abraham: "I will bless those who bless you and curse those who curse you, and in you, all the nations of the earth will be blessed."

Knowing this and reading the miracles along the way is what gives birth and credence to America's exceptionalism. America started as a community of faith with the Pilgrims and Puritans. They were looking, like Abraham, for a city who's builder and founder was God. There were many miracles along the way, from Valley Forge to George Washington surviving the French Indian Wars. Indeed, winning her independence from the mighty British empire was an incredible miracle. Those who would ignore such or record it some other way are betraying their motive to write God out of His own story. And they have about as much chance in the long run, as a fish becoming a bird or a monkey becoming a human. But I digress.

We are to bless Israel according to God. And His blessing for us is tied in some large measure to our obedience as individuals and nations to do so. It matters not that they are largely apostate or agnostic as a nation at the moment. God's word is God's word. And His dealing with His people is His to do. Just be faithful to do your part and show kindness and support for Israel anyway you can. Go visit if you can, with friends, and you'll be blessed. And you'll discover more pieces to the puzzle of Israel. This is not a hard puzzle unless you don't want to see it as it is. All the pieces are there and recorded in history, and the Bible, and the Land.

Also pray for the peace of Jerusalem. We're only instructed to pray for two cities in the Bible — our own city and Jerusalem. Obedience to do so carries with it another blessing from God. "Seek the welfare of the city where I have sent you into exile, and pray to the Lord on its behalf; for in its welfare you will have welfare" (Jeremiah 29:7). And: "Pray for the peace of Jerusalem: 'May they prosper who love you'" (Psalm 122:6).

Faithful Surgery the Same

If you read the Bible and look at history, you are keenly aware that when Israel is unfaithful to God and her promises, God is faithful to correct her and bring her to repentance, often involving a good bit of judgment.

It's the same for His bride, the church, or any community of faith local or global. God is able to care for His vineyard, whether it be a church or a nation. So don't get tripped up by this.

Remember: "'For those whom the Lord loves He disciplines, and He scourges every son whom He receives.' It is for discipline that you endure; God deals with you as with sons; for what son is there whom his father does not discipline? But if you are without discipline, of which all have become partakers, then you are illegitimate children and not sons. Furthermore, we had earthly fathers to discipline us, and we respected them; shall we not much rather be subject to the Father of spirits, and live? For they disciplined us for a short time as seemed best to them, but He disciplines us for our good, so that we may share His holiness. All discipline for the moment seems not to be joyful, but sorrowful; yet to those who have been trained by it, afterwards it yields the peaceful fruit of righteousness" (Hebrews 12:6-11).

And: "For it is time for judgment to begin with the household of God; and if it begins with us first, what will be the outcome for those who do not obey the gospel of God?" (1 Peter 4:17).

A New Creation and Development

Wikipedia reports: "As of 2020, the world's "core" Jewish population (those identifying as Jews above all else) was estimated at 14.8 million, 0.2% of the 7.95 billion worldwide population. .2% — tiny but potent, and important by God's standard, the standard that really counts.

Something worth watching, I believe, is how many of the world's 15 million Jews live in Israel. I say this because of many prophecies scattered throughout the Bible saying God will bring them back to the land at some future time. Now 51% of Jews live in the US, and 30% live in Israel accounting for 81%, while no other country has more than 3%, and 10 countries account for 17% of the remaining Jews living outside of Israel.

"Therefore say, 'Thus says the Lord God,' "I will gather you from the peoples and assemble you out of the countries among which you have been scattered, and I will give you the land of Israel" (Ezekiel 11:17).

"Behold, I am bringing them from the north country, and I will gather them from the remote parts of the earth, among them the blind and the lame, the woman with child and she who is in labor with child, together; a great company, they will return here. With weeping they will come, and by supplication I will lead them; I will make them walk by streams of waters, on a straight path in which they will not stumble; for I am a father to Israel, and Ephraim is My firstborn" (Jeremiah 31:8-9).

"For I will take you from the nations, gather you from all the lands and bring you into your own land" (Ezekiel 36:24).

"'At that time I will bring you in, even at the time when I gather you together; indeed, I will give you renown and praise among all the peoples of the earth, when I restore your fortunes before your eyes,' says the Lord" (Zephaniah 3:20).

It's just something to know and keep an eye upon.

Messianic Jews or Jewish Christians

The first time I went to Israel in 1994, I met a young Jewish man who worked for the Jerusalem Post. He drove me and three friends to meet his mother, who was a Jewish Christian, a rarity in those days. When he drove us back to the hotel, I asked if he was a Christian. He seemed uncomfortable with the question, then replied, "Yes, but if it were known I would lose my job." I then asked how many messianic Jews he knew. He said, "I could count them on one hand."

Fast forward to 2005, and I was on another trip to Israel with a college group touring and studying for course credit. I arranged to meet the same man before breakfast one morning at our hotel. He was now retired from his job and lived just outside Jerusalem. I asked him if what I remembered and recounted above was correct. He said it was. I then asked if that was still the case.

To my surprise he said, "Not at all. There are messianic congregations in almost every village in Israel, and every neighborhood in Jerusalem." Shocked, I asked, "What did the rabbis say about that?" He replied, "They hated it, and attacked it in the papers, synagogues, and every way they could. But it was like a spring of water coming up out of the ground, and they couldn't stop it."

This happened in only eleven years. I didn't hear anything about it on CNN, did you? But it seems like it signals something very new and different from the previous centuries of Christian-Jewish animosity, and of Jewish hardness to the Gospel of Jesus Christ. Excuse me, I mean Yeshua Hamachiach, Jesus the Messiah.

"For I say to you, from now on you will not see Me until you say, 'Blessed is He who comes in the name of the Lord!'" (Matthew 23:39).

In 2012 I was in Israel again on a private spiritual retreat and to visit friends. I attended a Messianic Jewish worship service in Hebrew, in Christ Church by the Jaffa Gate. It was on Shabbat, or Saturday, so as not to interfere with the normal Christian service on Sunday. Translators with headsets provided translation into English, Spanish, French, and a few other languages as needed or staff was available. The speaker was a Jewish pastor from the Galilee. It was a beautifully insightful teaching from the Scriptures. Amazing! Are we on the same planet as we were born? Things are changing so fast, and right under our noses.

[Visit oneforisrael.org if you would like to read more about the Messianic movement among Jewish people today.]

Keep an Eye on Israel and Jerusalem

Israel is a fairly new nation among the family of nations. Yet she is as old as it gets. The books of Daniel and Revelation tie a lot of end time prophecy to the nation of Israel. Indeed, she was reborn in a day after a 2000 thousand year scattering. But she's back and just about one generation old. My next door neighbor was born April 14, 1948, one month to the day before Israel became a nation again. He's seventy-four.

Jesus said this to His disciples in response to their questions about the end of time and the return of Christ: "Now learn this lesson from the fig tree: As soon as its twigs get tender and its leaves come out, you know that summer is near. Even so, when you see all these things, you know that it is near, right at the door. Truly I tell you, this generation will certainly not pass away until all these things have happened. Heaven and earth will pass away, but my words will never pass away" (Matthew 24:32-35).

Due to the context of Jesus' remarks, the disciple's question, and that a fig tree is often used as a metaphor for Israel, many have supposed that Jesus was saying: "The second advent will occur within one generation of Israel becoming a nation again." We'll see. There are lots of hints this eschatology could be true, but it also seems fuzzy for a reason.

Jesus' main message is for us to "watch" these things, so we're not unprepared. Certainly keep an eye on Israel, Jerusalem, and the Temple Mount. Do this while you pray for peace. *Shalom.*

PUZZLING CHAPTER 65

See God and Live

IF YOU'VE BEEN AROUND CHURCH or read the Bible much, you've likely come across the statement, "No one can see God's face and live." That is recorded in the Bible: "But He said, 'You cannot see My face, for no man can see Me and live!'" (Exodus 33:20).

But one might make the case that you need to see God's face to really live. I'll explain. First, this issue is fuzzy, like a few others I've discovered along the way as recorded in God's Word, the Bible. I say this because most spiritual people believed they would die if they were to see God's face, but then recorded instances where they did see God's face in some form or fashion and lived. They expected to die but didn't for some reason or another, and instead became more spiritually aware and alive. Let's look at a few examples.

The oldest example was Jacob, Abraham's grandson, around 2000 BC: "So Jacob named the place Peniel, for he said, '**I have seen God face to face, yet my life has been preserved** [emphasis added]'" (Genesis 32:30). The next recorded instance of this issue was in the life of

Moses, around 1500 BC. Moses asked God to see His glory, and God responded as follows.

"The Lord said to Moses, 'I will also do this thing of which you have spoken; for you have found favor in My sight and I have known you by name.' Then Moses said, 'I pray You, show me Your glory!' And He said, 'I Myself will make all My goodness pass before you, and will proclaim the name of the Lord before you; and I will be gracious to whom I will be gracious, and will show compassion on whom I will show compassion.' But He said, '**You cannot see My face, for no man can see Me and live!**' Then the Lord said, 'Behold, there is a place by Me, and you shall stand there on the rock; and it will come about, while My glory is passing by, that I will put you in the cleft of the rock and cover you with My hand until I have passed by. Then I will take My hand away and you shall see My back, but My face shall not be seen [emphasis added]'" (Exodus 33:19-23).

We see someone here bold enough to want to see God's face. And we see something of God Who wants to reward one and commune with one in some way who truly wants a relationship and will risk it.

The next time we run across a similar instance was when Gideon was Judge of Israel around 1150 BC: "When Gideon realized that it was the angel of the Lord, he exclaimed, '**Alas, Sovereign Lord! I have seen the angel of the Lord face to face!' But the Lord said to him, 'Peace! Do not be afraid. You are not going to die.**' So Gideon built an altar to the Lord there and called it The Lord Is Peace. To this day it stands in Ophrah of the Abiezrites [emphasis added]'" (Judges 6:22-24 NIV). Interestingly the first word the Lord spoke to Gideon was "*Shalom,*" or peace. And in Gideon's summary of their encounter, Gideon built an altar named "*Yahweh Shalom,*" The LORD is Peace.

During the life of Isaiah the prophet, about 750 BC, during a dark historical time for the kings of Israel, he records: "In the year of King Uzziah's death I saw the Lord sitting on a throne, lofty and exalted, with the train of His robe filling the temple. Then I said, '**Woe is me,** for I am ruined! Because I am a man of unclean lips, and I live among a people of unclean lips; for my eyes have seen the King, the Lord of hosts** [emphasis added]" (Isaiah 6:1,5). When Isaiah is in the presence of the Lord, he sees his sin and that of his people. We also see immediately the Lord forgives Isaiah's sin and takes it away, enabling him to serve the Lord by willingly speaking whatever truths the Lord gives him. Isaiah becomes the greatest prophet in ancient Israel or the greatest writing prophet.

The Most Mystifying Example

To make a point and draw this fuzzy affair into focus, let's look at one more bizarre instance of seeing God and living to tell about it during Moses' time.

Last year during a church support trip to Honduras, Pastor Dario, the senior regional pastor, told me he had been reading through his Bible for a year and discovered this instance. I told him I was sure I'd read it because I'd read the Bible a few times. But I didn't recall it, and it hadn't stood out to either of us before like it was at this moment. Exodus 24 tells the story: **"Moses and Aaron, Nadab and Abihu, and the seventy elders of Israel went up and saw the God of Israel.** Under his feet was something like a pavement made of lapis lazuli, as bright blue as the sky. **But God did not raise his hand against these leaders of the Israelites; they saw God, and they ate and drank** [emphasis added]" (Exodus 24:10).

This event raises more questions than it gives answers. They saw God! And they only recorded a description of the pavement under His feet? Maybe everything above His feet was too bright white light and indescribable? Perhaps the Spirit just recorded what He wanted to record? And they ate and drank. That's puzzling! I'm pretty sure they didn't take anything up there to picnic if you read the fearful context of the meeting. So this hospitality was God's idea and something He alone could provide in this setting, along with the invitation. It seems like it could be the first communion and a type of things to come, or something like the wedding supper of the Lamb we see described in Revelation. This meal is unexpected but tells about God's humility, willingness to commune with humanity, and His awe-inducing splendor.

It began with Moses' humble prayer asking God if some others could come up and experience God as he had (Exodus 19:23). God said yes later (Exodus 24:1-2) after the people received the law and agreed to the covenant. They would bear His image among themselves and to the world. It was a time to celebrate life and relationship. It was a new day of a community seeing God and living. It was a day of people being changed into His image because they saw Him as He is (1 John 3:2, 1 Corinthians 13:12).

A Word of Caution to the Religious

I hesitate to write about this because the risk of seeing God is worth it for anyone. Yet being trite about the privilege of access to the King of the Universe, the all-powerful Creator, must be avoided. Religious leaders are most at risk of falling into this trap due to the praise accorded them, resulting in pride and a particular familiarity trap due to often handling the things of God. Being on the mountain and seeing God affected Aaron's two sons this way.

"Nadab and Abihu were the first two sons of Aaron the Levite by his marriage to Elisheba, daughter of Amminadab from the tribe of Judah. ... During the Exodus journey, after the Israelites affirmed their covenant with God, Abihu and Nadab accompanied Moses, Aaron, and 70 elders up Mount Sinai" (Wikipedia). What happened to Aaron's sons, Nadab and Abihu?

We read that later: "Aaron's sons Nadab and Abihu took their censers, put fire in them and added incense; and they offered unauthorized fire before the Lord, contrary to his command. So fire came out from the presence of the Lord and consumed them, and they died before the Lord. Moses then said to Aaron, 'This is what the Lord spoke of when he said: "Among those who approach me I will be proved holy; in the sight of all the people I will be honored." Aaron remained silent'" (Leviticus 10:1-3). Moses then directed the young men's cousins: "'Come here; carry your cousins outside the camp, away from the front of the sanctuary.' So they came and carried them, still in their tunics, outside the camp, as Moses ordered" (Leviticus 10:4b-5).

The two brothers of the dead priests were told not to mourn but to honor their responsibilities to God before the people more than their family relationships. The rest of the camp and relatives were allowed to mourn the loss of life.

A reasonable question many might ask is: "Why did God kill Nadab and Abihu?" The apparent reason stated in the Bible is because, as ministers of God before the people, they offered: "unauthorized fire before the Lord, contrary to his command." They didn't show the people the proper respect of the Lord because they didn't have it. Throughout history, we see people usually eat what the leaders put in the pot.

Might it be like Uzzah and the Ark (2 Samuel 6:3-7) or Ananias and Sapphira (Acts 5:1-11)? When God is making a chapter change in history and making things new, He may see fit to reestablish the "fear of the LORD," for everyone's benefit. Just a thought!

We Must See God

We must see God is the main point. Moses tells us: "The Lord our God has shown us his glory and his majesty, and we have heard his voice from the fire. Today we have seen that a person can live even if God speaks with them" (Deuteronomy 5:24 NIV).

Until His last days on earth, people wanted to see God: "They came to Philip, who was from Bethsaida in Galilee, with a request. 'Sir,' they said, 'we would like to see Jesus'" (John 12:21).

Jesus told Nicodemus: "Just as Moses lifted up the snake in the wilderness, so the Son of Man must be lifted up, that everyone who believes may have eternal life in him" (John 3:14-15).

Jesus told a close disciple: "Don't you know me, Philip, even after I have been among you such a long time? Anyone who has seen me has seen the Father. How can you say, 'Show us the Father?'" (John 14:9).

All Will See Him — As He Is

Don't be put off by this fuzzy, seemingly contradictory situation — seeing God and living or dying. It's a bit obscure and hidden for a reason. I would suggest it is for God's motives. He could make it crystal clear if He wanted to do so. Besides, if you ignore hundreds and hundreds of pieces of the Bible puzzle and God's story, that does fit together because a few intricate pieces may not work until the very end; this says more about you and your desires to know God than about God.

I humbly suggest that by looking intently into the Word of God when there appear to be contradictions, controversies, or paradoxes, you have perhaps the most to gain or discover about God. It may take time, an intense gaze, and asking in prayer for revelation, but it's worth it in any age and all ages. He is our very great reward.

John, who knew Him best, tells us: "Dear friends, now we are children of God, and what we will be has not yet been made known. But we know that when Christ appears, we shall be like Him, for we shall see Him as He is" (1 John 3:2). And Paul adds: "For now we see only a reflection as in a mirror; then we shall see face to face. Now I know in part; then I shall know fully, even as I am fully known" (1 Corinthians 13:12).

About the end of earth time, we read: "For the Lord himself shall descend from heaven with a shout, with the voice of the archangel, and with the trump of God: and the dead in Christ shall rise first: then we which are alive and remain shall be caught up together with them in the clouds, to meet the Lord in the air: and so shall we ever be with the Lord" (1 Thessalonians 4:16-17 KJV).

In a glimpse of the end of the matter, we're told: "And they shall see his face; and his name shall be in their foreheads. And there shall be no night there; and they need no candle, neither light of the sun; for the Lord God giveth them light: and they shall reign for ever and ever" (Revelation 22:4-6 NIV).

I would suggest we need to see the Lord whenever and wherever we can. Looking intently at the person of Jesus of Nazareth with the aid of the Holy Spirit to guide and illuminate us would be the best plan.

Do so while you hold in mystery all the truths the Bible tells us about seeing God: "No one has ever seen God, but the one and only Son, who is himself God and is in closest relationship with the Father, has made him known" (John 1:18). And: "Who alone is immortal and who lives in unapproachable light, whom no one has seen or can see. To him be honor and might forever. Amen" (1 Timothy 6:16).

"The Lord bless you and keep you; the Lord make his face shine on you and be gracious to you; the Lord turn his face toward you and give you peace"

(Numbers 6:24-26).

PUZZLING CHAPTER 66

Blessings at Gerizim

"Nothing gives rest but the sincere search for truth."
Blaise Pascal

Deuteronomy 28

Where are we, and how did we get here — as a church and nation? Doesn't that seem puzzling? It is to most if they are even aware our churches and country have plunged into some moral morass. This swamp has economic, health care, political, national, energy, business, security, and international ramifications unheard of and unexpected two short decades ago.

Shortly after the COVID-19 outbreak began in 2020, I read this chapter in a daily quiet time of reflecting and engaging the Bible. Deuteronomy 28 is timely and timeless in describing what's happening in America and speaks to what we need to do in response. As our country went into isolation for the better part of two years, that gave us time and a chance to ponder our ways, consider what was happening, and why it might be happening.

This chapter of the Bible describes an isolated situation. Still, it's far from isolated in its summary and the story it tells for ancient Israel, Israel through the ages, all nations through the ages, and the USA today.

I encourage you to read and meditate on the entire chapter so you can see its relevance. The message is very plain — the imagery is clear and explicit.

The Blessings

"**Now it shall be, if you diligently obey the Lord your God, being careful to do all His commandments which I command you today, the Lord your God will set you high above all the nations of the earth**. All these blessings will come upon you and overtake you if you obey the Lord your God:

"**The Lord shall cause your enemies who rise up against you to be defeated before you**; they will come out against you one way and will flee before you seven ways. **The Lord will command the blessing upon you in your barns and in all that you put your hand to, and He will bless you in the land which the Lord your God gives you.** The Lord will establish you as a holy people to Himself, as He swore to you, **if you keep the commandments of the Lord your God and walk in His ways**. So all the peoples of the earth will see that you are called by the name of the Lord, and they will be afraid of you. **The Lord will make you abound in prosperity, in the offspring of your body and in the offspring of your beast and in the produce of your ground,** in the land which the Lord swore to your fathers to give you. The Lord will open for you His good storehouse, the heavens, to **give rain to your land in its season and to bless all the work of your hand; and you shall lend to many nations, but you shall not borrow. The Lord will make you the head and not the tail, and you only** will be above, and you will not be underneath, if you listen to the commandments of the Lord your God,** which I charge you today, to observe them carefully, **and do not turn aside from any of the words which I command you today, to the right or to the left, to go after other gods to serve them** [emphasis added]"

(Deuteronomy 28:1-14).

Consequences of Disobedience

"**But it shall come about, if you do not obey the Lord your God, to observe to do all His commandments** and His statutes with which I charge you today, that all these curses will come upon you and overtake you:

"**The Lord will send upon you curses, confusion, and rebuke, in all you undertake to do, until you are destroyed and until you perish quickly, on account of the evil of your deeds, because you have forsaken Me. The Lord will make the pestilence cling to you until He has consumed you from the land where you are entering to possess it.** The Lord will smite you with consumption and with fever and with inflammation and with fiery heat and with the sword and with blight and with mildew, and they will pursue you until you perish. The heaven which is over your head shall be bronze, and the earth which is under you, iron. **The Lord will make the rain of your land powder and dust; from heaven it shall come down on you until you are destroyed.**

"**The Lord shall cause you to be defeated before your enemies; you will go out one way against them, but you will flee seven ways before them,** and you will be an example of terror to all the kingdoms of the earth. Your carcasses will be food to all birds of the sky and to the beasts of the earth, and there will be no one to frighten them away.

"The Lord will smite you with the boils of Egypt and with tumors and with the scab and with the itch, from which you cannot be healed. **The Lord will smite you with madness and with blindness and with bewilderment of heart; and you will grope at noon, as the blind man gropes in darkness, and you will not prosper in your ways; but you shall only be oppressed and robbed continually, with none to save you.** You shall betroth a wife, but another man will violate her; you shall build a house, but you will not live in it; you shall plant a vineyard, but you will not use its fruit. …**Your sons and your daughters shall be given to another people,** while your eyes look on and yearn for them continually; but there will be nothing you can do. **A people whom you do not know shall eat up the produce of your ground and all your labors, and you will never be anything but oppressed and crushed continually. You shall be driven mad by the sight of what you see.** … **The Lord will bring you and your king, whom you set over you, to a nation which neither you nor your fathers have known, and there you shall serve other gods, wood and stone.** You shall become a horror, a proverb, and a taunt among all the people where the Lord drives you.

"You shall bring out much seed to the field but you will gather in little, for the locust will consume it. You shall plant and cultivate vineyards, but you will neither drink of the wine nor gather the grapes, for the worm will devour them. You shall have olive trees throughout your territory but you will not anoint yourself with the oil, for your olives will drop off. **You shall have sons and daughters but they will not be yours, for they will go into captivity.** The cricket shall possess all your trees and the produce of your ground. **The alien who is among you shall rise above you higher and higher, but you will go down lower and lower. He shall lend to you, but you will not lend to him; he shall be the head, and you will be the tail.**

"So all these curses shall come on you and pursue you and overtake you until you are destroyed, because you would not obey the Lord your God by keeping His commandments and His statutes which He commanded you. They shall become a sign and a wonder on you and your descendants forever.

"Because you did not serve the Lord your God with joy and a glad heart, for the abundance of all things; therefore you shall serve your enemies whom the Lord will send against you, in hunger, in thirst, in nakedness, and in the lack of all things; and He will put an iron yoke on your neck until He has destroyed you.

"**The Lord will bring a nation against you from afar, from the end of the earth, as the eagle swoops down, a nation whose language you shall not understand, a nation of fierce countenance who will have no respect for the old, nor show favor to the young.** Moreover, it shall eat the offspring of your herd and the produce of your ground until you are destroyed, who also leaves you no grain, new wine, or oil, nor the increase of your herd or the young of your flock until they have caused you to perish. **It shall besiege you in all your towns until your high and fortified walls in which you trusted come down throughout your land, and it shall besiege you in all your towns throughout your land which the Lord your God has given you.** ...

"**If you are not careful to observe all the words of this law which are written in this book, to fear this honored and awesome name, the Lord your God, then the Lord will bring extraordinary plagues on you and your descendants, even severe and lasting plagues, and miserable and chronic sicknesses.** ... **It shall come about that as the Lord delighted over you to prosper you, and multiply you, so the Lord will delight over you to make you perish and destroy you; and you will be torn from the land where you are entering to possess it.** Moreover, the Lord will scatter you among all peoples, from one end of the earth to the other end of the earth; and there you shall serve other gods, wood and stone, which you or your fathers have not known. Among those nations you shall find no rest, and there will be no resting place for the sole of your foot; but there **the Lord will give** you a trembling heart, failing of eyes, and despair of soul. So your life shall hang in doubt before you; and you will be in dread night and day, and shall have no assurance of your life.** In the morning you shall say, 'Would that it were evening!' And at evening you shall say, 'Would that it were morning!' **because of the dread of your heart which you dread,** and for the sight of your eyes which you will see. ... And there **you will offer yourselves for sale to your enemies as male and female slaves, but there will be no buyer"**

(Deuteronomy 28:15-68).

Israel Through the Ages

If you know a little history and your Bible, you'll recognize Israel through the ages when reading Deuteronomy 28. She has lived long enough to see this scenario played out many times.

The blessings and cursings are played out several times recorded in the book of Judges. They are repeated many times during the kings of Israel culminating in the conquest of the ten northern tribes in 722 BC and the two southern tribes in 586 BC. This second conquest resulted in the destruction of the temple and the end of the monarchy. Twenty-five hundred years later — May 14, 1948 — Israel again became an independent, sovereign nation.

At that time, she became a nation "born in a day" by her covenant God's word, grace, and mercy. She remains the national image-bearer for how God rules among the nations as they attempt to govern themselves with generous amounts of His grace interspersed with His judgments and corrections — another form of grace.

God gives us images of how nations should act according to just and moral laws and what happens to them in due time when they do not. He bestowed through Israel the moral law — the Ten Commandments — which informs the laws of most nations worldwide.

God tells us that the nations of the earth are somewhat insignificant to Him: "Behold, the nations are like a drop from a bucket, and are regarded as a speck of dust on the scales; behold, He lifts up the islands like fine dust" (Isaiah 40:15). But He also gives essential hints or guidance for how they can succeed: "Blessed is the nation whose God is the Lord" (Psalm 33:12a). And: "Righteousness exalts a nation, but sin is a disgrace to any people" (Proverbs 14:34). God goes on to say Who will judge such matters: "Before the Lord, for He is coming, for He is coming to judge the earth. He will judge the world in righteousness and the peoples in His faithfulness" (Psalm 96:13). And: "He ordered us to preach to the people, and solemnly to testify that this is the One who has been appointed by God as Judge of the living and the dead" (Acts 10:42).

Historical Perspective — Rome

So we've seen Biblical and historical perspectives on where we are and how we got here. Much of the rest of this puzzle is devoted to how we should live in these times. To aid in this, we should look at Roman times, because they mirror our times.

We see what was going on then is going on now. Paul gives us ways to address the truth. He starts his letter to the Romans blessing the Roman Christians: "To all in Rome who are loved by God and called to be his holy people: Grace and peace to you from God our Father and from the Lord Jesus Christ" (Romans 1:7). He tells them he's longed to be with them: "...so that I [Paul] may impart to you some spiritual gift to make you strong— that is, that you and I may be mutually encouraged by each other's faith" (Romans 1:11-12).

The book of Romans is a worthy read. It was written 6th of the 13 epistles but placed first by the church fathers and early church councils. It came to be known as the "Gate Keeper Epistle." Other books of the New Testament had to pass through Romans' lens of truth. John Piper said Romans is "the most important theological, Christian work ever written." Ben Merkle says: "No other letter in the history of the world has received as much attention or has been given as much consideration as Paul's letter to the church at Rome. . . . Paul's letter to the church at Rome is the greatest letter ever written because of its great impact in history, its grand theology about Christ, and its practical instructions for Christian living."

Martin Luther: "This epistle [Romans] is really the chief part of the New Testament, and is truly the purest gospel." John Calvin: "When any one understands this Epistle, he has a passage opened to him to the understanding of the whole Scripture." J. I. Packer: "All roads in the Bible lead to Romans, and all views afforded by the Bible are seen most clearly from Romans, and when the message of Romans gets into a person's heart there is no telling what may happen." Paul was martyred in Rome about 66 AD, a willing sacrifice for his King and the church, Christ's bride whom he loved. We can trust its timely, timeless message.

I am attending a semester-long Bible study on Romans at the moment. We're only three chapters into the book, but I want to share with you from these chapters how Romans ties in to Deuteronomy 28, written some 1500 years earlier. God is working His plan through every epoch, age, and culture, sharing His eternal truths with all, noticing who will listen, acting as judge, while dispensing mercy and grace.

When writing to the Roman Christians, Paul wasted no time getting right into an overview of the Gospel and his call and position of authority. He then stated his purpose and plan: "**I am under obligation both to Greeks and to barbarians, both to the wise and to the foolish. So, for my part, I am eager to preach the gospel to you also who are in Rome. For I am not ashamed of the gospel, for it is the power of God for salvation to everyone who believes**, to the Jew first and also to the Greek. For in it **the righteousness of God is revealed from faith to faith; as it is written, 'But the righteous man shall live by faith** [emphasis added]'" (Romans 1:14-17). These truths are incredibly insightful and profound in light of Scripture, and we're not even out of chapter one.

While still in the chapter, Paul launches into the biggest problems of the day with confrontational truth, confronting the culture and maybe the church: "For **the wrath of God is revealed from heaven against all ungodliness and unrighteousness of men who suppress the truth in unrighteousness**…Professing to be wise, **they became fools, and exchanged the glory of the incorruptible God for an image in the form of corruptible man**… Therefore **God gave them over in the lusts of their hearts to impurity, so that their bodies would be dishonored among them. For they exchanged the truth of God for a lie, and worshiped and served the creature rather than the Creator**, who is blessed forever. Amen [emphasis added]" (Romans 1:18, 22-23a, 24-25).

Paul continues to state the problems and reasons for them, all in chapter one, before explaining God's solution and plan in practical, legal, and spiritual ways in the remaining parts of the epistle: "**For this reason God gave them over to degrading passions; for their women exchanged the natural function for that which is unnatural, and in the same way also the men abandoned the natural function of the woman and burned in their desire toward one another, men with men committing indecent acts and receiving in their own persons the due penalty of their error.**

"And just as **they did not see fit to acknowledge God any longer, God gave them over to a depraved mind, to do those things which are not proper**, being filled with all unrighteousness, wickedness, greed, evil; full of envy, murder, strife, deceit, malice; they are gossips, slanderers, haters of God, insolent, arrogant, boastful, inventors of evil, disobedient to parents, without understanding, untrustworthy, unloving, unmerciful; and although they know the ordinance of God, that **those who practice such things are worthy of death, they not only do the same, but also give hearty approval to those who practice**

them [emphasis added]" (Romans 1:26-32).

You can't say it any better or plainer than that. And you might as well say it like it is. Remember the duck test: "If it looks like a duck, swims like a duck, and quacks like a duck, then it probably is a duck." Or the idiom: "If the shoe fits, wear it." Better yet, as the Scripture attests: "For **the word of God is living and active and sharper than any two-edged sword, and piercing as far as the division of soul and spirit,** of both joints and marrow, and **able to judge the thoughts and intentions of the heart** [emphasis added]" (Hebrews 4:12).

Chapters 1-2-3

That's only chapter one of Romans. Chapter two tells us God is impartial, and being Jewish isn't as important to Him as one's heart. The heart is the most-mentioned subject in the Bible, some 750 times — *kardia* is the heart, soul, you! John Eldridge tells us it's not as important what the Gospel does for us as what it does to us. The last words of chapter two read: "For he is not a Jew who is one outwardly, nor is circumcision that which is outward in the flesh. But he is a Jew who is one inwardly; and **circumcision is that which is of the heart, by the Spirit,** not by the letter; and **his praise is not from men, but from God** [emphasis added]" (Romans 2:28-29). As we're reminded many times in the Old Testament, "the Lord weighs hearts" (Proverbs 21:2, 2 Chronicles 16:9).

In Romans 3, Paul reminds us that God condemns the immoral, the moralist, the law-bound Jew with an uncircumcised heart, and all men equally: "**there is no distinction; for all have sinned and fall short of the glory of God**" (Romans 3:22b-23). Paul, in chapter three, quotes Isaiah about humankind's condition and cause: "**And the path of peace they have not known. There is no fear of God before their eyes** [emphasis added]" (Romans 3:17-18).

Romans has sixteen chapters and ends very relationally, calling several friends and saints by name before ending on this grace-filled note: "**Now to him who is able to establish you in accordance with my gospel, the message I proclaim about Jesus Christ**, in keeping with the revelation of the mystery hidden for long ages past, but now revealed and made known through the prophetic writings by the command of the eternal God, so that all **the Gentiles might come to the obedience that comes from faith— to the only wise God be glory forever through Jesus Christ! Amen** [emphasis added]" (Romans 16:25-27 NIV).

Grace Abounds

One of my favorite verses from Romans, and one that certainly fits our times is: "But **where sin abounded, grace abounded much more**, so that as sin reigned in death, even so grace might reign through righteousness to eternal life through Jesus Christ our Lord [emphasis added]" (Romans 5:20b-21 NKJV).

Deuteronomy 28 is not the end of the story. Romans adds and builds on God's ways, by adding the Gentiles into God's family, and being very clear about what God's ways are v.s. the culture of the Romans 57 AD. Romans illuminates the cause and effect of our ills as a church and nation. It would be wise if we could see that and own those ills, especially the church. Another favorite verse from Romans comes to mind: "… let God be found true, though every man be found a liar" (Romans 3:4b). God does not change, He is the same yesterday, today, and forever. But that is also why we are not consumed: "Remember my affliction and my wandering, the wormwood and bitterness. Surely my soul remembers and is bowed down within me. This I recall to my mind, therefore I have hope. The Lord's lovingkindnesses indeed never cease, for His compassions never fail. They are new every morning; great is Your faithfulness" (Lamentations 3:19-23).

I don't want to deviate far from the main point of this chapter:

where we are as a church and nation. A day of meditation on Deuteronomy 28, applying it to our country and church would be beneficial. We should agree with God and humble ourselves before Him, praying for mercy and forgiveness, healing and help.

There Is Mercy With God

The beautiful lament of the prophet Jeremiah continues below the verses cited above. I would recommend you read and meditate on all of Lamentations three. It was written during a time like ours, before Babylon carried ancient Israel away as prisoners.

Some portions stood out as I read them just now: "'**The Lord is my portion,**' says my soul, '**therefore I have hope in Him.' The Lord is good to those who wait for Him**, to the person who seeks Him. **It is good that he waits silently for the salvation of the Lord** [emphasis added]" (Lamentations 3:24-26).

"Let him **sit alone** and **be silent** since He has laid it on him. Let him put his mouth in the dust, **perhaps there is hope**. Let him give his cheek to the smiter, let him **be filled with reproach**. For **the Lord will not reject forever, for if He causes grief, then He will have compassion according to His abundant lovingkindness.** For He does not afflict willingly or grieve the sons of men. To crush under His feet all the prisoners of the land, to deprive a man of justice in the presence of the Most High, to defraud a man in his lawsuit— of these things the Lord does not approve. Who is there who speaks and it comes to pass, unless the Lord has commanded it? **Is it not from the mouth of the Most High that both good and ill go forth? Why should any living mortal, or any man, offer complaint in view of his sins? Let us examine and probe our ways, and let us return to the Lord**. We lift up our heart and hands toward God in heaven; '**The Lord is my portion,**' says my soul, therefore **I have hope** in Him [emphasis added]'" (Lamentations 3:28-41).

You can be active and should be involved in this time of judgment, correction, and pestilence. Pray to the Lord. Light a candle instead of cursing the darkness. Be aware of Who is in control and Who is making these corrections for our good. Expect grace (power) will abound to you as you pray and serve others, acting redemptively during this time, led by His Spirit. Also accept your part in what has happened. Amen.

Take Courage and Speak Up

Another thing comes to mind in how to act during these times of polarized good versus evil and darkness calling itself light — a time of deceit and deception becoming increasingly aggressive. That is, speaking up when you have the opportunity and leading to do so. Let the Spirit be your guide, but look for opportunities to speak to a neighbor, pointing to the Biblical truth of a matter gently and in love. Maybe write a newspaper article. Maybe start a blog, not arguing any point, but just stating Bible truth, and let the fact speak for itself. God's Word doesn't return to Him void but accomplishes what He sends it to do (Isaiah 55:11). And remember, the sword of the Spirit is the Word of God (Ephesians 6:17) — it's not your sword, so let Him wield it as He wishes. You are only the courageous messenger. You can humbly remind your audience: "Don't shoot the messenger." The Spirit of God can fend for Himself.

Speak Up

I add this note because a dear friend came over today and shared with me Eric Metaxas' new book, *Letter to the American Church*. I haven't started it yet, but Amazon's website says of it: "In an earnest and searing wake-up call, the author of the bestseller *Bonhoeffer: Pastor, Martyr, Prophet, Spy* warns of the haunting similarities between today's American church and the German church of the 1930s. Echoing Bonhoeffer's prophetic call, Eric Metaxas exhorts his fellow Christians to repent of their silence in the face of evil before it is too late.

"Can it really be God's will that His children be silent at a time like this? Decrying the cowardice that masquerades as godly meekness, Eric Metaxas summons the Church to battle.

"The author of a bestselling biography of Dietrich Bonhoeffer, Metaxas reveals the haunting similarities between today's American Church and the German Church of the 1930s. Echoing the German martyr's prophetic call, he exhorts his fellow Christians to repent of their silence in the face of evil.

"An attenuated and unbiblical 'faith' based on what Bonhoeffer called 'cheap grace' has sapped the spiritual vitality of millions of Americans. Paying lip service to an insipid 'evangelism,' they shrink from combating the evils of our time. Metaxas refutes the pernicious lie that fighting evil politicizes Christianity. As Bonhoeffer and other heroes of the faith insisted, the Church has an irreplaceable role in the culture of a nation. It is our duty to fight the powers of darkness, especially on behalf of the weak and vulnerable.

"Silence is not an option. God calls us to defend the unborn, to confront the lies of cultural Marxism, and to battle the globalist tyranny that crushes human freedom. Confident that this is His fight, the Church must overcome fear and enter the fray, armed with the spiritual weapons of prayer, self-sacrifice, and love."

Summing a major message of Dietrich Bonhoeffer, Metaxas writes: "Silence in the face of evil is itself evil. Not to speak is to speak. Not to act is to act. God will not hold us guiltless."

Live Faithful Lives Before God

Living faithful lives in obedience to God and His ways is a powerful deterrent to evil and God's judgment of the same. We read in Samuel's farewell address these remarks: "If you will fear the Lord and serve

Him, and listen to His voice and not rebel against the command of the Lord, then both you and also the king who reigns over you will follow the Lord your God. If you will not listen to the voice of the Lord, but rebel against the command of the Lord, then the hand of the Lord will be against you, as it was against your fathers" (1 Samuel 12:14-15).

The end of that sacred event speaks to living faithful lives and to our times: "Then all the people said to Samuel, 'Pray for your servants to the Lord your God, so that we may not die, for we have added to all our sins this evil by asking for ourselves a king.' Samuel said to the people, 'Do not fear. You have committed all this evil, yet do not turn aside from following the Lord, but serve the Lord with all your heart. You must not turn aside, for then you would go after futile things which can not profit or deliver, because they are futile. For the Lord will not abandon His people on account of His great name, because the Lord has been pleased to make you a people for Himself. Moreover, as for me, far be it from me that I should sin against the Lord by ceasing to pray for you; but I will instruct you in the good and right way. Only fear the Lord and serve Him in truth with all your heart; for consider what great things He has done for you. But if you still do wickedly, both you and your king will be swept away'" (1 Samuel 12:19-25).

Courage, Faith, Grace

Faithful, obedient lives are valuable to the Lord. They catch His ever-watchful eye. So do courage, faith, and His grace at work. I love the biographies of Michael Medved and agree with his assessment that America is exceptional in history in much the same way Israel is exceptional. Most would cite our founding fathers' sacrifice, service, search for religious freedom, and fear of God as the reasons for these similarities.

I love some of the founding leaders Medved picked to tell us their stories. In *God's Hand on America: Divine Providence in the Modern Era*, we have the stories of people not so noble who do have courage and seem to have destiny on their side for protection and success. In one of Medved's earlier books, his biography of Sam Houston is still my favorite — a must-read for any Texan or historian of how Texas came to be. Our nation's history is littered with these stories — any puzzler's dream.

John Adams, in 1765 wrote: "I always consider the settlement of America with Reverence and Wonder — as the Opening of a grand scene and Design in Providence, for the Illumination of the Ignorant and the Emancipation of the slavish Part of Mankind all over the earth."

Edmund Burke wrote in 1791: "As to great and commanding talents, they are the gift of Providence and some way unknown to us. They rise where they are least expected."

Abraham Lincoln, in 1840 wrote: "If ever I feel the soul within me elevate and expand to these dimensions not wholly unworthy of its Almighty Architect, it is when I contemplate the cause of my country...."

Pray to the God of heaven, don't give up on our country, and do what you can to invite and wield God's grace in helping America out of this impasse. Above all, fear God, keep His commandments — seek His peace, and know His love. Godspeed as you journey.

PUZZLING CHAPTER 67

Twenty Years

Holy God

Another piece of this puzzle ended with: "But the Lord killed seventy men from Beth-shemesh because they looked into the Ark of the Lord. And the people mourned greatly because of what the Lord had done. **'Who is able to stand in the presence of the Lord, this holy God?'** they cried out. **'Where can we send the Ark from here?'** So they sent messengers to the people at Kiriath-jearim and told them, 'The Philistines have returned the Ark of the Lord. Come here and get it! [emphasis added]'" (1 Samuel 6:19-21 NLT).

The people of God disrespected the Ark of the Presence. Many died, including seventy men from the village who looked into the Ark. Maybe they were ignorant and didn't know it was forbidden. Maybe just curious? We don't know their motives or what they knew, and it's a moot point. God's people should learn His ways by reading His Word and being taught by those set aside to teach His ways.

Grief-struck and confused, they sent a message to a village in the forest near Jerusalem to some God-fearing priests, asking them to come to take the Ark of the Presence away from them, exclaiming, "Who is able to stand in the presence of this holy God?" It's a good question, isn't it.

Seemed Abandoned

"So the men of Kiriath-jearim came to get the Ark of the Lord. They took it to the hillside home of Abinadab and ordained Eleazar, his son, to be in charge of it. **The Ark remained in Kiriath-jearim for a long time—twenty years** in all. During that time all **Israel mourned because it seemed the Lord had abandoned them** [emphasis added]" (1 Samuel 7:1-2).

This sounds very familiar, doesn't it? If you've heard conversations around the country, on social media, and in churches, you've listened to the same sentiment expressed. Is the Lord punishing us? Has he abandoned us — our church and our nation? "Who abandoned who?" might be a more appropriate question.

It feels like we're in the process of puzzling that out and kicking the can down the road to see what happens next. But the question hangs in the air. Twenty years is a long time for such a question to remain unanswered and evaluated. The way things seem to have sped up in our technologically advancing world, especially with communication, that time may equate to two years today. Who knows? He Who looks upon the heart knows, and it's His decision.

I'm not saying that the situation in ancient Israel is prophetically speaking about our situation as a church and culture. There are many times of apostasy and correction, followed by repentance or judgment, recorded in the Bible and history. In general, it fits. But I leave that for you to puzzle out.

Let's look at some details of how it played out in Israel, and you can decide what you think.

Something Changed

Something changed. The people made their decision during the twenty years when it seemed like the Lord had abandoned them. They wanted Him back if He would accept them again — a good plan and posture.

The Lord saw their repentant hearts and sent word to them by His prophet: "Then Samuel said to all the people of Israel, **'If you want to return to the Lord with all your hearts, get rid of your foreign gods and your images of Ashtoreth. Turn your hearts to the Lord and obey him alone; then he will rescue you from the Philistines**. So **the Israelites got rid of their images** of Baal and Ashtoreth **and worshiped only the Lord** [emphasis added]" (1 Samuel 7:3-4).

It doesn't always happen this way. Do 722 BC and 586 BC ring a bell? They should. In 722 BC, the ten northern tribes of Israel were conquered by Assyria and led away into captivity, never to be the same again. This was after years of apostasy, idolatry, and child sacrifice trying to look like the nations around them. God sent prophets to speak the truth to them in love about where their course was taking them. They did not listen or repent.

In 586 BC, the two southern tribes of Israel, Judah and Benjamin, commonly referred to as Judah, were carried into captivity by Babylon for the same reasons. This happened even after they saw what happened to their brothers to the north, had a few good kings exercising moral leadership, and prophets sent from God with the loving, truthful message about choices — where apostasy, idolatry, and unrighteous living was taking them. They didn't listen, and Babylon destroyed their temple, religious system, capital, and country. They were captives for seventy years in a foreign land of other gods and violent people. Then because of God's faithfulness and His promise to Abraham, Isaac, Jacob, David, and others, He brought them back into the land and a relationship with Him. It was due to His grace, His mercy, and to accomplish His plan to have a relationship with humans who would also choose

Him. This plan would involve a future king coming during the Roman empire and returning as a Lamb and a Lion at the end of the age.

God's invitation to righteous living and relationship usually comes to people of faith, the religious who have lost their way, or some covenant people — but not always. Do you remember the story of Jonah and Nineveh? It's a fascinating story told in the short book of Jonah in the Bible. It has many beautiful themes and even the intrigue of one of God's prophets running away from God. This prophet did not mind preaching that this evil city must repent or be destroyed. He rather enjoyed that part. But what he feared might happen did happen. The king and people repented, and God forgave them and showed mercy. This indicates God's heart and goodwill toward humans and the magnitude of His grace and mercy. It shows how much He values repentance and humility. It shows He is no respecter of persons or religions but views all people equally. He will also show favor to whom He wishes. He is the Lord.

Interestingly, Jonah prophesied only a few decades before Assyria, with its capital in Nineveh, attacked Israel and carried them away as a judgment from the Lord. But let's get back to Israel three hundred years earlier and our story of choices.

Put Away Your Idols

Above we read: "**So the Israelites got rid of their images of Baal and Ashtoreth and worshiped only the Lord** [emphasis added]" (1 Samuel 7:4). This is such a short verse, but it's so important. It's the crux of the whole matter. God acts the same yesterday, today, and forever. But people do not.

You might be surprised at what happens next, but you shouldn't be. It's ubiquitous in human experience and routinely recorded in these types of instances in the Bible. An enemy immediately attacks.

Attack!

The people have just rent their hearts before God. They made a quality decision to follow Him only and put away their idols. God made them painfully aware idol worship was destroying them and their relationship with Him.

So indeed, nothing terrible should happen to them now. You wouldn't think so, but the enemy is prone to attack at such times. And so it was: "Then Samuel told them, 'Gather all of Israel to Mizpah, and I will pray to the Lord for you.' So they gathered at Mizpah and, **in a great ceremony, drew water from a well and poured it out before the Lord. They also went without food all day and confessed that they had sinned against the Lord**. (It was at Mizpah that Samuel became Israel's judge.) **When the Philistine rulers heard that Israel had gathered at Mizpah, they mobilized their army and advanced. The Israelites were badly frightened** when they learned that the Philistines were approaching [emphasis added]" (1 Samuel 7:5-7).

I just noticed that it was at Mizpah Samuel became judge officially over Israel. Mizpah in Hebrew means "watchtower." Samuel watched what was going on in Israel during these twenty years in the people's hearts and heard the word of the Lord. It may symbolize that God is watching them always — He sees. But at this moment, someone in the watchtower saw their enemies approaching in military formation. They certainly hadn't expected something like this, weren't prepared for war, and were now in desperate straights.

The Philistines forgot God's plagues, pestilence, and power that had visited their land twenty years earlier. Maybe they had a new leadership? Perhaps they remembered how they loved it when the children of God served them and their gods. At any rate, they had military intelligence that the whole nation was gathered at Mizpah for some religious or national ceremony and unprepared for war. It was a perfect time for a surprise attack and maybe even to kill or capture their leader Samuel.

In hindsight, which they say is 20/20, this was a perfect time for Israel to be attacked. It benefited them greatly, as we shall see.

Here's a funny thought about hindsight being 20/20. If you read history and the Bible, it seems like hindsight isn't 20/20, at least for long. I remember a quote from my western civilization book in college: "History teaches us that man learns nothing from History." Winston Churchill said: "Is the only lesson of history to be that mankind is unteachable?" A wise one said: "What has been will be again, what has been done will be done again; there is nothing new under the sun" (Ecclesiastes 1:9 NIV). The truth of this matter may resolve into what I tell people lately, "I have a good memory, but it's short." Twenty years seems like a short time to forget such monumental lessons, but it happens. We'll see later that it happens in Israel again in about another twenty years.

But this day, with the enemy at the door having the advantage of surprise, Israel acts differently than when they dragged the Ark into battle with them. They pray and look to God for help and deliverance: "'Don't stop pleading with the Lord our God to save us from the Philistines!' they begged Samuel. So Samuel took a young lamb and offered it to the Lord as a whole burnt offering. He pleaded with the Lord to help Israel, and the Lord answered him" (1 Samuel 7:8-9).

God answered as only He can, delivering His people and putting a healthy fear of the Lord into His own and their enemies. What looked like a disaster in the making turned into a celebration of God's power, love, and protection — a triumph over those wishing to steal from them, kill them, and enslave them. The fighting and attacks stop, and peace reigns. The enemies of God's people lose interest in attacking God's people, at least for a while. They are living in the right relationship now and under God's protection.

The Bible describes the scene: "Just as Samuel was sacrificing the burnt offering, the Philistines arrived to attack Israel. But the Lord spoke with a mighty voice of thunder from heaven that day, and the

Philistines were thrown into such confusion that the Israelites defeated them. The men of Israel chased them from Mizpah to a place below Beth-car, slaughtering them all along the way" (1 Samuel 7:10-11).

I mentioned the name Mizpah means "watchtower." God is watching his people, their enemies, and all cultures and peoples of the earth. Interestingly, they pursued their enemies in a rout caused by the Lord, as far as Beth-car, which means "the place of the lamb." It seems that the battle stops here, and peace is restored here, for the people of God, the enemies of God, for everyone — at the place of the Lamb. It's just a thought.

Synchronicity

Oddly and coincidentally, our pastor taught from this text and story in his sermon last week. He said there was a time in his life when he was playing spiritual games. He was going through the motions expected in his religious life, but his private life was a mess. There were no big sins or moral issues, but his marriage wasn't going all that well, nor was the rest of his family and friendship life. Then he had a moment of clarity, and things started to change.

That's what happened in Israel if you didn't catch it. They heard Samuel speak what God was saying. Their reply was, "We have sinned against the Lord." They then put away their foreign gods, directed their hearts toward the Lord, and decided to serve him only. They even had a public day of ceremony where they poured out water to the Lord, fasted, and confessed they had sinned against the Lord.

They demonstrated their sincerity, albeit under duress, by praying and calling out to the Lord instead of trying to drag their religion into the situation. God let them fall on their face, and then he thundered in their hearing, protection, and defense.

Interestingly, Baal, the major Canaanite god, was thought to be the strongest and most dominant god of the region and the earth, the god of the storm: "Among Baal's titles were 'Rider of the Clouds,' 'Almighty,' and 'Lord of the Earth.' He was the god of both fertility and the thunderstorm, as well as a mighty warrior, sometimes a sun god and the protector of crops and livestock" (New World Encyclopedia). The God of Israel chose a storm and power display, the likes of which they had never experienced, to set the record straight and drive the enemy away.

The God of Israel sends a storm on the enemies of Israel. He doesn't give them the cold shoulder for their past transgressions but real help when they turn to him in sincere humility and repentance. The whole story of the Bible is that we can expect the same.

The Stone of Help

Samuel knew the people of God would need help to remember all that happened and break the twenty-year cycle: "Samuel then took a large stone and placed it between the towns of Mizpah and Jeshanah. He named it Ebenezer (which means 'the stone of help'), for he said, **'Up to this point the Lord has helped us!** [emphasis added]'" (1 Samuel 7:12). That's brilliant and shows what a seer Samuel was. It was as if he pointed out to the people that the Lord has graced them with His help "up to this point," but this isn't the end of the matter or warfare living in a pagan world. He knew they would need to experience and live in God's grace and help going forward. This has proved true to this very day and is an integral part of the valid Gospel message. Christianity is not a do-it-yourself project or proposition. Grace is required.

We can say with the faith community in ancient Israel: "Up until now," we can see the Lord has helped us. He's shown us some tough love by letting us see our needs. We've learned that no matter how far or long we've drifted away from the Lord, we only need to do a humble 180-degree turn to be restored to Him. Paul said it this way: "**But God**, being rich in mercy, because of His great love with which He loved us, even when we were dead in our transgressions, made us alive together with Christ (by grace you have been saved), and raised us up with Him, and seated us with Him in the heavenly places in Christ Jesus, so that in the ages to come He might show the surpassing riches of His grace in kindness toward us in Christ Jesus [emphasis added]" (Ephesians 2:4-7).

I asked my wife what she heard in the pastor's sermon. She replied, "Leave idols, commit to God, and follow through." You can't say it much more succinctly than that. It's what God asks of us and what we must do to experience Him anew and live a life of freedom from sin — a life of love, joy, and grace. They did, and we can too. The opportunity and invitation are out there for you. And by His Spirit, you'll have help. Just make the sincere, humble, quality decision and start walking. And it doesn't hurt to ask daily in prayer for His help — grace. His ear is open to your cry.

A Generation of Peace

God loves peace. You get that as you read the Bible. One of His names is Jehovah *Shalom* — God of Peace. He chose for His Name to dwell on the earth in Jerusalem — the City of Peace. The beautiful, ancient (3500-year-old) Aaronic blessing given by God to Moses for the High Priest Aaron to bless the sons of Israel goes like this: "The Lord bless you, and keep you; the Lord make His face shine on you, and be gracious to you; the Lord lift up His countenance on you, and give you peace" (Numbers 6:24-26).

Peace came to Israel because their change of heart and actions showed they wanted to walk again with God. So this is a "They lived happily ever after" story. The Bible tells it this way: "**So the Philistines were subdued and didn't invade Israel again for some time.** And throughout Samuel's lifetime, the Lord's powerful hand was raised against the Philistines. The **Israelite villages** near Ekron and Gath that the Philistines had captured **were restored to Israel**, along with the rest of the territory that the Philistines had taken. And **there was peace between Israel and the Amorites in those days** [emphasis added]" (1 Samuel 7:13-14).

It goes on to say: "**Samuel continued as Israel's judge for the rest of his life**. Each year he traveled around, setting up his court first at Bethel, then at Gilgal, and then at Mizpah. He judged the people of Israel at each of these places. Then he would return to his home at Ramah, and he would hear cases there, too. **And Samuel built an altar to the Lord at Ramah**" (1 Samuel 7:15-17).

This sounds like a beautiful end to a beautiful chapter in Samuel's life and of the people of God whom he led. And it is. The Spirit inspired the writer to indicate this accurate summary. You can feel the peaceful, happy life they lived walking with God under moral leadership. It is reminiscent of the New Testament definition of the Kingdom of God: "For the kingdom of God is … righteousness and peace and joy in the Holy Spirit" (Romans 14:17).

Twenty Years Strikes Again

Looking at the Bible, the next chapter starts like this: "**As Samuel grew old, he appointed his sons to be judges over Israel**. Joel and Abijah, his oldest sons, held court in Beersheba. But **they were not like their father, for they were greedy for money. They accepted bribes and perverted justice** [emphasis added]" (1 Samuel 8:1-3).

Chapter seven of First Samuel shows national repentance and a peaceful, prosperous time in Israel as the people seek and obey the Lord. But trouble is brewing again. If the restoration mentioned above came in the middle of Samuel's life, he might have reasonably been forty years old, with his oldest sons being twenty years old. Now they are old enough to be judges in the important city on Israel's southern border, Abraham's abode one thousand years earlier, Beersheba. We're not given the chronology, but the elapsed time could likely be twenty years.

I know what you're thinking, "How could the sons of righteous Samuel turn out as poorly as the sons of Eli, the previous judge?" There are some distinctions. God reprimanded Eli for not correcting his sons. We don't see this in the case of Samuel. Samuel named his oldest two boys Joel, which means "Jehovah is God," and Abijah, which means "Jehovah is my father." And he sent them to serve the people in Beersheba, which means "well of the sevenfold oath," a reminder they were to be a covenant-keeping people. But they made their own decisions.

This demonstrates the adage that God has no grandchildren, only children. And it shows the acorn doesn't always fall close to the tree. We see in God's sight and the elders of Israel's sight that character, not chromosomes, determines fitness to lead. So here we are, about twenty years later, and Israel is staring at a vacuum in leadership.

The Bible puts it this way: "Finally, all the elders of Israel met at Ramah to discuss the matter with Samuel. '**Look,' they told him, 'you are now old, and your sons are not like you. Give us a king to judge us like all the other nations have** [emphasis added]'" (1 Samuel 8:4-5).

The Scripture doesn't pull any punches. It gets right to the point. But this is a new twist in the people's hearts — they are asking for a king. Or is it an old twist resurfacing that they want to be like the nations around them — a subculture, not a counter-culture, which God's people most always are and are to be? You can decide.

You already have enough pieces of the puzzle to decide if you think this time and situation in Israel's history speaks to our time and what might be in store for our churches and nation. So I want to wrap this up, and make a few attendant observations.

Are we in a vacuum of leadership too? Does this go hand in hand with people getting lukewarm in their relationship with God? Have we started to put our trust in man and government? And then, will God give us what we ask for as punishment and reward? Let's look a bit farther into these issues.

This is a crucial moment in Israel. Samuel has been a towering figure as a leader, but Israel seems to be in a time of change. The other nations around them have warrior kings. They tell Samuel, "We want one too!"

Samuel's response was predictable because he knew, feared, and loved the Lord: "Samuel was displeased with their request and went to the Lord for guidance. '**Do everything they say to you,**' the Lord replied, '**for they are rejecting me, not you.** They don't want me to be their king any longer. Ever since I brought them from Egypt they have continually abandoned me and followed other gods. And now they are giving you the same treatment. Do as they ask, but **solemnly warn them about the way a king will reign over them** [emphasis added]'" (1 Samuel 8:6-9).

Samuel did as the Lord instructed: "**So Samuel passed on the Lord's warning to the people who were asking him for a king**. 'This is how a king will reign over you,' Samuel said. '**The king will draft your sons** and assign them to his chariots and his charioteers, making them run before his chariots. Some will be generals and captains in his army, **some will be forced to plow in his fields and harvest his crops**, and **some will make his weapons and chariot equipment. The king will take your daughters from you** and force them to cook and bake and make perfumes for him. **He will take away the best of your fields and vineyards and olive groves and give them to his own officials. He will take** a tenth of your grain and your grape harvest and distribute it among his officers and attendants. **He will take** your male and female slaves and demand the finest of your cattle and donkeys for his own use. **He will demand** a tenth of your flocks, and **you will be his slaves. When that day comes, you will beg for relief from this king you are demanding, but then the Lord will not help you** [emphasis added]'" (1 Samuel 8:10-18).

So are you looking for someone to fight your battles? It will cost you your freedom and a lot more. Are you looking for the government to supply your needs? It will cost you your freedom and a lot more. The king will take and then take some more. In the end, you won't be happy about it. Does that sound like something that could be happening? In the church? In the culture? In the USA and the West?

Israel's answer is predictable. Their minds are made up. The allure of being like the people around them is just too much for them. And we see the Lord's answer in the matter: "But **the people refused to listen to Samuel's warning. 'Even so, we still want a king,' they said. 'We want to be like the nations around us.** Our king will judge us and lead us into battle.' So Samuel repeated to the Lord what the people had said, and the Lord replied, 'Do as they say, and give them a king.' Then Samuel agreed and sent the people home [emphasis added]" (1 Samuel 8:19-22).

A Prophecy and Instructions for a King

Reading through Deuteronomy a few years ago, I saw the most fantastic thing. Five hundred years before the time of Samuel in this discussion, God told Moses that eventually, His people Israel would ask for a king. When they do, God told Moses, these will be the rules or guidelines for the king: "You are about to enter the land the Lord your God is giving you. When you take it over and settle there, you may think, 'We should select a king to rule over us like the other nations around us. If this happens, be sure to select as king the man the Lord your God chooses. You must appoint a fellow Israelite; he may not be a foreigner" (Deuteronomy 17:14-15).

"The king must not build up a large stable of horses for himself or send his people to Egypt to buy horses, for the Lord has told you, 'You must never return to Egypt.' The king must not take many wives for himself, because they will turn his heart away from the Lord. And he must not accumulate large amounts of wealth in silver and gold for himself" (Deuteronomy 17:16-17).

"When he sits on the throne as king, he must copy for himself this body of instruction on a scroll in the presence of the Levitical priests. He must always keep that copy with him and read it daily as long as he lives. That way he will learn to fear the Lord his God by obeying all the terms of these instructions and decrees. This regular reading will prevent him from becoming proud and acting as if he is above his fellow citizens. It will also prevent him from turning away from these commands in the smallest way. And it will ensure that he and his descendants will reign for many generations in Israel" (Deuteronomy 17:18-20).

This describes a shepherd king, not a warrior king. This is a servant king under God's authority and protection, a spokesman for God, and not a replacement for God. God values your trust and knows confidence in man will not end well. "The fear of man brings a snare, but he who trusts in the Lord will be exalted" (Proverbs 29:25 NASB). "Some trust in chariots and some in horses, but we trust in the name of the Lord our God" (Psalm 20:7 ESV).

Where is your trust? A telling statement might be: "Having a retirement account isn't a problem — putting your trust there is!"

Be careful where you place your trust. Be careful what you ask. God often gives us what we want or ask as a reward or punishment.

Our founding fathers got what they asked of God — the greatest country the world has ever known, with the most freedom. They were God-fearing, Bible-believing, and trusted God with their fate and fortunes. God gave them God-fearing leaders for quite a long time. When King George III heard that Washington would resign his commission to a powerless Congress, he told the painter Benjamin West: "If he does that, he will be the greatest man in the world." That he did because his trust was in God, Who he saw as the ruler of all humanity.

Recently, what have we the people asked of God by our actions and votes? To be left alone, perhaps, or to be like the nations around us.

God may not save you from yourself or protect you from bad choices. His judgments are true and altogether righteous. Our pastor ended his message from First Samuel: "Sometimes God doesn't bless us with failure, but punishes us with success." It's worth pondering in light of the Bible and our times.

At a very successful time in Israel's history, about five hundred years before Samuel's time, Joshua, their leader, challenged the people: "If it is disagreeable in your sight to serve the Lord, **choose for yourselves today whom you will serve**: whether the gods which your fathers served which were beyond the River, or the gods of the Amorites in whose land you are living; but as for me and my house, we will serve the Lord [emphasis added]" (Joshua 24:15).

God isn't into big numbers but appreciates sincerity, honesty, humility, and trust. Your decision is very personal and precious to Him. Choose wisely, first for yourself and then for your family. Then walk it out trusting and by His grace — Godspeed as you journey.

PUZZLING CHAPTER 68

Quips and Quotes

IF I HAVE INFORMED YOU or helped you see we live in a deceived time, a time of rampant deception actually, so that you are aware and more free from it, this book has been worth the effort. If you can help others see it and push back against the lies and deception with truth and prayer, I have been successful.

If you have seen the necessity and beauty of living in both solitude and community, I am grateful. I am happy for you and your Creator. This book was written during the COVID-19 years, years I lived in solitude and community. I believe this approach to life is beautiful, rewarding, and compelling. It's our Master's plan for success and joy in our journey.

If you can see deception for what it is, where it began, and its various shapes you are becoming wise. If you see it could be from the Lord, and therefore be serving His purposes, and ours, you are becoming a person of faith.

If you can see deception without cursing the darkness, but instead light a candle and keep it lit, you are becoming a person of hope.

If you can see our times as they are with intense spiritual warfare, injury, devastation, dust, and the debris of the battlefield, you might call yourself a seer. And if you can focus on the care of the wounded and the safety of those in harm's way, while keeping yourself strong, you are becoming a person of love.

If you believe that where sin abounds, grace much more abounds, you are feeling the strength of your Father. You are becoming more and more a child of the King, and a son or daughter of Grace.

"Now abide faith, hope, and love, these three, but the greatest is love."

Always pray and don't lose heart.

Love your enemies and pray for those who persecute you.

Wash yourself with the water of the Word. Take up the Word of God, which is the sword of the Spirit. Always remember Whose sword it is.

Forgive!

Seek peace and pursue it. As far as possible be at peace with all men.

Owe no man anything, except to love him.

Maybe on these pages you've learned something of how to live in these times. Live in prayer, in the Word, with some solitude, and in community, encouraging one another all the more as you see the day approaching. Try to live a quiet and peaceful life, working with your hands.

Shiloh has come. Shiloh is coming — soon. Maybe He's right at our door. Live like it, making the most of your time because the days are evil.

When the days are evil, you can know judgment comes swiftly. So enjoy each day you have, and make the most of every opportunity to serve the King and His flock.

Men, lead your wives, your children, and the family of God. Lead in your entire realm or sphere of influence. It honors and pleases God, and He will help you.

Women, submit to and honor the men of authority in your lives, especially your husbands. It will be life-giving and life-enriching for both of you, and a boost to your children in life. It will honor and please God.

Stand against evil, in the Spirit, in prayer, and in action. Call evil what it is without fear, but in love. Trust God to answer your prayers and support you.

Speak the truth, in love.

Be faithful to family, friends, your church community, and most importantly to your God. He has been faithful and gracious to you.

Enjoy your life for the gift that it is.

Not as much depends on you as you probably think. The gracious One made life for you to enjoy. Remember that he is God, and you are not. Christianity is not a do-it-yourself project.

Live the life God's graciously giving you. He takes joy in your enjoyment of it. Treasure each day, person, and experience He brings your way.

Joy is the hallmark of a Christian. In God's presence is fullness of joy. Are you dwelling in His presence? Are you making your life and self a place of joyful hospitality and habitation for Him to enjoy with you?

Witness. Jesus said you shall be my witnesses to the ends of the earth. Tell people what you've seen, believe to be true, and have experienced.

Get rid of religious baggage if need be, and language. Don't defend or take your identity in your church, denomination, or community, but in Christ alone.

Be in community, of course, God commands it. Don't call Him Lord, and not do what He says. You're deceiving yourself. But find an expression of the church that follows the Bible, exalts the King, and loves people with abandon.

It's a time of warfare. People are on the move. Be open to help and embrace spiritual refugees, and move yourself if need be, or if the Lord leads.

Be strong in the Lord and in the power of His might. Remember always that the joy of the Lord is your strength. Go where you find joy, strength, purpose, and life. God has a destiny for you. Follow your dreams.

Don't waste your life! It is a gift to be enjoyed and lived with purpose and commitment to the King, and to his children, your spiritual siblings.

Don't make excuses. Don't feel entitled. You are not. It's a trap.

You have been given the gift of life. Grace is yours for the asking and taking. Make the most of your life! Take responsibility and trust God to help you on the journey. It is His plan.

Throw away the race card. It's a trap. God says it's not to be important to you. He communicates this in His creation, His word, and His actions. If you say it is, then you are at odds with God and putting yourself higher than Him. Are you sure you want to do that? Or will you trust His judgments, His ways, and His grace to help everyone equally in our main struggle, which is with self and against sin.

"There is neither Jew nor Greek, there is neither slave nor free man, there is neither male nor female; for you are all one in Christ Jesus. And if you belong to Christ, then you are Abraham's descendants, heirs according to promise" (Galatians 3:28-29).

Wisdom is fighting the right enemy, and the right battles. Wisdom is also calling a thing by its right name.

What does the Lord require of you? Only to do justly, love mercy, and walk humbly with your God. That's what he told us (Micah 6:8).

Hear, people of God, that the Lord our God, the Lord is One. You shall love Him with all your heart, with all your soul, and with all your strength. You do this when you obey His commands and honor His ways.

Impress His commands on your children. Tell them about His ways when you sit at home, and when you walk along the way, and when you lie down, and when you get up.

Be careful that you do not forget the Lord, who brought you out of slavery.

Men, you must lead. It makes it easier for your wives to submit and show you honor. But do it anyway.

Read history that interests you from reliable, truthful sources — not those histories rewritten with an agenda. Share what you read with others.

Men, lead your wives and family in prayer.

Men, lead your wives and family in reading the Word.

Try to understand mental health and prayer. Ask God for leading and revelation if this affects you or someone you love. This is not new. It's not unique to you. The battle rages. It's mainly a battle of thoughts and the will, what is believed and why. It's perhaps handled best with prayer and counseling, not drugs. But if drugs are already in play, a person should get skilled, professional help to discontinue them if that decision is made.

Is God a common god? Have you forgotten His Majesty? Ask for help and revelation in prayer if you have.

"If a thing is free to be good it is also free to be bad. And free will is what has made evil possible. Why, then, did God give them free will? Because free will, though it makes evil possible, is also the only thing that makes possible any love or goodness or joy worth having" (C.S. Lewis).

"If in His absolute freedom God has willed to give man limited freedom, who is there to stay His hand or say, 'What doest thou?' Man's will is free because God is sovereign. A God less sovereign could not bestow moral freedom upon His creatures. He would be afraid to do so" (A.W. Tozer).

"Where there is no freedom of choice there can be neither sin nor righteousness, because it is the nature of both that they be voluntary" (A.W. Tozer).

Remember Tozer's quote: "What you think about God is the most important thing about you." Try to know Him as well as you can, and think rightly about Him. Those who know their God will do valiantly. Be still, and know.

Fear not little flock. God knows what you need before you ask.

"Better save money! No one will take care of you." Of course there is some truth in that. It's wise to not eat all of your seed (spend all your money), but save some to plant. Proverbs tells us: "Go to the ant, O sluggard, observe her ways and be wise, which, having no chief, officer or ruler, prepares her food in the summer and gathers her provision in the harvest" (Proverbs 6:6-8).

But is that the whole story, or even the most important part? Is it what Jesus tells us in the Sermon on the Mount (Matthew 5-7)? "Look at the birds of the air, for they neither sow nor reap nor gather into barns; yet your heavenly Father feeds them. Are you not of more value than they?" (Matthew 6:26).

The other side of the story is the guy in Jesus' parable who who tore down good barns and built bigger barns, then died before he could enjoy or use any of it. Jesus advises us to spend it as we go, to sow into others, and to enjoy the lives God has by His grace given us. Note the parable of the talents and stewards (Matthew 25:14-30). "Take risk, invest, occupy (stay in the market place) until I come," Jesus told his disciples. Believe God is good, and He will take care of you, and He will be with you until your graying years (Isaiah 46:4).

To the guy with the new barns, trusting in his wealth and only accumulating to that end, Jesus said: "'You fool! This very night your soul is required of you; and now who will own what you have prepared?' So is the man who stores up treasure for himself, and is not rich toward God" (Luke 12:20-21). Find out what it means to be rich toward God!

"Remember also your Creator in the days of your youth, before the evil days come and the years draw near when you will say, 'I have no delight in them'" (Ecclesiastes 12:1). Live your life with joy, and with purpose, savoring each day with thanksgiving. Remember your Maker.

Enjoy your cell phone. But see it for what it is, possibly a life enhancing device, and possibly a life destroying device. It may suck away the life of its possessor. It's in my mind the biggest technical marvel of the modern world, with wide-reaching capabilities for evil and for good. Make sure it serves you and others, and that you don't end up serving it, or those who write software, peddle their wares, or their thoughts into your very private, personal space 24/7/365. The tail should never wag the dog.

"And the Lord will continually guide you, and satisfy your desire in scorched places, and give strength to your bones; and you will be like a watered garden, and like a spring of water whose waters do not fail" (Isaiah 58:11).

"Those from among you will rebuild the ancient ruins; you will raise up the age-old foundations; and you will be called the repairer of the breach, the restorer of the streets in which to dwell" (Isaiah 58:12).

A successful businessman and friend recently stood to speak at an early morning men's meeting I attended. He started by reading this text his wife sent while he was driving to the meeting: "I just wondered if you ever had a chance to share about your dad's losing a mother at childbirth, having his dad commit suicide when the boys were 13 and then being split up from his twin but still managing to make a successful life without being a victim even though fraught with functioning alcoholism later possibly due to those things combined with World War II issues. Not by might, not by power, but by my Spirit." Contemplating this makes one think, "no entitlement, no whining, and no bad days."

Grief may come in for the night, but joy returns in the morning.

Your days were all numbered before not one of them was lived.

"A man can do noting better than to eat and drink and find satisfaction in his work. This too, I see, is from the hand of God, for without him, who can eat or find enjoyment? To the man who pleases him, God gives wisdom, knowledge, and happiness" (Ecclesiastes 2:24).

"He has made everything beautiful in its time. He has also set eternity in the human heart; yet no one can fathom what God has done from beginning to end" (Ecclesiastes 3:11 NIV).

"The root of the righteous flourishes" (Proverbs 12:12 WEB).

"With the goodness of God to desire our highest welfare, the wisdom of God to plan it, and the power of God to achieve it, why do we lack? Surely we are the most favored of all creatures" (A.W. Tozer, *The Wisdom of God*).

"An open secret," could be a beautiful, insightful, timely conclusion to *The Knowledge of the Holy* by A.W. Tozer.

"In the year king Uzziah died, I saw the Lord" (Isaiah 6).

"Let me never fall into the vulgar mistake of dreaming I am persecuted whenever I am contradicted" (Ralph Waldo Emerson).

"A man's heart determines his speech" (Matthew 12:34 TLB).

"The curse of the Lord is on the house of the wicked, but He blesses the dwelling of the righteous" (Proverbs 3:33).

"Little children, you are from God and have overcome them, for He who is in you is greater than he who is in the world. They are from the world; therefore they speak from the world, and the world listens to them. We are from God. Whoever knows God listens to us; whoever is not from God does not listen to us. By this we know the Spirit of truth and the spirit of error" (1 John 4:4-6).

"The human spirit is the lamp of the Lord that sheds light on one's inmost being" (Proverbs 20:27 NIV).

"We need to use our past as a springboard, not a sofa — a guidepost, not a hitching post" (Celebrate Recovery Bible Notes).

"Be strong and courageous. Do not be afraid; do not be discouraged, for the Lord your God will be with you wherever you go" (Joshua 1:9).

"Watch yourselves, so that you may not lose what we have worked for, but may win a full reward. Everyone who goes on ahead and does not abide in the teaching of Christ, does not have God. Whoever abides in the teaching has both the Father and the Son" (2 John 8-9 ESV).

"The high minded man must care more for the truth than what people think" (Aristotle).

"The road to tyranny, we must never forget, begins with the destruction of the truth" (Bill Clinton, US President).

"Whenever you find yourself on the side of the majority, it is time to pause and reflect" (Mark Twain, American writer).

"But above all things truth beareth away the victory" (Plato).

"A lie gets halfway around the world before the truth has a chance to get its pants on" (Winston Churchill).

"Three things cannot be long hidden: the sun, the moon, and the truth" (Buddha).

"Rather than love, than money, than fame, give me truth" (Henry David Thoreau).

"All truth passes through three stages. First, it is ridiculed. Second, it is violently opposed. Third, it is accepted as being self-evident" (Arthur Schopenhauer).

"No legacy is so rich as honesty" (William Shakespeare).

"Truth is so obscure in these times, and falsehood so established, that, unless we love the truth, we cannot know it" (Blaise Pascal).

PUZZLING CHAPTER 69

Puzzling Summary

WHEN COVID-19 BROKE OUT in the United States in early 2020, I was amazed and shocked at the fear and panic that seized the church and our nation. Had the pandemic occurred during the previous generation, our parents or grandparents would have said, "It looks like a bad strain of the flu. We better be careful, wash our hands, and get back to work." There was a different level of faith and fear in the country and church then.

I railed against the fear response, especially of the church, until I realized the plague was from the Lord. The response was just introducing us to ourselves, putting some to sleep, and waking others up to what is happening in the spiritual and natural realms. God is doing some cosmic surgery, cutting the cancer of sin and apathy out of His church and our culture. He's merciful and skilled, so His scalpel won't go deeper than needed, but He is thorough and capable, so He will reveal and deal with the problem. We must trust Him to do that and only do our small parts as asked.

As I watched the sad saga we essentially brought on ourselves by turning further away from God unfold, I started to ponder how we got here. Where are we in the sequence of judgment and correction? And how should we live during times like these? I felt the Spirit encourage me to write what I saw.

I turned to God's Word and history for insight and instruction. I asked His Spirit for revelation and His leading during this time and all the time I have left. I asked for help to live a life of grace and redemption, adventure and service in these days that the Lord planned for me from the beginning of time. I want to light a candle and not curse the darkness, as I hear so many doing.

I want to soar in the Spirit and know experientially that healing and redemption come not by power or by might but by His Spirit. I want to feel His Spirit flow through me to those nearby who need a healing or enlightening touch. And I want to know better the LORD, His Christ, and His Spirit. I've come to see He wants the same thing for us! Where sin abounds, His grace (unmerited favor and power) abound more for life and living.

Our times are not unique in this regard. This same scenario has played out many times in history and in the Bible. God is timeless, and so are His ways. These times are unique only because we're farther along God's timeline for the earth and humankind, and these are our times.

You need to know a few things to be a warrior or warrioress in the days ahead. You need to know the Word of God well. You must see the heart of God and the nature of Christ well. You must experience the indwelling Holy Spirit to lead and guide you along the way and give you power for your journey.

This book attempts to inform you of those facts and add to your arsenal ways of thinking, and methods of handling the truths of the Bible, empowered by the Spirit. You must commit humbly to being a lifetime learner and practicing the art of living with God — because, in Him, we live and move and have our being. Knowing Him is our very great reward.

Hopefully, you've learned or caught a glimpse that it doesn't all depend on you. That's Christian humanism, which should be an oxymoron, but sadly in our day, it is not—Christian humanism is a close cousin of secular humanism or self-exaltation in place of God. If you have an accurate and ever-sharpening view of God, you'll know by revelation and experience that battles are won not by power or might but by God's Spirit (Zechariah 4:6).

You hopefully have learned the valuable lesson: "In repentance and rest is your salvation, and in quietness and trust is your strength" (Isaiah 30:15). You can seek to live a quiet and peaceful life and work with your hands. If you abide in Him as He abides in you, you'll know what to do, when, and have the power to accomplish it (John 15:5).

Prayer is perhaps the most important spiritual discipline, especially if you have an accurate glimpse of the One to Whom you pray. God's power, grace, mercy, love, and His sincere invitation to pray make praying compelling (Hebrews 4:16). God feels joy when you pray (Proverbs 15:8). And you bring the benefits of the kingdom of God to others when you pray (Psalm 18:6-14, James 5:16, Revelation 8:1-5). May you come to picture yourself like the highly favored queen Esther, coming into the presence of her king, who raises his scepter and bids her come. Or see yourself like Mary, the mother of Jesus, praying, "They have no wine." Care enough about others to bring them or their plight into the presence of the King (Mark 2:4-5).

Community and knowing the Word are equally crucial for living, surviving, and thriving in our day — a day of deception with evil and sin abounding. I wrote this book during these two puzzling years of COVID-19 — a time of solitude but also community. These truths and experiences came from living in solitude and community, the way of the Spirit, the way of the Lord, the ancient and future path — practicing His presence alone and with others.

I have learned many of the lessons shared during the last two years. I met many of those mentioned during the same time. It's been a time of learning in community, a time of journaling and worship in solitude and silence, a time of adventure and joy with others. I recommend these practices wholeheartedly.

The Lord blessed us just before this time with a beautiful, comfortable cabin in the mountains, a place with an airstrip, where we have spent time in solitude, also enjoying each other and friends. The Lord's goodness and grace seem overwhelming, and it went before us. I discovered a new verse during this time: "For of His fullness we have all received, and grace upon grace" (John 1:16).

I still shake my head in happy disbelief that during July 2021, only one short year ago, while much of the world and church crouched down in fear, the Lord led me on an adventure flying my own airplane to Honduras. With a like-minded brother, we facilitated drilling a water well in a village, supported the leadership of a local church, and encouraged and enjoyed their youth leaders. Those who wait upon the Lord, He will renew their strength. They will mount up with wings like eagles, indeed. My faith, in many ways, is becoming sight. It's the Lord's doing, marvelous in my eyes and experience.

I can say it is well with my soul. "The waves and wind still know His name," as the lyrics of a popular song proclaim. And I'm more confident than ever that He knows my name. That's my prayer for you, the reader — that you press into the Lord anew and partake of the grace that is flowing during this correction or judgment: "O taste and see that the Lord is good; how blessed is the man who takes refuge in Him!" (Psalm 34:8).

Perhaps it's to be your destiny and honor to be redemptive during this time, mentoring and encouraging the next generation for the unique mission God has in store for them: "Those from among you will rebuild the ancient ruins; you will raise up the age-old foundations; and you will be called the repairer of the breach, the restorer of the streets in which to dwell" (Isaiah 58:12). "One generation shall praise Your works to another, and shall declare Your mighty acts" (Psalm 145:4).

Unplug from your cell phone and social media often and much — television and the media in general. It's a tether to the world powerfully promoting the lust of the flesh, the lust of the eyes, and the boastful pride of life, all of which are contrary to God's will for you (1 John 2:16). This media stream is also an umbilical cord to life-robbing deception in our day. It spews the poison of fear, sensationalism, and self-exalting secular humanism. Instead of drinking from this poison well daily, make it your practice to dwell alone with God and in God-fearing communities. You'll sleep better, think better, and enjoy the life God has graced you — a life of love, power, and peace. God's plan for us and a description of His kingdom is: "righteousness, peace and joy in the Holy Spirit" (Romans 14:17).

Seek to be at peace and rest. Religion says, "Do this and do that and you'll be right or righteous." But Christ says, "It's not about works, lest anyone should boast." "No boasting!" may be a summation of the Gospel of Jesus Christ. He did what only He could do. We can rest in that, accept His almost-unfathomable gift of righteousness and eternal life, then say only, "Thank you." We can then continue to respond to Him in love and admiration — worshiping the beauty of His holiness with wonder.

"For whoever has entered God's rest has also rested from his works as God did from his. Let us therefore strive to enter that rest, so that no one may fall by the same sort of disobedience" (Hebrews 4:10-11 ESV).

You'll be in the minority. The Bible tells us: "Enter through the narrow gate; for the gate is wide and the way is broad that leads to destruction, and there are many who enter through it. For the gate is small and the way is narrow that leads to life, and there are few who find it" (Matthew 7:13-14). God isn't into numbers but the quality of character and humility. He's constantly screening or searching the earth for people who would be good candidates to make up a church, a bride, for His Son the King — saved by His grace, then changed by His grace.

So the question comes to be, "Would you rather please God or man?" Or, "Do you fear God or man?" You get to choose. You choose daily. After they crossed the Jordan and possessed their land, Joshua told Israel, "Choose this day whom you will serve" (Joshua 24:15).

But don't feel you're all alone, or going it alone, even if you are in the minority. God says He will be with you to the end of the age and that He is a strong tower. If you are wise, you'll run to Him (Proverbs 22:3). Elijah once thought he was the only one who feared God left in Israel. God reminded him that He had preserved 7000 men in Israel during that evil time who hadn't bowed their knees to Baal or kissed his idol.

With their mass communication capabilities, the media in our day make it appear that secular humanism is the wave of the future and the power of this new day. Beware of this insidious group think. It's an old lie but now powered by unprecedented technology— deception on a massive scale.

How do you fight against deception? You can win the fight by seeking the truth, knowing the truth, and speaking the truth. You can see what's true, and know the Truth Himself. He will make you free and keep you free. That's what Jesus told us (John 8:32, John 14:6).

But what if it's an evil time and people hate the truth, or there is seemingly no market for truth? Admittedly it's more tricky in these times. But God's Word guides us. In one place, it says: "Therefore at such a time the prudent person keeps silent, for it is an evil time" (Amos 5:13). Don't cast your pearls before swine. And don't feel like you're God, that it all depends on you. By being quiet, you can show your quiet faith that God will judge every word and deed and doesn't need your assistance. Instead, be still and know that He is God (Psalm 46:10).

But the Bible also tells us: "Then we will no longer be infants, tossed back and forth by the waves, and blown here and there by every wind of teaching and by the cunning and craftiness of **people in their deceitful scheming**. Instead, **speaking the truth in love**, we will grow to become in every respect the mature body of him who is the head, that is, Christ [emphasis added]" (Ephesians 4:14-15). So if you love people and know it's the truth that sets them free, you will courageously tell them the truth in love. But realize it's the job of the Holy Spirit to change or convince them. Your job is to pray, love, and speak the truth in love. "And He [the Holy Spirit], when He comes, will convict the world concerning sin and righteousness and judgment" (John 16:8).

Which is it, keep silent or tell them the truth in love? It's either or both depending on the situation and what you sense the Holy Spirit tell you to do: "Whether you turn to the right or to the left, your ears will hear a voice behind you, saying, 'This is the way; walk in it'" (Isaiah 30:21). The Holy Spirit speaking behind you or within you is a significant part of the puzzle. Even Jesus didn't go it alone but said what He heard the Father say through the Spirit (John 12:49). Learn the Word, and be led by the Spirit.

Practice. It's like walking a log, a rail fence, or the balance beam. In the case of the balance beam, you must not fail to practice with courage and have a coach committed to your safety and success. Remember: "Faithful is He who calls you, and He also will bring it to pass" (1 Thessalonians 5:24).

You may recall the Proverbs conundrum from a previous puzzle piece: "Do not answer a fool according to his folly, or you yourself will be just like him. Answer a fool according to his folly, or he will be wise in his own eyes" (Proverbs 26:4-5 NIV). So you must know the Bible and the truth of the matter to have an answer. And you must have the leading of the Holy Spirit as to when and how to answer someone who says there is no God or is ignorant of God's ways.

We must gain an experiential walk with the Holy Spirit. To do so, we may need to forget what our denominations taught us. We must go back to what Jesus told us, and the Apostles demonstrated, and learn to sail with the Spirit, when and where He is moving, like the wind (John 3:8). It's a relationship. You know Him by being near and experiencing Him and His presence. And you learn by obeying His voice — practice obedience. "But we have this treasure in jars of clay to show that this all-surpassing power is from God and not from us" (2 Corinthians 4:7).

This spiritual connection has always been essential, and it always will be. It's an eternal truth determined by the eternal God, Who has put eternity in our hearts, yet God keeps things mystical and hidden. The "Teacher sent from God" told the "Teacher of Israel" as much in John 3. The Spirit must introduce us to the spiritual realm, which is more real and important than the natural realm. Hearing the Spirit is critical in times of extreme lies and deception obscuring our vision and wrecking our lives, leading us away from the eternal One. God wants us to live life with Him, now and for eternity.

Deception is difficult to discuss but perhaps the most important thing to see. It is the reason for much of the chaos and confusion in our time. It's rampant in our churches and culture, and we're mostly blind to it. You don't know if you're deceived. To see it, one must have an epiphany, revelation, and help from the Holy One. The Bible warns us about this, but people have been deceived to not see the Bible for what it is — God's Word and the antithesis of lies and deception. Thus we become blind leaders of the blind. Don't let this happen to you. Humble yourself before the Word and be light and salt — help and guide those around you. "Don't curse the darkness; light a candle" has become my mantra. Maybe a more basic mantra is: "Don't curse the darkness, be a candle."

What changes if God has sent this delusion or darkness? The two principal verses cited to speak to darkness and deception in our times are in the same chapter of the Bible: "**Let no one deceive you by any means**; for **that Day** ["of the Lord," the second coming of Christ the

King] **will not come unless the falling away comes first**" (2 Thessalonians 2:3). And: "They did not receive the love of the truth so as to be saved. For this reason **God will send upon them a deluding influence so that they will believe what is false** [emphasis added]" (2 Thessalonians 2:10b-11).

It's folly to stand between God and something He's doing or between God and someone He's correcting. You'll be injured if not destroyed. So if you believe, as I do, that this deception and pestilence is from God, then it's time to let Him have His wise and merciful way for our healing and benefit. It will serve us best to explain God's ways, exclaim His goodness, and help those who are lost find their way with God's leading and in the power of His Spirit.

Look up! An accurate image of God, *imago dei* in Latin, is our charge and destiny. God created humankind in His image (Genesis 1:27). We are to bear His image for our joy and let others see His image in us. Scripture tells us: "For now we see through a glass, darkly; but then face to face: now I know in part; but then shall I know even as also I am known" (1 Corinthians 13:12). "It has not appeared as yet what we will be. We know that when He appears, we will be like Him, because we will see Him just as He is" (1 John 3:2). When we see more of God, by revelation or in someone else, we become more like Him. Our primary focus should be seeing Him and bearing His image to others.

"And we all, who with unveiled faces contemplate the Lord's glory, are being transformed into his image with ever-increasing glory, which comes from the Lord, who is the Spirit" (2 Corinthians 3:18). "Get yourself up on a high mountain, O Zion, bearer of good news, lift up your voice mightily, O Jerusalem, bearer of good news; lift it up, do not fear. Say to the cities of Judah, 'Here is your God!'" (Isaiah 40:9).

These are the answers to how we should live in this present day and time. Hopefully they've come into clearer focus as you've puzzled these pieces together, viewing them closely, and then stepping back to view the whole. Godspeed as you journey from here, in His strength, power, love, leading, and grace.

> "You make known to me the path of life;
> you will fill me with joy in your presence,
> with eternal pleasures at your right hand"
> (Psalm 16:11 NIV).

PUZZLING CHAPTER 70

Afterword

IT'S BEEN SAID, "THE PEN is mightier than the sword." And those who pay too little attention to the pen of the Spirit, the Bible, may soon experience the sword. That's a thought that came to me when thinking about this book just now. It's proven true throughout history.

The pens of men and women made righteous by God, having experienced His initial and continuing Grace, I believe are mightier than the enemy's sword of lies and deception. They bring the Bible to light in the power of the Spirit, bringing truth, courage, and love of life to the hearts of their readers, peers, and friends.

The journey of writing this book has had the unusual quality of being written for me. It's almost as if I discovered or rediscovered these truths as I wrote about them. They seemed to apply mainly to me. And I was fine with that. It's about the relationship. It's about the journey with God.

That journey includes journeying with others, a community of faith. These truths were discovered, some rediscovered, and all celebrated in community — a thing of beauty and joy, the Bride of Christ.

I am keenly aware of the last written words of the wisest man who ever lived. Solomon tells us: "The writing of many books is endless, and excessive devotion to books is wearying to the body" (Ecclesiastes 12:12b).

Then his last written words are the most profound imaginable, as one would expect: "The conclusion, when all has been heard, is: fear God and keep His commandments, because this applies to every person. For God will bring every act to judgment, everything which is hidden, whether it is good or evil" (Ecclesiastes 12:13-14). "Fear God and keep His commandments." Have we heard this before? Perhaps from the beginning to the end of Scripture, His Holy Bible. Distilled wisdom and truth from the wisest of the wise, inspired by God's Holy Spirit. Amen.

Concerning this book, Solomon's words also describe what's in my heart for this book and you the reader: "The Preacher sought to find delightful words and to write words of truth correctly. The words of wise men are like goads, and masters of these collections are like well-driven nails; they are given by one Shepherd" (Ecclesiastes 12:10-11). "Words of truth, written correctly, given by one Shepherd" has been my passion and goal. It will be up to you as to how well I communicated these truths, and up to the Spirit as to how deeply into some of these things you are able to peer. I pray it's deep, because deep calls to deep (Psalm 42:7-8).

Life is a mysterious — beautiful mystery. I can hardly believe all the ways God has led my wife and I, and cared for us in this chapter of our lives, the decade of our 60s. It has been "grace upon grace" indeed (John 1:16). My heart says with the Psalmist, "You are good and your mercies endure forever" (Psalm 136:1).

When I retired early from the airline, it never entered my mind that I might have an airplane, or a mountain-top cabin with an airstrip for solitude and hosting friends. I certainly never dreamed I'd fly my own airplane with friends to Alaska, Idaho, and Honduras, in addition to crisscrossing the Ozarks' backcountry. I never dreamed we'd move to a new city, make new friends, visit old friends, and find a loving church community, committed to teaching the Word unapologetically, and living life together with the Spirit leading and providing grace for the moment. And there is more.

I feel I must tell it to the next generation, and to anyone with ears to hear. I must live and enjoy it too! The reality of God's goodness He means for us to enjoy! Grace filled lives are easier to talk about as you experience and live them. You start to get it. That the power is from God — the love, leading, and life too.

I want to give thanks, with no boasting, except in God. The Psalmist declares: "My soul shall make its boast in the Lord; the humble shall hear of it and be glad" (Psalm 34:2 NKJV). A major theme of this book has been: "For by grace you have been saved through faith, and that not of yourselves; it is the gift of God, not of works, lest anyone should boast" (Ephesians 2:8-9 NKJV).

Paul the Apostle of Jesus Christ wrote that, and yet at one point in his ministry he indulged in boasting about his trials, hardships, the grace God poured out on him, the adventures he experienced, and the love God continued to show him and pour into his heart. That is quite a change from a murderous Pharisee sent from the High Priest to imprison and kill Christians. Grace can change a person, as does the Holy Spirit, when and after one believes.

Paul had much he could boast about if he wanted. One of the few times he did in Scripture was to the church in Corinth when there was some deception and deceivers at work. He wanted to call them out, to ensure the church's true devotion to Christ (2 Corinthians 11:16-33). That was his motive for boasting expressed in his own words: "I hope you will put up with me in a little foolishness. Yes, please put up with me! I am jealous for you with a godly jealousy. I promised you to one husband, to Christ, so that I might present you as a pure virgin to him. But I am afraid that just as Eve was deceived by the serpent's cunning, your minds may somehow be led astray from your sincere and pure devotion to Christ" (2 Corinthians 11:1-3 NIV).

Paul boasted in his qualifications, and in his sufferings to help the church see through some deception and uncover some deceivers so they could continue on the path of devotion to Christ. Other than that he boasted in his weakness: "'**My grace is sufficient for you, for my power is made perfect in weakness.**' Therefore **I will boast all the more gladly about my weaknesses, so that Christ's power may rest on me.** That is why, for Christ's sake, I delight in weaknesses, in insults, in hardships, in persecutions, in difficulties. **For when I am weak, then I am strong** [emphasis added]" (2 Corinthians 12:9b-10 NIV).

Boasting is summed up in the thought: "Some boast in chariots and some in horses, but we will boast in the name of the Lord, our God" (Psalm 20:7). And in the prophet Jeremiah's words: "Thus says the Lord, '**Let not a wise man boast of his wisdom, and let not the mighty man boast of his might, let not a rich man boast of his riches; but let him who boasts boast of this, that he understands and knows Me, that I am the Lord who exercises lovingkindness, justice and righteousness on earth; for I delight in these things,' declares the Lord** [emphasis added]'" (Jeremiah 9:23-24).

Immediately afterwards, the prophet tells us the Lord is about to punish the religious (church) and the culture for their unfaithfulness to Him and the truth: "'Behold, the days are coming,' declares the Lord, 'that I will punish all who are circumcised only in the flesh'" (Jeremiah 9:25 NIV).

Paul did a little boasting but tastefully, embarrassed almost. No, he was totally embarrassed! But he did it anyway as a testimony to God's grace — pure and simple.

He did it meekly. Meekness is not weakness, but power under control. Perhaps that's a goal or a good definition of grace. It's power under control, understated, acknowledging the goodness and power of the Source to others as you offer your worship — declaring the worthiness of the Gift Giver, His Grace, our God, even the LORD and His Son Jesus Christ. Amen.

It appears this book will go out on that note. It is done, but not finished, attempted but not perfected, acknowledging His grace and returning to life and living to explore its depths and feel the awe and blessings of his grace again and again, until the end — which will be a new beginning in a new heaven and a new earth, with His Grace and by His Grace. Amen.

"For the Lord God is a sun and shield; the Lord gives grace and glory; No good thing does He withhold from those who walk uprightly. O Lord of hosts, how blessed is the man who trusts in You!" (Psalm 84:11-12).

"… we have this treasure in jars of clay to show that this all-surpassing power is from God and not from us" (2 Corinthians 4:7 NIV).

What a beautiful thought and cover under which to live a beautiful, rested, joy-filled life. Let's do it! Follow the Lamb wherever He may go. His eternal, restful, joyful *shalom* be yours in abundance. Amen.

"The grace of the Lord Jesus be with all. Amen" (Revelation 22:21).

Appendix

Simple Approximate Time Line
(For Your Use and Reference)

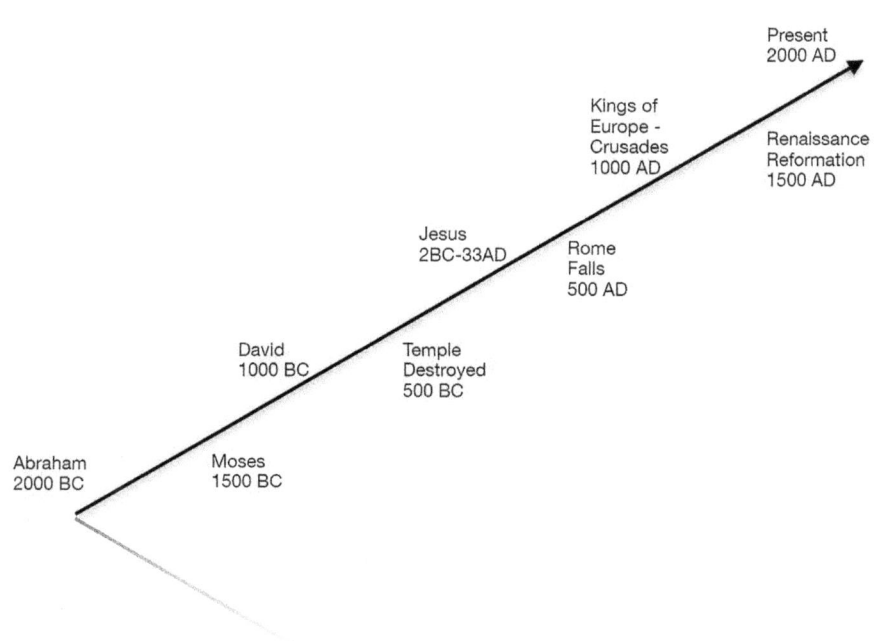

www.ingramcontent.com/pod-product-compliance
Lightning Source LLC
Chambersburg PA
CBHW050336010526
44119CB00037B/468/J